GUIDE TO
THE PROBATE INVENTORIES
OF THE BRISTOL DEANERY OF
THE DIOCESE OF BRISTOL
1542–1804

2

The Inventory of Thomas A Deane 1688

GUIDE TO
THE PROBATE INVENTORIES
OF THE BRISTOL DEANERY OF
THE DIOCESE OF BRISTOL
(1542–1804)

E. and S. GEORGE

ISBN 0-901538-09-4

To our daughter
MARGARET McGREGOR

Published by Bristol Record Society and the Bristol and
Gloucestershire Archaeological Society with the help of generous
donations from the Bristol and West Building Society and the
Marc Fitch Fund

Produced by Alan Sutton Publishing Ltd., 30 Brunswick Road,
Gloucester.
Printed in Great Britain.

CONTENTS

ACKNOWLEDGEMENTS

We should like to thank all those who have helped to make this volume possible. Miss Elizabeth Ralph initiated the project when she was Bristol City Archivist. Her successor Miss E.M. Williams, the present City Archivist Mr J.S. Williams, the staff of the Bristol Record Office and Professor McGrath have given us continual help and encouragement.

Without the practical assistance of Reginald and Philomena Jackson it would have been difficult to complete the work. Mr Richard Bryant of Alan Sutton Publishing Ltd. has given very helpful practical advice, and Mr Edwin Turnbull has assisted with the presentation of the map. We are grateful to Mr. J.S. Williams for permission to reproduce the inventory of Thomas A Deane.

Finally, our thanks are due to the Bristol Record Society, the Bristol and Gloucestershire Archaeological Society, the Bristol and West Building Society and the Marc Fitch Fund for grants which have enabled this work to be published.

E. and S. George

FOREWORD

The importance of the inventories of probate records as sources of information about our ancestors cannot be overstressed. The genealogists have long realized this, now the social and economic historians are awakening to the possibilities of a new field of research. For the social historian, home life at all levels of the scale is reflected in them. Bristol being an important centre of trade and commerce, the inventories are a vaulable source of information on trade and industry.

This index of probate inventories covering the period 1542–1804 is the result of the detailed examination of over seven thousand inventories. It is an index of names, places, trades and occupations. For the researcher in this field it is an essential piece of equipment. In addition Mr and Mrs George have prepared abstracts of all the documents indexed and transcribed some 300 inventories especially relevant to the City trades. They are still continuing this work and many of the abstracts and transcriptions remain in manuscript. These show the extent of the task undertaken and demonstrate the difficulty of printing them in full. They intend, eventually, to deposit these abstracts in the Bristol Record Office, from which in the meanwhile details can be obtained about this aspect of their work.

Edwin and Stella George should be congratulated on the good workmanlike treatment of the available information.

Elizabeth Ralph

PREFACE

The object of the guide is to record the probate inventories of the City and Deanery of Bristol which are held in the Bristol Record Office, thus showing what is available and making the contents more readily accessible for study. Details of the main series of testamentary records to which these inventories belong are to be found in the Bristol Diocesan *Catalogue of the Records of the Bishop and Archdeacons and of the Dean and Chaper.*[1]

Our interest in the inventories began in 1966 when at a University Extra-Mural Class Miss Ralph suggested that the inventories of Temple Parish could be profitably examined to see what information they could add to the history of the parish. Thirteen inventories were studied, and a paper was produced at the end of the session.[2]

The bundles of wills and inventories which had been stored in the Bristol Probate Registry came to the Bristol Record Office in 1958. Many of the wills had their corresponding inventories folded inside them. By 1966 most of these inventories had been separated from the wills and added to the main inventory collection. We were then asked if we would prepare an index to these inventories; and we decided to make abstracts of them at the same time. We were able to include some 200 inventories which were still remaining either with the wills, the administrations or which were included in the collection of cause papers.[3] All letters, accounts and documents included in the bundles of inventories have been recorded in this guide. We have also made detailed abstracts of their contents, and have fully transcribed over 300 city inventories selected as being representative of the major trades of the city. Work is still continuing on improving the abstracts and extending the transcriptions. Up-to-date information on the progress may be obtained from the Bristol Record Office.

[1] Compiled by Isabel M. Kirby, Bristol Corporation, 1970, pg 56.
[2] *Notes on Bristol History No. 7,* typescript in Bristol Record Office.
[3] Bristol Record Office, EP/J/2.

THE CITY AND DEANERY OF BRISTOL (1542–1836)

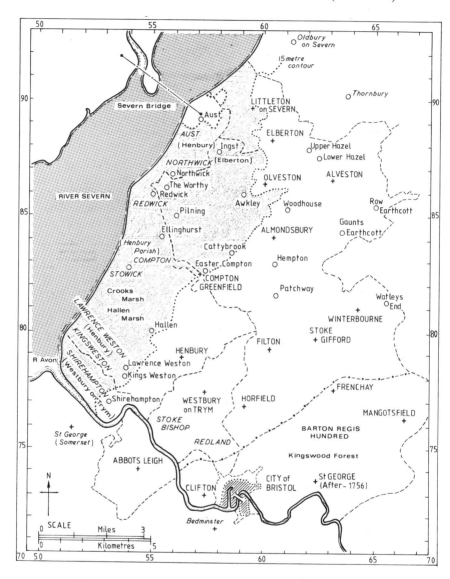

REFERENCES

Parish and parish church	+ FILTON
Tithings	*COMPTON*
Hamlets, estates or farms	○ Patchway
Parish, and City, boundaries	— — — — — —
(built up area of City shaded)	
Barton Regis Hundred boundary	.—.—.—.—.—.
The Severn Marsh	
land below 15 metre (50') contour stippled	

The numbers in the margin correspond with the kilometre square of the National Grid.

INTRODUCTION

Probate

The last will and testament of a dying man was a serious spiritual matter as the preamble to sixteenth century wills makes abundantly clear. Consequently, ensuring that his wishes were faithfully carried out without fraud became the responsibility of the ecclesiastical rather than the secular courts. The first step was proving the will: establishing that the will produced to the court was in fact the last will of the deceased person, that it was valid and that the executors presenting it were justified in acting on behalf of the deceased.

Ecclesiastical courts were set up by the bishops to control the affairs of each diocese. These courts retained their probate jurisdiction until 1857, but could only act within their own diocese. If the deceased had property or goods outside its domain, the diocesan court was powerless to call witnesses or investigate any irregularities. The will had then to be proved in the Archbishop's Court, the Prerogative Court of Canterbury, which had jurisdiction over the whole province. Such probate was all that was needed, but nevertheless copies of wills and inventories produced before it were often deposited with the Diocesan Registry and appear with the local documents. Sometimes wills that could have been proved satisfactorily in the diocesan registry appear to have been taken to the prerogative court as if to give them added authority, but it is more likely to have been a precautionary measure. Bonds due to the deceased were part of his goods and chattels, and if a bond-holder lived or moved outside the diocese difficulties could arise. The following extract taken from the inventory of Elizabeth Moore illustrates the problem:

"John Hall of Compton, one of the overseers of the will of John Moore has in his possession, having no authority to keep and moving out of the Diocese, the sum of £10 which he refuseth to deliver or take out any administration for during the minority of Elizabeth Moore and which is part of her father's legacy."[1]

[1] Inventory of Elizabeth Moore, 1609/53, *infra* p. 158.

An executor had to assume responsibility for the goods, credits and debts of the deceased and distribute them according to the provisions of the will. The presumption in law was that the deceased's affairs were in good order and that all legacies, debts and expenses could be met out of the estate; but if a proper inventory of the deceased's goods and credits had been accepted by the probate court its declared value became the limit of his liability. At first the court insisted that a 'true and perfect inventory' should be submitted to it before giving the executor permission to act, but with the passage of time the court relaxed this requirement and would grant probate provided that it was satisfied that an inventory could be produced if demanded. The cause papers contain many citations to produce such inventories. Sixty inventories, most of them very detailed, have been included from that source, the earliest being dated 1684.

In 1704 a different type of inventory begins to appear. These are for mariners who died during their service at sea, often on H.M. ships of war. These documents served to safeguard their dependents and are limited to a statement of the wages due for the deceased's last voyage, the name of the ship and sometimes that of the master or captain. In some cases at least, the information was provided by the Navy Office.

Ecclesiastical law laid down the provisions to be followed in making inventories and gave guidance about the items to be included. It is sufficient to say here that the object of probate was to safeguard the creditors, legatees and dependents, and that a proper inventory was in the interest of the administrator.

A minimum of two appraisers was required, one of whom was to be a creditor if possible, while one of the others should be sufficiently knowledgeable to evaluate the goods adequately. If specialised goods were involved, a fellow craftsman or tradesman was usually called in to assist.

Internal evidence suggests that instructions were available for the guidance of appraisers. There is considerable similarity in the layout of inventories at any given time. The earlier ones almost invariably start with 'Wearing apparel' and 'Money in Purse' as if those two items headed the list. Later the wearing apparel may occur in one of the rooms and the money near the end together with the debts. There were standard prices for livestock; and for crock metal, brass, pewter and iron, which were taken by weight. After 1634 the use of the words 'trumpery' and 'and other small things', which had been common up to then, changed in favour of the expression 'and other implements'. The change, although not absolute, is sufficiently well marked to suggest a change in the guidance given to the appraisers was made about that time.

The goods to be included in the inventories were the deceased's personal possessions, his moveable goods, trade goods, tools of trade, farm stock, cultivated crops and any chattel leases, but not freehold property or those fixtures belonging to the house or farm which the heir or incoming occupier would expect to find. Wainscot and window leaves, which we now regard as fixtures, were usually included, but large cider presses were not.

It was realized that the executor might sometimes have to sell some or all of the goods in his charge to pay debts and to settle the legacies for which he was responsible. The appraisers were expected to bear this in mind and to value the goods accordingly "at such price as they may be sold for at the time". This accounts for such descriptive statements as those from the following inventories:

"an old blind horse hurt with a pike and like to die"[2]
"a gray mare with one eye; a bay mare with a bald face"[3]
"bedding, some being rotten and worn out during his sickness"[4]
"12 yards of motheaten kersie",[5]
"8 very aged stools; 5 old torn flock beds & bedding; worm eaten chest"[6]

With the inventories of the less wealthy inhabitants the appraisers may have tended to put low values on the goods in order to reduce the probate administration fees which were based on the value of the inventory. For those below £5 the fee was 1/– divided equally between the scribe and the commissioners; from £5 to £40 the scribe received 1/– and the commissioners 2/6; and for values over £40 the fee was 5/– of which the scribe received half. Not until 1758 were reduced fees introduced for 'widows and others acting on behalf of inferior officers and men dying in H.M. navy'. The fee then became 1/– for inventories below £5, 2/– between £5 and £40, and 3/– for those over £40 in total value.

In *Bristol Observed* Dr J.H. Bettey gives the population of the City of Bristol as not above 12,000 during the sixteenth century; about 15,000 on the eve of the Civil War (1642); 20,000 by 1700, rising to some 68,000 by the end of the century.[7] Over the three years 1641–1643 there is an average of 45 city inventories a year or about three per thousand of the population. By 1700 the average had fallen to 20 a year representing one per thousand of the population. The series of year-bundles ceases in 1764 after which only occasional inventories remain. These originate either from the probate administrations, the Court of Ecclesiastical Causes or through being permanently attached to their wills.

Information included in this guide

We have listed the probate inventories in alphabetical order arranging the information in six columns. The first records the year of the

---

[2] Wade, 1609/75, *infra* pg. 238.
[3] Marshe, 1623/42, *infra* pg. 150.
[4] Pentegrace, 1624/52, *infra* pg. 176.
[5] Aspley, 1633/2, *infra* pg. 6.
[6] Dr. Hussey, 1635/48, *infra* pg. 121.
[7] J.H. Bettey, *Bristol Observed*, Bristol, 1986, pp. 28, 43 & 61.

bundle of inventories in which that particular one is stored, together with its position in that bundle. The second gives the name of the person to whom it refers, and the third the parish or area from which it came. The fourth gives the deceased's occupation or status; the fifth the value of the goods in the inventory, and the final column contains any necessary notes. The occupation and status given in the fourth column is the subject of a separate index; while the distribution of inventories year by year and the occurrence of a large and distinctive class of mariners' inventories in the eighteenth century are shown in the appendixes.

Column 1. Date of inventory bundle and other references

The probate inventory documents (for they are not all inventories) are stored in the year-bundles in which they were received by the Bristol Record Office, regardless of whether it was the year of appraisal, the year of exhibition, or the year in which they were received at the probate registry.

The inventories, which are folded and numbered on the outside, often have more than one set of numbers. In the earlier bundles they were already grouped alphabetically according to the first letter of the deceased's name and numbered in ink; but by 1697 this arrangement was not always observed. Consequently, starting with the year 1700, each bundle has been re-arranged by us in strict alphabetical order and the documents re-numbered in pencil to correspond. These are the numbers which, with the date of the year-bundle, form the specific reference to every document and which are given in the first column of this Guide. Thus 1692/4 indicates that the inventory is the fourth document in the bundle for 1692. The original numbering showed that there had been a loss of less than eight inventories per thousand between 1667 and 1720, that one was missing from the 1722 bundle and five from 1760.

Executor's accounts occur regularly among the documents. They may consist of just a lew lines added at the end of an inventory, or they may be on separate sheets and very detailed. For the years between 1677 and 1680 there are groups of accounts at the end of each bundle, and these are noticeably in a worse state of preservation than the inventories themselves. Accounts were not always completed until several years after the inventory was made, and then being in a different year, they remained unrelated until brought together in this Guide.

Occasionally inventories were written at the foot of a will,[7] or were fastened to it with a seal. These, of necessity, remain with the wills, but they have been numbered into their place in the alphabetical sequence, although physically missing from the year-bundles. Should a gap in the numbering be noticed when looking through the actual

---

[7] See, for example, Sarah Aland, 1689/–, *infra* p. 3.

inventories, reference to the separate year-lists[8] and then to this Guide will show if this is the explanation. Some inventories were required for proceedings in the consistory court and they also remain with those records. They are identified in the Guide by the letters 'CP' showing that they are with the 'Cause Papers'.[9] They may occur in those records several years after the date of the inventory.

When probate inventories have been found with the wills or administrations and have been introduced by us into the existing sequence, the number on the document preceeding the insertion has been given the suffix 'A' and the inserted one 'B'. Second copies of an inventory, or multiple documents relating to the same person (for example Ann Leaper's eleven documents)[10] have been given lower case letters after their sequence number. Between the years 1748 and 1758 there are several examples of inventories being written on the back of discarded documents, and in one case on the back of an earlier inventory.[11] These earlier documents cover a variety of subjects: a coal-works at Bitton,[12] a storm at sea,[13] the slave trade,[14] two excommunications[15] and a marriage allegation.[16]

We have made lists of all the Bristol wills covering the period of the inventories, recording both parish and occupation. When the name, date, parish and occupation given on a will were found to agree with an inventory the entry in the Guide is prefixed 'W', and the date of the will given if it is more than a year earlier than that of the inventory. If there is some difference between the information on an inventory and a will that might be relevant to it the prefix '(w)' has been used. The parish may not be the same, the occupation may be described differently or it may be a husband's will followed by his widow's inventory. Examination of the will may nevertheless be of interest.

When an inventory is found in a year-bundle which is much later than its appraisal date there is usually some special reason. It may be the coming of age of a minor, the sale of a lease, or a delay in the receipt of rent or of debts due to the estate. Occasionally it appears that another death in the family drew attention to the need for an inventory not previously provided. This tendency is more noticeable in the rural areas. A specific example is provided by the inventories of Thomas Adlam senior and Thomas Adlam junior which are in the same year-bundle although the father died two years before his son.[17]

---

[8] Available in Bristol Record Office.
[9] Bristol Record Office EP/J/2.
[10] Ann Leaper, 1634/44, *infra* pg. 138.
[11] See entry for Martin Lynch, 1758/4B, *infra* pg. 147.
[12] James Field, 1750/11, *infra* pg. 79.
[13] Thomas Bromby, 1753/4, *infra* pg. 29.
[14] Thomas Parry, 1749/57, *infra* pg. 173.
[15] George Beard, 1748/6 *infra* pg. 17, and Thomas Maddocks, 1749/42 pg. 148.
[16] Thomas Liberton, 1749/39, *infra* pg. 141.
[17] Thomas Adlam snr and jr., 1726/1 and 1726/2, *infra* pg. 3.

Column 2. Names

The name of a person to whom the inventory refers may well appear on it three times, written by three different people and with a different spelling each time.

Inventories usually open with the words: "A true and perfect inventory of all the goods and chattels of *John Smith* of the parish of *St. Stephen* . . ." followed by his occupation. This statement contains the appraiser's spelling of the name, and unless it is illiterate or phonetic it is the one given preference in this Guide. The name may also appear in the exhibition statement if the copy has been presented for probate; and there is a latinised form of the name, written in a professional hand, as a heading, on the outside of the folded document. This is not always free from error: Edward Hynam appears in the 1669 year-bundle between Clary and Cox because his occupation, cooper, was taken as his surname;[18] and John Clement who lived in Shirehampton and was buried at Westbury-on-Trym, is credited with belonging to Henbury parish.[19] Nevertheless, these latin headings are valuable as they sometimes confirm the parish, or help to clarify an ambiguity such as whether an inventory of (say) "Widow Hollister's goods" arises from her own death or that of her late husband.

Giving preference to the spelling used by the appraiser results in a variety of closely similar spellings being indexed for the same generic name. There has been no attempt to group or classify them, or to include every minor variation. Each document has been indexed under the most reasonable spelling of the person's name that occurs on it. Alternative spellings have only been given a separate entry when needed for clarification. The exhibition notice often contains information about the family or next of kin, but after 1676, the year in which fresh legislation was introduced,[20] it is more likely to be a simple endorsement of the fee paid.

The spelling of a name on a will may differ significantly from that on the corresponding inventory; for example Duplant/Deplant and Jennings/Genning. Consequently, when looking for a specific name it is necessary to check all possible spellings. The curious name 'Wethon Wewol' has been interpreted as Welthian Vowel (reading the 'V' as doubled to form a capital letter and with the vowels accidentally transposed). Katherine Frances Neck (1723/20) is one of the few people with more than one christian name.

After 1704 numerous mariners' inventories appear, and introduce many foreign and unfamiliar names: Oman, Peuryfy, Syfere, Touffi, Thair, Thydall, Varah and many others who joined their ships in Bristol, registered their wills here, and never returned.

The social conditions of the time often made it expedient for a

[18] Edward Hynam, 1669/17, *infa* pp. 121.
[19] John Clement, 1648/4, *infra* pp. 46.
[20] 29 Charles II, c.3.

widow to marry again within a short period of her husband's death, perhaps before the administration of his estate was complete. Thus we have the inventory of Robert Marlowe dated December 1634, and a grant of administration to Elizabeth Mason, alias Marlowe, wife of John Mason and relict of Robert Marlowe, dated March 1634.[21] This resulted in a woman being known by more than one name; and to clarify her identity her previous name was kept as an alias. An alias may also arise from the wife's maiden name or originate from her husband's occupation. Such aliases served to maintain the legal identity of the individual, and were important when legacies or property were involved. Sons and daughters would be known by either name according to the circumstances, and their aliases might continue for many years. The various entries for John, Joyce and Richard Adams and for Marie Tilladams between 1618 and 1667 demonstrate this. With aliases, both names have been recorded and cross-referenced in the Guide.

In the same way that an alias recorded on an inventory helped to preserve a person's identity, so inventories were occasionally used as a means of recording an interest in certain property. William Redman's inventory[22] regarding the annual value of an old inn called the 'Worlds End' at Lawford's Gate may have been made with this in mind.

Column 3. Parishes and areas

The area from which these inventories are drawn contains almost an equal number of city and rural parishes. The inventories give the city parishes according to their dedication and the rural ones according to their locality.

The term 'parish' is used here in the rather liberal sense in which it appears on the inventories. Castle Precincts was a non-parochial area adjacent to St. Peter's church and many of its inhabitants were likely to describe themselves as being of St. Peter's parish. St. Mark's on College Green, originally the chapel of the Gaunt's Hospital, was acquired by the Corporation in 1542 and granted to the French Protestant refugees who worshipped there until 1722. The term 'Barton Regis' was frequently used for that part of the parish of St. Philip and St. Jacob which lay outside the city boundary, but it would be unrealistic to assume that 'SS. Philip & Jacob' always referred to the in-parish and 'Barton Regis' to the out-parish. Inventories are included from the parishes of Bedminster and St. George, Easton-in-Gordano, but these were never part of the city and deanery of Bristol.

All the earlier city inventories bear the name of the parish, but increasingly after 1660, and especially after 1675, they frequently state just 'City of Bristol', while the rural ones continue to give their

---

[21] Robert Marlowe, 1634/49 (a) and (d), *infra* pg. 150.
[22] William Redman, 1640/53, *infra* pg. 190.

place of origin. The names of the parishes have been given their modern form, but in one or two places (i.e. Broad Street and Wine Street) only the street named can be given, as it is impossible to know in which of two neighbouring parishes the deceased lived.

TABLE I

The parishes or areas from which the inventories arise

City parishes or wards	Rural parishes or areas
All Saints	Abbots Leigh
*Castle Precinct	Almondsbury
Christchurch	Alveston
St. Augustine	*Barton Regis
St. Ewen	Clifton
St. George (after 1756)	Compton Greenfield
St. James	Elberton
St. John	Filton
St. Leonard	Frenchay
*St. Mark (le Gaunts)	Henbury
St. Mary-le-Port	Horfield
St. Mary, Redcliffe	Littleton-on-Severn
St. Michael	Mangotsfield
St. Nicholas	Olveston
St. Peter	St. George,
SS. Philip & Jacob	Easton-in-Gordano
St. Stephen	Stapleton
St. Thomas	Stoke Gifford
St. Werburgh	Westbury-on-Trym
Temple	Winterbourne

The areas asterisked are not ecclesiastical parishes.

In the inventories from the rural areas the part of the parish is often given. This applies particularly to a large parish such as Westbury-on-Trym with its three tithings of Westbury-on-Trym, Redland and Shirehampton. Shirehampton, being near the mouth of the River Avon, had a maritime interest and its inhabitants included a number of sailors, mariners and pilots. Westbury also had a number of isolated farms or 'island sites' out on the Severn Marsh, an area normally associated with Henbury. Such apparent anomalies as 'Henbury (Lawrence Weston)' and 'Westbury-on-Trym (Lawrence Weston)' are both technically correct. A similar situation arises with the smaller parish of Compton Greenfield which lies within the tithing of Compton in the parish of Henbury. Such descriptions are indexed in the form in which they occur. On the other hand, Aust, with its ancient church near the end of the Severn Bridge, always remained a chapelry of Henbury and all references to it are included in that parish. The two rural parishes of Alveston and Olveston are so similar in name that they are easily confused when reading the handwriting.

With the rural parishes the name given in brackets may be quite specific and refer to individual farms which still exist or can be traced today. Cattybrook, Elinors, The Worthy, Woodlands and Ingst are examples. It would be interesting to study their fortunes over the years as several inventories exist for each property.

Column 4. Occupations

The occupation or status, marital or otherwise, given in this column is taken when possible from the opening words of the inventory. Otherwise it was obtained from the will; or, failing that, from the contents of the inventory if the trade goods are sufficiently distinctive. Angular brackets have been used if the occupation is not expressly stated on the inventory. In any case, the declared occupation of the deceased may not always agree with the goods listed by the appraisers. David Potter (1720/26) is described as a surgeon, but his inventory is that of a man keeping a thriving inn of 23 rooms, while John Bittfield (1624/12), a soap-maker of St. Thomas, has an inventory filled with a miscellany of items from his general store. Such secondary occupations must remain outside the scope of this index; although with David Potter a note is included, as his inventory is such a good example of an important city inn.

The inventories from the country parishes cover a limited number of occupations and crafts such as yeoman, husbandman, blacksmith or labourer, and these can yield valuable information on the agricultural economy of the district. It is, however, from the occupations of those dwelling in the city that a picture of a more complex style of life emerges. The comprehensive list is impressive, and although several of the trade descriptions overlap or are synonymous, there are over 240 distinct occupations mentioned. These are given in the Occupation Index which allows the inventories to be traced in the main index.

One cannot work with these inventories for long without realizing how closely parish and occupation are linked. It is well known that weaving centred on Temple (the Weaver's Guild Chapel was in Temple Church); butchers operated from the Shambles in St. Mary-le-Port, and St. Thomas was alive with the arrival and departure of coaches from its several inns. What is less evident until the relationship between parish and occupation is studied in detail is how far these trades spilled over into neighbouring areas, and to what extent related trades went hand in hand. The inventories show that the butchery trade was not limited to St. Mary-le-Port or the adjacent parish of St. Nicholas but was also thriving in SS. Philip & Jacob on the city boundary where the animals arrived 'on the hoof' and were found suitable grazing until they were needed. Most hauliers came from St. John where many of the merchants lived; while the five

TABLE II

Main trades and occupations in the City of Bristol
(Occupations for which ten or more City inventories exist)

No. of inventories	Trade or occupation	No. of inventories	Trade or occupation
44	Bakers	12	Maltsters
16	Barber-surgeons	19	Masons
32	Blacksmiths	46	Merchants
66	Butchers	16	Pewterers
32	Brewers	10	Pin-makers
25	Carpenters	10	Saddlers
15	Clothiers	11	Sail-makers
136	Coopers	21	Shearmen
63	Cordwainers	11	Ship-carpenters
13	Farriers	69	Shipwrights
16	Felt-makers	17	Shoe-makers
16	Gardeners	13	Soap-boilers
15	Glaziers	22	Soap-makers
14	Grocers	54	Surgeons
14	Haberdashers	60	Tailors
15	Hauliers	14	Tanners
30	Hoopers	18	Tilers
24	House-carpenters	80	Victuallers
43	Inn-holders	29	Weavers
39	Joiners	14	Whitawers

There are inventories of 33 coal-miners, coal-drivers and colliers from the Barton Regis, Stapleton and Mangotsfield districts.

Many of the surgeons were ships' surgeons, and many of the coopers and shipwrights worked on board sea-going vessels.

carriers whose inventories we have are from SS. Philip & Jacob or Barton Regis near the Old Market.

Ship-building and its allied trades – shipwrights, ship-carpenters, joiners, sail-makers, riggers, coopers, block-makers and pump-makers – congregated in St. Stephen's parish while another group of shipwrights lived in Abbots Leigh. Was it just coincidence that they liked to live on that side of the city, or was shipbuilding then in progress at Crockern Pill? There is also a shipwright's inventory from St. George, Easton-in-Gordano and a ship-carpenter from Abbots Leigh, so this seems a distinct possibility.

The rural nature of SS. Philip & Jacob during this period is shown by the number of husbandmen and gardeners living there, by the charcoal burner, and the forest ranger. The development of Barton

Regis can also be followed; and the rise of a brick-making industry there is shown by inventories dated 1717, 1736 and 1737.

Redcliffe was favoured by chapmen. Perhaps they liked to live near the inns and hostelries of St. Thomas where travelling merchants came to display their wares. It was also the centre for the woollen industry and its trades included felt-hat making and hair-weaving. Drapers' inventories come chiefly from St. Stephen and St. Nicholas which suggests that much of their livelihood came from supplying ships and their personnel. St. James' parish included many of the trades related to building, such as house-carpenters, masons, rough-masons and paviers.

A full examination of the occupations carried out in each parish cannot be made without taking into account the information given in the wills and this goes beyond the scope of this Guide. We have prepared such lists hoping that they will give a reliable insight into the life of the various parts of the city throughout this period.

The other type of information given in this column deals with the status, marital or otherwise, of the individual concerned. It ranges from lieutenant-colonel, captain, doctor of laws to pensioner, almsman, pauper and prisoner in Newgate. The goods of a married woman were regarded as those of her husband, so it is surprising to find the term 'wife' used at all. When it does occur it is usually because there is some uncertainty as to whether her husband is still alive. Among the unmarried citizens' inventories there is an imbalance of 134 spinsters to 14 bachelors.

In the occupations and status index those widows with an inventory valued at over £100 have been specifically included because of the part many of them played in the economy of the city by loaning money on bond or by using it for adventures at sea. The less wealthy widows, together with yeomen, husbandmen and mariners, are so numerous that it is impracticable to index each entry separately.

Column 5. Values

The values given in this column have been rounded to the nearest pound and look straightforward, but there is an inherent danger that they may be misunderstood and interpreted too literally. They are 'inventory values' taken for a specific purpose. They are not a direct measure of the person's wealth, but only an evaluation of his moveable goods and chattels (including any chattel leases) and the value of any cultivated crops. They do not include the value of any freehold property he might own, any income he may have or the goodwill of his business. Neither are the goods appraised at their full value, but only at the second-hand value they would be expected to fetch if the executors were forced to sell them to clear the deceased's debts and to pay his legacies. Iron, brass, pewter, silver and gold are valued at a standard rate per pound or ounce regardless of the workmanship of the article involved. In addition, there may sometimes have been a conscious effort on the part of the appraisers to put low values on the goods to keep the fees of the probate court at a minimum. Furthermore, because people from all walks of life were called upon to appraise inventories there are bound to be inconsistencies and inaccuracies in the results, but these do not detract from the overall interest and usefulness of the figures.

Many inhabitants could, if they wished, afford to pay educated people to prepare inventories for them, or perhaps find someone among their friends or from their craft guild able to undertake this task. The distinctive writing of Samuel Fox can be recognized in several inventories of the 1680 period (e.g. Walter Howell 1680/30), and Mary Smith, a widow who ran a writing school in Church Lane, St. Thomas, wrote several mariners inventories between 1730 and 1735, of which that of Mordecai Oman 1735/31 is the last. Poorer people would press into service any neighbour who could write at all. There are inventories in which both appraisers were illiterate and who approved the document by making their mark. Under these conditions all kinds of inaccuracies could arise. The calculations may be wrong, the addition incorrect, and in at least one case the funeral expenses were included in the assets of the deceased (David Vowell, 1640/80). Such erroneous inventories were admitted for probate, and remained unchecked unless challenged. Consequently we found it necessary to check the totals of all the inventories, and to correct approximately one in five for amounts ranging from a few pence to a hundred pounds. This was in the inventory of Edward Tolson (1643/89) which has an appraisers' total of £371–14–10 instead of £271–14–10. The chief causes of error by the appraisers were found to be (1) failure to arrange their figures in distinct columns, (2) a tendency to total 10/– as an additional £1, (3) the misreading of altered or blotted figures when making the addition, and (4) the ease with which some roman numerals can be misread.

The period of these inventories covers that of the introduction of arabic numerals. Around 1610 they occur in about 10% of the inventories, but by 1650 the proportion had risen to 90%, the change being most marked after 1642. At the height of the change-over awkward hybrid values appear, such as xs 8d, £i–vj–8 and £x–0–4.

There is also the question of debts which may be due to the deceased. Sometimes these are put under two headings 'sperate' and 'desperate', but frequently they are put together as 'debts good and bad'. Consequently, to be consistent, all debts have had to be included in these values. Even if they were never recovered, such debts serve to illustrate the extent of the deceased's trading interests. Thus, in the case of John Young (1658/3) the inventory total was £2,960–18–5, and his desperate debts £2,240–19–0. The appraisers' errors and the inclusion of bad debts explains why the total value shown in this Guide often differs from that given on the inventory. Nevertheless, the inventory values give an important insight into the social status and lifestyle of each individual. The scavenger John Barwick (1687/4) with an inventory value of £125 was better-off than one would expect, while Henry Martin (1683/38) and Thomas Deane

(1745/6), both described as 'Gent.', had values of £2 and £3 respectively. The values also serve to distinguish between different inventories bearing the same name, and can point to how successfully a widow carried on the business of her late husband, or show the fortunes of a farm as it passed from father to son.

The inventory values cannot be used to provide statistically valid evidence of the distribution of wealth in the area, as many important inventories were proved in the Prerogative Court of Canterbury and do not appear in this collection; but they do afford a valuable indication of its distribution between the various trades.

Column 6. Notes

The final column of the index has been added to allow brief comments to be included where necessary. Among other things it permits reference to duplicate copies of inventories and to alternative names. It also serves to draw attention to the more comprehensive accounts of executors' expenditure. Many inventories have some reference to funeral and other expenses, but only the more informative of them are marked 'inv. & account'.

Most of the eighteenth century mariners whose names appear in the index lost their lives at sea either through sickness or wounds while on active service or through privateering activities. Their inventories consist of a formal statement of the wages due for their last voyage and may include the name of the ship and its master. There are 1486 inventories of this type during the period 1704–1764, more than half the total number. The first is typical:

Benjamin Tarr, cooper, July 1704
"Deceased's wages due on the ship Expectation of Bristol £16."

With these inventories, if the occupation is given as something other than mariner or sailor the entry is marked 'died at sea' to show it is one of this type. The occupations concerned are usually those needed on board ship: shipwrights, sailmakers, carpenters, coopers and surgeons; but there are others, for example, yeoman, cabinet-maker and stone-carver.

On the few occasions when more extensive information is needed, it has been given a full line of text and needs no further comment.

SHORT BIBLIOGRAPHY

1. *Ecclesiastical Law*, R. Burn, London, 9th edition 1842 (Vol. IV).
2. 'Probate Inventories, the Legal Background', in *The Local Historian*, Vol. 16, nos. 3 & 4, August 1984.
3. *Probate Records and the Local Community*, edited Philip Riden, Gloucester, 1985.
4. *Bristol Observed*, J.H. Bettey, Bristol, 1986.

For transcribed inventories see:

The Goods & Chattels of our Forefathers, edited J.S. Moore, Phillimore 1976. (Frampton Cotterell & District Probate Inventories 1539–1804).

Clifton & Westbury Probate Inventories 1609–1761, edited J.S. Moore, Avon Local History Association, Bristol, 1981.

City Chamberlain's Accounts of the sixteenth and seventeenth centuries, edited D. Livock, Bristol Record Society Volume xxiv, 1966, contains a transcription of Nicholas Meredith's inventory of 1639.

NOTES ON ABBREVIATIONS AND LAY-OUT

(for full details of method used, see Introduction)

In addition to the extended notes, round brackets enclose information written on the inventory.

Angular brackets enclose information taken from the will or derived from the inventory contents.

Year reference Column

This gives the year of the bundle in which the inventory is to be found and its position in that bundle.

Upper case letters mark an introduction into the numbered sequence, 'A' being the document preceeding the insertion.

Lower case letters differentiate documents relating to the same individual.

'CP' distinguishes inventories included with the Ecclesiastical Cause Papers.

W as a prefix indicates that the corresponding will exists.
(w) indicates a related, or possibly relevant, will.

Names

The spelling used by the appraiser is normally indexed unaltered.

Value

to make these comparable all values include good and bad debts and have been corrected for errors made by the appraisers in their addition. Inventory values are of moveable goods only and may not represent total wealth.

In the note on page 85 'BRS XXVI' refers to the Bristol Record Society's publication *Minute Book of the Men's Meeting of the Society of Friends in Bristol 1667–1686.*

BRISTOL PROBATE INVENTORIES

1542–1804

THE GUIDE

Year ref.	W	Name	Parish or area	Occupation or status	Value	Notes
1629/1		- anon -	'St. Mary' (damaged, name and value missing)			
1646/45		- anon -	(no name, no date and no parish)			
1682/1		Abbot, John	Temple	Pipe-maker	£2	
1748/1		Abercumby, John	City of Bristol	Mariner	£15	
1892/4	W	Abington, Martha	City of Bristol	Widow	£15	
1620/1	W	Abley, John	(see Able)		£96	
1620/1	W	Ablie, John	St. Stephen	Joiner	£239	
1669/1		Ably, Henry	St. Nicholas	Mariner	£75	
1635/1	W	Aburge, Robert	Winterbourne	⟨Husbandman⟩	£45	
1714/1	W	Adams, Abel	City of Bristol	Butcher	£41	
1685/1	W	Adams, Daniel	City of Bristol	Ropemaker	£179	
1707/2		Adams, Elizabeth	St. Stephen	Widow	£71	
1695/3A	W	Adams, Grace	Almondsbury	Widow	£136	
1678/1		Adams, Joan	St. Nicholas	Widow	£47	
1618/1		Adams, John	St. Nicholas	Butcher	£11	alias Tilledge
1664/50		Adams, John	(alias Tillis, which see)			
1740/1		Adams, John	City of Bristol	Mariner	£12	
1667/1	W	Adams, Joyce	St. Mary-le-Port	⟨Widow⟩	£481	alias Tyllis
1732/1	W	Adams, Lewis	City of Bristol	Mariner	£12	
1613/1	W	Adams, Nicholas	St. Ewen	Yeoman	£33	
1640/76	W	Adams, Richard	(alias Tyllis, which see)			
1703/1		Adams, Richard	City of Bristol	Mariner	£49	
1707/1	W	Adams, Richard	Olveston	⟨Husbandman⟩	£303	
1668/3		Adams, Robert	St. Thomas	Tailor	£2	
1704/1	W	Adams, Roger	⟨City of Bristol⟩	⟨Tailor⟩	£5	
1617/1		Adams, Thomas	St. Stephen	--	£21	
1682/2	W	Adams, William	Almondsbury	Husbandman	£137	
1683/2		Addams, Henry	St. Stephen	--	£34	
1715/1	W	Addams, George	City of Bristol	Mariner	£13	
1620/4	W	Addelie, Agnes	(see Audley)			
1720/1	W	Addes, Robert	(see Addis)			

W	Ref.	Name	Place	Occupation	Value	Notes
W	1635/2	Addice, Richard	St. Michael	<Gunsmith>	£23	
	1728/1	Addis, John	City of Bristol	Cider merchant	£5	
W	1635/2	Addis, Richard	(see Addice)			
W	1720/1	Addis, Robert	City of Bristol	Mariner	£15	
	1649/1	Addis, Thomas	St. Michael	--	£5	
	1739/1	Adeane, Mathew	St. Leonard	Wine-cooper	£3,113	inv. & account
	1620/2	Adeane, Thomas	St. Leonard	Cooper	£31	
W	1637/16	Adeane, Thomas	(see Deane)			
	1668/1	Adeane, Thomas	City of Bristol	Organist	£15	
	1732/2	Adeane, Thomas	City of Bristol	Mariner	£4	
W	1620/3	Adee, William	Henbury	Blacksmith	£49	
	1648/1a	Ades, Henry	St. James	House-carpenter	--	schedule
	1648/1b	Ades, Henry	St. James	House-carpenter	£2	inventory
W	1617/2	Adies, Isabell	Olveston <Woodhouse>	Widow	£4	
	1643/1	Adlam, John	Henbury	--	£181	
W	1666/1	Adlam, Mathew	Westbury-on-Trym	Husbandman	£28	
W	1669/2	Adlam, Thomas	Westbury-on-Trym	<Yeoman>	£133	
W	1726/1	Adlam, Thomas	Henbury	Yeoman	£305	inv. dated 1724
W	1726/2	Adlam, Thomas <jnr>	Henbury	Yeoman	£199	inv. dated 1726
	1733/1	Adlam, Thomas	Henbury	Gent.	£103	
W	1689/4	Adridge, Robert	(see Aldridge)			
	1714/2	Agnew, Joseph	City of Bristol	Mariner	£5	
	1702/1	Agrove, William	Winterbourne	--	£54	
	1716/1	Akramants, John	SS. Philip & Jacob	Brass-worker	£5	
W	1689/-	Aland, Sarah	<St. Peter> (no inventory, schedule of goods listed in will)	<Spinster>	--	
W	1709/1	Albert, Joane	Winterbourne (Hambrook)	Widow	£84	
	1642/1	Alcraft, Jefferie	St. James	<Oatmeal-maker in will>	£3	
	1732/3	Aldgate, Abraham	City of Bristol	--	£6	
W	1748/1	Aldran, John	City of Bristol	Mariner	£19	
	1691/1	Aldridge, John	City of Bristol	Baker	£14	
W	1689/4	Aldridge, Robert	City of Bristol	Mariner	£7	

	Year ref.	Name	Parish or area	Occupation or status	Value	Notes
W	1624/1	Aldworth, Francis	St. Peter	Merchant	£1,555	
W	1688/1	Alexander, Ann	Alveston	Widow	£116	
W	1719/1	Alexander, John	City of Bristol	Mariner	£7	
W	1756/1	Alexander, John	City of Bristol	Mariner	£19	
	1698/2	Alford, Sarah	City of Bristol	Spinster	£9	
	1618/2A	Alford, William	Olveston	Labourer	£11	
	1736/1	Allbright, Nicholas	Winterbourne	Mason	£10	
W	1698/1	Allbury, Mary	(see Oldbury)			
	1687/3	Allchurch, Richard	(see Orchard)			
W	1731/1	Allchurch, William	City of Bristol	\<Schoolmaster\>	£8	
	1719/2	Allen, James	(alias Allway, which see)			
W	1642/2	Allen, John	Olveston (Tockington)	Husbandman	£34	
W	1741/1	Allen, John	St. James	Glazier	£489	
	1724/15	Allen, Judith	(see Smith)			
	1636/1	Allen, Martin	(see Allin)			
W	1674/1	Allen, Randolph	St. Thomas	Inn-holder	£140	
	1627/1	Allen, Richard	Elberton	--	£7	
W	1749/1	Allen, Samuel	City of Bristol	Mariner	£10	
	1633/1	Allen, Thomas	(see Allin)			
W	1625/1	Allen, William	Knolle, Co. Warwick \<Hampton-in-Arden\>	Yeoman	--	alias Eringtone
W	1743/1	Alleston, Collen	City of Bristol	Mariner	£9	
W	1661/2	Allford, Thomas	St. Stephen	Cooper	£144	
	1707/3	Allin, John	City of Bristol	Mariner	£18	
	1636/1	Allin, Martin	St. Augustine	--	£15	
W	1627/2	Allin, Robert	Almondsbury (Over)	\<Husbandman\>	£64	
	1633/1	Allington, Thomas	St. Mary-le-Port	--	£3	
	1750/1	Allison, Walter	\<City of Bristol\>	Mariner	£4	
W	1734/1	Allway, James	Horfield	\<Mariner\>	£8	
	1719/2	Allword, Thomas	St. Michael	Yeoman	£205	alias Allen
	1668/2			Surgeon	£9	

	Reference	Name	Place	Occupation	Value	Notes
	1640/1	Alpas, Richard	Henbury (Charlton) & Horfield	Husbandman	£56	
	1618/2B	Ambrose, James	Temple	Cloth-worker	£6	
	1625/2	Ambrose, Thomas	Almondsbury	--	£64	
	1714/3	Amos, Daniel	City of Bristol		£18	inv/acct: damaged
	1753/1	Amos, John	SS. Philip & Jacob	Cooper	£22	
	1731/2	Anderson, Christopher	City of Bristol	Porter	£6	
	1730/1	Anderson, Joseph	City of Bristol	Mariner	£6	
w	1742/1	Anderson, William	City of Bristol	Mariner	£3	
	1681/1	Andras, Andrew	City of Bristol	Strong-water distiller	£146	
	1697/5	Andras, Elianore	Clifton	--	£19	
	1642/3	Andras, Samuel	St. Michael	<Mariner>	£8	
w	1684/2	Andrewes, Edward	City of Bristol	Mariner	£4	
	1669/3	Andrewes, Thomas	SS. Philip & Jacob	Charcoal maker	£193	
	1680/1	Andrewes, William	City of Bristol	Butcher	£5	
	1697/5	Andrews, Elianor	(see Andras)			
w	1678/2	Andrews, John	City of Bristol	--	£21	
w	1749/2	Andrews, Lawrence	City of Bristol	Mariner	£5	
	1687/2	Andrews, Samuel	Westbury-on-Trym	Yeoman	£70	
	1644/1	Andrews, Thomas	St. Stephen	--	£8	
	1750/2	Andrews, William	City of Bristol	Peruke-maker	£14	
	1628/1	Androes, Arthur	St. Thomas	Weaver	£4	
	1642/3	Andros, Samuel	(see Andras)			
	1636/2	Androwes, Walter	Olveston	Husbandman	£69	inv. caveat. letter
	1711/1	Appleby, Richard	<SS. Philip & Jacob>	Inn-holder	£1	
	1734/2	Archer, James	City of Bristol	Mariner	£2	
w	1705/1	Arden, John	Stoke Gifford	Yeoman	£32	
w	1707/4	Arden, Sarah	Stoke Gifford	<Widow>	£7	
w	1684/3	Arden, William	Stapleton	Tailor	£83	
w	1707/5	Arden, William	City of Bristol	Mariner	£6	
w	1625/3	Ardington, Christian	Westbury-on-Trym	--	£4	also 2nd copy
	1618/3	Armestronge, Thomas	St. Thomas	--	£32	
	1709/2	Armstrong, Richard	City of Bristol	Mariner	£14	

	Year ref.	Name	Parish or area	Occupation or status	Value	Notes
	1663/1	Arnee, John	St. Thomas	--	£38	
	1664/2	Arnee, Mary	St. Thomas	Widow	£79	
	1736/2	Arnell, John	City of Bristol	Mariner	£9	
W	1701/1	Arney, Thomas ⟨snr⟩	⟨City of Bristol⟩	Baker	£115	
W	1716/2	Arney, Thomas	⟨SS. Phillip & Jacob⟩	Baker	£81	
	1642/4	Arnie, William	SS. Phillip & Jacob	--	£10	
	1683/1	Arnold, Thomas	City of Bristol	Cordwainer	£16	
	1674/2	Arnoll, William	SS.Phillip & Jacob	Ranger	£3	
W	1707/5	Aron, William	(see Arden)			
	1748/3	Arpin, George	City of Bristol	Mariner	£15	
W	1691/3	Arrundell, Elizabeth	St. Nicholas	Widow	£137	
W	1663/3	Arters, Ann	St. Mark	Widow	£85	
W	1745/1	Arters, Charles	City of Bristol	Mariner	£15	
	1625/3	Arthington, Christian	(see Ardington)			
W	1745/1	Arthur, Charles	(see Arters)			
W	1718/1	Arthur, James	SS. Phillip & Jacob	Pensioner ⟨Mariner⟩	£8	
	1671/1	Arthur, Samuel	City of Bristol	Mariner	£5	
W	1754/1	Arthurs, Hyett	City of Bristol	Hooper	£10	died at sea
	1748/4	Arthurs, John	Stapleton	Carpenter	£10	
	1663/2	Arundell, Margaret	SS. Phillip & Jacob	Widow	£22	
	1711/2	Asbury, Nicholas	City of Bristol	Mariner	£7	
W	1740/2	Ashby, Edward	City of Bristol	Mariner	£3	
	1747/1	Ashfield, John	City of Bristol	Mariner	£10	
W	1763/1A	Ashford, Charles	City of Bristol	Mariner	£10	
	1628/2	Ashford, William	SS. Phillip & Jacob	Yeoman	£140	
W	1713/1	Ashley, John	Henbury	Cordwainer	£73	
W	1679/3	Ashley, Robert	St. John	Cordwainer	£8	
W	1611/1	Ashlin, Thomas	SS. Phillip & Jacob	Husbandman	£174	
	1609/1	Askewe, John	Henbury	Baker	£51	
	1633/2	Aspley, Thomas	St. Nicholas	--	£158	
	1703/2	Astin, Richard	(see Austin)			

	Reference	Name	Place	Occupation	Value
W	1627/3	Atkins, Agnes	Filton	Widow	£11
	1723/1	Atkins, Anthony	City of Bristol	Mariner	£8
W	1698/30	Atkins, Elizabeth	(alias Simons, which see)		
	1661/3	Atkins, Joan	(see Atkyns)		
W	1679/1	Atkins, Joan	Elberton	Widow	£11
W	1691/2	Atkins, John	City of Bristol	Mariner <Cooper>	£12
	1697/3	Atkins, John	--	--	£7
W	1685/2	Atkins, John	<City of Bristol>	<Cordwainer>	£21
W	1680/42	Atkins, Robert	(alias Sansom, which see)		
	1701/2	Atkins, Thomas	St. Stephen	Joiner	£252
W	1613/2	Atkins, William	City of Bristol	Mariner	£72
	1717/1	Atkinson, Joseph	Almondsbury <Over>	Widow	£6
W	1661/3	Atkyns, Joan	St. Thomas	Freemason	£309
	1668/4	Attkins, Thomas	Stapleton	Widow	£86
W	1649/2	Attwood, Agnes	Olveston	Widow	£338
	1684/1	Attwood, Ann	Mangotsfield	Widow	£11
W	1706/1	Attwood, Bridget	Barton Regis	Widow	£155
W	1689/1	Attwood, Francis	Stapleton	Felt-maker	£13
	1609/2	Attwood, Henry	Winterbourne	--	£69
W	1623/1	Attwood, Henry	Stoke Gifford	--	£24
W	1609/3	Attwood, John	Stoke Gifford	Husbandman	£25
W	1635/3	Attwood, John	(Stapleton)	Husbandman	£14
	1637/1	Attwood, John	Stapleton	Husbandman	£420
W	1697/2	Attwood, Mary	City of Bristol	Widow	£9
W	1694/1	Attwood, Rebecca	Stapleton	Widow	£34
W	1661/4	Attwood, Richard	Winterbourne (Hambrook)	<Yeoman>	£76
W	1664/1	Attwood, Richard	Stapleton	Yeoman	£125
	1676/1	Attwood, Richard	SS. Philip & Jacob	Husbandman	£5
W	1697/7	Attwood, William	Mangotsfield	Yeoman	£190
W	1729/1	Atwood, Barnaby	<SS. Philip & Jacob>	<Soapmaker>	£329
W	1627/4	Atwood, Joan	Stapleton	<Widow>	£9

	Year ref.	Name	Parish or area	Occupation or status	Value	Notes
	1696/1	Atwood, John	--	--	£2	
W	1705/2	Atwood, Joseph	Winterbourne <Hambrook>	--	£77	
W	1686/3	Atwood, Phillip	Stapleton	<Yeoman>	£67	
W	1634/1	Atwood, Sara	Stapleton	Single-woman	£26	
W	1705/3	Atwood, Thomas	<City of Bristol>	<Shipwright>	£48	
W	1648/2	Atwood, William	Stapleton	Yeoman	£216	
W	1685/3	Atwood, William	City of Bristol	Felt-maker	£37	
W	1620/4	Audley, Agnes	Almondsbury	Single-woman	£13	
W	1661/1	Austen, John	St. Mary, Redcliffe	Chapman	£93	
	1667/2	Austin, Humphrey	St. Thomas	Butcher	£20	alias Scarlett
W	1710/1	Austin, John	Olveston (Tockington)	Blacksmith	£47	
W	1746/32	Austin, John	City of Bristol	Mariner	£11	
	1703/2	Austin, Richard	Henbury (Stowick)	Fisherman	£13	
	1682/3	Austin, William	St. Mary, Redcliffe	Wire-drawer	£17	
	1609/4	Austine, George	Abbots Leigh	--	£21	
W	1697/6	Avery, Jacob	Henbury (Kingsweston)	Yeoman	£88	
	1679/2	Avery, Richard	SS. Philip & Jacob	<Whip-maker>	£2	
W	1720/2	Avery, Thomas	City of Bristol	Stuff-maker	£297	
	1716/3	Awre, John	City of Bristol	Cooper	£12	
	1687/1	Axford, Jonathan	St. Peter	Pewterer	£147	
	1670/1	Axson, Thomas	St. James	Mariner	£42	
W	1704/2	Ayleffe, Robert	City of Bristol	Mariner	£3	
	1705/4	Ayliffe, Elizabeth	City of Bristol	Widow	£50	
	1689/3	Ayloff, Anthony	City of Bristol	--	£62	
	1732/4	Aylward, Thomas	City of Bristol	Mariner	£3	
W	1620/5	Ayton, Elizabeth	Henbury	Widow	£50	
W	1635/4	Ayton, Henry	Temple	Brewer	£110	1635 will
W	1636/3	Ayton, William	Henbury <Kingroad>	Yeoman	£222	
W	1611/2	Aytton, Christopher	Almondsbury	Husbandman	£28	

	Reference	Name	Place	Occupation	Value	Note
W	1692/9	Baber, Alice	⟨City of Bristol⟩	⟨Widow⟩	£10	
	1689/46	Baber, John	--	Blacksmith	£17	
W	1675/8	Baber, John (snr)	⟨Mangotsfield⟩	⟨Husbandman⟩	£29	
W	1678/12	Baber, Richard	St. Thomas	Tobacconist	£60	
	1613/4	Baccat, Thomas	City of Bristol	--	£4	
	1708/1	Backwell, Henry	St. Nicholas	Water-bailiff	£20	
	1758/1	Bacon, Jonas or Jonathan	City of Bristol	Yeoman	£19	
W	1639/1	Bacon, John	Henbury	--	£108	
	1710/2	Bacon, Richard	City of Bristol	Grocer	£1,415	
W	1628/3	Badcocke, Nicholas	St. Mary, Redcliffe	--	£4	
W	1673/1	Baddam, Susanna	St. John	⟨Widow⟩	£33	
	1661/7	Baddum, George	St. Stephen	Surgeon	£18	
(w)	1773/CP	Badger, Daniel	City of Bristol	Tailor	£44	
W	1666/8	Bagg, Margaret	St. Nicholas	Widow	£76	
	1675/4	Bagg, Thomas	City of Bristol	Butcher	£7	
	1675/11	Bagg, Thomas	(duplicate of 1675/4, above)				
	1665/4	Bagg, William	St. Nicholas	Butcher	£23	
W	1611/5	Bailie, William	Clifton	⟨Husbandman⟩	£68	
	1609/7	Baily, John	Mangotsfield	--	£71	
	1679/5	Baily, William	St. Nicholas	Joiner	£31	
	1685/11	Baker, Abraham	City of Bristol	Porter	£14	
	1678/9	Baker, Alice	St. Stephen	Widow	£23	alias Porter
	1611/3	Baker, Arthur	Westbury-on-Trym (Shirehampton)	--	£43	
W	1635/5	Baker, George	SS. Phillip & Jacob	--	£17	
W	1698/5	Baker, Henry	City of Bristol	Merchant	£37	
W	1624/2	Baker, John	Compton Greenfield	--	£127	
	1671/3	Baker, John	St. John	Gent	£30	
W	1701/3	Baker, John	Henbury (Aust)	Yeoman	£842	
	1721/1	Baker, John	City of Bristol	Surgeon	£4	died at sea
W	1731/3	Baker, Malline	Henbury	--	£178	
	1684/7	Baker, Margery	City of Bristol	--	£29	

Year ref.		Name	Parish or area	Occupation or status	Value	Notes
1717/2		Baker, Philip	Abbots Leigh	Mason	£10	
1707/6	W	Baker, Robert	Henbury	Yeoman	£208	
1642/5		Baker, Thomas	St. Thomas	Hooper	£8	
1643/2	W	Baker, Thomas	Henbury (Aust)	Tailor	£33	
1662/5		Baker, Thomas	Henbury	Husbandman	£322	
1613/45	W	Baker, Walter	(alias Petipace, which see)	--		
1611/6	W	Baker, William	Henbury (Charlton)	Carpenter	£55	
1746/1		Baker, William	City of Bristol	Mariner	£5	
1666/2		Baldwin, William	St. Stephen	--	£362	
1639/2		Baldwin, Thomas	Henbury	Husbandman	£187	
1613/5	W	Baldwin, George	<St. Augustine>	Gent.	£480	
1709/3		Balies, Josiah	City of Bristol	Whitawer	£17	
1684/9		Ball, Andrew	St. James	--	£19	
1669/10		Ball, George	SS. Philip & Jacob	Prisoner	£7	
1687/13	W	Ball, Margaret	City of Bristol	Widow	£60	
1635/6	W	Ball, Margery	Mangotsfield	Widow	£62	
1678/3	W	Ball, Martha	SS. Philip & Jacob	Widow	£36	
1625/4	W	Ball, John	Mangotsfield	<Husbandman>	£83	
1637/3	W	Ball, John	Mangotsfield	<Husbandman>	£69	
1715/2	W	Ball, John	City of Bristol	Victualler	£7	
1613/3		Ball, Thomas	Mangotsfield	Husbandman	£38	
1678/7	W	Ball, William	St. James	--	£33	
1678/66		Balldin, Thomas	St. James (see Baldwin)	--	£33	account only
1639/2		Baller, Joseph	City of Bristol	Mariner	£7	
1734/3	W	Ballor, William	Abbots Leigh	--	£7	
1669/7		Ballwell, William	Christchurch	Carpenter	£164	
1699/1	W	Balmont, William	City of Bristol	Mariner	£17	
1745/2		Bambridge, William	City of Bristol	Mariner	£9	
1742/2		Bampton, Henry	Mangotsfield	<Yeoman>	£176	
1670/5	W	Bampton, Nicholas	St. Peter	Butcher	£82	
1646/1						

	Ref.	Name	Place	Occupation	Value	Notes
W	1669/12	Bampton, Samuel	Mangotsfield	Yeoman	£100	
	1716/4	Band, Thomas	--	Lighterman	£26	
	1693/3	Bane, John	Stapleton	--	£4	
W	1618/4	Banfield, Elizabeth	St. James	Widow	£3	
W	1641/1	Banister, Henry	Abbots Leigh	<Yeoman>	£175	will 1640
W	1673/6	Banks, Mary	Stapleton	Widow	£5	
	1696/6	Bannatine, Ronald	City of Bristol	Mariner	£20	
	1646/1	Bannton, Nicholas	(see Bampton)		--	
	1641/2	Banton, William	St. Peter	Seaman		
W	1690/3	Baptist, John	SS. Philip & Jacob (Barton Hill)	Wax-chandler	£187	
	1643/3	Barenfield, Richard	St. Mary, Redcliffe	--	£4	
	1715/5	Barjew, Margaret	City of Bristol	Widow	£123	
	1707/7	Barjew, Thomas	City of Bristol	Baker	£382	
W	1637/4	Barker, Sarah	St. Mary, Redcliffe	Widow	£78	
	1663/9	Barker, Thomas	St. Nicholas	Merchant	£55	
W	1718/2a	Barker, Thomas	City of Bristol	Mariner	£7	
W	1718/2b	Barker, Thomas	(the account of Sarah Jones, administratrix)			
W	1620/6	Barker, William	St. Werburgh	Merchant	£249	
	1717/3	Barkwell, Simon	City of Bristol	Mariner	£12	
	1737/1	Barlow, Edward	City of Bristol	Wine-cooper	£12	died at sea
W	1611/4	Barlye, Thomas	Olveston (Tockington)	Mason	£27	
W	1624/3	Barnard, Henry	St. Stephen	--	£84	
	1746/2	Barnard, Matthew	City of Bristol	Mariner	£8	
	1736/3	Barnard, Robert	City of Bristol	Mariner	£4	
	1681/5	Barnard, William	City of Bristol	Blockmaker	£11	
W	1639/3	Barnes, Alice	Henbury <Lawrence Weston>	Widow	£41	
	1624/4a	Barnes, John	Temple	--	£25	
	1624/4b	Barnes, John	Temple	--	--	
			(unpriced list of goods and apparel)			
W	1717/4	Barnes, John	Henbury <Compton Greenfield>	--	£72	

Year ref.		Name	Parish or area	Occupation or status	Value	Notes
W	1727/1	Barnes, John	London	Mariner	£3	
W	1625/5	Barnes, Nicholas	Clifton	⟨Lighterman⟩	£93	
	1730/2	Barnes, Nicholas	City of Bristol	Mariner	£7	
W	1715/3	Barnes, Robert	⟨St. Thomas⟩	Cordwainer	£69	
	1646/2	Barnes, Thomas	Alveston	Husbandman	£102	
W	1626/1	Barnes, William	Temple	Clothworker	£12	
	1635/7	Barnes, William	Temple	Clothier	£13	
	1752/1	Barns, Edward	City of Bristol	Mariner	£3	
W	1749/6	Barnsby, William	City of Bristol	Mariner	£10	
W	1714/4	Barnwell, John	City of Bristol	Mariner	£4	
	1628/4	Barram, Richard	St. Augustine	—	£11	
W	1672/6	Barrat, Anna	Almondsbury	Widow	£210	
	1628/6	Barrat, Thomas	St. Michael	—	£10	
W	1639/5	Barratt, Ann	St. Nicholas	Widow	£179	
W	1748/5	Barratt, Edward	City of Bristol	Haulier	nil	
W	1679/6	Barre, Elizabeth	Westbury-on-Trym (Shirehampton)	Widow	£29	
			—	—	£3	
W	1694/3	Barren, Alexander	(see Barrat)			
W	1672/6	Barret, Anna	Almondsbury	Yeoman	£258	
W	1668/11	Barret, Robert	(see Barratt)			
W	1639/5	Barrett, Ann	St. Peter	Widow	£23	
	1634/2	Barrett, Elizabeth	City of Bristol	Spinster	£4	
	1721/2	Barrett, Sarah	City of Bristol	Mariner	£6	
W	1747/2	Barrett, William	City of Bristol	Mariner	£5	
W	1749/3	Barrett, William	City of Bristol	Mariner	£10	with wills
W	1766/1	Barrey, James	—	—	£4+	
	1691/7	Barrey, Peter	St. Augustine	—	£10	
	1639/4	Barrie, Alice	St. Augustine	—	£8	
	1634/3	Barrie, Anthony	City of Bristol	Mariner	£5	
W	1740/3	Barry, Andrew	City of Bristol	Cooper	£5	died at sea
W	1739/2	Barry, David				

	Ref.	Name	Place	Occupation	Value	Notes
W	1766/2	Barry, James	City of Bristol	Mariner	£3	with wills
	1620/7	Bartayn, Elinor	(see Barton)			
W	1617/3	Barten, Richard	St. Augustine	Blacksmith	£41	
	1624/5	Barter, Thomas	St. Thomas	--	£5	
	1741/2	Bartholomew, Benjamin	Westbury-on-Trym	Cordwainer	£43	
W	1618/5	Bartlet, Edward	Almondsbury	Yeoman	£130	
	1634/4	Bartlet, Edward	Almondsbury (Compton)--		£28	
W	1669/14	Bartlet, Edward	Almondsbury <Patchway>		£163	
W	1694/7	Bartlet, Elizabeth	Almondsbury	Widow	£79	
	1641/3	Bartlett, Alice	Almondsbury	Widow	£16	
	1745/3	Bartlett, Ambrose	City of Bristol	Cooper	£14	
	1744/1	Bartlett, John	City of Bristol	Brush-maker	£117	
	1620/7	Barton, Elinor	St. Augustine	Widow	£6	
	1704/3	Barton, Francis	--	--	£12	
W	1664/9	Barton, John	Littleton-on-Severn	--	£69	
W	1678/29	Barton, John	Henbury (Compton Greenfield)	<Cordwainer>	£114	also marked 'Grenvil' outside
	1679/12	Barton, John	Henbury (Compton Greenfield)	Cordwainer	£29	
	1755/1	Barton, Richard	City of Bristol	Mariner	£7	
	1678/11	Barton, Thomas	Henbury (Compton Greenfield)	--	£115	compare 1678/64
	1678/64	Barton, Thomas	Henbury (Compton Greenfield)	--	£111	compare 1678/11
	1633/3	Barton, William	St. Augustine	Lighterman	£8	
W	1665/5	Barwell, Jonas	St. Thomas	Cloth-worker	£20	
	1687/4	Barwick, John	City of Bristol	Scavenger	£125	
	1714/5	Barwick, John	City of Bristol	Mariner	£45	
	1717/5a	Barwick, John	<St. Michael>	Mariner	£17	inv. & account
	1717/5b	Barwick, John	<St. Michael>	Mariner	£35	
		(additn. inv. & account of Christopher Smith, administrator)				
W	1620/9	Basely, Joanna	(see Baslee)			

	Year ref.	Name	Parish or area	Occupation or status	Value	Notes
	1740/4	Basker, Thomas	(see Bosker)			
W	1620/9	Baslee, Joanna	St. Michael	Widow	£23	
W	1675/6	Bason, Katherine	City of Bristol	Widow	£83	
W	1673/2	Bason, Thomas	Castle Precinct	\<Distiller\>	£229	
W	1744/2	Bass, Antony	City of Bristol	Mariner	£28	
	1609/5	Bass, Margaret	--	--	£17	alias Philpott
	1723/2	Bass, William	City of Bristol	Mariner	£5	
	1731/4	Bassat, William	City of Bristol	House-carpenter	£10	
	1686/6	Basset, John	City of Bristol	Tobacconist	£29	
	1731/4	Basset, William	(see Bassat)			
W	1768/CP	Bastable, Nancy	City of Bristol	Widow	£169	inv. & account
W	1637/2	Batchiler, Susan	St. James	Widow	£116	
	1620/8	Bateman, Edward	Westbury-on-Trym (Shirehampton)	--	£4	
	1633/4	Bateman, William	Westbury-on-Trym (Shirehampton)	Yeoman	£94	
	1736/4	Bates, Jonas	City of Bristol	Weaver	£117	inv. & account
W	1617/4	Batman, Elizabeth	Westbury-on-Trym	Widow	£98	
	1735/1	Batt, Abraham	SS. Philip & Jacob	Distiller	£199	
	1640/2	Batt, Henry	St. Mary, Redcliffe	Sailor	£1	
	1702/2	Batten, Francis	City of Bristol	Inn-holder	£132	
	1685/10	Batten, George	City of Bristol	Cooper	£176	
	1694/4	Batten, George	--	--	£11	
	1663/4	Batten, Griffin	St. Stephen	Cooper	£346	
	1749/4	Batten, James	City of Bristol	Mariner	£10	
	1639/6	Batten, Joan	St. Augustine	--	£113	
	1643/4	Batten, Joan	City of Bristol	--	£28	
W	1611/7	Batten, John	Stoke Gifford (Harry Stoke)	Husbandman	£59	
	1701/4	Batten, Margaret	City of Bristol	Widow	£66	
W	1647/1	Batten, Thomas	Winterbourne	--	£36	

	Ref.	Name	Place	Occupation	Value	Notes
W	1661/5	Batten, Thomas	St. Augustine	--	£21	
	1678/8	Batten, Thomas	St. Augustine	Mariner	£16	
	1733/2	Battin, Henry	City of Bristol	Mariner	£9	
	1682/5	Battman, Stanton	City of Bristol	--	£11	inv. & account
W	1666/7	Baugh, Elizabeth	St. James	Widow	£320	
	1704/4	Baugh, Hester	City of Bristol	Widow	£212	
	1639/7	Baugh, Richard	Christchurch	--	£21	
	1609/6	Baughe, John	St. Stephen	Turner	£5	
	1669/5	Baune, George	Winterbourne	Baker	£103	
	1693/3	Baune, John	(see Bane)			
	1754/2	Bave, Martha	City of Bristol	Widow	£10	formerly Bright
	1667/11	Bawne, Nathaniel	Stapleton	Miller	£30	
W	1687/10	Baxter, Sarah	City of Bristol	Widow	£142	
W	1742/3	Baxter, William	City of Bristol	Mariner	£3	
	1757/1	Bayler, Peter	City of Bristol	Mariner	£9	
	1681/2	Bayley, Isaac	Stoke Gifford	Yeoman	£31	
	1620/10	Bayley, John	St. Augustine	--	£4	
W	1618/7	Bayley, Thomas	Almondsbury	Tailor	£8	
W	1676/2	Bayley, William	(see Baylie)			
W	1679/4	Bayley, William	City of Bristol	Joiner	£40	
	1667/4	Baylie, Ann	Winterbourne	Widow	£43	
W	1620/11	Baylie, Francis	Temple	Cloth-worker	£994	
	1609/7	Baylie, John	(see Baily)			
	1685/9	Baylie, John	--	--	£47	
W	1625/6	Baylie, Katherine	Clifton	--	£8	also 2nd copy
	1633/5	Baylie, Nicholas	Olveston (Tockington)	Husbandman	£73	
W	1641/4	Baylie, Thomas	Winterbourne <Hambrook>			
	1623/2	Baylie, William	Clifton	Yeoman	£517	
W	1676/2	Baylie, William	Almondsbury	--	£5	
W	1637/5	Bayly, Agnes	Clifton	Yeoman	£111	
			(a 1637 will of Anne Baylie of Clifton exists)	Widow	£8	
	1723/3	Bayly, Edward	City of Bristol	Mariner	£226	inv & account

Year ref.	Name	Parish or area	Occupation or status	Value	Notes
W 1711/4	Bayly, Elianor	City of Bristol	Widow	£123	
W 1676/6	Bayly, Elizabeth	Winterbourne (Hambrook)	Widow	£409	
1677/60	Bayly, Elizabeth	Winterbourne (Hambrook)	--	£409	account only
W 1620/11	Bayly, Francis	(see Baylie)			
1692/7	Bayly, George	Winterbourne (Frenchay)	Husbandman	£139	
W 1624/6	Bayly, Joan	St. Michael	Widow	£3	
W 1668/10	Bayly, John	St. Stephen	Shipwright	£65	
1687/14A	Bayly, John (snr)	SS. Philip & Jacob	--	£105	2 inventories
1687/14B	Bayly, John (jnr)	SS. Philip & Jacob	--	£5	
1727/2	Bayly, John	Winterbourne	Cordwainer	£18	
W 1620/12	Bayly, Margaret	Westbury-on-Trym	Single-woman	£30	
1667/6	Bayly, Michael	St. Peter	--	£32	
W 1624/7	Bayly, Richard	Temple	Weaver	£8	
W 1686/8	Bayly, Robert	City of Bristol	Merchant	£224	
W 1618/6	Bayly, Roger	--	--	£2	
W 1711/3	Bayly, Thomas	Winterbourne (Hambrook)	Yeoman	£672	
1672/3	Bayly, Thomas	--	--	£178	
W 1618/8	Bayly, William	Winterbourne (Hambrook)	--	£166	
1667/10	Bayly, William	Almondsbury	--	£229	
W 1708/2	Bayly, William	Henbury	Yeoman	£46	
1611/8	Baylye, John	Almondsbury	--	£26	
W 1634/5	Baylye, William	St. James	⟨Felt-maker⟩	£81	
1663/7	Baynton, Edward	St. Peter	Inn-holder	£6	
1669/9	Beacham, Samuel	Temple	Yeoman	£40	
1634/6	Beacon, Grace	St. Peter	--	£14	
1613/6	Beadwell, Richard	--	--	£6	

	Reference	Name	Place	Occupation	Value	Notes
	1624/9	Beaken, John	St. Nicholas	--	£7	
	1639/8	Beaker, Elias	Henbury	--	£173+	
	1634/7	Beakey, Francis	St. Michael		£23	
	1634/6	Beakon, Grace	(see Beacon)			
	1754/3	Beal, Hugh	City of Bristol	Dyer	£15	
W	1662/1	Beale, Andrew	<Henbury> (Aust)	Boatman	£29	
	1697/9	Beale, Matthew	St. Michael	--	£5	
	1609/8	Beale, Robert	Henbury (Aust)	--	£91	
	1675/5	Beames, Elizabeth	--	--	£11	
	1671/2	Beames, John	Stoke Gifford	Yeoman	£101	
	1667/3	Beames, Roger	St. Augustine	Carpenter	£14	
W	1710/3	Beams, Richard	Mangotsfield (Downend)	Mariner		<Quarrier in will>
W	1748/6	Beard, George	City of Bristol	Mariner	£6	
W	1674/4	Beaton, George	<St. Peter>	Grocer	£850	(copy of 1675/12, but with items valued £131 omitted)
	1675/12	Beaton, George	<St. Peter>	Grocer	£981	(written on back of a document of excommunication) see also 1674/4
	1761/1	Beaton, Levi	City of Bristol	Mariner	£19	
W	1718/3	Beavan, George	City of Bristol	Mariner	£5	
	1738/1	Beavan, Michael	City of Bristol	Mariner	£6	
	1704/5	Beazar, Edward	(see Beeser)			
W	1649/3	Becher, Phane	City of Bristol	Lieut-Col.	£589	
W	1734/4	Beck, John	City of Bristol	Mariner	£15	
	1716/5	Beck, Richard	City of Bristol	Mariner	£13	
W	1665/1	Bedford, John	All Saints	Hosier	£136	
	1731/5	Bedford, Robert	City of Bristol	--	£13	
	1642/6	Beeke, Thomas	St. Peter	Whitawer	£22	
W	1711/5	Beeks, Richard	City of Bristol	Cordwainer	£17	
W	1736/5	Beer, John	City of Bristol	Mariner	£3	
	1624/10	Beere, John	SS. Phillip & Jacob	--	6s 6d	
W	1677/2	Beese, William	(see Bissye)			
	1704/5	Beeser, Edward	Barton Regis	Husbandman	£15	

Year ref.	Name	Parish or area	Occupation or status	Value	Notes
W 1624/8	Beker, John	Stoke Gifford	Husbandman	£10	
1665/3	Beker, Richard	Castle Precincts	Tinmaker	£84	
W 1696/2	Belcher, James	Almondsbury	Husbandman	£35	
W 1669/11	Belcher, James <snr>	Winterbourne	<Weaver>	£363	
W 1716/6	Belcher, Joseph	--	<Mariner>	£34	
1633/6	Belcher, Thomas	(see Bellsheere)			
1677/5	Belcher, Thomas	(see Bellsher, James)			
1719/3	Bell, Daniel	City of Bristol	Mariner	£9	
1680/4	Bell, Elizabeth	SS. Philip & Jacob	Widow	£10	
1679/9	Bell, Francis	SS. Philip & Jacob	<Bodice-maker>	£25	
1636/4	Bell, James	SS. Philip & Jacob	Tailor	£1	
1609/9	Bell, John	City of Bristol	--	£4	
1733/3	Bell, John	City of Bristol	Mariner	£4	
W 1741/3	Bellamy, John	SS. Philip & Jacob	<Victualler>	£11	
1620/13	Bellarmyne, Elizabeth	Temple	--	£18	
1700/20	Bellenger, Francis	--	--	£31	
W 1730/3	Bellew, Hugh	City of Bristol	Mariner	£6	
1677/5	Bellsheere, James	--		£89	
1633/6	Belsher, Robert	St. James	Stonemason	£14	
W 1618/9	Belsher, Sarah	Winterbourne	Husbandman	£88	
W 1751/1	Belshire, Robert	<St. Mary, Redcliffe>	Widow	£13	
W 1618/9	Benett, Margaret	(see Belsher)			
W 1628/5	Benfeld, Thomas	Clifton	<Single-woman>	£33	
W 1681/3	Bennet, Ann	SS. Philip & Jacob	<Gardener>	£26	
W 1671/4	Bennet, John	Almondsbury <Gaunts Earthcott>	<Widow>	--	
1687/11	Bennet, John	Horfield	--	£141	
1690/5	Bennet, John	Almondsbury	--	£7	
W 1715/4	Bennet, Philip	Mangotsfield	Carpenter	£4	
1660/1	Bennet, Ralph	St. Thomas	--	£22	
W 1708/3	Bennet, Richard	City of Bristol	Mariner	£6	

	Ref.	Name	Place	Occupation	Value	Notes
W	1698/3	Bennet, Samuel	City of Bristol	Writing-master	£206	
	1662/6	Bennett, John	SS. Philip & Jacob	Yeoman	£87	died at sea
W	1759/1	Bennett, John	City of Bristol	Yeoman	£17	
	1628/5	Bennett, Margaret	(see Benett)			
	1731/CP	Bennett, Mary	--	Widow	£478	also 2nd copy
	1733/4	Bennett, Philip	Mangotsfield	Cordwainer	£20	
W	1706/2	Bennett, Thomas	Mangotsfield (Moorend)	Carpenter	£25	
W	1682/4	Bennett, Thomas	Horfield	<Yeoman>	£82	
	1752/2	Bennett, William	City of Bristol	Brewer	£15	
W	1643/5	Benson, Barnard	<St. Thomas>	Pewterer	£897	
	1609/10	Benson, Christopher	--	--	£8	
	1730/4	Benson, Edward	City of Bristol	Yeoman	£76	
	1649/4	Benson, George	St. John	Barber-surgeon	£31	
W	1646/3	Benson, Mary	St. Thomas	Widow <Pewterer>	£518	compare 1643/5
W	1623/3	Benson, Maude	St. Mary, Redcliffe	Widow <Pewterer>	£59	
W	1763/1B	Bent, Joseph	City of Bristol	Mariner	£4	with 1765 wills
W	1721/3	Berckbeck, William	City of Bristol	Mariner	£11	
	1715/5	Berjew, Margaret	(see Barjew)			
	1717/6	Berjew, Richard	City of Bristol	Mariner	£3	
	1707/7	Berjew, Thomas	(see Barjew)			
	1644/4	Berkeley, Richard	City of Bristol	Esq.	£8	
	1644/2	Berkin, Abraham	(see Birkin)			
	1644/3	Berkin, Richard	(see Birkin)			
	1760/1	Berquast, Erick	City of Bristol	Mariner	£5	
W	1661/13	Berriman, Anne	St. James	Widow	£51	
	1650/1	Berriman, Richard	St. James	Tobacco-pipe maker	£29	a/c only: 3 documents
	1635/8	Berrow, Charles	St. John	--	£228	see Berrowe 1634/8
W	1676/3	Berrow, Edmund	St. Stephen	<Shipwright>	£19	
	1667/7	Berrow, Phillip	St. James	Cooper	£3	
	1690/2	Berrow, Philip	--	--	£18	
	1683/4	Berrow, William	--	<Glazier>	£49	
W	1725/1	Berrow, William	City of Bristol	Painter	£26	

	Year ref.	Name	Parish or area	Occupation or status	Value	Notes
	1634/8	Berrowe, Charles	St. John	Cooper	£228	see Berrow 1635/8
	1639/9	Berrowe, John	St. Stephen	Pump-maker	£32	
	1679/7	Berry, George	Westbury-on-Trym (Shirehampton)	Mariner	£54	
W	1670/2	Berry, John	Westbury-on-Trym (Shirehampton)	<Pilot>	£170	
W	1689/5	Besse, Ann	(see Bissie)			
	1647/2	Best, George	Mangotsfield	Gent.	£44	
	1675/2	Best, George	Mangotsfield	Cordwainer	£64	
	1677/57	Best, George	Mangotsfield	--	£66	account only
W	1628/7	Betterton, William	St. Thomas	Cloth-worker	£16	also 2nd copy
	1716/7	Betton, Thomas	(see Bitten)			
	1737/2	Betts, William	City of Bristol	Mariner	£5	
W	1711/6	Bevan, Daniel	Olveston	--	£53	
	1692/6	Bevan, George	--	--	£11	
	1742/4	Bevan, Joanna	City of Bristol	Widow	£7	
	1686/9	Bevan, John	City of Bristol	Tobacco-roller	£20	
	1676/4	Bevan, Thomas	--	--	£6	
W	1717/7	Beven, Sarah	Littleton-on-Severn	Spinster	£50	
	1691/8	Beverston, Richard	--	Baker	£16	
W	1678/5	Bevill, John	City of Bristol	Arms-painter	£70	
W	1686/4	Bevin, Augustine	Henbury (Lawrence Weston)	Yeoman	£54	
W	1639/10	Bevin, Elway	St. Augustine	--	£34	
	1666/3	Bewhenning, Robert	St. John	Yeoman	£3	
	1687/12	Bey, Robert	Henbury	<Skinner>	£148	
W	1637/6	Bibbie, Thomas	St. Peter	--	£707	
	1676/5	Bickham, William	--	--	£5	
	1625/7	Bicknell, Nicholas	SS. Philip & Jacob	Blacksmith	£4	
W	1662/2	Bicknell, William	SS. Philip & Jacob	<Cutler from will>	£18	

Ref	W	Name	Place	Occupation	Value	Notes
1681/4		Bicknoll, George	Horfield	Smith	£17	
1666/5		Biddle, Joan	St. Michael	--	£70	
1629/2	W	Biddle, <John>	<St. Michael>	--	£4	
1644/5		Biddlestone, Rowland	City of Bristol	--	£--	
1689/8		Bide, John	City of Bristol	Miller	£8	
1724/1		Bide, Robert	Stapleton	--	£9	
1668/6		Bigelstone, Richard	--	<Locksmith>	£9	(Inv. of trade goods shared between Richard & Phillip)
1687/7		Biggs, Elinor	-- (Wine Street)	Inn-keeper	£91	
1682/9		Biggs, Henry	St. James	Tailor	£32	
1669/6		Biggs, Richard	City of Bristol	--	£19	
1677/1	W	Biggs, Thomas	<Christchurch>	Inn-holder	£171	long roll
1620/14		Billing, Richard	St. Michael	--	£4	
1641/5		Binney, Erasmus	St. Nicholas	--	£4	
1713/2		Binney, Joseph	Henbury (Stowick)	--	£73	
1742/5	W	Birch, Joseph	City of Bristol	Mariner	£16	
1736/6		Birch, Thomas	City of Bristol	Mariner	£18	
1643/6	W	Bircken, Walter	St. Nicholas	Cooper	£19	
1624/11		Birckhead, Christopher	St. Nicholas	--	£88	
1762/1A	W	Bird, Henry	City of Bristol	Mariner	£6	with wills
1680/9	W	Bird, Israel	City of Bristol	Freemason	£90	
1648/3	W	Bird, John	SS. Philip & Jacob	<Yeoman>	£16	
1639/17	W	Bird, John	St. Nicholas	<Yeoman>	£105	
1639/14	W	Bird, William	St. Mary, Redcliffe	--	£8	
1642/7		Bird, William	St. James	--	£19	
1639/11	W	Birde, Robert	St. Thomas	Cutler	£84	
		Birkbeck, William	(see Berckbeck)			
1721/3	W	Birkin, Abraham	St. Thomas	Baker	£118	
1644/2		Birkin, James	St. Stephen	<Soap-boiler>	£106	
1668/9	W	Birkin, John	City of Bristol	Soap-boiler	£263	
1672/7		Birkin, Mary	City of Bristol	Widow		
1681/7	W	Birkin, Richard	<The Quay>	--	£496	
1644/3		Birkin, Richard	St. Nicholas	Cooper	£139	

Year ref.	W	Name	Parish or area	Occupation or status	value	Notes
1613/7		Birte, John	St. Stephen	Cooper	£21	
1674/7		Bishop, John	St. Nicholas	Bachelor	£16	
1748/7		Bishop, Joseph	City of Bristol	Mariner	£14	
1668/8	W	Bishop, Thomas (snr)	Temple	Tailor	£79	
1692/8		Bishop, Thomas	Westbury-on-Trym	Glover	£3	
1685/8		Bishopp, Thomas	City of Bristol	Mariner	£243	
1713/3	W	Bishoppe, Mary	Mangotsfield	Widow	£10	
1669/8		Biss, Richard	St. Mary, Redcliffe	Weaver	£22	
1683/5	W	Biss, Susanna	City of Bristol	Widow	£156	
1748/8	W	Bisse, Edward	City of Bristol	Mariner	£14	
1628/8		Bisse, John	City of Bristol	Wire-drawer	£6	
1689/5	W	Bissie, Ann	Filton	Widow	£80	see also Bissye
1691/5		Bissop, Robert	--	--	£6	
1677/2	W	Bissye, William	Filton	Yeoman	£40	
1716/7		Bitten, Thomas	City of Bristol	Pewterer	£11	
1624/12		Bittfield, John	St. Thomas	Soapmaker	£26	
1717/7	W	Biven, Sarah	(see Beven)			
1623/4	W	Blachley, Thomas	Almondsbury <Over>	--	£66	inv. & account
1720/3	W	Blachley, William	City of Bristol	Tailor	£22	1719 will
1674/6		Black, Edward	--	--	£16	(document marked 'Edmond Blayth' outside)
1672/51		Blackbourne, John	--	--	£15	see Stevens, Edward
1731/6	W	Blackett, William	City of Bristol	Mariner	£4	
1639/12	W	Blackford, John	Henbury	Husbandman	£18	
1625/8	W	Blackford, Elizabeth	Henbury	Widow	£16	
1747/3	W	Blackly, Francis	City of Bristol	Mariner	£8	
1692/5	W	Blackmore, Margaret	City of Bristol	Widow	£298	
1758/2	W	Blackmore, Hugh	City of Bristol	Mariner	£14	
1711/7	W	Blackway, Hannah	City of Bristol	Spinster	£131	
1637/7		Blackwell, Margaret	St. Peter	Widow	£5	2 documents

W	Ref	Name	Place	Occupation	Value
	1692/10	Blackwell, Samuel	St. Thomas	--	£21
W	1697/8	Blackwell, Thomas	Stoke Gifford	Yeoman	£63
	1695/4	Blaiden, Ann	--	Widow	£3
	1749/5	Blair, Samuel	City of Bristol	Mariner	£13
	1646/4	Blake, Clement	St. James	--	£100
W	1690/1	Blake, Grace	Filton	<Widow>	£196
W	1726/4	Blake, Isaac	City of Bristol	Mariner	£3
W	1682/8	Blake, John	Filton	Cordwainer	£190
	1706/3	Blake, John	Henbury	--	£13
W	1719/4	Blake, John	Henbury <Lawrence Weston>		£13
W	1726/3	Blake, John	City of Bristol	Yeoman	£355
	1640/3	Blake, William	Temple	Mariner	£10
W	1661/8	Blanch, Alice	Stoke Gifford	Labourer	£4
	1629/3	Blanch, Ellen	Stoke Gifford	Widow	£27
W	1661/9	Blanch, Robert	City of Bristol	Widow	£21
W	1690/4	Blanch, Susanna	<Almondsbury, (Gaunts Earthcott)>	Yeoman	£7
	1711/8	Blatchley, Abraham	City of Bristol	Widow	£153
	1674/6	Blayth, Edmond	(see Black, Edward)	Victualler	£137
	1613/9	Blayth, William	St. Nicholas	Cooper	£6
	1643/7	Bletchley, Katherine	Almondsbury	Widow	£70
W	1727/3a	Bletsoe, John	City of Bristol	Mariner <Doctor>	£60
W	1727/3b	Bletsoe, John	(account of Edward Hallden concerning Dr. John Bletsoe)	<Cooper>	£64
	1681/10	Blewett, Charles	St. Leonard	--	£3
	1620/15	Blindman, John	St. Michael	Mariner	-- no other details
	1760/2	Blinkinson, William	City of Bristol	Mariner	£13
	1672/1	Blinman, John	(see Blynman)	Minister of the Gospel	
	1708/4	Blinman, Nathaniel	City of Bristol	Mariner	£13
W	1681/6	Blinman, Richard	City of Bristol		£40
W	1620/16	Blockly, Thomas	Henbury	--	£4
	1634/9	Blount, John	SS. Philip & Jacob	Gent.	£329

Year ref.		Name	Parish or area	Occupation or status	value	Notes
W	1731/7	Blow, John	City of Bristol	Mariner	£7	
W	1625/9	Blundie, Christian	St. Nicholas	Widow	£27	
	1634/9	Blunte, John	(see Blount)			
	1672/1	Blynman, John	City of Bristol	Ropemaker	£99	also 2nd copy
	1665/2	Board, Margaret	Stapleton	Widow	£16	
	1623/5	Bobbett, George and Margaret		--	£2	
	1678/10	Bodenham, John	St. Augustine	Mariner	£4	
W	1731/8	Bodge, Henry	City of Bristol	Mariner	£15	
	1753/2	Body, James	City of Bristol	Mariner	£10	
W	1750/3	Boles, John	City of Bristol	Mariner	£7	
	1766/CP	Bolt, Thomas	St. Augustine	⟨Surgeon in will⟩ Sexton	£327	inv. & account
	1633/10	Boman, Anthony	Winterbourne (Hambrook)			
	1719/5	Bond, John	City of Bristol	Mariner	£27	
	1702/3	Bone, Joseph	--	--	£8	
	1674/5	Bonfield, George	SS. Philip & Jacob	--	£7	
	1644/6	Bonham, Roger	(see Bonum)	Colour-merchant	£21	
	1746/3	Bonnell, Richard	City of Bristol	Mariner	£7	
	1672/5	Bonners, William	St. Michael	--	£4	
	1644/6	Bonum, Roger	Christchurch	--	£4	also Bonham
	1694/2	Boobier, Humphrey	City of Bristol	Shipwright	£3	
W	1625/14	Boock, Richard	SS. Philip & Jacob	⟨Husbandman⟩	£29	
	1644/7	Boonde, Christopher	St. Nicholas	⟨Cooper⟩	£6	
W	1709/4	Boone, John	City of Bristol	Vintner	£64	
	1702/3	Boone, Joseph	(see Bone)			
W	1620/17	Boone, Thomas	(see Bownd)			
	1667/22	Booth, Alice	(alias Edwards which see)			
	1672/2	Booth, Samuel	Stoke Gifford	Carpenter	£66	
W	1734/5	Borrett, Thomas	City of Bristol	Mariner	£13	

	Reference	Name	Place	Occupation	Value	Notes
W	1629/4	Bosden, Susan	<St. Werburgh>	Widow	£64	
	1740/4	Bosker, Thomas	City of Bristol	Mariner	£5	
	1664/7	Bosley, Thomas	St. Peter	--	--	
	1759/2	Bosscher, James	City of Bristol	Mariner	£9	
	1678/6	Bosse, Anne	St. John	Widow	£34	
	1747/5	Bossow, Peter	City of Bristol	Mariner	£10	
	1628/9	Boswell, Thomas	--	--	£6	
	1690/6	Bottom, Abraham	Almondsbury	--	£24	
	1644/8	Bottomley, Joyce	All Saints	Widow	£41	
W	1614/1	Boucher, Katherine	(see Bowcher)			
W	1734/6	Boucher, Thomas	City of Bristol	Mariner	£8	
	1633/8	Boullye, Thomas	St. Mary, Redcliffe	--	£7+	damaged
	1624/13	Boulton, --	St. Thomas	--	£6	
	1758/5	Boulton, James	City of Bristol	Mariner	£9	
W	1634/10	Boulton, Joan	Olveston	--	£7	
W	1628/10	Boulton, John	St. Stephen	--	£606	
W	1633/9	Boulton, Richard	Olveston	--	£35	
W	1685/5	Boulton, William	<Olveston> Tockington	Carpenter <Yeoman in will>	£168	
W	1628/11	Boultton, Walter	Temple	--	£26	
W	1623/6	Bourne, William	St. Mary, Redcliffe	Merchant	£139	
	1683/3	Bourne, William	City of Bristol	Woollen-draper	£97	
	1611/12	Boushe, William	(see Bushe)			
	1725/2	Boutcher, John	City of Bristol	Barber-surgeon	£19	
W	1748/9	Bovatt, William	City of Bristol	Mariner	£5	
W	1643/8	Bowcher, George	St. John	<Merchant>	£462	
W	1625/10	Bowcher, Henry	(see Butcher)			
W	1607/-	Bowcher, Katherine	City of Bristol	--	--	<alias Grove> with 1610 wills will gives 'Butcher' alias Grove
W	1614/1	Bowcher, Katherine	City of Bristol (items in her house at Rochester: extra to 1614/1)	Widow	£2,409	
W	1742/6	Bowden, Marmaduke	--	Mariner	£11	
	1644/9	Bowden, Richard	City of Bristol	Grocer	£14	

Year ref.	Name	Parish or area	Occupation or status	value	Notes
W 1718/4	Bowen, Mary	Westbury-on-Trym	Widow	£10	
W 1751/2	Bowen, North	City of Bristol	Mariner	£16	
1714/6	Bowen, John	City of Bristol	--	£27	inv. & account with wills
W 1766/3	Bowen, John	City of Bristol	Mariner	£10	
1686/5	Bowen, William	--	--	£15	
W 1752/3	Bowen, William	City of Bristol	Mariner	£11	
1670/4	Bowering, Susan	Henbury	Widow	£204	
1633/8	Bowlie, Thomas	(see Boullye)			
1633/10	Bowman Anthony	(see Boman)			
W 1733/5	Bowman, William	City of Bristol	Mariner	£16	
W 1620/17	Bownd, Thomas	Temple	Mariner	£130	
1618/10	Boxwell, Richard	St. Thomas	Inn-keeper	£91	
W 1684/8	Boyce, Thomas	Castle Precincts	Tailor	£33	
W 1642/8	Boyce, William	Littleton-on-Severn	Yeoman	£94	
W 1644/8	Boyce, William	City of Bristol	Tailor	£10	
1724/1	Boyd, Robert	(see Bide)			
1643/9	Boyns, Morris	St. Stephen	--	£23	
W 1642/9	Brace, Richard	St. Augustine	Physician (Gent.)	£135	
1694/9	Bracy, John	Winterbourne	Yeoman	£34	
W 1674/3	Bracy, Mary	Almondsbury <Over>	--	£205	
1707/8	Bracy, Mary	Almondsbury (Over)	Widow	£355	
W 1701/5	Bracy, Richard	Almondsbury (Over)	Yeoman	£806	also 2nd copy
W 1663/8	Bracy, Thomas	Almondsbury	--	£274	
W 1717/8	Bracy, Thomas	Almondsbury <Over>	Cordwainer	£86	
W 1740/5	Braddy, John	SS. Philip & Jacob	Stocking-maker	£4	
1753/3	Bradford, Arthur	City of Bristol	Mariner	£8	
W 1662/3	Bradford, Thomas (snr)	St. Mary-le-Port	Cordwainer	£321	
W 1670/3	Bradley, George	Henbury <Bilsome>	Yeoman	£219	
W 1630/1	Bradley, John	<Henbury> Northwick	--	£61	
W 1682/7	Bradley, Mary	<City of Bristol>	<Widow>	£80	
W 1677/3	Bradly, Robert	City of Bristol	Merchant	£277	

Ref	W	Name	Place	Occupation	Value	Notes
1748/10		Bradly, William	City of Bristol	Chaser	£8	
1633/11		Bradlye, John	<Henbury> Northwick	--	£20	
1694/8		Bradoke, John	--	--	£3	
1715/6	W	Bradwick, John	City of Bristol	Mariner	£14	
1740/5		Brady, John	(see Braddy)			
1675/3		Brage, George	SS. Philip & Jacob	Mr.	£170	see also Bragg 1677/59
1675/3		Bragg, George	(see Brage)			
1677/59		Bragg, George	SS. Philip & Jacob			account only
1704/6		Bragington, George	St. Peter	Tobacco-roller	£180	
1696/3		Braine, James	City of Bristol	Cooper	£13	
1709/5		Braine, Thomas	City of Bristol	Haulier	£289	
1710/4	W	Bramble, John	City of Bristol	Blacksmith	£9	
1693/2	W	Bramlee, Elizabeth	Henbury	--	£176	
1623/7		Bramley, Thomas	St. Stephen	--	£89	
1708/5		Brampton, John	Barton Regis	Tailor	£6	
1696/4		Branch, Edmond	City of Bristol	Surgeon	£8	
1663/10	W	Branch, Henry	Temple	Silk-weaver	£19	
1689/43		Branch, Martha	Clifton	Widow	£123	
1716/16		Branch, Sarah	(alias Crooks, which see)		£28	
1685/7		Branch, Thomas	--	--	£33	
1663/11		Brandon, William	St. Stephen	Tailor	£211	
1749/6	W	Bransby, William	(see Barnsby)			
1640/4		Brantly, Edward	SS. Philip & Jacob		£5	
1675/10	W	Brawler, Anne	City of Bristol	Widow	£38	
1661/6		Brawler, Robert	St. Stephen	Shipwright	£10	
1620/18		Brawne, John (also called Richard)	St. Augustine	--	£5	
1736/7		Bray, John	City of Bristol	Mariner	£5	
1731/9	W	Bray, Robert	City of Bristol	Mariner	£5	
1715/7		Brayne, Charles	City of Bristol	Mariner	£6	
1668/13		Brayne, John	St. Thomas	--	£22	
1688/3		Brayne, Thomas	City of Bristol	Haulier	£16	
1689/44		Brayne, Widow	City of Bristol	Haulier	£15	wife of John Brayne

Year ref.	W	Name	Parish or area	Occupation or status	value	Notes
1719/6		Bready, Jacob	St. Thomas	Hooper	£17	
1688/2	W	Breane, Agnes	City of Bristol	Spinster	£32	
1620/21	W	Bredges, Richard	(see Bridges)			
1677/4		Brent, Humphrey	St. Thomas	Minister	£270	
1668/7		Brereton, Henry	Westbury-on-Trym	--	£109	
1749/7		Brewer, Henry	City of Bristol	Shopkeeper	£15	
1644/10		Brewer, James	SS. Philip & Jacob	--	£5	
1689/47		Brewer, John	--	--	£1	
1653/1		Brewer, Nicholas	<City of Bristol>		£--	
1664/3		Brewer, Thomas	SS. Philip & Jacob	<Grocer>	£6+	shop goods unvalued
1664/4		Brewer, Thomas	SS. Philip & Jacob	--	--	
1730/5		Brewer, Walter	Almondsbury	Yeoman	£230	
1634/12		Brewster, Joan	St. Peter	<Widow>	£17	four documents
1636/5		Brewster, Joan	City of Bristol	Widow	£18	
1697/10	W	Brewton, Mary	Almondsbury	--	£19	
1639/13	W	Briant, Elinor	St. Peter	--	£29	
1642/10		Brian, Joan	St. Augustine	Widow	£33	
1666/4		Briant, Thomas	St. Augustine	Linen-draper	£10	
1629/5	W	Brickdale, Thomas	St. Werburgh	Cook-Victualler <Clerk in will>	£44	
1636/7		Brickdall, John	St. Werburgh	--	£2	
1643/10	W	Bricker, John	SS. Philip & Jacob	--	£212	
1663/12		Bricker, Lawrence	Temple	Carrier	£152	
1662/4		Bricker, Roger	Castle Precinct	Clothier	£29	
1620/21	W	Bridges, Richard	St. Augustine	Linen-draper	£16	
1635/9	W	Bridges, Richard	St. Nicholas	Tailor	£13	
1636/7		Brigdall, John	(see Brickdall)			
1629/5	W	Brigdall, Thomas	(see Brickdale)			
1754/28		Bright, Joan	(see Young)			
1754/10		Bright, Mary	(see Butler)			
1754/2		Bright, Martha	(see Bave)			

Ref.	W	Name	Place	Occupation	Value	Notes
1629/6		Bright, Richard	City of Bristol	⟨Butcher⟩	£3	
1754/4		Bright, Richard	City of Bristol	Carpenter	£15	
1680/8	W	Bright, Robert	Barton Regis	Barber-surgeon	£85	
1754/5		Bright, Thomas	City of Bristol	Cloth-worker	£18	
1634/11		Bright, Walter	St. Mary-le-Port	Butcher	£6	
1713/4	W	Brimsden, Anne	City of Bristol	Spinster	£9	
1713/5	W	Brimsmead, Thomas	(alias Burrowes, which see)			
1689/7		Brin, Nicholas	---		£11	
1713/4	W	Brindham, Anne	(see Brimsden)			
1643/11		Brine, Isaac	City of Bristol	Virginal maker	£5	
1727/4		Brinkworth, Richard	City of Bristol	Cordwainer	£26	
1691/4		Brinn, Henry	---		£1	
1731/10		Brisbane, John	City of Bristol	Mariner	£5	
1685/4	W	Bristoll, Richard	(see Bristow)			
1685/4	W	Bristow, Richard	SS. Philip & Jacob	Lime-burner	£98	
1684/5		Brittan, George	St. Peter	Tanner	£254	
1687/CP		Brittaine, Thomas	City of Bristol	---	£21	account only
1698/6	W	Britten, Joseph	City of Bristol	Mariner	£4	
1716/8		Britten, Samuel	City of Bristol	Mariner	£8	
1686/7		Britten, Thomas	---		£21	
1687/6		Britten, Thomas	---		£42	
1680/3		Brock, Ellinor	St. Mary, Redcliffe	Widow	£47	
1710/5	W	Brock, James	City of Bristol	Shipwright	£18	
1731/11	W	Brock, John	---	⟨Mariner⟩	£5	
1731/12	W	Brock, Laurance	City of Bristol	Mariner	£5	
1699/5		Brock, Peter	St. James	---	£3	
1618/11	W	Brock, Richard	Almondsbury	Husbandman	£40	
1723/4		Brock, Sarah	City of Bristol	Widow	£38	inv. & account
1641/6		Brocke, Phillip	St. Stephen	⟨Mariner⟩	£8	
1675/13		Brockes, Roger	---	Mariner	£7	
1753/4		Bromby, Thomas	City of Bristol	---	£7	(written on document claiming damage to goods in storm at sea)
1704/7		Brome, Ann	Abbots Leigh	---	£29	

Year ref.		Name	Parish or area	Occupation or status	value	Notes
1681/8		Bromhall, Richard	SS. Phillip & Jacob	Inn-holder	£430	
1758/3		Bronsdon, Benjamin	City of Bristol	Mariner	£14	
1613/10		Brooke, Alice	Alveston	Widow	£8	
1624/14		Brooke, Joan	St. Stephen	--	£3	
1734/7		Brooke, Robert	City of Bristol	Peruke-maker	£10	
1643/12	W	Brooke, Thomas	St. Stephen	House-carpenter	£42	
1617/5		Brooke, William	St. Leonard	--	£2	
1693/4		Brookes, Grace	--	Widow	£30	
1624/15		Brookes, Margaret	St. Mary, Redcliffe	--	£3	
1679/13	W	Brookes, Margaret	Olveston	Widow	£89	
1698/8	W	Brookes, Nicholas	Stoke Gifford	Yeoman	£158	
1706/4		Brookes, Thomas	City of Bristol	Victualler	£21	
1671/47		Brookes, Thomas	Henbury	Yeoman	£181	alias Witherly
1625/11		Brookman, William	St. Thomas	<Skinner>	£42	
1733/6		Brooks, John	SS. Philip & Jacob	Mason	£15	
1680/50	W	Brooks, Maudlin	City of Bristol	Widow	£15	alias Tuther
1721/4	W	Brooks, Peter	City of Bristol	Mason	£51	
1643/13	W	Brooks, Robert	Henbury (Charlton)	Yeoman	£284	alias Wytherly
1742/7	W	Brooks, Robert	City of Bristol	Mariner	£8	
1635/10		Brooks, William	St. Thomas	--	--	
1636/6		Brooks, William	St. Thomas	Haberdasher	£3	
1714/7		Brooks, William	City of Bristol	Mariner	£1	
1620/19	W	Broome, John	St. James	Pin-maker	£13	
1659/1		Broome, Richard	Abbots Leigh	Shipwright	£49	
1753/5	W	Brotherstone, Mary	City of Bristol	Widow	£10	
1721/5		Brouse, John	--	<Hatter>	£14	
1731/13		Brown, Alice	Henbury (Hallen)	Widow	£160	
1720/4		Brown, Benjamin	City of Bristol	Mariner	£12	
1733/7	W	Brown, Francis	City of Bristol	Tiler	£221	
1722/1		Brown, Henry	Henbury	Yeoman	£187	
1761/2		Brown, James	City of Bristol	Mariner	£12	

W	Reference	Name	Place	Occupation	Value	Notes
W	1751/3	Brown, John	City of Bristol	Mariner	£8	
	1756/2	Brown, John	City of Bristol	Brazier	£42	
W	1758/4A	Brown, John	<St. James>	Victualler	£19	
	1748/12	Brown, Margaret	City of Bristol	Widow	£5	
	1728/2	Brown, Mary	City of Bristol	--	£5	
W	1625/12	Brown, Robert	Clifton	Yeoman	£382	
	1732/5	Brown, Robert	City of Bristol	Shipwright	£5	
	1718/5	Brown, Thomas	City of Bristol	Victualler	£21	
	1728/3	Brown, Thomas	--	<Haberdasher>	£348	also 2nd copy
	1728/CP	Brown, Thomas	--	Hosier	£354	
	1628/12	Browne, Ann	St. Thomas	Widow	£8	
	1669/4	Browne, Anthony	City of Bristol	--	£102	
	1640/5a	Browne, Charles	Henbury	Husbandman	£21	
	1640/5b	Browne, Charles	(Northwick/Redwick)			
	1706/5	Browne, Edward	(document re administration)	--	£8	
W	1644/11	Browne, Gabriell	--	Dyer	£141	
W	1698/4	Browne, George <snr>	City of Bristol	Musician	£91	
	1663/5	Browne, Gifford	City of Bristol	Seaman	£118	
	1644/12	Browne, Henrie	St. Stephen	Boatswain	--	
	1613/11	Browne, Henry	Christchurch	Shoemaker	£2	
	1673/3	Browne, Henry	City of Bristol	--	£93	
	1744/3	Browne, James	City of Bristol	Mariner	£30	
W	1620/20	Browne, Joan	St. Stephen	Widow	£14	
W	1628/13	Browne, John	St. Mary, Redcliffe	Wheelwright	£20	
	1629/7	Browne, John	Castle Precinct	Dyer	£7	
	1679/8	Browne, John	City of Bristol	Shipwright	£23	
W	1697/11	Browne, John	Barton Regis	Butcher	£29	
	1719/7	Browne, John	City of Bristol	Mariner	£15	
W	1635/11	Browne, Margery	St. Nicholas	Widow	£19	
	1643/14	Browne, Nicholas	SS. Philip & Jacob	--	£44	
	1662/8	Browne, Richard	St. Mary-le-Port	Shoemaker	£142	

	Year ref.	Name	Parish or area	Occupation or status	Value	Notes
W	1682/6	Browne, Robert	Almondsbury (Hempton)	Gent.	£58	
	1684/4	Browne, Sarah	City of Bristol	Widow	£25	
W	1611/9	Browne, Thomas	Almondsbury <Over>	<Husbandman>	£60	
	1647/3	Browne, Thomas	Winterbourne	--	£11	
W	1680/7	Browne, Thomas	City of Bristol	Watchmaker	£42	
W	1675/7	Browne, Thomas	St. Stephen	<Pump-maker>	£61	
W	1734/8	Browne, Thomas	City of Bristol	Mariner	£14	
W	1637/8	Browne, Thomas	Stapleton	Yeoman	£51	
W	1643/15	Browne, Walter	St. Stephen	Joiner	£49	
W	1651/1	Browne, William	Henbury	Husbandman	£134	
W	1701/6	Browne, William	Henbury <Stowick>	<Yeoman>	£276	
W	1724/2	Browne, William	City of Bristol	Mariner	£12	
	1687/15	Browning, Francis	--	--	£1	
	1662/7	Browning, Jasse	SS. Philip & Jacob	--	£13	
W	1754/7	Browning, John	City of Bristol	Joiner	£5	
	1688/4	Browning, Nathaniel	City of Bristol	Shipwright	£42	
	1705/5	Browning, Richard	--	Pipe-maker	£27	
W	1715/8	Browning, Robert	City of Bristol			
	1664/5	Browning, Sarah	St. Stephen	Widow	£14	
W	1739/3	Browning, William	City of Bristol	Mariner	£14	
	1735/2	Bruce, Ann	City of Bristol	Widow	£19	
	1625/13	Bruce, William	St. Peter	Ship-carpenter	£5	died at sea
	1634/13	Bruer, John	St. Peter	--	£13	
	1634/12	Bruer, John	(see Brewster)	--	--	grant of admin.
		Bruister, Joan	Almondsbury (Rednend)			
W	1617/6	Bruton, Gregory	--	Husbandman	£95	
	1618/12	Bruton, Thomas		--	£3	
	1742/8	Bryan, Dennis	City of Bristol	Mariner	£7	
W	1760/3	Bryan, George	City of Bristol	Mariner	£5	
	1712/1	Bryan, Henry	Barton Regis	Mariner	£5	

	Ref	Name	Place	Occupation	Value	Notes
W	1749/8	Bryan, John	City of Bristol	Mariner	£3	
W	1732/6	Bryan, William	City of Bristol	Mariner	£5	
W	1736/8	Bryan, William	<City of Bristol>	Mariner	£8	
	1691/9	Bryant, Christopher	--	--	£1	
	1680/6	Bryant, Francis	St. Werburgh	--	£3	
W	1653/2	Bryant, George	St. Augustine	--	£27	
W	1733/8	Bryant, George	City of Bristol	Mariner	£13	
	1741/4	Bryant, Joseph	City of Bristol	<Mariner>	£12	
	1723/5	Buchanan, John	<Abbots Leigh>	Mariner	£7	
W	1628/15	Buck, Elizabeth	Stapleton	Widow	£27	
W	1694/10	Buck, Richard	Stapleton	Nailer	£34	
	1661/10	Bucke, Edward	(see Boock)	Collier	£41	
W	1625/14	Bucke, Richard	Stapleton	--	£25	dated 1662
	1663/6	Bucke, Richard	St. Thomas	--	£15	
	1643/16	Buckford, Joan	City of Bristol	Widow	£9	
W	1719/8	Buckland, Dorothy	City of Bristol	Grocer	£25	inv. & account
	1721/6	Buckler, Daubeny	City of Bristol	Mariner	£5	
W	1754/8	Buckler, John	City of Bristol	Mariner	£15	
W	1747/4	Buckston, Richard	(see Budding)			
	1675/9	Budden, Edward	Olveston	Yeoman	£267	
W	1675/9	Budding, Edward	City of Bristol	Spinster	£17	
W	1712/2	Bulbrick, Blanch	City of Bristol	Serge-maker	£147	
W	1689/45	Bulgin, John	--	--	£2	
	1667/8	Bull, George	City of Bristol	Widow	£14	
W	1714/8	Bull, Mary	City of Bristol	Farrier	£17	
	1712/3	Bull, Percival	Almondsbury	Husbandman	£25	
	1623/12	Buller, John	Christchurch	Pewterer	£50	
	1694/5	Bullock, Anthony	City of Bristol	Mariner	£11	
	1729/2	Bullock, Daniel	St. Leonard	Cooper	£29	
	1664/6	Bullock, Henry	St. Stephen	--	£108	
W	1644/13	Bullock, William	St. John	--	£7	
	1649/5	Bullock, William	City of Bristol	--		
W	1711/9	Bullock, William	City of Bristol	Tiler	£34	

Year ref.		Name	Parish or area	Occupation or status	Value	Notes
1761/3		Bullocke, George	City of Bristol	Gent.	£361	inv. & account
1720/5		Bulmer, William	City of Bristol	Mariner	£6	
1700/19	W	Bumstead, John	<City of Bristol>	<Shipwright>	£8	
1643/17		Bumsted, Frances	St. Stephen	Widow	£85	
1675/14	W	Bumpsteed, Sarah	<City of Bristol>	Widow	£482	
1743/2	W	Burch, Henry	City of Bristol	Mariner	£10	
1719/9		Burchel, Robert	Winterbourne	Yeoman	£13	
1625/15	W	Burckott, Thomas	St. Stephen	Baker	£165	
1668/12		Burd, John	St. Stephen	Blockmaker	£425	
1678/4	W	Burd, Katharine	City of Bristol	Widow	£40	
1639/11	W	Burd, Robert	(see Birde)			
1639/14	W	Burd, William	(see Bird)			
1617/7	W	Burdnell, Alice	Almondsbury <Patch-head>	Widow	£9	
1613/12	W	Burdnell, Thomas <snr>	Almondsbury	Husbandman	£29	also 2nd copy
1635/12	W	Burford, Christopher	St. Peter	Rough-mason	£39	
1661/12	W	Burford, Thomas	St. Peter	Currier	£103	
1635/12	W	Burford, Christopher	(see Burford)			
1688/5	W	Burges, Benjamin	Stapleton	Horse-driver	£26	
1642/11	W	Burges, Elizabeth	St. Nicholas	--	£27	
1672/4		Burges, Leonard	Stapleton	--	£39	
1723/6	W	Burges, Samuel	SS. Philip & Jacob	<Victualler>	£10	
1623/9		Burges, Thomas	SS. Philip & Jacob	Tailor	£3	
1721/7	W	Burges, William	City of Bristol	Surgeon	£12	
1696/5	W	Burgess, Anthony	Henbury (Lawrence Weston)	Yeoman	£127	
1680/2		Burgess, Henry	City of Bristol	Sieve-maker	£2	
1611/10	W	Burgesse, John	St. Mary, Redcliffe	Felt-maker	£23	
1728/4	W	Burgh, Thomas	City of Bristol	Surgeon	£7	
1702/4		Burgiss, Samuel	--	--	£38	
1749/9	W	Burk, William	City of Bristol	Mariner	£6	

Ref.	Name	Place	Occupation	Value	Notes
W 1754/6	Burk, William	City of Bristol	Mariner	£15	
W 1663/6	Burke, Richard	Stapleton	--	£12	
W 1625/15	Burkett, Thomas	(see Burckott)			
1639/15	Burkston, Walter	Christchurch	--	£5	
1667/9	Burly, William	St. Nicholas	Cordwainer	£26	
1644/14	Burnaberey, Bridget	St. Stephen	Widow	£55	
W 1642/12	Burnaberye, James	St. Stephen	--	£62	
1644/14	Burnabury, Bridget	(see Burnaberey)			
W 1639/16	Burnell, Edward	Olveston	Carpenter	£91	
1668/5	Burnell, Elioner	St. Stephen	Widow ⟨Hooper⟩	£231	
1609/11	Burnell, Joan	Almondsbury	--	£47	
W 1742/9	Burnell, Mary	Olveston	⟨Widow⟩	£21	
W 1717/9	Burnett, David	City of Bristol	Mariner	£7	died at sea
1740/6	Burrage, Peter	City of Bristol	Sail-maker	£9	
1684/6	Burroughs, John	City of Bristol	Mariner	£156	alias Brimsmead
W 1713/5	Burrowes, Thomas	City of Bristol	Yeoman	£91	inv. & account her debts 30/-
1759/3	Burt, Agnes	City of Bristol	Widow	--	
1689/48	Burt, John	--	Cooper	£9	
1679/10	Burton, Almadad	St. James	--	£26	
1728/5	Burton, Benjamin	City of Bristol	Mariner	£13	
1685/6	Bush, George	City of Bristol	Victualler	£6	
1708/6	Bush, George	City of Bristol	Butcher	£46	
1695/3B	Bush, Gregory	City of Bristol	Cordwainer	£258	
1687/8	Bush, Hannah	SS. Philip & Jacob	--	£9	
1735/3	Bush, Hannah	City of Bristol	Widow	£39	
1707/9	Bush, John	City of Bristol	Cooper	£15	
1717/10	Bush, John	City of Bristol	Mariner	£10	
1695/12	Bush, Richard	--	--	£6	inv. also marked Richard Edwards
1709/6	Bush, Thomas	City of Bristol	Shipwright	£15	
1727/5	Bush, Thomas	Winterbourne (Frenchay)	--	£14	compare next entry

	Year ref.	Name	Parish or area	Occupation or status	Value	Notes
	1727/6	Bush, Thomas	Winterbourne	Miller	£19	see previous entry
W	1643/19	Bush, Walter	—	—	£2	
	1754/9	Bushby, John	City of Bristol	Mariner	£9	
	1623/10	Bushe, Alice	St. Mary, Redcliffe	Widow	£5	
	1643/18	Bushe, George	St. Nicholas	—	£39	
	1623/11	Bushe, Henry	St. Mary, Redcliffe	Tanner	£11	
W	1611/11	Bushe, Joan	St. Mary-le-Port	Widow	£21	
W	1643/20	Bushe, Joan	St. Nicholas	Widow	£29	
	1611/12	Bushe, William	SS. Philip & Jacob	—	£2	
W	1629/8	Busher, Katherine	<Henbury> Aust	Spinster	£9	
	1634/14	Busher, William	St. Ewen	—	--	note re administration
	1635/13	Busher, William	St. Ewen	—	£4	also 2nd copy
	1633/12	Bushell, Thomas	Mangotsfield	—	£22	
	1666/6	Bussell, Ann	St. Nicholas	Widow	£111	
W	1628/16	Bussell, Henry	St. Nicholas	Mariner	£34	
	1747/5	Bussow, Peter	(see Bossow)			
	1742/10	Buslum, James	City of Bristol	Mariner	£7	
	1625/10a	Butcher, Henry	Clapton, Somerset	Clerk	£202	
	1625/10b	Butcher, Henry	Clapton, Somerset	Clerk	(list of some household goods with values)	
	1623/8	Butcher, John	St. Werburgh	Alderman	£3,515	three copies
	1748/13	Butcher, Joseph	City of Bristol	Mariner	£4	
W	1614/1	Butcher, Katherine	(see Bowcher)			
W	1628/14	Butcher, Nathaniel	City of Bristol <St. Werburgh>	Merchant	£6,954	
	1673/4	Butcher, Thomas	Stoke Gifford	Gent.	£7	
W	1693/1	Butcher, William	Winterbourne (Hambrook)	Maltster	£523	
W	1716/9	Butler, William	City of Bristol	Upholsterer	£1,134	
W	1617/8	Butler, Alice	St. Peter	Spinster	£2	
W	1723/7	Butler, Ann	<City of Bristol>	<Widow>	£22	

Reference	W	Name	Place	Occupation	Value	Notes
1649/6		Butler, Benjamin	City of Bristol	Tailor	£3	
1679/11		Butler, Christopher	St. Stephen	Cordwainer	£2	
1746/4	W	Butler, Edmund	City of Bristol	Mariner	£15	
1724/3		Butler, Hugh	City of Bristol	Mariner	£19	
1730/6	W	Butler, James	City of Bristol	Mariner	£5	
1732/7	W	Butler, James	City of Bristol	Mariner	£17	
1633/13	W	Butler, John	Winterbourne	Yeoman	£108	
1635/14	W	Butler, John	Winterbourne	Yeoman	£19	
1754/10	W	Butler, Mary	City of Bristol	Widow	£18	formerly Bright
1758/6		Butler, Richard	—	Mariner	£9	
1713/6		Butler, Samuel	City of Bristol	Mariner	£9	
1689/6		Butler, Thomas	SS. Philip & Jacob	—	£29	
1637/9		Butler, William	St. Stephen	—	£72	
1748/11	W	Butson, Thomas	City of Bristol	Mariner	£6	
1720/6	W	Butter, Edward	City of Bristol	Mariner	£11	
1661/11	W	Button, Joan	Westbury-on-Trym	—	£3	
1694/6	W	Buxton, Samuel	Westbury-on-Trym (Shirehampton)	—	£11	
1702/5		Buy, Elizabeth	Henbury (Kingsweston)	Gent.		
1712/4	W	Byam, John	City of Bristol	Barber-surgeon	£26	
1669/13	W	Byde, John	St. Peter	<Millwright>	£13	
1629/9	W	Byde, Robert	Temple	Shearman	£71	
1704/8	W	Bye, Edward	Barton Regis	<Gallipot maker>	£57	
1756/3	W	Bye, James	SS. Philip & Jacob	—	£19	
1680/5	W	Bynam, Mary	St. Stephen	Widow	£19	
1708/7		Bynon, Morgan	City of Bristol	Mariner	£17	
		Byrd, John	(see Bird)			
1639/17	W	Byrd, John	St. Augustine	—	£10	
1620/22	W	Byshop, Henry	Alveston	Husbandman	£66	
1667/5		Byshop, Thomas	St. Mary, Redcliffe	Clothier	£93	
1613/8	W	Bysshop, William	St. Thomas	Cloth-worker	£25	
1633/7	W				£168	also 2nd copy

Year ref.	Name	Parish or area	Occupation or status	Value	Notes
W 1667/13	Cabbell, John	St. Werburgh	Barber	£9	
W 1691/13	Cable, Mary	City of Bristol	Widow	£14	
W 1694/12	Cable, George	City of Bristol	Blockmaker	£298	
1611/13	Cadde, Lawrence	St. Leonard	--	£27	
1776/CP	Cadell, Philip	City of Bristol	Tea-man	£123	inv. & account
1699/2	Cadle, John	St. Stephen	--	£31	
W 1746/5	Cadogan, Roger	City of Bristol	Mariner	£15	
1647/4	Cadoogan, Richard	City of Bristol	Bachelor	£4	
1636/8	Cadwell, Christopher	<City of Bristol>	--	--	
1761/4	Cahill, William	City of Bristol	Mariner	£8	
1740/7	Caines, James	City of Bristol	Mariner	£9	
W 1746/6	Calahan, Daniel	City of Bristol	Hooper	£9	died at sea
1727/7	Calderhead, James	City of Bristol	Chapman	£10	
1726/5	Caldicott, Henry	City of Bristol	Mariner	£19	
1707/10	Cale, Gilbert	City of Bristol	Gent.	£70	
W 1763/2	Callaghan, John	City of Bristol	Mariner	£15	
W 1733/9	Callahan, Edward	City of Bristol	Mariner	£11	
1756/4	Callone, Daniel	City of Bristol	Blacksmith	£6	
1741/5	Callow, Robert	St. James	Mariner	--	
1636/9	Callowhill, Philip	--	--	£106	
W 1715/9	Cambourne, Richard	Westbury-on-Trym (Lawrence Weston)	Yeoman	£322	
W 1688/7	Cambridge, Mary	City of Bristol	Widow	£39	
W 1752/4	Cambridge, Samuel	City of Bristol	Mariner	£10	
1661/15	Cambridge, Thomas	SS. Philip & Jacob	Yeoman	£32	
W 1754/11	Camens, Thomas	--	<Mariner>	£3	
W 1719/10	Campbell, Neale	City of Bristol	Mariner	£13	
1751/4	Campbell, Patrick	City of Bristol	Mariner	£71	
W 1625/16	Campe, Agnes	Henbury (Compton Greenfield)	Widow	£107	

	Ref.	Name	Place	Occupation	Value	Notes
W	1623/13	Campe, John	Henbury (Compton Greenfield)	Tailor	£135	
	1752/5	Campin, George	City of Bristol	Mariner	£6	
W	1736/9	Campion, John	City of Bristol	Mariner	£12–£14	
W	1697/14	Cann, Richard	Compton Greenfield	Gent.	£184	
W	1754/11	Cannens, Thomas	(see Camens)			
	1719/11	Cannings, William	City of Bristol	Shoemaker	£67	
	1712/5	Cantell, Moses	City of Bristol	Cordwainer	£5	
W	1639/18	Canter, William	(see Cantor)			
W	1639/18	Cantor, William	Westbury-on-Trym (Southmead)	Yeoman	£379	
W	1745/4	Cantrell, Anne	City of Bristol	Widow	£13	
	1748/14	Cantrell, Martha	City of Bristol	Spinster	£13	
	1627/5	Capie, William	<Henbury> Aust	Waterman	£4	
W	1682/11	Caple, James	City of Bristol	Wire-drawer	£208	
	1641/7	Cappell, John	Aston Blank (Glos)	Labourer	£22	also 2nd copy
	1640/6a	Car, Andrew	St. Leonard	Sailor	£5	
	1640/6b	Car, Andrew	(note re administration)			
W	1633/14	Care, William	St. Nicholas	<Draper>	£222	
W	1639/19	Carie, Lettice	St. Werburgh	Widow	£421	
	1743/3	Carncross, Thomas	City of Bristol	Mariner	£8	
W	1758/7	Carney, Thomas	City of Bristol	Mariner	£5	
	1740/8	Carney, William	City of Bristol	Mariner	£9	
	1637/10	Caro, Alexander	St. Mary, Redcliffe	Gent.	£501	
W	1639/20	Caro, Anne	St. Mary, Redcliffe	Widow	£46	
W	1665/12	Caro, George	St. Mary, Redcliffe	<Gent.>	£265	
W	1690/7	Caro, George	St. Thomas	Inn-keeper	£162	
	1643/21	Carpenter, John	St. Michael	<Grocer in will>	£24	
W	1754/12	Carpenter, Martha	City of Bristol	Widow	£19	
	1680/11	Carpenter, Walter	City of Bristol	Baker	£33	
W	1625/17	Carrant, Edmond	<Christchurch>	Gent.	£54	
W	1620/23	Carrell, Richard	Henbury	Carpenter	£108	

	Year ref.	Name	Parish or area	Occupation or status	Value	Notes
	1758/8	Carrels, Carreb	City of Bristol	Mariner	£5	
	1649/7	Carrent, George	St. Michael	--	£23	
W	1679/18	Carrier, Josiah	Henbury (Stowick)	Yeoman	£129	
W	1684/10	Carrier, Margaret	Henbury	<Widow>	£69	
	1724/4	Carter, George	City of Bristol	Mariner	£16	
	1748/15	Carter, George	City of Bristol	Mariner	£10	
W	1628/17	Carter, Nicholas	<Almondsbury?>	--	£36	
W	1662/10	Cartwright, Henry	SS. Philip & Jacob	<Cutler & knife-maker>	£107	
	1669/16A	Cary, Grace	City of Bristol	Widow	£19	
W	1628/18	Case, Ann	St. James	Widow	£37	
	1627/6	Casey, John	St. James	Tobacco-pipe maker	£2	
	1617/9	Casse, Miles	St. James	Tobacco-pipe maker	£7	
	1756/5	Cassin, Mary	City of Bristol	Widow	£13	
W	1758/9	Castle, Sarah	City of Bristol	Widow	£15	
	1625/18	Cattelena, --	Almondsbury	Single-woman	£6	a negro
	1677/7	Cause, Giles	City of Bristol	Bachelor	£48	
	1639/21	Cause, Philip	SS. Philip & Jacob	Tanner	£214	
	1675/15	Cause, Richard	SS Philip & Jacob	--	£61	
	1620/24	Cause, Thomas	(see Cawse)			
W	1726/6	Cavena, Robert	City of Bristol	Mariner	£5	
	1745/5	Cavanaugh, James	City of Bristol	Mariner	£19	
	1639/22	Cawley, Robert	(see Cawlie)			
	1639/22	Cawlie, Robert	St. Michael	--	£1	
	1677/7	Cawse, Giles	(see Cause)			
	1620/24	Cawse, Thomas	St. Peter	--	£11	
W	1730/7	Cayford, William	City of Bristol	Mariner	£11	
W	1678/13	Cealy, Mary	Temple	Spinster	£32	
	1706/6	Cecile, Richard	--	--	£3	
	1700/2	Cecill, Benjamin	City of Bristol	Joiner	£15	
	1682/14	Cecill, James	City of Bristol	Cordwainer	£7	

W	Ref	Name	Place	Occupation	Value	Note
W	1650/2	Cecill, Joan	St. Mary, Redcliffe	<Widow>	£118	
	1695/11	Cecill, Peter	--	--	£9	
W	1678/13	Celey, Mary	(see Cealy)			
W	1639/23	Cessell, Alice	Temple	Widow	£14	
	1686/11	Challoner, Francis	City of Bristol	Inn-holder	£131	
	1623/14	Chalmer, William	St. Stephen	--	£6	
	1675/16	Chaloner, Francis	City of Bristol	Merchant	£69	
W	1667/14	Chalwell, John	St. James	--	£26	
	1677/9A	Chambers, Ann	St. Stephen	Widow	£40	account only
	1678/65	Chambers, Ann	St. Stephen	Widow	£40	
	1636/10	Chambers, John	St. Augustine	Tailor	£2	
	1712/6	Chamlea, William	City of Bristol	Mariner	£8	
W	1629/10	Chamnes, Mary	Almondsbury	--	£134	compare Champnis
W	1731/14	Champin, Charles	<St. George: Pill>	Mariner	£4	
	1728/6	Champion, George	City of Bristol	Mariner	£8	
	1609/12	Champion, William	Mangotsfield	--	£41	
W	1636/11	Champion, William	St. Michael	Inn-holder	£233	
W	1677/6	Champneis, Mary	<SS. Philip & Jacob>	<Widow>	£18	
W	1642/13	Champneys, John	Almondsbury	<Yeoman>	£93	
W	1674/9	Champneys, John	(see Champnies)			
W	1668/17	Champnies, Agnes	Elberton	--	£72	
	1749/10	Champnies, Arah	Henbury	<Widow>	£189	
W	1623/15	Champnies, Edmond	Littleton-on-Severn	<Yeoman>	£342	
	1674/10	Champnies, Edward	Almondsbury	Yeoman	£304	
	1716/10	Champnies, James	Henbury (Chittening)	--	£67	
	1609/13	Champnies, John	--	--	£13	
W	1674/9	Champnies, John <snr>	Almondsbury	Yeoman	£620	
	1663/15	Champnies, Toby	Elberton	--	£280	
W	1629/11	Champnis, Thomas	Elberton	--	£232	compare Chamnes
W	1613/13	Champnyes, Anne	Elberton	Widow	£61	
	1720/7	Chandler, David	City of Bristol	Lighterman	£19	
W	1687/18	Chandler, Joseph	SS. Philip & Jacob	Cordwainer	£14	

Year ref.		Name	Parish or area	Occupation or status	Value	Notes
1671/7		Chandler, Martha	Clifton	Widow	£41	compare 1670/7
1678/14	W	Chandler, Philip	SS. Philip & Jacob	⟨Cordwainer⟩	£9	
1676/8		Chandler, Thomas	St. Nicholas	Haulier	£8	
1670/7		Chandler, William	City of Bristol	--	£52	
1699/4	W	Chaney, Henry	(see Cheney)			
1742/11		Chapman, George	City of Bristol	Mariner	£3	
1625/19a	W	Chapman, Robert	St. James (Barton)	⟨Gardener⟩	£12	
1625/19b	W	Chapman, Robert	St. James	Gardener	--	with wills
1623/16		Chappel, Bartholomew	St. Michael	Gent: Dr. of Physic	£5	
1669/19	W	Chappell, Mary	St. Nicholas	Widow	£125	
1690/12		Chappell, Mary	--	--	£30	
1747/6	W	Chappell, Robert	City of Bristol	Mariner	£8	
1680/10		Chappell, Thomas	City of Bristol	Soap-boiler	£12	
1642/14		Charles, Gartry	St. Stephen	Widow	£5	
1737/3		Charles, Issac	Abbots Leigh	Pilot	£46	
1618/13		Charles, John	St. Werburgh	--	£9	
1685/14		Charles, William	City of Bristol	Bachelor	£3	
1705/6		Chatten, Charles	(see Chatton)			
1728/7		Chatterton, Richard	City of Bristol	Mariner	£11	died at sea
1740/9		Chatto, Robert	City of Bristol	Surgeon	£8	
1705/6		Chatton, Charles	City of Bristol	Glover	£1	
1672/8		Chatton, Mary	⟨Christchurch⟩	Widow	£168	
1613/14	W	Chaundler, William	Clifton	Sailor	£58	
1613/15	W	Chaundler, William	Temple	Lighterman	£8	
1698/9		Check, George	--	--	£2	
1709/7	W	Chelley, William	City of Bristol	Mariner	£19	
1741/6		Chenevard, Isaac	City of Bristol	Factor	£7	
1699/4	W	Cheney, Henry	Stapleton	Yeoman	£63	
1611/14	W	Cherrington, Alexander	Temple	Cloth-worker	£29	
1754/13	W	Cherry, Sarah	City of Bristol	Widow	£8	

Ref	Name	Place	Occupation	Value	Notes
W 1612/2	Cheshire, John	Westbury-on-Trym (Shirehampton)	--	£43	alias Smale
W 1752/6	Cheslet, Barnaby	City of Bristol	Mariner	£10	
1667/15	Chester, Walter	SS. Philip & Jacob	Gent.	£67	
W 1683/8	Chester, William	Barton Regis	Gent.	£135	
1704/9	Chestle, John	--	--	£5	
W 1746/7	Chevalier, John	City of Bristol	Mariner	£8	
1708/8	Chick, John	City of Bristol	Mariner	£4	
1715/10	Chicken, Joseph	City of Bristol	Mariner	£7	
1734/9	Chilcott, Richard	City of Bristol	Mariner	£9	
W 1669/21	Child, Edward	Henbury <Berwick>	Yeoman	£165	
1688/10	Child, Edward	City of Bristol	Cutler	£1	
1708/9	Child, Francis	City of Bristol	Tobacconist	£15	
W 1696/7	Child, Jane	Henbury (Kingsweston)	Widow	£47	
W 1663/13	Child, Joan	Christchurch	Widow	£13	
W 1706/CP	Child, Joyce	Henbury (Hallen)	--	£88	inv. & account (bad condition)
1693/5	Child, Morriss	Henbury (Kingsweston)	Yeoman	£39	
1678/15	Child, Richard (jnr)	Henbury (Kingsweston)	--	£36	
W 1719/12	Child, Sam	Henbury <Kingsweston>	<Yeoman>	£926	
W 1662/9	Child, Samuel	Henbury <Kingsweston>	Yeoman	£692	
1634/15	Childe, William	Christchurch	Mariner	£101	
W 1749/11	Chilton, Elianor	<St. James>	Widow	£7	
W 1732/8	Chilton, Thomas	Westbury-on-Trym	<Yeoman>	£47	
1609/14	Chilton, William	(see Chylton)			
W 1640/7	Chilvester, Nicholas	St. Michael	<Cordwainer>	£37	
W 1629/12	Chisheere, Joan	Westbury-on-Trym (Shirehampton)	Single-woman	£13	alias Smalle

	Year ref.	Name	Parish or area	Occupation or status	Value	Notes
	1679/15	Chitts, Richard	Olveston (Tockington)	--	£32	
	1671/5B	Chivers, Henry	--	--	£8	
	1668/19	Chock, John	St. Thomas	Bodice-maker	£345	
	1641/8	Chock, Richard	St. Nicholas	--	£2	
W	1733/11	Church, Miles	City of Bristol	Mariner	£12	
W	1709/8	Church, Thomas	City of Bristol	Mariner	£9	
		Churchy, John	(see Churchill)			
W	1705/7	Churchill, John	Barton Regis	Blacksmith	£63	
W	1709/9	Churchill, Robert	--	Mariner	£15	
W	1718/6	Churchill, Susana	SS. Philip & Jacob	Widow	£64	
	1666/12	Churchman, John	<Henbury> Aust	--	£200	
	1709/10	Churchouse, Samuel	City of Bristol	Mariner	£17	
	1635/19	Chrispe, Henry	(see Crispe)			
	1734/10	Christmas, Henry	City of Bristol	Mariner	£9	
	1711/10	Christopher, Valentine	City of Bristol	Mariner	£6	
W	1688/8	Christopher, William	<St. Ewen>	Merchant Tailor	£559	
	1733/10	Christy, John	City of Bristol	Mariner	£17	
	1609/14	Chylton, William	SS. Philip & Jacob	--	£3	
W	1639/23	Cissell, Alice	(see Cessell)			
	1635/13	Cissell, David	St. Thomas	Shearman	£3	
	1662/13	Cissell, Richard (jnr)	St Mary-le-Port	--	£17	
	1682/14	Cissill, James	(see Cecill)			
	1641/10	Clackson, Robert & Sarah	SS. Philip & Jacob	--	£17	
	1641/10	Clackson, Sarah	(see Clackson, Robert)			
	1761/5	Clapp, William	City of Bristol	Mariner	£12	
W	1642/15	Clarie, Edward	St. Stephen	Joiner	£257	
W	1731/15	Clark, James	City of Bristol	Mariner	£5	
	1740/10	Clark, James	City of Bristol	Mariner	£4	
	1702/6	Clark, John	Olveston	--	£68	

W	Ref	Name	Place	Occupation	Value	Notes
W	1707/11	Clark, John	City of Bristol	House-carpenter <Cooper in will>	£12	
	1730/8	Clark, Joseph	City of Bristol	Mariner	£9	
W	1761/6	Clark, Robert	City of Bristol	Mariner	£12	
	1717/11	Clark, Thomas	City of Bristol	Mariner	£3	
	1737/4	Clark, William	City of Bristol	Mariner	£15	
W	1679/23	Clarke, Anne	Alveston	Widow	£14	
	1673/9	Clarke, Catherine	--	--	£16	
W	1639/24	Clarke, Edward	--	--	£222	
	1738/2	Clarke, Eleanor	Henbury (Northwick)	Widow	£447	
	1644/15	Clarke, George	Christchurch	Yeoman	--	
W	1641/9	Clarke, Giles	Clifton	Yeoman	£298	
	1620/25	Clarke, Henry	Elberton	Master of Arts	£35	
W	1661/22	Clarke, Henry	Stoke Gifford	Husbandman	£67	
W	1668/16	Clarke, John	Stapleton	--	£168	
		Clarke, John	(alias Tyler which see)			
W	1672/10	Clarke, Mary	Almondsbury	Spinster	£30	
W	1617/10	Clarke, Richard	St. Thomas	Husbandman	£10	
W	1625/20	Clarke, Richard <snr>	Stapleton	Baker	£63	
W	1779/CP	Clarke, Susannah	St. Augustine	Widow	£68	also 2nd copy
	1689/10	Clarke, Thomas	City of Bristol	--	£7	
	1665/8	Clarke, William	Mangotsfield	Farrier	£62	
	1671/8	Clarke, William	St. Peter	--	£15	
W	1698/10	Clarke, William	Clifton	House-carpenter	£37	
	1711/11	Clarke, William	City of Bristol	Gent.	£45	
	1746/8	Clary, Daniel	City of Bristol	<Mariner>	£12	
	1669/16B	Clary, John	City of Bristol	Cooper	£36	
W	1635/16	Clavell, Elinor	St. Stephen	Widow	£15	
	1641/10	Claxon, Sarah	St. Mary-le-Port (see Clackson, Robert)			
W	1680/13	Claxton, James	St. Peter	Weaver	£59	
	1686/14	Clay, Richard	City of Bristol	Porter	£27	
	1637/11	Claybrooke, Challoner	St. Nicholas	Servant	£9	
W	1693/6	Clayton, Jane	Mangotsfield	Widow	£15	

Year ref.		Name	Parish or area	Occupation or status	Value	Notes
1666/9		Cleament, Elizabeth	(see Clement)			
1742/12		Clear, John	City of Bristol	Mariner	£7	
1677/8	W	Cleare, Ann	City of Bristol	Widow	£97	also 2nd copy
1618/14	W	Clement, Thomas	(see Clement)			
1666/9		Clement, Elizabeth	Mangotsfield	Widow	£61	
1737/5		Clement, George	City of Bristol	Pewterer	£3	
1661/19	W	Clement, Joan	Barton Regis	Widow	£9	
1628/19a		Clement, John	--	--	£14	
1628/19b		Clement, John	--	--	£14	account
1648/4		Clement, John	Westbury-on-Trym (Shirehampton)		£5	
1734/11	W	Clement, John	Henbury	Butcher	£9	
1625/22		Clement, Peter	St. Mary, Redcliffe	--	£3	
1588/1		Clement, Robert	City of Bristol	Carpenter	£72	
1618/14	W	Clement, Thomas	St. Peter	Haberdasher	£34	
1628/20		Clement, Thomas	St. Nicholas	Saddler	£285	also 2nd copy
1668/15	W	Clement, Thomas	SS. Philip & Jacob	Butcher	£58	
1679/16		Clements, Alice	SS. Philip & Jacob	Yeoman	£12	
1637/12		Clements, Arthur	Henbury	Widow		alias Maynard 2 documents
1639/25		Clements, Cicely	St. Thomas	Widow	£12	
1712/7		Clements, Edward	Barton Regis	Coal-driver	£5	
1635/17		Clements, John	St. James	〈Tanner〉	£54	
1676/9		Clements, John	Temple	Weaver	£15	
1667/16		Clements, Robert	Stapleton	Miller	£28	
1744/4		Clements, Sarah	--	--	£18	
1620/26	W	Clements, Thomas	SS. Philip & Jacob & Westbury-on-Trym	Yeoman	£214	
1640/8		Clements, Thomas	SS. Philip & Jacob	--	£71	
1668/15	W	Clements, Thomas	SS. Philip & Jacob	Yeoman 〈Coal-driver in will〉	£31	

	Ref.	Name	Place	Occupation	Value	Notes
W	1682/13	Clements, Thomas	Barton Regis	⟨Yeoman⟩	£45	
	1714/9	Clements, William	SS. Philip & Jacob	--	£94	
	1741/7	Clemonds, Richard	(see Clemonds, Roger)			
	1741/7	Clemonds, Roger	City of Bristol	Mariner	£1	died at sea
	1730/9	Cleverly, John	City of Bristol	Shipwright	£14	
	1686/13	Cleverly, William	City of Bristol	Ropemaker	£22	
	1618/15	Clifford, James	St. James	Brewer	£41	
W	1732/9	Clifford, Thomas	City of Bristol	Mariner	£11	
W	1661/16	Clifford, William	--	--	£12	
W	1670/6	Clinck, Owen	Temple	--	£85	
W	1746/9	Clinton, Thomas	City of Bristol	Cooper	£9	died at sea
W	1635/18	Clissold, Henry	St. Mary-le-Port	Soapmaker	£156	also 2nd copy
W	1731/19	Clottenburg, Clois	City of Bristol	Mariner	£9	
	1627/7	Clovill, Humfrey	Christchurch	Goldsmith	£144	
	1746/10	Cloyne, Richard	City of Bristol	Mariner	£16	
	1732/10	Clunn, William	City of Bristol	Mariner	£2	
	1735/4	Clutson, Hugh	(see Clutsum)			
	1735/5	Clutson, Richard	SS. Philip & Jacob	--	£10	
	1735/4	Clutsum, Hugh	Westbury-on-Trym	--	£30	
	1680/12	Clymer, Dorothy	St. Stephen	Blockmaker	£66	
			(document states 'Thomas Clymer' outside)			
W	1679/20	Clymer, Richard	St. Stephen	Blockmaker	£32	
	1666/10	Clymer, William	St. John	--	£18	
	1646/5	Coale, Anis	SS. Philip & Jacob	Widow	£9	
W	1665/9	Coale, Edward	Winterbourne	⟨Yeoman⟩	£167	
W	1732/11	Coalman, Samuel	Stapleton	--	£79	
	1696/10	Coarte, John	--	--	£5	
	1637/13	Coats, Agnes	Henbury	Widow	£17	compare 1636/12
	1636/12	Coats, --	⟨Henbury⟩	Widow	--	letter re goods
W	1618/16	Cobden, Thomas	Westbury-on-Trym	--	£91	
W	1709/11	Cock, Elizabeth	City of Bristol	Spinster	£16	
W	1712/8	Cockaine, Thomas	St. Stephen	Victualler	£294	
W	1683/7	Cocke, Anthony	City of Bristol	Bay-maker	£591	

	Year ref.	Name	Parish or area	Occupation or status	Value	Notes
W	1628/21	Cocke, Thomas	Temple	Cloth-worker	£17	
W	1671/9	Cockes, Ezekiel	Mangotsfield	⟨Husbandman⟩	£38	
	1639/26	Cockey, Edward	SS. Philip & Jacob	Brazier	£3	
	1729/3	Cockling, Jeremy	City of Bristol	Mariner	£3	
W	1633/15	Codner, Robert	St. Werburgh	—	£716	
W	1685/12	Codner, William	City of Bristol	Soapmaker	£18	
W	1717/12	Codner, Susanna	City of Bristol	Widow	£44	
	1613/17	Coke, Edith	(see Cook)			
W	1740/11	Colbard, Patrick	City of Bristol	Mariner	£9	
	1692/11	Cole, Abraham	City of Bristol	Merchant	£33	
	1675/17	Cole, Edward	(see Coole)			
W	1640/9	Cole, George	Alveston	⟨Weaver⟩	£62	
	1649/8	Cole, Henry	St. Michael	—	£5	
W	1729/4a	Cole, Henry	City of Bristol	Mariner	£7	
W	1729/4b	Cole, Henry	City of Bristol	Mariner	£14	revised inv.
W	1711/12	Cole, Hezekiah	Winterbourne	Yeoman	£821	
	1726/7	Cole, Humphry	SS. Philip & Jacob	Glass-maker	£361	
	1633/16	Cole, John	St. James	⟨Mariner⟩	£4	
	1636/13	Cole, John	Christchurch	Tailor	£204	
	1746/11	Cole, John	City of Bristol	Mariner	£6	
	1747/7	Cole, John	City of Bristol	Mariner	£8	
W	1679/21	Cole, Margaret	Winterbourne	Widow	£24	
W	1716/11	Cole, Margaret	Winterbourne	⟨Widow⟩	£320	
W	1678/19	Cole, Robert	Winterbourne (Hambrook)	⟨Clothier⟩	£73	
	1613/16	Cole, Thomas	St. Augustine	—	£13	
	1733/12	Cole, Thomas	City of Bristol	Mariner	£12	
	1735/6	Coleman, Daniel	(see Colman)			
W	1725/3	Coleman, John	Limerick	Mariner & Cooper	£10	
	1664/11	Coleman, Richard	Christchurch	—	£110	
	1633/17	Coleman, Richard	(see Couleman)			

W	Ref	Name	Place	Occupation	Value	Notes
W	1732/11	Coleman, Samuel	(see Coalman)			
	1611/15	Coles, Alice	Almondsbury	--	£23	
	1617/11	Colle, Alice	St. Augustine	--	£38	
	1678/19	Colle, Robert	(see Cole)			
	1661/14	Collens, John	Filton	Husbandman	£40	
	1691/12	Collens, John	--	<Hatter>	£6	
	1620/27	Collens, Richard	SS. Philip & Jacob	--	£5	
W	1747/8	Collett, John	City of Bristol	Mariner	£5	
	1673/11	Colliers, John	St. Mary, Redcliffe	Cooper	£2	
W	1635/20	Collier, Giles	Temple	Instrument maker	£41	
	1647/5	Collier, Thomas	St. Mary-le-Port	Inn-holder	£182	'The Swan'
W	1696/8	Collier, William	City of Bristol	Baker	£45	
W	1639/29	Collimoor, Edward	(see Cullimor)			
W	1699/-	Collings, John	City of Bristol	Cordwainer		
			(not an inventory; schedule of goods listed in will)			
	1696/9	Collings, Mary	Mangotsfield	Widow	£10	
W	1663/17	Collongs, Timothy & Elnor	Littleton-on-Severn	Yeoman	£261	
W	1641/11	Collins, Arnold	St. Mary-le-Port	Cook	£136	
	1732/12	Collins, Charles	SS. Philip & Jacob	Stay maker	£26	
	1742/13	Collins, David	City of Bristol	Mariner	£6	
	1746/12	Collins, Elianor	Temple	Widow	£16	
	1716/12	Collins, Henry	City of Bristol	Maltster	£403	
	1748/16	Collins, James	City of Bristol	Mariner	£4	
	1640/10	Collins, John	Henbury (Lawrence Weston)	Husbandman	£34	
	1664/10	Collins, John	St. John	Soap-boiler	£25	
W	1669/20	Collins, John	St. Stephen	Turner	£8	
	1709/12	Collins, John	City of Bristol	Mariner	£15	
W	1727/8	Collins, John	City of Bristol	Yeoman	£87	
	1783/CP	Collins, John	City of Bristol	Mariner	£66	also 2nd copy
	1672/11	Collins, Owen	Mangotsfield	Husbandman	£50	
	1731/16	Collins, Peter	City of Bristol	Mariner	£18	
	1620/27	Collins, Richard	(see Collens)			

Year ref.	Name	Parish or area	Occupation or status	Value	Notes
W 1669/22	Collins, Richard	St. Thomas	Smith	£58	
1720/8	Collins, Richard	City of Bristol	Gent.	£15	
W 1625/24	Collins, Robert	Mangotsfield	⟨Husbandman⟩	£67	
1662/14	Collins, Robert	Mangotsfield	Shoemaker	£46	
1643/22	Collins, Thomas	SS. Philip & Jacob	--	£327	
1643/23	Collins, Thomas	Westbury-on-Trym (Shirehampton)		£149	
W 1767/1	Collins, Thomas	Elberton	Yeoman	--	
1633/18	Collins, Walter	St. Thomas	Wire-drawer	£13	
W 1663/16	Collins, William	Westbury-on-Trym	⟨Miller⟩	£72	
W 1712/9	Collins, William	--	⟨Mariner⟩	£19	
W 1718/7	Collins, William	Mangotsfield (Downend)	⟨Husbandman⟩	£320	
1742/14	Collins, William	City of Bristol	Mariner	£8	
1735/6	Colman, Daniel	City of Bristol	Mariner	£18	
1743/4	Colnot, Alice	City of Bristol	Widow	£5	
1757/2A	Colquhoun, David	City of Bristol	Mariner	£7	
1625/23	Colston, Robert	St. John	Merchant	£17	
1688/6	Colthorpe, George	City of Bristol	Inn-keeper	£7	
W 1690/10	Colton, Margaret	St. James	Widow	£12+	
1760/4	Colton, Peter	City of Bristol	Mariner	£4	
W 1637/15	Combe, Florence	Horfield	Widow	£25	
1697/15	Combe, John	Horfield	Gent.	£36	
1712/10	Comdone, Thomas	City of Bristol	Mariner	£3	
W 1687/17	Comberbatch, John	City of Bristol	Horner	£666	will 1685
		(see also Cumberpatch, 1689/CP)			
1707/12	Comley, William	City of Bristol	Cooper	£18	
1743/5	Commons, Thomas	City of Bristol	Mariner	£8	
1611/17	Compton, John	St. Peter	Butcher	£35	
W 1691/14	Compton, Susanna	⟨St. Mary, Redcliffe⟩	Widow	£504	
W 1690/9	Compton, Thomas	St. Mary, Redcliffe	Hair-weaver	£531	

	1635/21	Compton, William	St. James	—	£1	
W	1728/8	Conelly, Solomon	City of Bristol	Mariner	£5	
W	1740/12	Conigam, Barnetgiam	City of Bristol	Mariner	£9	
W	1740/12	Conigham, Barnetgiam	(see Conigam)			
	1749/12	Connell, Cornelius				died at sea
W	1728/9	Conniber, John	City of Bristol	Mariner	£18	
	1750/4	Connor, Charles	City of Bristol	Mariner	£4	
	1748/17	Connor, Luke	City of Bristol	Hooper	£10	
W	1730/10	Connor, Peter	City of Bristol	Mariner	£7	
W	1752/7	Connor, Thomas	City of Bristol	Mariner	£12	
	1637/14	Consett, Mathew	St. Nicholas		£5	
	1741/8	Conway, Matthew	City of Bristol	Mariner	£13	2 documents
W	1731/17	Conway, William	City of Bristol	Mariner	£4	
	1721/8	Cook, Abraham	Abbots Leigh	Shipwright	£2	
	1613/17	Cook, Edith	Winterbourne		£14	
W	1691/11	Cook, Grace	Henbury	<Single-woman>	£15	
	1716/13	Cook, James	City of Bristol	Cooper	£65	
	1649/9	Cook, John	St. Stephen	Mariner	£14	
	1735/7	Cook, Morris	—	—	£774	
W	1715/11	Cook, Thomas	Almondsbury	<Yeoman>	£280	
	1671/5A	Cook, Thomas	St. Michael	Mariner	£140	
W	1694/13	Cooke, Ann	St. Michael	Widow	£29	
	1687/21	Cooke, Edward	City of Bristol	Haberdasher	£43	
	1634/16	Cooke, Elizabeth	Henbury	Widow	£195	
W	1679/19	Cooke, Frances	Christchurch	Widow	£13	
W	1625/25	Cooke, Gabriell	Temple	Almsman	£47	
	1673/5	Cooke, Henry	Christchurch	Merchant Tailor	£16	
	1624/16	Cooke, John	St. Stephen	Cooper	£17	
	1624/17	Cooke, John	St. John & Sneyd Park, Co. Glos.		£77	
W	1690/8	Cooke, John	St. Michael	Gent.	£20	
	1756/6	Cooke, John	St. James	Surgeon	£96	
	1647/20	Cooke, Katheryn	(alias Maye, which see)	Sail-maker	£12	

Year ref.	Name	Parish or area	Occupation or status	Value	Notes
W 1666/11	Cooke, Phillip	St. Michael	<Mariner>	£133	
1735/8	Cooke, Samuel	City of Bristol	Mariner	£5	
W 1661/21	Cooke, Thomas	Almondsbury	<Yeoman>	£805	
1694/11	Cooke, Thomas	--	--	£7	
W 1611/16	Cooke, William	Almondsbury (alias May, which see)	--		
W 1642/32B	Cooke, William	City of Bristol	Mariner	£8	
W 1749/13	Cookney, Richard	Almondsbury (Sundays Hill)		£10	
1711/13	Cooksey, Thomas	City of Bristol	--	£105	
1731/18	Cookson, Rachael	Winterbourne	Yeoman	£15	
1675/17	Coole, Edward	--	Mariner	£63	
1710/6	Coole, Francis	Stapleton	Yeoman	£16	
W 1636/14	Coombe, William	Winterbourne (Hambrook)	--	£117	
1694/14	Coombes, John	City of Bristol	Mariner	£10	
1726/8	Coombs, Amos	City of Bristol	Mariner	£8	
1740/13	Coombs, Benjamin	St. Mary-le-Port	Cordwainer	£8	
W 1697/12	Coombs, Thomas	<City of Bristol>		£1	
W 1705/8	Coomer, Frances	Temple	Widow	£19	
1624/18	Cooper, Elizabeth	City of Bristol	Widow	£14	
1760/5	Cooper, Henry	All Saints	Mariner	£19	
1640/11	Cooper, Humphry	City of Bristol	Goldsmith	£162	
W 1764/1	Cooper, John	St. James	Mariner	£7	with wills
1636/15	Cooper, John	City of Bristol	--	£253	
1720/9	Cooper, Peter	St. Augustine	Mariner	£6	
1640/12	Cooper, Rachaell	City of Bristol	--	£160	
1760/6	Cooper, Robert	City of Bristol	Mariner	£19	
W 1720/10	Coose, John	City of Bristol	Cooper	£17	died at sea
1670/23	Cope, John	(see Hoope)			
1733/13	Coppenger, Edmond	City of Bristol	Mariner	£16	
1695/7	Corbett, John	St. Stephen	--	£3	

Reference	W	Name	Place	Occupation	Value
1663/14		Cording, John	City of Bristol	Mariner	£24
1695/9 A	W	Cording, William	City of Bristol	Mariner	£15
1624/19		Corie, John	SS. Philip & Jacob	--	£170
1644/16		Corie, Robert	St. Augustine	--	£54
1629/13		Corie, Thomas	St. Mary, Redcliffe	Dyer	£1
1711/14		Cornish, Elizabeth	City of Bristol	Widow	£37
1713/7		Cornish, James	City of Bristol	Tailor	£3
1715/12		Cornish, John (jnr)	City of Bristol	Tiler	£59
1641/12		Cornock, Thomas	Temple	Weaver	£41
1668/18		Correy, Elizabeth	St. James		£13
1667/18		Corry, John	(see Cory)		
1674/8	W	Corsley, Elizabeth	City of Bristol	Widow	£442
1674/11		Corsley, John	City of Bristol	Chapman	£117
1726/9		Cortt, George	City of Bristol	Mariner	£5
1702/7		Cory, Elizabeth	Barton Regis	Widow	£15
1667/18		Cory, John	SS. Philip & Jacob	Coal-driver	£22
1627/8		Cory, Thomas	St. Mary, Redcliffe	--	£--
1726/10	W	Cory, William	City of Bristol	Mariner	£10
1732/13		Coshlan, Henry	City of Bristol	Mariner	£18
1733/14	W	Cosins, James	City of Bristol	Mariner	£9
1742/15	W	Cotham, John	City of Bristol	Mariner	£8
1678/16		Cott, Henry	St. Stephen	--	£15
1742/15	W	Cottam, John	(see Cotham)		
1688/11	W	Cottemore, Thomas	<SS. Philip & Jacob>	<Miller>	£358
1717/13		Cottel, Richard	Alveston (Row Earthcott)	--	£214
1660/2		Cotterill, Christopher	St. Peter	--	£8
1629/14	W	Cotterill, Thomas	Almondsbury	Yeoman	£62
1736/10	W	Cottle, Joan	City of Bristol	Widow	£85
1685/13	W	Cottle, William	St. James	Joiner	£217
1673/10		Cottrell, William	Westbury-on-Trym	--	£10
1633/17		Couleman, Richard	Henbury (Kingsweston)	Yeoman	£211

Year ref.	Name	Parish or area	Occupation or status	Value	Notes
W 1706/7	Coules, Edward	Horfield	Yeoman	£566	
W 1628/22	Coules, Walter	Olveston (Auckley)	<Husbandman>	£88	
W 1629/15	Couleman, John	Stapleton	<Husbandman>	£38	
1644/17	Coulter, William (jnr)	St. Peter	Clothier	£51	
1743/6	Couples, Edward	City of Bristol	Mariner	£14	
W 1646/6	Court, Edward	St. Stephen	<Turner>	£54	
1669/15	Court, John	St. Stephen	Mariner	£15	
W 1679/22	Court, John	Clifton	--	£6	
1723/8	Court, John	City of Bristol	Sail-maker	£8	
1753/6	Courtauld, Augustin	City of Bristol	Mariner	£9	
W 1726/11	Courtis, Thomas	(see Curtis)			
1753/6	Courtland, Augustin	(see Courtauld)			
1739/4	Courtney, Stephen	City of Bristol	Mariner	£4	
1713/8	Cousten, Henry	Stapleton	Coal-miner	£162	
W 1716/14	Coventry, Sarah	City of Bristol	Widow	£7	
W 1634/17	Cowdell, Ann	St. Peter	Widow	£65	
1629/16	Cowdill, John	St. Peter	--	£47	
W 1748/18	Cowhird, William	City of Bristol	Mariner	£19	
W 1629/17	Cowles, Daniel	Olveston (Aukley)	Husbandman	£95	
W 1648/5	Cowles, Edward	Filton	Yeoman	£174	
W 1661/20	Cowles, Thomas	Horfield	<Yeoman>	£47	
1670/8	Cowlton, Thomas	--	--	£14	
1636/15	Cowper, John	(see Cooper)			
1726/15	Cowslipp, Elizabeth	City of Bristol	Widow	£110	
W 1644/18	Cox, Abraham	Winterbourne (Hambrook)	--	£120	
1749/14	Cox, Edward	City of Bristol	Mariner	£6	
W 1713/9	Cox, Elizabeth	Almondsbury	Widow	£1,354	
1713/10	Cox, Hester	Almondsbury (Ellinors)	Widow	£378	

	Reference	Name	Place	Occupation	Value	Notes
W	1690/11	Cox, Joan	<St. Nicholas>	Single-woman <Widow in will>	£9	also 2nd copy
	1668/14	Cox, John	Olveston	Yeoman	£90	
	1678/17	Cox, John	Olveston	Yeoman	£51	
	1695/6	Cox, John	Almondsbury	Yeoman	£648	
	1709/13	Cox, John	City of Bristol	Gent.	£11	
	1644/19	Cox, Martha	Westbury-on-Trym	Widow	£73	
	1697/13	Cox, Nicholas	Westbury-on-Trym	--	£20	
	1643/24	Cox, Robert	Henbury	Husbandman	£19	
	1716/15	Cox, Robert	Alveston	Yeoman	£62	
	1717/14	Cox, Robert	Olveston	Yeoman	£62	
W	1629/18	Cox, Thomas	St. Nicholas	--	£30	
W	1669/18	Cox, Thomas	Almondsbury	<Yeoman>	£362	
	1684/11	Cox, Thomas	Almondsbury	Yeoman	£396	
	1687/19	Cox, Thomas	Olveston (Tockington)	--	£94	
	1687/20	Cox, Thomas	Henbury	Husbandman	£15	
	1689/11	Cox, Thomas	--	--	£86	
	1699/3	Cox, Thomas	Almondsbury	Yeoman	£283	
	1646/7	Cox, William (jnr)	SS. Philip & Jacob	Rough-mason	£39	
W	1675/18	Cox, William	SS. Philip & Jacob	<Mason>	£50	
	1683/6	Cox, William	Westbury-on-Trym (Lawrence Weston)	--	£45	
W	1636/16	Coxe, Charles	Westbury-on-Trym	Yeoman	£202	
W	1620/28	Coxe, Margaret	Henbury	Widow	£5	
	1618/17	Coxe, Thomas	St. Stephen	--	£3	
	1633/19	Coyse, Thomas	St. Nicholas	Cooper	£10	
	1673/8	Coyte, John	St. James	--	£11	
	1687/22	Cozens, Andrew	City of Bristol	Mariner	£16	
W	1679/14	Crabb, John	Temple	Weaver	£167	
	1639/27	Crabb, Thomas	Temple	<Weaver>	£12	
W	1612/3	Cradocke, William	St. Michael	Shoemaker	£376	
W	1612/4	Cradocke, Alice	St. Michael	Widow	£378	

	Year ref.	Name	Parish or area	Occupation or status	Value	Notes
	1743/7	Craford, John	City of Bristol	Mariner	£9	
W	1750/5	Craford, Thomas	City of Bristol	Mariner	£10	
W	1722/2	Craggs, Adam	City of Bristol	Mariner	£14	
	1764/CP	Crane, Edward	City of Bristol	Coach-painter	£692	inv. & account
	1740/14	Crane, Henry	City of Bristol	Surgeon	£8	died at sea
W	1703/3	Crane, Roger	City of Bristol	Merchant	£121	
	1733/15	Crane, Thomas	City of Bristol	Mariner	£7	
	1741/9	Cranfield, John	City of Bristol	Mariner	£5	
	1629/19	Crase, John	SS. Philip & Jacob	--	£3	
W	1722/3	Crawley, James	Limerick, Ireland	Shipwright	£12	died at sea
W	1730/11	Crawson, John	City of Bristol	Mariner	£4	
W	1742/16	Creagh, Matthew	City of Bristol	Mariner	£10	
	1713/11	Crease, Edmond	Henbury (Northwick) (see Creess)	Yeoman	£160	
W	1732/14	Creese, Peter	Henbury <Berwick>			
W	1691/10	Creed, Alice	Westbury-on-Trym <Shirehampton>	Widow	£19	
W	1649/10	Creed, Edward	Henbury (Compton Greenfield)	Clerk	£10	
W	1686/10	Creed, Elizabeth		Single-woman	£178	
	1712/11	Creed, John	City of Bristol	Cooper	£11	
	1662/12	Creed, Richard	Henbury	--	£361	
	1688/16	Creed, Widow	--	Widow	£7	
W	1665/11	Creed, William <snr>	St. Stephens	Cooper	£190	
W	1689/9	Creed, William	Henbury	Husbandman	£103	
W	1732/14	Creess, Peter	City of Bristol	Mariner	£2	
W	1748/19	Creighton, James	City of Bristol	Mariner	£19	
	1695/1	Crendall, John	--	Vintner	£88	
W	1673/7	Crew, Francis	SS. Philip & Jacob	Farrier	£2	
	1668/21	Crew, Joan	Almondsbury	Widow	£82	
	1672/9	Crew, Sarah	SS. Philip & Jacob	Widow	£14	
	1665/7	Crewe, John	St. Augustine	--	£4	

	Ref	Name	Place	Occupation	Value	Alias
	1617/12	Crewe, Richard	Henbury	Servant	£5	
	1695/10	Cribb, Abraham	--	--	£3	
W	1640/13	Crich, Sarah	St. Augustine	Widow	£389	
W	1646/8	Crichley, Robert	(see Crytchlie)			
	1741/10	Crisp, Thomas	City of Bristol	Hooper	£60	
	1635/19	Crispe, Henry	St. Augustine	Seaman	£3	
	1649/11	Croade, Edward	(see Crode)			
	1613/18	Crocker, George	St. Michael	--	£14	
	1639/28	Crocker, William	Olveston	--	£16	
W	1694/16	Crocker, William	St. Michael	--	£25	
W	1753/7	Crockford, William	City of Bristol	Cordwainer	£19	
	1649/11	Crode, Edward	St. Thomas	--	£21	
	1752/8	Croft, James	--	--	£20	
W	1687/16	Croft, Sarah	St. Mary, Redcliffe	Widow	£89	
	1688/9	Crofts, Sarah	St. Mary, Redcliffe	Spinster	£82	
	1756/7	Crom, John	City of Bristol	Mariner	£6	
	1634/18	Crombe, Thomas	St. Peter	--	£1	
W	1714/10	Crooker, Thomas	\<Compton Greenfield\>	\<Yeoman\>	£623	alias Branch
	1716/16	Crooks, Sarah	City of Bristol	Widow	£18	
	1701/7	Croom, Richard	Henbury	Yeoman	£171	
	1682/10	Crosman, Hester	Almondsbury	Widow	£316	
W	1633/20	Crosman, Walter	Almondsbury	\<Yeoman\>	£102	
W	1662/15	Cross, Francis	Abbots Leigh	\<Widow\>	£186	
	1609/15	Cross, William	Almondsbury	--	£66	alias Crossman
W	1729/5	Cross, William	Westbury-on-Trym (Shirehampton)	Mariner	£63	
W	1762/1B	Cross, William	City of Bristol	Tidesman	£11	
	1617/13	Crosse, Elizabeth	Westbury-on-Trym	Widow	£7	
	1667/12	Crosse, Jasper	St. Michael	Surgeon	£7	
	1647/6	Crossman, John	Almondsbury	Husbandman	£37	
W	1662/11	Crossman, Margaret	Almondsbury	Single-woman	£49	
W	1681/13	Crossman, Thomas	Almondsbury \<Over\>	Yeoman	£92	
	1609/15	Crossman, William	(alias Cross, which see)			

Year ref.	Name	Parish or area	Occupation or status	Value	Notes
1636/17	Crouch, John	St. Mary, Redcliffe	--	£18	
1682/12	Crouch, Robert	St. Werburgh	Baker	£78	
1634/18	Croumb, Thomas	(see Crombe)			
W 1716/17	Crow, Edward	City of Bristol	Mariner	£11	
1714/11	Crow, Frances	Barton Regis	--	£3	
1741/11	Crowney, Andrew	City of Bristol	Mariner	£5	
1736/11	Crump, Isaac	City of Bristol	Grocer	(£73)	
		(statement & account of William Hibbs, administrator)			
W 1688/12	Crump, Thomas	City of Bristol	Whitawer	£92	
1748/20	Crusa, Baptist	City of Bristol	Mariner	£20	
1741/12	Cruss, John	City of Bristol	Mariner	£3	
W 1646/8	Crytchlie, Robert	Temple	Baker	£44	
1731/20	Cuddy, James	City of Bristol	Mariner	£5	
1730/12	Cue, Robert	City of Bristol	Mariner	£4	
1668/20	Culliford, George	St. James	Whitawer	£25	
W 1700/21	Cullimer, Robert	<Henbury; Compton Greenfield>	<Husbandman>	£66	
W 1639/29	Cullimor, Edward	Henbury (Berwick)	--	£279	
1609/16	Cullimore, George	Almondsbury (Rednend)	--	£34	
W 1612/1	Cullimore, Joan	Olveston	Widow	£4	
W 1676/7	Cullimore, Joan	Elberton	Widow	£19	
1708/10	Cullimore, John	City of Bristol	Mariner	£9	
1713/12	Cullimore, Joseph	City of Bristol	Mariner	£7	
W 1718/8	Cullimore, Nicholas	City of Bristol	Mariner	£5	
1617/14	Cullimore, Thomas	<City of Bristol>	Smith	£2	
1725/4	Cullimore, Thomas	Westbury-on-Trym	Yeoman	£4	
1731/21	Cullmer, Henry	City of Bristol	Mariner	£9	
W 1714/12	Cullum, Anne	Mangotsfield (Downend)	Widow	£82	
		(see Culme)			
W 1688/13	Cullum, Mrs.				

W	Ref	Name	Place	Occupation	Value	Notes
	1695/9B	Cullum, Peter	St. Nicholas	Haulier	£12	
	1731/22	Culmar, Robert	City of Bristol	Mariner	£5	
W	1688/13	Culme, Mrs. <Ann>	Mangotsfield	<Widow>	£22	
W	1722/4	Culme, Thomas	Mangotsfield	Cordwainer	£5	
	1681/12	Cumbe, Francis	City of Bristol	--	£6	
	1747/9	Cumberland, Isaac	City of Bristol	Mariner	£19	
W	1689/CP	Cumberpatch, John	--	Horner	£666	account only (inv. see Comberbatch, 1687/17; will 1685)
	1681/14	Cunderick, John	SS. Philip & Jacob	--	£80	
	1624/20	Cunn, John	St. Stephen	Sailor	£1	
	1696/11	Cunningham, John	City of Bristol	Mariner	£5	
	1679/17	Cupid, Anthony	St. Thomas	Mariner	£8	
	1718/9	Cupit, Andrew	SS. Philip & Jacob	Mariner	£5	
W	1733/16	Curll, Mary	City of Bristol	Widow	£154	
	1699/8	Cursell, William	City of Bristol	Mariner	£12	
W	1633/21	Curthoyes, Richard	Olveston	Yeoman	£67	
		Curtice, Anne	(see Curtis)			
		Curtice, Anne	(document re administration)			
W	1636/18	Curtis, Anne	SS. Philip & Jacob	Widow	£29	
W	1633/21	Curtis, Elizabeth	Barton Regis	Spinster	£11	
W	1686/12	Curtis, Elizabeth	City of Bristol	Spinster	£10	
	1718/10	Curtis, Henry	Stapleton	Yeoman	£222	
W	1634/19	Curtis, John	SS. Philip & Jacob	Yeoman	£21	
	1661/17	Curtis, John	SS. Philip & Jacob	Yeoman	£21	compare 1661/17
	1665/6	Curtis, Joseph	St. Stephen	Shipwright	£3	
	1678/18	Curtis, Michael	St. Stephen	Cooper	£82	
	1697/82	Curtis, Michael	St. Stephen	Cooper	£82	account only
	1748/21	Curtis, Sarah	City of Bristol	--	£10	
W	1726/11	Curtis, Thomas	City of Bristol	Cooper	£8	
	1636/19	Curtis, William	Stapleton	Single-man	£59	
W	1757/2B	Cutler, Richard	City of Bristol	Mariner	£19	died at sea
W	1729/6	Cutts, George	City of Bristol	Mariner	£11	<impressed>
	1712/12	Cutts, John	City of Bristol	Mariner	£10	

Year ref.		Name	Parish or area	Occupation or status	Value	Notes
1709/14		Dabs, Edmund	City of Bristol	Mariner	£8	
1701/8	W	Dagg, Joan	Almondsbury	<Spinster>	£177	
1683/10		Dagge, John	Almondsbury	Yeoman	£651	
1634/20		Dagge, Thomas	Winterbourne	Yeoman	£7	
1629/20		Dakers, Thomas	City of Bristol	Plumber	£70	
1732/15	W	Dale, Abraham	City of Bristol	Mariner	£5	
1644/20		Dale, Robert	St. Stephen	Haberdasher	£5	
1758/10	W	Dally, Richard	City of Bristol	Mariner <Maltster>	£10	
1736/12	W	Dalton, Peter	SS. Philip & Jacob	Brickmaker	£120	
1741/13	W	Dalton, William	City of Bristol	Mariner	£14	
1748/22		Daly, Owen	City of Bristol	Mariner	£4	
1687/26	W	Dancy, William	City of Bristol	Brewer	£68	
1661/26	W	Dander, John	St. John	Cooper	£16	
1741/16		Dandey, Joseph	City of Bristol	Mariner	£2	
1776/CP	W	Dando, Edward	Winterbourne <Whatley's End>	Yeoman	£351	
1681/15	W	Dandy, Joyce	St. John	Widow	£18	
1611/18		Dane, John	Temple	--	£2	
1618/18		Dane, William	SS. Philip & Jacob	Weaver	£10	
1728/10		Danelly, Thomas	City of Bristol	Mariner	£10	
1748/23		Dangerfield, Thomas	City of Bristol	Gent.	£12	
1680/14	W	Daniel, Jane	City of Bristol	Spinster	£36	
1721/9		Daniel, John	City of Bristol	Mariner	£10	
1729/7		Daniel, Joseph	City of Bristol	Wine-cooper	£169	
1732/16a		Daniel, Richard	City of Bristol	Gent.	£28	
1732/16b	W	Daniel, Richard	(the account of Katherine Daniel, relict)			
1742/17		Daniel, Thomas	<Christchurch>	Mariner	£10	
1624/21	W	Daniel, William	Henbury <Stowick>	Husbandman	£97	
1677/12	W	Daniell, Enoch	St. Stephen	--	£2	
1681/19		Daniell, James	Abbots Leigh	Yeoman	£151	appraised 1671
1759/4		Daniell, Joseph	City of Bristol	Mariner	£12	

	Ref	Name	Place	Occupation	Value	
W	1711/15	Daniell, Mary	<Abbots Leigh>	<Widow>	£64	
W	1676/11	Daniell, William	Abbots Leigh	Yeoman	£64	
	1749/15	Darbyshire, Henry	City of Bristol	Mariner	£10	
	1611/19	Darnsway, Samuel	City of Bristol	Mariner	£19	
	1611/19	Darsett, Arthur	SS. Philip & Jacob	Mason	£3	
		Dassy, Arthur	(see Darsett)			
W	1710/7	Daunsey, Thomas	Stapleton	Gent.	£217	
	1714/13	Davedge, John	City of Bristol	Mariner	£8	
	1681/17	David, George	Castle Precinct	--	£7	
W	1740/15	David, John	City of Bristol	Mariner	£10	
	1712/13	David, Lewis	City of Bristol	Mariner	£9	
	1713/13	David, Thomas	City of Bristol	Mariner	£8	
	1714/13	Davidge, John	(see Davedge)			
	1694/19	Davidge, Mary	--	Widow	£8	
W	1717/15	Davies, Anthony	City of Bristol	Mariner	£6	
W	1631/1	Davies, John	(see Davis)			
W	1710/8	Davies, John (snr)	St. Mary, Redcliffe	<Carpenter>	£219	
W	1646/9	Davies, Mary	St. Michael	Widow	£57	
W	1611/20	Davies, Mathew	St. Mary, Redcliffe	--	£16	
	1731/27	Davies, Samuel	City of Bristol	Victualler	£12	
	1731/23	Davies, Thomas	City of Bristol	Mariner	£10	
W	1640/15	Davis, Ann	St. Leonard	Widow	£87	
	1759/5	Davis, Benjamin	City of Bristol	Mariner	£12	
W	1722/5	Davis, Catharine	SS. Philip & Jacob	<Widow>	£38	
W	1690/13	Davis, Christopher	Winterbourne	Yeoman	£192	died at sea
W	1730/13	Davis, Daniel	City of Bristol	Hooper	£17	
W	1743/8	Davis, David	City of Bristol	Mariner	£7	
W	1753/8	Davis, David	City of Bristol	Mariner	£6	
	1731/24	Davis, Edward	Stapleton	Yeoman	£16	
	1731/25	Davis, Edward	City of Bristol	Mariner	£4	
W	1681/16	Davis, Elizabeth	St. Peter	Spinster	£5	
W	1734/12	Davis, Faithfull	City of Bristol	Mariner	£16	

	Year ref.	Name	Parish or area	Occupation or status	Value	Notes
	1635/22	Davis, George	St. Mary, Redcliffe	--	£9	(a 1635 will of George Davis, felt-maker, of St. Phillip, exists)
W	1683/9	Davis, George	St. Mary, Redcliffe	--	£2	
W	1715/13	Davis, George ⟨snr⟩	City of Bristol	Pin-maker	£18	
W	1734/13	Davis, George	City of Bristol	Mariner	£7	
	1663/18	Davis, Henry	Temple	Clothier	£138	
W	1635/23	Davis, Hugh	St. Mary-le-Port	⟨Tailor⟩	£51	
W	1748/24	Davis, James	City of Bristol	Cordwainer	£19	
W	1631/1	Davis, John	St. Stephen	Mariner	£72	
W	1635/24	Davis, John	City of Bristol	Haulier	£302	
	1640/14	Davis, John	St. Augustine	Mariner	£1	
	1643/25	Davis, John	St. John	Haulier	£28	
	1687/23	Davis, John	St. Peter	⟨Blacksmith⟩	£59	
	1708/11	Davis, John	SS. Philip & Jacob	Felt-maker	£4	
	1712/14	Davis, John	Clifton	Shoemaker	£4	
	1715/15	Davis, John	City of Bristol	Mariner	£14	
W	1716/18	Davis, John	City of Bristol	Mariner	£4	
	1729/8	Davis, John	City of Bristol	Mariner	£13	
W	1731/26	Davis, John	City of Bristol	Coach-harness maker	£14	
	1741/14	Davis, John	City of Bristol	Mariner	£4	
	1741/15	Davis, John	City of Bristol	Surgeon	£13	
	1746/13	Davis, John	City of Bristol	Mariner	£4	
W	1748/25	Davis, John	⟨City of Bristol⟩	⟨Mariner⟩	£8	
W	1750/6	Davis, John	⟨St. Mary, Redcliffe⟩ (see Dandey)	Glass-maker	£199	
	1741/16	Davis, Joseph	City of Bristol	Mariner	£3	
	1726/12	Davis, Joseph	Henbury	Yeoman	£345	
W	1677/9B	Davis, Lewis	City of Bristol	Widow	£182	
W	1753/9	Davis, Margaret	⟨St. James⟩	Tailor	£10	
W	1758/12	Davis, Miles	City of Bristol	Mariner	£4	
	1702/8	Davis, Miles	--	--	£13	
		Davis, Morris				

Ref	W	Name	Place	Occupation	Value	Notes
1707/13		Davis, Nathaniel	--	Barber-surgeon	£54	
1733/17		Davis, Peter	City of Bristol	Mariner	£8	
1625/26		Davis, Rafe (Radulphi)	--	--	£3	
1746/14		Davis, Richard	City of Bristol	Mariner	£7	
1670/9		Davis, Robert	Christchurch	--	£69	
1731/27		Davis, Samuel	(see Davies)			also 2nd copy
1714/14	W	Davis, Stephen	City of Bristol	Mariner	£9	
1640/16		Davis, Thomas	Henbury (Aust)	Tapster	£8	
1738/3	W	Davis, Thomas	City of Bristol	Victualler	£325	
1741/17	W	Davis, Thomas	Naugle, Pembroke	Mariner	£17	
1742/18		Davis, Thomas	City of Bristol	Mariner	£5	
1751/5	W	Davis, Thomas	Westbury-on-Trym	--	£5	
1724/5		Davis, Tymothy	City of Bristol	Mariner	£10	
1617/15	W	Davis, Walter	St. Leonard	--	£22	
1681/21	W	Davis, William	City of Bristol	Practitioner of Physick	£60	
1701/9	W	Davis, William	Westbury-on-Trym (Shirehampton)	--	£78	
1711/16		Davis, William	Barton Regis	Victualler	£20	
1729/9	W	Davis, William	City of Bristol	Mariner	£3	
1730/14		Davis, William	City of Bristol	Mariner	£10	
1733/18	W	Davis, William	City of Bristol	Blacksmith	£8	
1758/11		Davis, William	City of Bristol	Mariner	£7	
1729/10	W	Davison, John	City of Bristol	<Mariner>	£3	
1729/11	W	Daw, Samuel	City of Bristol	<Salt boiler>	£348	
1613/19		Dawe, John	Henbury	--	£11	
1760/8		Dawkins, Mary	Stapleton	--	£2	
1733/19		Dawly, Jeremiah	City of Bristol	Mariner	£6	
1611/21	W	Dawson, Henry	St. Leonard	Haberdasher	£4	
1716/19		Dawson, Isaac	City of Bristol	Cork-cutter	£902	
1761/7	W	Dawson, John	City of Bristol	Mariner	£10	
1609/17		Dawson, William	St. Leonard	Sailor	£6	
1725/5		Day, Hester	City of Bristol	Widow	£189	

	Year ref.	Name	Parish or area	Occupation or status	Value	Notes
	1761/8	Day, John	City of Bristol	Pump-maker	£18	
W	1679/24	Day, Mary	Temple	Widow	£37	
W	1709/15	Day, Mary	SS. Philip & Jacob	Widow	£209	
	1694/17	Day, Robert	St. Stephen	Cooper	£139	
W	1672/14	Day, Sibyl	St. Thomas	Widow	£25	
	1704/10	Day, Thomas	City of Bristol	--	£152	
W	1717/16	Day, William	SS. Philip & Jacob	Victualler	£20	
W	1726/13	Day, William	City of Bristol	Ship-carpenter	£11	died at sea
	1628/23	Daye, Margaret	St. Thomas	Widow <Glover>	£26	
	1623/17	Daye, Thomas	St. Thomas	Soapmaker	£7	
	1646/10	Dayes, Alice	--	--	£15	
	1640/17	Dayes, Richard	Temple	Silk-weaver	£15	
W	1730/15	Dazon, Thomas	City of Bristol	Mariner	£7	
W	1685/15	Deakers, Elizabeth	St. Stephen	Widow	£24	
W	1737/6	Deal, William	City of Bristol	Mariner	£9	
	1761/9	Dealy, Edward	City of Bristol	Mariner	£7	
	1753/10	Dean, John	City of Bristol	Mariner	£3	
	1736/13	Dean, Morgan	Henbury	Yeoman	£120	
W	1696/12	Dean, Sarah	<St. Stephen>	Widow	£31	
	1682/15	Deane, Elinor	St. Mary, Redcliffe	Widow	£7	
W	1634/21	Deane, Thomas	Henbury	Thatcher	£18	2 documents
W	1637/16	Deane, Thomas	St. Thomas	Grocer	£1,368	
	1745/6	Deane, Thomas	St. James	Gent.	£3	
	1618/18	Deane, William	(see Dane)			
W	1681/18	Deane, William	Henbury (Charlton)	Blacksmith	£50	
	1643/26	Deanne, Gabriel	Christchurch	Tailor	£45	
W	1716/20	Dedicott, Mary	City of Bristol	Widow	£26	
	1759/6	Dee, David	City of Bristol	Victualler	£117	inv. & account
	1636/20	Dee, John	St. Nicholas	<Cooper>	£8	
W	1611/22	Dee, Katherine	St. Mary-le-Port	<Widow>	£13	

	Ref.	Name	Place	Occupation	Value	Notes
W	1687/27	Dee, Peter	Westbury-on-Trym (Shirehampton)	Yeoman	£154	
	1628/24	Dee, Richard	--	--	£3	
W	1776/CP	Deere, John	<St. Michael>	Inn-holder	£71	
W	1727/9	Deering, Thomas	City of Bristol	Mariner	£11	
W	1730/16	Deios, John Alexander	City of Bristol	Mariner	£17	
W	1712/16	Demery, Daniel	City of Bristol	Mariner	£6	
W	1648/6	Demmery, Robert	St. Michael	<Yeoman>	£246	
	1675/47	DeMuling, Peter	--	--	£84	
	1629/21	Dence, William	St. Stephen	Goldsmith	£166	
	1754/14	Dennett, Michael	City of Bristol	Mariner	£7	
	1683/12	Dennis, Isaac	City of Bristol	Glover	£392	
	1663/19	Dennis, Thomas	St. Stephen	Mariner	£42	
	1713/14	Dent, Richard	City of Bristol	Gent.	£16	
W	1749/17	Dentford, Robert	City of Bristol	Mariner	£10	
	1720/11	Denton, John	City of Bristol	Mariner	£8	
W	1742/CP	Deplant, John	City of Bristol	Mariner	£10	Duplant, in will
W	1745/7	Deport, Francis	City of Bristol	Mariner	£15	
W	1640/33	Derby, John	(alias Hine, which see)			
	1731/28	Deright, John	City of Bristol	Mariner	£7	
W	1731/29	Derrick, Dennis	City of Bristol	Mariner	£9	
W	1667/21	Derrick, Leonard	Henbury <Stowick>	Husbandman	£135	
	1730/17	Derrick, Rees	Westbury-on-Trym	--	£1	
	1675/19	Derrick, Thomas	Henbury (Kingsweston)	Yeoman	£106	
W	1642/18	Derricke, Francis	St. Stephen	--	£271	
	1742/19	Desanto, Joseph	City of Bristol	Mariner	£3	
	1748/26	Deschamps, John	SS. Philip & Jacob	--	£47	
	1748/80	Devascote, William	(alias Williams, which see)			
W	1639/30	Deverell, John	(see Deverill, Robert)			
	1778/CP	Deverell, John	City of Bristol	Millwright	£67	inv. & account
W	1639/30	Deverill, Robert	Stoke Gifford	Yeoman	£12	
	1738/4	Devonshire, John	City of Bristol	Mariner	£16	
W	1634/22	Dew, Alice	St. Thomas	Widow	£17	

	Year ref.	Name	Parish or area	Occupation or status	Value	Notes
	1617/16	Dewe, Thomas	St. Thomas	Cloth-worker	£4	
W	1714/15	Dexter, Elizabeth	City of Bristol	Widow	£23	inv. & account
	1666/14	Deyer, Jane	(see Dyer)			
	1646/10	Deyos, Alice	(see Dayes)			
W	1731/30	Dickenson, John	City of Bristol	Mariner	£15	
	1708/12	Dickenson, Joseph	City of Bristol	Tiler	£4	
W	1643/27	Dickenson, Philip	St. Leonard	\<Merchant\>	£96	2 documents
W	1683/11	Dickenson, William	\<City of Bristol\>	Button-maker	£34	
	1757/3	Dickerson, Joel	City of Bristol	Mariner	£10	
W	1708/13	Dickinson, James	City of Bristol	Tiler	£195	
W	1735/9	Dickinson, James	City of Bristol	Mariner	£16	
	1734/14	Dickson, Thomas	City of Bristol	Mercer	£190	
	1665/13	Diddall, Anne	Temple	Widow	£8	
	1628/25	Diddall, Christopher	Temple	Boatman	£24	
	1633/77	Diddall, Thomas	(see Thydall)			
	1643/28	Diddall, Walter	St. Nicholas	--	£15	
W	1613/20	Dier, Elizabeth	Westbury-on-Trym (Shirehampton)	Widow	£52	
	1634/23	Dier, John (jnr)	Henbury	--	£98	
	1669/23	Diggons, Michael	St. Leonard	Mariner	£34	
	1634/24	Dighton, Isaac	St. James	Brewer	£188	
W	1749/18	Dillon, John	City of Bristol	Mariner	£8	
W	1648/6	Dimerie, Robert	(see Demmery)			
	1637/17	Dimery, John (jnr)	Alveston	--	£4	
W	1664/12	Dimmery, Henry	\<Henbury\> (Aust)	Minister of the Gospel	£146	
	1677/13	Dimock, John	Castle Precincts	House-carpenter	£17	
	1666/13	Dimocke, William	Westbury-on-Trym	Yeoman	£55	
W	1613/21	Dimrye, Richard	Olveston (Greding)	Yeoman	£190	
	1747/10	Dingle, Thomas	City of Bristol	Mariner	£14	
	1675/19	Dirrick, Thomas	(see Derrick)			

W	1746/16	Ditcham, John	‹City of Bristol›	‹Mariner›	£6	
	1728/11	Dite, Elisha	City of Bristol	Mariner	£17	
W	1628/26	Ditty, Enoch	Temple	Clothier	£1126	
	1671/10	Ditty, Margery	Temple	Widow	£20	
W	1624/22	Dobbes, William	St. Mary, Redcliffe	Chapman	£136	
	1746/15	Dobbin, Thomas	City of Bristol	Mariner	£24	
	1672/12	Dobbs, James	City of Bristol	‹Mariner›	£6	
	1633/22	Dockett, Thomas	St. Werburgh	--	£80	
W	1735/10	Dodd, Robert	City of Bristol	Mariner	£10	
W	1763/3	Dodderell, James	City of Bristol	Mariner	£15	
W	1623/18	Dodding, Richard	Olveston ‹Tockington›	--	£5	
	1752/9	Dodds, Edward	City of Bristol	Mariner	£4	
W	1629/22	Dodemeade, Theophila	St. Stephen	Widow	£93	
	1629/23	Dodemeade, Thomas	St. Stephen	--	£76	
W	1693/7	Dodie, Bridget	Henbury	Widow	£11	
	1710/9	Dodson, John	(see Dotson)			
	1634/26	Doewell, John	(see Dowell)			
	1611/24	Dole, Francis	St. Mary-le-Port	--	£13	
	1669/25	Dole, Francis	Castle Precinct	Glazier	£17	
	1732/17	Dole, John	City of Bristol	Mariner	£10	
	1717/17	Dole, Tobias	Barton Regis	Cordwainer	£13	
	1667/20	Dolphin, John	SS. Philip & Jacob	Cordwainer	£5	
	1691/15	Dolton, John	SS. Philip & Jacob	--	£30	
	1709/16	Donne, John	City of Bristol	Gent.	£11	
	1734/15	Donnison, Richard	City of Bristol	Mariner	£18	
	1732/18	Donnovan, Timothy	City of Bristol	Mariner	£9	
	1753/11	Donovan, Daniel	City of Bristol	Mariner	£18	
	1745/8	Donovan, Richard	City of Bristol	Mariner	£9	
	1745/9	Donovan, Timothy	City of Bristol	Mariner	£9	
W	1677/10	Dooding, Avis	Winterbourne	‹Widow›	£29	
W	1742/20	Dooly, John	City of Bristol	Cooper	£11	died at sea
W	1739/5	Dorey, James	City of Bristol	Joiner	£18	
W	1636/21	Dorney, Christopher	Stoke Gifford	Yeoman	£375	also 2nd copy

Year ref.	Name	Parish or area	Occupation or status	Value	Notes
W 1639/31	Dorney, Christopher	Stoke Gifford	Yeoman	£136	
1704/11	Dorney, John	--	--	£78	
W 1634/25	Dorney, Thomas	Stoke Gifford	Yeoman	£103	also 2nd copy
W 1648/7	Dorney, Thomas	Stoke Gifford	Husbandman	£134	
1761/10	Dorothy, Charles	City of Bristol	Mariner	£5	
1738/5	Dorrington, Thomas	City of Bristol	Mariner	£6	
W 1739/5	Dory, James	(see Dorey)			
W 1746/17	Dory, Jonas	City of Bristol	Mariner	£10	
W 1620/30	Dossey, Cicely	Westbury-on-Trym (Shirehampton)			
1609/19	Dossett, Dorothy	Henbury	--	£14	
1674/14	Dossett, Dorothy	Henbury	Widow	£40	
W 1674/12	Dossett, John <snr>	Henbury	--	£36	
1710/9	Dotson, John	City of Bristol	--	£58	
1647/7	Doughtie, John	(see Dowty)	Yeoman	£3	
1623/19	Doules, John	St. Peter	Glazier	£204	
W 1625/27	Dove, William	Horfield	<Husbandman>	£38	
1722/6	Dovefield, Walter	City of Bristol	Gent.	£15	
1731/31	Dover, John	City of Bristol	Mariner	£10	
1669/24	Dowd, John	St. Michael	--	--	
W 1650/3	Dowding, Edward	Henbury	Tailor	£35	
W 1620/29	Dowdinge, George	(see Dudding)			
1713/15	Dowding, John	City of Bristol	Mariner	£5	
1635/25	Dowding, Thomas	Henbury <Charlton>	Husbandman	£18	2 documents
W 1661/23	Dowding, Thomas	Henbury <Charlton>	--	£66	
W 1635/26	Dowding, William	Henbury (Charlton)	Yeoman	£71	
W 1644/21	Dowding, William	Henbury	Husbandman	£120	
W 1661/24	Dowell, Ralph	Filton	--	£38	
W 1706/8	Dowell, Richard	Almondsbury <Hempton and Patchway>	<Gent.>	£125	
W 1640/19	Dowell, Joan	St. Thomas	Widow	£94	

Ref	W	Name	Parish/Place	Occupation	Value	Notes
1634/26		Dowell, John	St. Thomas	Grocer	£41	
1634/27		Dowle, George	St. Peter	--	£2	
1670/10		Dowle, Peter	City of Bristol	Victualler	£17	alias Gotley
1707/15		Dowle, Richard	City of Bristol	Mariner	£19	
1623/19		Dowles, John	(see Doules)			
1642/16	W	Dowlsworth, William	St. Stephen	⟨Sawyer⟩	£15	alias Wheeler
1731/32	W	Dowman, Richard	City of Bristol	Mariner	£10	
1749/19		Downs, Thomas	City of Bristol	Mariner	£10	
1669/27		Dowting, Anne	Temple	Widow	£44	
1647/7		Dowty, John	St. Mary, Redcliffe	⟨Blacksmith⟩	£4	
1681/20	W	Drew, John	⟨Castle Precinct⟩	House-carpenter	£182	inv. & account
1688/17	W	Drew, Margaret	Christchurch	Widow	£148	
1624/23		Drewe, John	SS. Philip & Jacob	--	£16	
1676/10		Dring, William	St. Thomas	--	£23	
1731/33		Driscoll, Timothy	City of Bristol	Farrier	£10	
1740/16	W	Driscoll, Timothy	City of Bristol	Mariner	£7	died at sea
1745/10		Driscoll, Timothy	City of Bristol	Hooper	£5	
1753/12		Driscoll, William	City of Bristol	Mariner	£11	
1609/18		Drume, Christopher	--	--	£2	
1743/9		Drummon, George	City of Bristol	Mariner	£6	
1688/14		Dubberlin, Elinor	--	--	£1	
1707/14		Dubell, Thomas	--	--	£13	
1738/6		Duboyne, Alexander	St. James	Mariner	£15	
1748/27		Duckett, John	City of Bristol	Cordwainer	£16	
1620/29		Dudding, George	Olveston	Husbandman	£5	
1663/20	W	Duddleston, Edward	St. Thomas	Tailor	£224	
1719/13	W	Duddlestone, Susanna	City of Bristol	Dame; Widow	£297	
1748/28	W	Dudridge, Gabriel	City of Bristol	Mariner	£19	
1722/6		Duffield, Walter	(see Dovefield)			
1665/10		Duggan, Alice	St. James	Spinster	£145	
1733/20		Duggan, Matthew	City of Bristol	Mariner	£9	
1737/7	W	Duglas, Thomas	City of Bristol	Victualler	£11	
1749/20	W	Duhigg, William	City of Bristol	Mariner	£10	

Year ref.	W	Name	Parish or area	Occupation or status	Value	Notes
1718/11		Dully, Thomas	Barton Regis	Glass-maker	£17	
1646/11		Dummer, Jasper	St. Thomas	Shearman	£5	
1685/16	W	Dunbarr, John	City of Bristol	Surgeon	£14	
1726/14		Duncombe, Alexander	City of Bristol	Mariner	£18	
1715/14		Dunn, Francis	City of Bristol	Mariner	£6	
1707/16	W	Dunn, James	City of Bristol	Mariner	£9	
1624/24		Dunn, John	St. Mary-le-Port	--	£1	
1624/25		Dunn, John	St. Stephen	Fishmonger	£551	
1686/15		Dunn, Edward	--	--	£3	
1706/9		Dunn, Adam	City of Bristol	Pin-maker	£7	
1742/21	W	Dunn, John	City of Bristol	Mariner	£7	
1762/2	W	Dunn, John	City of Bristol	Mariner	£4	
1731/34		Dunn, Richard	City of Bristol	Mariner	£7	
1687/25		Dunning, Thomas	St. Stephen	Blockmaker	£49	
1647/8		Dunninge, Sarah	St. Stephen	--	£31	
1639/32a		Dunton, Mary	St. Peter	<Widow>	£19	
1639/32b		Dunton, Mary	(letter re orphan children)			
1742/CP	W	Duplant, John	(see Deplant)			
1613/22	W	Durberne, Henry	Westbury-on-Trym (Shirehampton)	<Mariner>	£8	
1735/11		Durbin, John	Littleton-on-Severn	Yeoman	£195	
1737/8		Durham, James	City of Bristol	Mariner	£9	
1609/20		Durnell, Ambrose	St. Ewen	Button-maker	£5	
1737/9	W	Durnin, Charles	City of Bristol	Mariner	£12	
1620/31	W	Dussell, Anne	St. Stephen	--	£102	
1617/17		Dussell, Thomas	St. Stephen	--	£16	
1682/16	W	Dusy, John	Almondsbury	Joiner	£31	
1728/12		Dutton, William	City of Bristol	Cordwainer	£125	inv. (1718) & a/c
1729/CP		Duval, John	City of Bristol	--	£2,621	
1668/22		Dwight, George	St. Peter	Wine-merchant	£101	
1711/17	W	Dyer, Dorothy	Olveston (Freezwood)	Inn-holder	£154	

	Reference	Name	Place	Occupation	Value	Notes
	1613/23	Dyer, Edward	St. Stephen	Mariner	£32	
W	1694/18	Dyer, Edward (jnr)	Henbury	Single-man	£64	
	1694/20	Dyer, Elizabeth	Henbury	Single-woman	£62	
W	1700/3	Dyer, Elizabeth	Henbury	Widow	£28	
W	1666/14	Dyer, Jane	Christchurch	--	£66	
	1609/21	Dyer, John	--	--	£16	
W	1641/13	Dyer, John	Henbury (Northwick)	Yeoman	£162	
W	1660/25	Dyer, John	Olveston	Blacksmith	£346	
W	1687/24	Dyer, John	Henbury	<Husbandman>	£20	
	1672/13	Dyer, Maurice	Henbury	Yeoman	£771	
W	1636/22	Dyer, Richard	Olveston (Tockington)	Weaver	£91	
W	1700/22	Dyer, Richard	Henbury (Stowick)	Yeoman	£151	
	1609/22	Dyer, Thomas	Henbury	Yeoman	£136	
W	1706/10	Dyer, Thomas	Winterbourne	Cordwainer	£60	
	1682/17	Dyke, Robert	City of Bristol	Mariner	£63	
W	1756/8	Dymer, Daniel	City of Bristol	Victualler	£19	
	1669/26	Dymer, Francis	St. Stephen	Cooper	£25	
W	1611/23	Dymmery, John	Alveston	<Husbandman>	£5	
	1677/11	Dymock, Mary	--	Spinster	£98	
	1674/13	Dymock, Robert	City of Bristol	Carpenter	£213	
	1710/10	Dymock, Thomas	City of Bristol	Shipwright	£9	
W	1661/25	Dymock, Tobias	St. James	House-carpenter	£39	
	1678/20	Dymuck, Joan	St. James	Widow	£48	relict of Tobias
	1673/13	Dynham, Henry	--	--	£20	
	1673/13	Dynnam, Henry	(see Dynham)			
W	1667/21	Dyrrick, Leonard	(see Derrick)			
	1759/7	Eadey, Charles	City of Bristol	Mariner	£10	
	1713/16a	Eagle, Thomas	City of Bristol	Mariner	£31	
	1713/16b	Eagle, Thomas	(the account of Hannah Eagle, relict)			
W	1643/29	Eagles, William	St. James	Tanner	£86	
	1609/23	Earle, Christian	Olveston (Cote)	--	£71	
W	1640/20	Earle, James	Elberton	--	£59	

	Year ref.	Name	Parish or area	Occupation or status	Value	Notes
	1620/32	Earle, Joan	Littleton-on-Severn	Widow	£4	
W	1611/25	Earle, John	Filton	Single-man	£37	
W	1707/17	Earle, Roger	Barton Regis	Basket-maker	£19	
	1609/24	Earle, Thomas	'Compton'	--	£5	
W	1699/6	Easment, Thomas	(see Eastment)			
W	1733/21	East, William	City of Bristol	Mariner	£12	
	1734/16	Easterbrook, Thomas	City of Bristol	Mariner	£14	
W	1699/6	Eastment, Thomas	St. Augustine	Haulier	£100	
	1701/10	Eastment, Thomas (jnr)	--	--	£10	
	1666/15	Ecroyde, Francis	St. Michael	Schoolmaster	£2	
	1642/17	Eddie, John	--	--	£10	
W	1687/28	Edding, Edward	Barton Regis	Yeoman	£27	
W	1618/19	Eddy, Margaret	St. Mary, Redcliffe	Widow	£10	
	1760/9	Edenberg, Jonas	City of Bristol	Mariner	£2	
W	1740/17	Edgell, Benjamin	City of Bristol	Mariner	£7	
	1680/19	Edgley, Stephen	St. Stephen	Baker	£12	
	1683/13	Edmonds, Alice	Olveston (Ingst)	Widow	£230	
W	1640/21	Edmonds, Edward <snr>	Henbury (Northwick)	<Yeoman>	£290	
W	1674/15	Edmonds, Edward	Olveston	Yeoman	£168	
	1679/25	Edmonds, Edward	Almondsbury (Over)	--	£28	
W	1685/17	Edmonds, Edward	Henbury (Lawrence Weston)	<Gent.>	£231	
W	1635/27	Edmonds, John (snr)	Olveston (Ingst)	--	£288	
W	1665/14	Edmonds, John	Olveston (Ingst)	Yeoman	£578	
	1680/18	Edmonds, John <snr>	Olveston (Ingst)	Yeoman	£175	
W	1716/21	Edmonds, Margerie	Elberton	Yeoman	£36	
	1611/26	Edmonds, Margerie	Henbury (Stowick)	Widow	£3	
	1611/27	Edmonds, Robert	Henbury	Widow	£5	
	1672/15	Edmonds, Robert	Henbury	--	£83	
W	1716/22	Edmonds, Robert	Henbury (Stowick)	Yeoman	£20	
	1704/12	Edmonds, Theophilus	--	--	£10	

	Reference	Name	Place	Status	£	Notes
	1633/23	Edmonds, Thomas	Westbury-on-Trym	Yeoman	£7	also 2nd copy
	1611/28	Edmonds, William	Elberton	--	£40	
	1611/29	Edmonds, William	Elberton	--	£53	
W	1643/30	Edmonds, William	Henbury	<Yeoman>	£122	
W	1661/27	Edmonds, William	St. Augustine	Mariner	£12	
W	1693/8	Edmonds, William	Henbury (Kingsweston)	Yeoman	£92	
	1648/8	Edson, John	City of Bristol	Mariner	£21	
	1643/31	Edwarde, Griffin	St. Mary, Redcliffe	--	£5	
	1688/15	Edwardes, Edward	Almondsbury (The Worthy)	Yeoman	£451	
	1699/7	Edwardes, Thomas	--	Blacksmith	£327	
W	1628/27	Edwards, Agnes	Horfield <Downing>	<Widow>	£18	
	1667/22	Edwards, Alice	Stoke Gifford	Widow	£34	alias Booth
W	1669/29	Edwards, Anne	St. John	Widow	£14	
	1720/12	Edwards, Charity	Stapleton	Widow	£16	
	1674/18	Edwards, Daniel	City of Bristol	Shoemaker	£227	
W	1673/12	Edwards, David	Clifton	Lime-burner	£20	
	1678/69	Edwards, David	Clifton	Lime-burner	£20	
	1761/11	Edwards, David	City of Bristol	Mariner	£15	account only
W	1737/10	Edwards, Edward	City of Bristol	<Shipwright in will>	£15	
W	1694/23	Edwards, Elizabeth	Temple	Widow	£94	
W	1727/10	Edwards, Elizabeth	Henbury <Chittening>	Widow	£321	
	1702/9	Edwards, James	St. James	Cordwainer	£6	
W	1664/14	Edwards, Joan	Henbury	<Widow>	£130	
	1668/23	Edwards, Joan	SS. Philip & Jacob	Widow	£5	
W	1730/CP	Edwards, Joan	Henbury	<Widow>	£538	
	1675/20	Edwards, John	City of Bristol	--	£15	
W	1677/14	Edwards, John	Henbury (Northwick)	Yeoman	£120	
W	1686/16	Edwards, John	Henbury (Northwick)	Yeoman	£135	
W	1707/18	Edwards, John	City of Bristol	Mariner	£19	
	1736/14	Edwards, John	Olveston (Woodhouse)	Yeoman	£131	inv. & account
	1742/22	Edwards, John	City of Bristol	Mariner	£10	

Year ref.	Name		Parish or area	Occupation or status	Value	Notes
W 1750/7	Edwards,	John	City of Bristol	Mariner	£5	
1717/18	Edwards,	Joshua	City of Bristol	Mariner	£171	
1681/22	Edwards,	Katherine	Temple	Widow	£29	
1639/33	Edwards,	Margaret	Henbury	Single-woman	£56	
1701/11	Edwards,	Martha	--	Widow	£19	
1674/17	Edwards,	Mary	Stapleton	--	£15	
W 1624/26	Edwards,	Maurice (Morric)	St. Nicholas	Victualler	£17	
1703/4	Edwards,	Nathaniel	--	--	£14	
1635/28	Edwards,	Richard	Stapleton	--	£42	
1695/12	Edwards,	Richard	(see Bush)			
W 1715/15	Edwards,	Robert	City of Bristol	Surgeon	£154	
1752/10	Edwards,	Robert	City of Bristol	Painter	£7	
1688/18	Edwards,	Sarah	St. Nicholas	--	£44	
W 1691/16	Edwards,	Sarah	Westbury-on-Trym (Shirehampton)			
W 1709/17	Edwards,	Susannah	Stapleton	Widow	£61	
W 1697/16	Edwards,	Thomas	Henbury (Lawrence Weston)	Widow	£75	
W 1728/13	Edwards,	Thomas	City of Bristol	Yeoman	£274	
1620/33	Edwards,	William	St. Thomas	Mariner	£12	
1627/9	Edwards,	William	St. Peter (Castle)	--	£15	
1669/28	Edwards,	William	St. John	--	£14	
1682/18	Edwards,	William	Christchurch	--	£4	
1689/14	Edwards,	William	--	--	£2	
1696/13	Edwards,	William	Henbury (Stowick)	--	£50	
W 1710/11	Edwards,	William	City of Bristol	--	£20	
1641/14	Eighton,	Thomas	Clifton	Yeoman	£104	
1609/25	Elborowe,	Alice	Henbury (Charlton)	Shipwright	£15	
1627/10	Elboroes,	Thomas	St. Michael	<Husbandman>	£336	
1750/9	Elder,	Thomas	City of Bristol	--	£57	
				--	£18	
				Mariner	£10	

W	1757/4	Eley, John	City of Bristol	Mariner	--	
	1732/19	Elkington, James	City of Bristol	Mariner	£8	also 2nd copy
	1629/24	Elleott, Bartholomew	--	--	£187	
W	1680/16	Ellery, Richard	Winterbourne	--	£100	
W	1680/15a	Elliatt, William	City of Bristol	Woollen-draper	(£39)	goods
W	1680/15b	Elliatt, William	City of Bristol	Woollen-draper	(£346)	list of debts
W	1680/20	Elliatt, William	(parchment copy of 15a and 15b)			
W	1636/23	Elliott, Ann	City of Bristol	Widow	£509	
	1743/10	Elliott, George	City of Bristol	Mariner	£15	
	1692/13	Elliott, John	--	--	£4	
W	1663/21	Ellis, Edmond	St. Augustine	<Minister>	£145	
	1620/34	Ellis, Elizabeth	--	--	£107	
	1611/30	Ellis, Humphrey	City of Bristol	Haberdasher	£15	
	1635/29a	Ellis, John	St. Peter	--	£5	
	1635/29b	Ellis, John	(account concerning funeral charges for John & his wife)			
W	1750/8	Ellis, John	City of Bristol	Mariner	£9	
	1633/24	Ellott, Adam	St. Michael	Seafarer	£23	
	1629/24	Ellott, Bartholomew	(see Elleott)			
	1646/12	Ellot, George	St. Thomas	Wire-drawer	£8	
	1738/7	Elmer, Walter	City of Bristol	Mariner	£7	
W	1618/20	Elmes, Joseph	St. Mary, Redcliffe	Joiner	£35	
	1609/56	Elmes, Robert	(see Nelmes)			
	1676/12	Elson, James	--	--	£10	
	1676/13a	Elton, Jacob	St. Stephen	Cooper	£4	
	1676/13b	Elton, Jacob	(document re administration)			
	1663/22	Emason, Elizabeth	(see Emmerson)			
W	1760/10	Emerson, John	City of Bristol	Mariner	£19	
W	1680/17	Emlen, Nicholas	Winterbourne	--	£28	
	1664/13	Emmerson, Andrew	Mangotsfield	Tiller	£83	
W	1663/22	Emmerson, Elizabeth	Mangotsfield	Widow	£183	
W	1720/13	England, Joan	City of Bristol	Widow	£76	
W	1636/24	England, John	SS. Phillip & Jacob	--	£2	
W	1666/17	England, John	St. Augustine	Mariner	£27	

	Year ref.	Name	Parish or area	Occupation or status	Value	Notes
	1719/14	England, John	City of Bristol	Butcher	£12	
	1729/13	England, John	Westbury-on-Trym	Butcher	£57	
	1639/34	England, Thomas	St. Mary, Redcliffe	Chapman	£10	
W	1689/13	England, Thomas ⟨snr⟩	Barton Regis	Butcher ⟨Victualler in will⟩	£6	
W	1734/17	England, Thomas	City of Bristol	Shipwright	£5	died at sea
W	1729/12	England, William ⟨snr⟩	Westbury-on-Trym (Shirehampton)	Butcher	£68	
	1670/11	Eoynion, Katherin	--	--	£8	
	1682/19	Erberry, William	St. Thomas	--	£4	
	1682/19	Erbury, William	(see Erberry)			
W	1625/1	Eringtone, William	(alias Allen, which see)			
	1753/13	Ervin, George	City of Bristol	Mariner	£6	
	1674/16	Escot, John	City of Bristol	--	£10	
	1628/28	Eson, John	City of Bristol	Salt-maker	£13	
	1750/10	Essex, Thomas	City of Bristol	Mariner	£4	
	1678/70	Estcourt, Ursula	City of Bristol	Widow	£33	inv. & account
	1662/23	Estemed, John	Almondsbury	Yeoman	£80	alias Hunt
W	1662/23	Estmead, John	(see Estemed)			
W	1662/16	Euans, William	SS. Philip & Jacob	Brewer	£10	
	1731/35	Eustace, Joshua	City of Bristol	Mariner	£35	
	1719/15	Evan, Morgan	City of Bristol	Mariner	£5	
	1719/16	Evan, Williams	Henbury	Yeoman	£17	
W	1726/15	Evans, Daniel	City of Bristol	Mason	--	
			(for inventory of Daniel Evans' widow, see Elizabeth Cowslipp)			
	1644/22	Evans, Francis	Winterbourne	--	£1	
	1681/23	Evans, George	City of Bristol	--	£72	
W	1692/12	Evans, Griffith	St. Nicholas	--	£23	
	1613/24	Evans, Henry & Sibell	Mangotsfield	--	£66	joint inventory
	1714/16	Evans, Henry	City of Bristol	Tobacco-cutter	£7	
W	1636/25	Evans, James	SS. Philip & Jacob	--	£54	

	Reference	Name	Place	Occupation	Value	Notes
	1643/32	Evans, James	SS. Philip & Jacob	--	£1	
	1667/23	Evans, John	Littleton-on-Severn	Clerk	£46	
W	1678/21	Evans, John	City of Bristol	Mason	£16	
	1726/16	Evans, John	--	<Cooper>	£197	
	1742/23	Evans, John	City of Bristol	Mariner	£9	
	1754/15A	Evans, John	City of Bristol	Mariner	£6	
	1755/2	Evans, John	City of Bristol	Mariner	£12	
	1698/11	Evans, Joseph	--	Mariner	£1	
	1688/19	Evans, Llewellin	St. Thomas	Tobacco-pipe maker	£183	
W	1749/21	Evans, Margaret	City of Bristol	Spinster	£7	
	1718/12	Evans, Mary	(see Evens)			
W	1703/5	Evans, Mr.	(will of Sarah Evans, City of Bristol, widow, relates)		£53	
	1732/20	Evans, Owen	City of Bristol	Mariner	£7	
	1715/16	Evans, Richard	Westbury-on-Trym	Labourer	£10	
	1678/22	Evans, Robert	City of Bristol	Freemason	£13	
W	1741/18	Evans, Robert	City of Bristol	Mariner	£10	
W	1703/5	Evans, Sarah	(see Evans, Mr.)			
	1613/24	Evans, Sibell	(see Evans, Henry)			
	1689/12	Evans, Simon	Winterbourne	Husbandman	£47	
	1686/17	Evans, Thomas	St. James	Baker	£22	
	1690/14	Evans, Thomas	--	--	£18	
	1694/24	Evans, Thomas	--	--	£13	
	1708/14	Evans, Thomas	--	Mariner	£15	
W	1733/22	Evans, Thomas	City of Bristol	Apothecary	£7	
W	1748/29	Evans, Thomas	City of Bristol	Mariner	£4	
	1662/16	Evans, William	(see Euans)			
	1734/18	Evans, William	City of Bristol	Mariner	£2	
	1644/22	Evens, Francis	(see Evans)			
	1718/12	Evens, Mary	City of Bristol	Spinster	£19	
W	1703/5	Evens, Mr.	(see Evans)			
	1641/15	Everard, Edward	St. Stephen	Shipwright	£639	
W	1675/21	Everet, James	<SS. Philip & Jacob?>	Tobacco-cutter	£162	died at sea

	Year ref.	Name	Parish or area	Occupation or status	Value	Notes
W	1668/24	Everett, Thomas	Castle Precinct	Tobacco-cutter	£146	
	1752/11	Every, George	City of Bristol	Gardener	£6	
W	1708/15	Eves, John	⟨Henbury; Kingroad⟩	Mariner	£19	see also Euans 1662/16
W	1708/15	Evies, John	(see Eves)			
	1662/16	Ewans, William	SS. Philip & Jacob	Brewer	£10	
	1642/18	Ewins, Margaret	St. Stephen	Widow	£16	
	1746/10	Eyers, John	City of Bristol	Gent. ⟨Mariner⟩	£5	died at sea
W	1666/16	Eyton, Ralph	St. Thomas	Clothier	£206	
	1628/29	Eyton, Thomas	Henbury (Berwick)	Yeoman	£51	
W	1636/3	Eyton, William	(see Ayton)			
W	1716/23	Faire, Thomas	City of Bristol	Mariner	£14	
	1642/19a	Fanklin, Thomas	St. Michael	--	--	
	1642/19b	Fanklin, Thomas	(renunciation by the Widow Grace)			
W	1706/11	Farding, John	City of Bristol	Mariner	£14	
W	1635/30	Farewell, Richard	(see Farwell)			
	1625/29	Farington, John	Westbury-on-Trym		£4	
W	1625/28	Farmer, Alexander	Christchurch	⟨Vintner⟩	£27	
W	1685/20	Farmer, Thomas	Barton Regis	Butcher	£25	
W	1711/31	Farmer, William	(alias Neck, which see)			
	1692/14	Farnell, Anne	Olveston	Widow	£156	
W	1683/15	Farnom, Emmanuel	SS. Philip & Jacob	--	£21	
W	1730/18	Farr, John	Henbury	Yeoman	£170	
	1675/23	Farr, Martha	Henbury	--	£7	
	1730/19	Farrell, Roger	City of Bristol	Mariner	£11	
	1700/23	Farrenden, Joshua	St. Stephen	Needle-maker	£85	
W	1635/30	Farwell, Richard	Winterbourne	⟨Gent.⟩	£51	
W	1640/22	Fayland, John	St. Stephen	Joiner	£20	
	1734/19	Fear, John	City of Bristol	Mariner	£3	
	1685/22	Fear, William	Christchurch	Cordwainer	£7	
W	1733/23	Fearn, Gilbert	City of Bristol	⟨Mariner⟩	£10	

W	Ref	Name	Place	Occupation	Value	Notes
W	1665/16	Feates, William	Stapleton	⟨Collier⟩	£67	
	1761/12	Fee, John	City of Bristol	Mariner	£15	
W	1633/25	Feild, Mary	Olveston (Tockington)	Widow	£19	
W	1625/64	Felps, George	(see Phelps)			
W	1634/56	Felpes, Israel	(see Phelpes)			
W	1633/51	Felpes, Joan	Almondsbury	--	£32	
	1717/19	Fender, William	City of Bristol	Mariner	£18	
	1689/15	Fenn, Ann	--	--	£25	
W	1724/6	Fennell, Thomas	St. John	Haulier	£16	will 1723
W	1719/17	Fenton, Benjamin	(see Fentten)			
	1749/22	Fenton, George	City of Bristol	Sail-maker	£491	
W	1719/17	Fentten, Benjamin	City of Bristol	⟨Cooper⟩	£9	
	1754/15B	Fenwick, Thomas	City of Bristol	Mariner	£5	
	1742/24	Fernands, Anthony	(see Fornands)			
W	1640/23	Field, Anthony	Olveston (Tockington)	Yeoman	£44	see also Field
W	1678/26	Field, Edward	St. Peter	Collar-maker	£241	
	1750/11	Field, James	City of Bristol	Weaver	£5	(inv. at foot of document concerning coal works at Bitton)
W	1695/13	Field, John	Almondsbury	Yeoman	£390	
W	1633/25	Field, Mary	(see Feild)			
W	1713/17	Field, Richard	City of Bristol	Carpenter/Mariner	£6	
	1718/13	Field, Thomas	St. Stephen	--	£58	
	1717/20	Fifoot, John	City of Bristol	Ship-carpenter	£19	
W	1681/24	Fild, Edward (snr)	Almondsbury	Yeoman	£83	
W	1634/28	Fill, Elinor	Almondsbury	⟨Widow⟩	£90	
W	1623/20	Fill, John	Almondsbury	⟨Husbandman⟩	£86	alias Guggin
W	1695/13	Fill, John	(see Field)			
	1636/44	Filpot, James	(see Philpot)			
	1759/8	Finch, Daniel	City of Bristol	Mariner	£15	
	1685/18	Finch, Richard	St. Thomas	Merchant	£144	
	1661/28	Fines, Thomas	St. James	Mariner	£95	

	Year ref.	Name	Parish or area	Occupation or status	Value	Notes
	1764/2	Finlay, John	City of Bristol	Mariner	£53	inv. & account
W	1731/36	Finlayson, William	City of Bristol	Mariner	£5	
	1750/12	Finn, Henry	City of Bristol	Jeweller	£10	
W	1746/19	Finnell, John	--	Mariner	£12	
W	1700/4	Finney, John	City of Bristol	Merchant	£5,060	
	1640/24a	Fipps, William	Mangotsfield	Tiller	£10	
	1640/24b	Fipps, William	(document re administration)			
	1691/19	Fisher, Ann	St. Michael	Widow	£224	
W	1662/19	Fisher, Edward	St. Peter	\<Clothier\>	£209	
	1612/5	Fisher, Emanuel	SS. Philip & Jacob	--	£20	
W	1762/3A	Fisher, Henry	City of Bristol	Mariner	£12	
W	1719/18	Fisher, Jonathan	City of Bristol	Joiner	£13	
W	1677/16	Fisher, Joseph	\<St. Michael\>	\<Clothier\>	£232	tobacconist's goods
	1691/18	Fisher, Joseph	St. Michael	Clothier	£23	
	1687/29	Fisher, Richard	City of Bristol	Wire-drawer	£1	
	1661/29	Fisher, Thomas	St. Thomas	Inn-holder	£395	the 'Red Lyon'
	1735/12	Fisher, William	City of Bristol	Hooper	£16	died at sea
	1733/24	Fishley, Robert	City of Bristol	Mariner	£4	
	1665/15	Fishpill, Robert	St. Michael	Mariner	£37	
	1618/21	Fishpill, Thomas	(see Fyshpool)			
W	1675/25	Fishpoole, John	Henbury (Charlton)	Yeoman	£116	
W	1678/25	Fitticate, Edward	\<Temple\>	Cloth-worker	£48	
W	1741/19	Fitzgerald, Edmund	City of Bristol	Mariner	£12	
	1732/21	Fitzgerald, Patrick	--	\<Mariner\>	£9	
	1757/5	Fitzgerald, William	City of Bristol	Cooper	£8	died at sea
	1748/30	Fitzgerrald, William	City of Bristol	Mariner	£16	
	1741/20	Flanery, Patrick	City of Bristol	Hooper	£10	died at sea
	1753/14	Flanigan, Thomas	City of Bristol	\<Mariner\>	£4	
	1639/35	Flatcher, Thomas	SS. Philip & Jacob	--	£40	
W	1746/20	Flear, Robert	City of Bristol	Mariner	£11	
	1617/18	Fleet, William	St. John	Merchant	£140	

Ref.	W	Name	Place	Occupation	Value	Notes
1763/4		Fleming, Elizabeth	City of Bristol	Widow	£67	
1733/25		Fleming, John	City of Bristol	Mariner	£2	
1640/25		Flemons, James	St. James	--	£1	
1728/14		Fletcher, Abraham	City of Bristol	Porter	£29	
1646/13		Fletcher, John	St. John	Seaman	--	(not valued)
1730/20	W	Fletcher, Richard	City of Bristol	Mariner	£15	
1748/31		Fling, Michael	City of Bristol	Mariner	£18	
1743/11		Fling, Thomas	City of Bristol	Mariner	£8	
1733/26	W	Fling, William	City of Bristol	Mariner	£8	
1760/11		Flook, Joseph	Mangotsfield	Quarrier	£18	
1748/32		Flooke, Richard	City of Bristol	Mariner	£16	
1682/30		Floud, Elizabeth	Winterbourne	Widow	£29	
1620/35		Flower, Anne	Christchurch	Widow	£69	
1646/14		Flower, Christopher	St. Nicholas	Mariner	--	(not valued)
1646/15		Flower, George & Mary	St. John	<Tailor>	£114	2 documents
1733/27	W	Flower, John	City of Bristol	Victualler	£98	
1646/15		Flower, Mary	(see Flower, George)			
1865/19		Flower, Robert	City of Bristol	Butcher	£11	
1674/19		Flower, Walter	St. John	--	£83	
1765/1	W	Floyd, Griffin	City of Bristol	Mariner	£5	with wills
1707/19		Floyd, Joseph (jnr)	City of Bristol	Mariner	£12	
1717/21		Floyd, Joseph	Westbury-on-Trym	Victualler	£371	
1750/13		Floyd, Samuel	City of Bristol	Fan-maker	£19	
1750/14		Floyd, Samuel	City of Bristol	Yeoman	£8	
1733/28		Floyd, Thomas	City of Bristol	Mariner	£7	
1662/18	W	Floyde, John	Almondsbury	<Yeoman>	£156	
1678/39		Flueling, William	(see Llewellin)			
1618/23		Fluellen, Ann	City of Bristol	--	--	
1732/22		Fluellin, Ann	(see Fluellen)			
1718/14		Fly, Richard	City of Bristol	<Mariner>	£6	
1661/32		Foley, Samuel	SS. Philip & Jacob	Blacksmith	£3	
1751/6	W	Foley, Richard	St. Thomas	--	--	damaged, values missing
		Folsame, John	City of Bristol	Mariner	£4	

Year ref.	Name	Parish or area	Occupation or status	Value	Notes
W 1634/29	Folwell, Elizabeth	St. Michael	<Spinster>	£5	
W 1684/13	Fookes, Fereman	City of Bristol	Merchant Tailor	£225	
W 1625/31	Foord, John	Alveston	Labourer	£8	
W 1745/11	Foord, John	City of Bristol	Mariner	£9	
1773/CP	Foot, Hannah	City of Bristol	Victualler	£242	inv. & account
1683/16	Ford, Gilbert	Temple	Pewterer	£9	
W 1689/16	Ford, Joan	City of Bristol	Widow	£44	
W 1639/36	Ford, Richard	Almondsbury	--	£65	
W 1697/17	Ford, Robert	City of Bristol	Weaver	£70	
W 1703/6	Ford, William	Mangotsfield (Downend)	Coal-miner	£11	
1749/23	Ford, William	City of Bristol	Mariner	£9	
W 1738/8	Foreman, William	City of Bristol	Mariner	£8	
1741/21	Forester, Lawrence	City of Bristol	Mariner	£5	
1742/24	Fornands, Anthony	City of Bristol	Mariner	£3	
1685/21	Forrest, Joseph	City of Bristol	Button-maker	£13	
1730/21	Forsithe, Adam	City of Bristol	Mariner	£3	
1749/24	Fortune, James	City of Bristol	Mariner	£5	
1716/24	Forward, Nicholas	City of Bristol	Sergeant-at-Mace	£8	
1675/27	Foster, William	City of Bristol	Smith	£34	
1677/61	Foster, William	St. Stephen	--	£39	account only
W 1698/12	Fowler, Christopher	Mangotsfield	Felt-maker	£25	
W 1735/13	Fowler, David	City of Bristol	Mariner	£8	
1696/14	Fowler, John	Olveston (Tockington)	Yeoman	£121	
W 1636/26	Fowler, Joyce	Winterbourne (Hambrook)	Widow	£23	
1618/22	Fowler, Richard	Littleton-on-Severn	--	£13	
W 1641/16	Fowler, Richard	Elberton	--	£161	
W 1678/24	Fowler, Robert	City of Bristol	Cooper	£213	
1661/30	Fowler, William	St. Nicholas	Pinner	--	

W	1676/15	Fowles, Alice	City of Bristol	Widow	£8	
W	1675/22	Fowles, Samuel	City of Bristol	Cooper	£38	
W	1635/31	Fownes, John	<St. John>	Merchant	£846	
	1726/17	Fowsett, Mary	City of Bristol	Widow	£127	
W	1677/15	Fox, Alice	SS. Philip & Jacob	Widow	£46	
	1716/25	Fox, Anne	City of Bristol	Widow	£43	
	1740/18	Fox, Charles	City of Bristol	Mariner	£11	died at sea
	1708/11	Fox, Edward (jnr)	(see Davis, John)			
	1668/26	Fox, Hanna	SS. Philip & Jacob	Widow	£76	
	1754/16	Fox, Isaac	City of Bristol	Hooper	£19	
	1649/12	Fox, John	Abbots Leigh	Gent.	£24	
	1713/18	Fox, John	City of Bristol	Butcher	£8	
W	1611/31	Fox, Katherine	--	<Widow>	£10	
W	1730/22	Fox, Phillip	Castle Precincts	Soapmaker	£27	
	1682/20	Fox, Poyns	City of Bristol	Carpenter	£523	
	1661/31	Fox, Richard	St. Peter	Farrier	£51	
W	1733/29	Fox, Richard	City of Bristol	Mariner	£6	
W	1668/25	Fox, William	SS. Philip & Jacob	Yeoman	£84	
	1737/11	Fox, William	City of Bristol	Pavier	£1	inv. & account
	1739/6	Foxall, Charles	(see Foxell)			
	1739/6	Foxell, Charles	City of Bristol	Joiner	£580	
	1643/33	Foxe, Henry	Christchurch	Barber-surgeon	£33	
	1618/24	Foxe, Thomas	St. James	--	£4	
	1620/36	Foxe, Thomas	St. Thomas	Butcher	£14	
	1710/12	Frances, William	SS. Philip & Jacob	--	£11	
W	1641/17	Francis, Agnes	(see Fraunces)			
	1637/18	Francis, Christopher	Henbury		£38	
	1715/17	Francis, Richard	Henbury (Redwick)	Yeoman	£277	
	1637/19	Francis, Thomas	SS. Philip & Jacob	Yeoman	£11	
	1706/12	Francisco, John	Oporto, Portugal	Mariner	£19	
W	1709/18	Franckham, Robert	Olveston	Yeoman	£10	died at sea
	1640/26	Francklinge, John	St. Michael	Sailor	£14	

Year ref.	Name	Parish or area	Occupation or status	Value	Notes
W 1699/9	Franckome, Margaret	Olveston (Tockington)	Widow	£332	
W 1712/17	Francomb, John	Almondsbury (Hortham)	Yeoman	£480	
1681/25	Frankcombe, Robert	Olveston	Yeoman	£53	
W 1714/17	Frank, Samuel	Barton Regis	Tailor	£277	
1733/30	Franklin, Samuel	City of Bristol	Mariner	£6	
1690/15	Frape, Robert	City of Bristol	Shoemaker	£3	
1700/24	Frapwell, Richard	SS. Philip & Jacob	Ropemaker	£56	
W 1641/17	Frauncis, Agnes	Henbury	Widow	£35	
W 1748/33	Frauncis, Valentine	City of Bristol	Mariner	£15	
W 1612/6	Frayes, Mary	St. Stephen	<Widow>	£15	
1609/26	Frayes, Thomas	--	Sailor	£15	
1639/37	Freeman, John	St. Nicholas	Victualler	£70+	
1705/9	Freind, John	--	--	£16	
1620/101	Freind, Thomas	(see Frennd)			
W 1732/23	French, John	City of Bristol	Mariner	£5	
W 1750/15	French, John	Westbury-on-Trym <Shirehampton>	Yeoman	£12	
1620/101	Frennd, Thomas	Mangotsfield	--	£60	
1711/18	Friend, John	--	Surgeon	£26	
1620/101	Friend, Thomas	(see Frennd)			
1620/37	Frithe, John	SS. Philip & Jacob		£4	
W 1680/21	Frogley, Robert	Barton Regis	<Inn-holder>	£140	
W 1678/23	Fry, Avis	City of Bristol	Widow	£43	
W 1684/12	Fry, Anne	City of Bristol	Widow	£34	
1759/9	Fry, James	City of Bristol	Mariner	£9	
W 1676/14	Fry, Jane	<City of Bristol>	<Widow>	£134	
1662/17	Fry, John	St. Mary, Redcliffe	<Wool-carder or Merchant>	£69	
W 1689/17	Fry, John	City of Bristol	Tailor	£672	

Ref	W	Name	Place	Occupation	Value	Notes
1623/21		Fry, Owen	St. Michael	—	£26	
1706/13		Fry, Priscilla	<St. Peter>	Widow	£317	
1670/12	W	Fry, Robert	SS. Philip & Jacob	Grocer	£18	
1691/17		Fry, Samuel	City of Bristol	Cooper	£44	
1675/24	W	Fry, William	<St. Mary-le-Port>	Cordwainer	£387	BRS XXVI p.200
1609/27		Frye, Thomas	St. James	Chapman	£55	
1609/28		Frye, William	—	—	£65	
1677/17		Fudger, Stephen	St. Peter	Virginal maker	£7	
1683/14		Fuller, Jacob	—	—	£4	
1717/22	W	Fulton, James	City of Bristol	Mariner	£10	
1735/14	W	Furlong, Charles	City of Bristol	Mariner	£11	
1747/11	W	Furlong, James	City of Bristol	Mariner	£10	
1762/3B	W	Furnace, Samuel	City of Bristol	Mariner	£4	
1663/23		Fursill, Mary	St. James	—	£30	
1672/16		Fussell, Josias	Henbury	—	£85	
1705/10		Fyfoot, William	City of Bristol	Shipwright	£6	
1618/21	W	Fyshpool, Thomas	Henbury	Husbandman	£17	
1618/25	W	Gabb, Johan	Almondsbury	Single-woman	£16	
1698/15		Gaffer, William	—	—	£2	
1762/4		Gage, James	City of Bristol	Mariner	£16	
1676/17		Gagecomb, Thomas	City of Bristol	Mariner	£3	
1714/18	W	Gagg, Barbara	City of Bristol	Widow	£41	inv. & account
1679/27		Gagg, Edmund	City of Bristol	Soap-boiler	£157	
1680/25		Gagg, John	City of Bristol	Soapmaker	£49	
1685/CP		Gagg, John	City of Bristol	Soapmaker	£50	inv. & account, and compare 1680/25
1754/17		Gagle, Francis	City of Bristol	Victualler	£10	
1667/28		Gainer, Rowland	Olveston	Yeoman	£121	
1732/24		Gainer, William	—	—	£15	
1743/12		Gale, John	City of Bristol	—	£14	
1715/18		Gallaspy, John	City of Bristol	Mariner	£16	
1707/20		Gallop, William	—	Mariner	£18	

(with wills)

	Year ref.	Name	Parish or area	Occupation or status	Value	Notes
	1720/15	Gamage, John	City of Bristol	Mariner	£4	
	1720/14	Gamage, Thomas	City of Bristol	Mariner	£7	
W	1672/19	Gamlen, John	<Henbury> Compton Greenfield	Cordwainer	£673	
W	1703/7	Gandy, Hannah	St. John	Widow	£23	
W	1700/5	Gandy, John <snr>	City of Bristol	Blacksmith	£17	
	1701/12	Gandy, John	--	<Blacksmith>	£51	
W	1740/19	Ganthony, Peter	St. Michael	Mariner	£6	
W	1717/23	Gardener, Joan	City of Bristol	Spinster	£60	
W	1635/32	Gardiner, Ellinor	St. John	<Widow>	£10	
	1706/14	Gardner, Katherine	St. James	--	£4	
W	1723/9	Garing, Harman	City of Bristol	Mariner	£13	
W	1731/37	Garland, Elizabeth	Mangotsfield	Widow	£3	
W	1625/37	Garland, John	Almondsbury	<Husbandman>	£78	
W	1705/11	Garland, John	<St. Nicholas>	<Lighterman>	£321	
W	1715/19	Garland, Mary	City of Bristol	Widow	£168	
W	1680/24	Garland, Thomas	Clifton	Mariner	£579	
W	1611/32	Garland, William	--	<Single-man>	£22	
W	1766/4	Garnet, Nicholas	City of Bristol	Mariner	£11	with wills
W	1721/10	Garrard, Thomas	City of Bristol	Gent.	£24	
	1714/19	Garraway, Ann	City of Bristol	Spinster	£48	see also 1712/18
W	1712/18	Garraway, Anne	City of Bristol	Spinster	£40	see also 1714/19
W	1733/31	Garrett, Nicholas	City of Bristol	Mariner	£10	
	1671/11	Gastrill, Roger	SS. Philip & Jacob	Coal-driver	£25	
	1737/12	Gatcombe, Richard	City of Bristol	Mariner	£13	
	1716/26	Gay, Richard	City of Bristol	Mariner	£18	
	1695/15	Gayner, Thomas	--	--	£5	
	1640/27	Geathing, John	St. Stephen	Seaman	£4	
W	1637/22	Gebbens, Robert	(see Gibbens)	--		
	1639/38	Gee, Elizabeth	Henbury	--	£7	
W	1660/28	Gee, John	Henbury	<Tailor>	£45	

W	Reference	Name	Place	Occupation	Value	Notes
W	1618/26	Geeve, Ann	St. Peter	Widow	£59	
	1612/7	Genninges, Adam	SS. Philip & Jacob	--	£24	
W	1620/38	Gennings, Marie	SS. Philip & Jacob	Widow	£18	Jennings on will
	1666/21	George, David	Abbots Leigh	Husbandman	£11	
W	1633/26	George, Edward	SS. Philip & Jacob	Collier	£134	
W	1665/19	George, Eleanor	St. Thomas	Spinster	£3	
	1633/27	George, John	Westbury-on-Trym	Husbandman	£24	
	1719/19	George, John	City of Bristol	Mariner	£6	
	1672/20	George, Lambert	--	<Mariner>	£20	
	1695/14	George, Maurice	Westbury-on-Trym (Shirehampton)	--		
W	1628/30	George, Robert	Westbury-on-Trym (Shirehampton)	--	£51	
	1689/20	George, Thomas	City of Bristol	Mariner	£28	
W	1664/15	Gerett, Charles	St. Mary, Redcliffe	--	£11	
W	1637/20	Gerratt, Martha	St. Mary, Redcliffe	<Widow>	£8	1636 will; 2 MSS
W	1635/51	Gerrett, William	(see Jerrett)		£8	
W	1768/CP	Gerrish, Charles	City of Bristol	Basket-maker	£114	inv. & account
W	1646/16	Gethen, Ann	Temple	Widow	£44	
	1597/1	Gethen, William	City of Bristol	<Cooper>	£4	
	1643/34	Gethin, Edward	City of Bristol	Mariner	£5	
	1669/31	Gethin, William	St. John	--	£10	
W	1637/21	Gibbens, Margaret	St. John	Widow	£29	
W	1637/22	Gibbens, Robert (snr)	SS. Philip & Jacob	<Blacksmith>	£41	
W	1613/25	Gibbes, Miles	Henbury (Kingsweston)	--	£30	
	1643/35	Gibbins, John	(see Stibbins)			
	1623/23	Gibbon, John	St. Nicholas	Widow	£17	alias Starke
	1663/24	Gibbons, Anne	SS. Philip & Jacob	Widow	£30	
	1733/32	Gibbons, Jacob	City of Bristol	Mariner	£2	
	1623/22	Gibbons, John	St. John	<Baker>	£214	
W	167/26	Gibbons, John & Elizabeth	SS. Philip & Jacob	--	£93	
W	1713/19	Gibbons, Leonard	City of Bristol	Mariner	£12	
	1671/13	Gibbons, Robert	--	--	£14	

	Year ref.	Name	Parish or area	Occupation or status	Value	Notes
	1704/13	Gibbons, Robert	SS. Philip & Jacob	Farrier	£277	
	1670/14	Gibbs, Edward & Alice	City of Bristol	Mariner	£85	Edward: unknown if alive or dead
W	1748/35	Gibbs, Jacob	City of Bristol	Mariner	£4	
	1689/19	Gibbs, John	SS. Philip & Jacob	--	£57	
	1609/29	Gibbs, Thomas	Olveston	--	£1	
	1671/24	Gibson, John	St. Stephen	Mariner	£5	
	1700/7	Gibson, Joseph	City of Bristol	Organist (Cathedral)	£11	
	1617/19	Giee, Edward	(see Guie)			
W	1688/22	Gifford, Anne	City of Bristol	Widow	£31	
	1703/8	Gilbert, John	--	--	£5	
	1754/18A	Gilbert, Richard	City of Bristol	Yeoman	£19	
	1744/5	Gilbert, Thomas	City of Bristol	Mariner	£10	
	1624/27	Gilbert, Thomas and Joan	Winterbourne	--	£79	
	1728/15	Giles, Richard	SS. Philip & Jacob	Blacksmith	£8	
W	1706/16	Giles, Thomas	<St. Stephen>	Baker	£158	
	1625/32	Gill, Tacy	St. Peter	Wife	£3	husband's will
W	1686/21	Gill, Thurstone	<City of Bristol>	Glover	£93	
W	1731/38	Gillam, Joseph	City of Bristol	Mariner	£8	
	1761/13	Gilles, Robert	City of Bristol	Mariner	£5	
	1647/10	Gillet, Phillip	St. Thomas	Mariner	£2	
	1751/7	Gillfoy, James	City of Bristol	Mariner	£8	
	1642/20	Gillings, John	Henbury	Husbandman	£6	
	1689/21	Gillmore, John	--	Pewterer	£14	
	1691/21	Gillson, John	St. Mary, Redcliffe	Tiler	£4	
	1643/36	Gilston, Giles	Stapleton	Gent.	£236	
	1708/16	Gingell, William	Barton Regis	Weaver	£5	
	1709/19	Gingell, William	Stoke Gifford	Yeoman	£173	
W	1750/16	Glen, Alexander	City of Bristol	Mariner	£10	
W	1723/10	Glody, Nicholas	City of Bristol	Mariner	£8	
	1730/23	Glover, John	City of Bristol	Mariner	£3	

Ref.	W	Name	Place	Occupation	Value	Notes
1666/19		Glyde, Roger	St. Thomas	Brewer	£31	
1666/20		Glyde, Roger	St. Thomas	Brewer	--	2nd document
1667/24	W	Goard, Edward	St. Augustine	Tiler	£88	
1635/34		Goare, John	(see Goure)			
1647/11	W	Goddard, Margaret	Alveston	Widow	£39	
1617/20	W	Godden, John	Olveston	--	£3	
1756/9		Godfrey, George	City of Bristol	Mariner	£15	
1636/27		Godman, Christopher	St. Nicholas	--	£11	also a 2nd copy and caveat
1704/14		Godman, Dorothy	Clifton	Widow	£13	
1663/25		Godsall, John	St. Stephen	Carpenter	£23	
1672/17		Godsell, William	Barton Regis	--	£14	
1663/25		Godshall, John	(see Godsall)			
1749/25	W	Godson, Richard	City of Bristol	Mariner	£6	
1686/19		Godwin, John	--	Butcher	£206	
1620/39		Godwyn, Henry	SS. Philip & Jacob	--	£6	
1687/31	W	Godwyn, Susanna	Henbury	Widow	£104	
1675/31		Godwyn, Thomas	Stapleton	Clerk	£36	
1694/28		Goff, Henry	City of Bristol	Merchant	£24	
1721/11	W	Gold, Dorothy	(see Gould)			
1752/12	W	Golden, Edward	Mangotsfield	Coal-miner	£4	
1733/33	W	Golden, John	City of Bristol	Mariner	£4	
1636/28	W	Goldinge, Margaret	St. Mary, Redcliffe	Widow	£62	
1675/30	W	Goldsmith, John (snr)	St. Thomas	Pin-maker	£406	
1620/42		Goldsmith, Richard	Temple	Tucker	£36	
1634/30		Goninge, Thomas	St. John	Merchant	£50	
1642/21		Gonning, Edward	Henbury	--	£127	
1674/21		Good, John	St. Stephen		£19	
1704/15	W	Good, Thomas (jnr)	Mangotsfield	<Husbandman>	£18	
1620/40		Good, William	St. Peter	Pewterer	£27	
1733/34	W	Goodall, Charles	City of Bristol	Mariner	£3	
1712/19		Goodall, Nathaniel	City of Bristol	Mariner	£15	
1649/13		Goode, Alice	City of Bristol	Widow	£20	alias Williams

	Year ref.	Name	Parish or area	Occupation or status	Value	Notes
	1661/34	Goode, John	Clifton	Gent.	£66	
w	1635/33	Goodeare, Ephraim	St. Ewen	Goldsmith	£412	
w	1664/19	Goodeare, Toby	St. Ewen	Goldsmith	£43	
w	1634/31	Goodin, Richard	St. Thomas	Chandler	£73	
	1743/13a	Goodlade, Arthur	City of Bristol	Mariner	£8	
	1743/13b	Goodlade, Arthur	(affidavit of Mary Brace, widow, re debt due from deceased)			
w	1729/14	Goodman, Arthur	City of Bristol	Mariner	£13	
w	1634/32	Goodman, Bridget	St. Stephen	Widow	£53	
w	1639/39	Goodman, Edward	Olveston (Tockington)	--	£107	
w	1624/28	Goodman, Ellen	Olveston \<Tockington\>	\<Widow\>	£14	
w	1629/25	Goodman, Henry	St. Stephen	Carpenter	£77	
	1623/24A	Goodman, John	Olveston (Tockington)	--	£7	
	1620/41	Goodman, John	St. Stephen	--	£16	
w	1678/28	Goraway, Walter	St. Mary, Redcliffe	--	£25	
	1672/28	Gorden, John	(see Jorden)			
	1674/20	Gording, John	St. James	--	£23	
	1747/12	Gordon, James	City of Bristol	Mariner	£12	
w	1752/13	Gordon, Sarah	City of Bristol	Widow	£8	
	1671/14	Gorge (Mr.)	--	--	£16	
w	1750/17	Gorman, Richard	City of Bristol	Mariner	£10	
	1705/12	Gorway, John	City of Bristol	--	£38	
	1542/1	Gorwey, John	St. Mark	--	£13	
	1693/10	Goss, John	Henbury (Kingsweston)			
	1678/72	Goswell, John	St. John	Shepherd	£7	
	1670/10	Gotley, Peter	(alias Dowle, which see)	Merchant Tailor	£29	account only
	1675/32	Gough, Edward	St. Thomas	--	£5	
	1646/17	Gough, Henry	St. Thomas	Haberdasher	£7	
	1646/18	Gough, Israel	St. John	\<Cooper\>	£98	
	1661/33	Gough, Israel	St. Stephen	Cooper	£38	
w	1634/33	Gough, John	Alveston	Rough-mason	£23	

	Ref.	Name	Place	Occupation	Value	Notes
	1744/6	Gould, Anthony	City of Bristol	Mariner	£9	
W	1721/11	Gould, Dorothy	Barton Regis	Widow	£10	
W	1685/24	Gould, Elizabeth	City of Bristol	Widow	£13	<Cordwainer's goods>
W	1686/18	Gould, John	SS. Philip & Jacob	--	£47	
	1684/14	Gould, William	Castle Precinct	Cordwainer	£57	
	1661/35	Gouldsmith, Thomas	St. James	Rough-mason	£39	
	1644/23	Gouldsmyth, Humphrey	Temple	Cloth-worker	£221	
	1635/34	Goure, John	St. Thomas	Butcher	£1	
	1749/26	Govier, John	City of Bristol	Mariner	£19	
	1732/25	Govier, Thomas	City of Bristol	Soap-boiler	£26	
W	1706/17	Grace, John	City of Bristol	Weaver	£20	
W	1712/20	Grace, John	Henbury	Yeoman	£79	
W	1741/22	Gradg, David	City of Bristol	Mariner	£17	
	1646/19	Grafton, Nicholas	--	--	£1	
	1629/26	Grafton, Thomas	St. Mary, Redcliffe	<Mariner>	£146	
	1748/36	Gragamore, Thomas	City of Bristol	--	£5	(written on back of a deposition re prize taking, Sept. 1746)
	1749/27	Graham, James	City of Bristol	Mariner	£10	
W	1757/6	Grames, John	City of Bristol	Mariner	£18	
	1740/20	Granger, William	City of Bristol	Mariner	£19	
W	1636/29	Grant, Edward	Winterbourne <Hambrook>	--	£68	
	1677/18	Grant, Peter	City of Bristol	Victualler	£25	
	1677/54	Grant, Peter	City of Bristol	Victualler	£25	inv. & accounts 3 documents
	1694/25	Grant, Roger	Westbury-on-Trym	--	£76	
	1671/12	Grant, Thomas	St. Nicholas <Henbury>	Upholsterer	£11	
W	1711/19	Grant, William	Kingsweston	Yeoman	£76	
	1730/24	Grantland, Katherine	City of Bristol	--	£10	
W	1624/29	Gravell, Edith	St. Nicholas	Widow	£14	
W	1682/21A	Graves, Sarah	Christchurch	Widow	£9	

	Year ref.	Name	Parish or area	Occupation or status	Value	Notes
W	1669/32	Gray, Joan	Westbury-on-Trym	⟨Widow⟩	£66	
	1740/21	Gray, Tobias	City of Bristol	Mariner	£4	
W	1733/35	Gray, William	City of Bristol	Mariner	£3	
W	1613/26	Graye, Elizabeth	St. Thomas	Single-woman	£36	
	1609/30	Graye, William	--	--	£19	
	1720/16	Graye, Susanna	(see Greated)			
W	1667/25	Green, Ann	St. James	Widow	£74	
W	1665/18	Green, Jane	St. Augustine	Single-woman	£6	
W	1663/26	Green, John	Westbury-on-Trym ⟨Shirehampton⟩	⟨Yeoman⟩	£174	inv. & obligation
	1665/20	Green, John	St. Mary, Redcliffe	Glazier	£26	
	1715/20	Green, John	City of Bristol	Shipwright	£13	
W	1738/9	Green, John	⟨St. James⟩	Haberdasher of hats	£18	
	1667/27	Green, Joseph	(see Green, John)			
W	1668/27	Green, Margaret	Westbury-on-Trym ⟨Shirehampton⟩	⟨Widow⟩	£42	
	1694/26	Green, William	Barton Regis	Distiller	£34	
W	1699/10	Greenald, Thomas	Winterbourne	Yeoman	£181	
W	1675/28	Greene, Anne	Henbury (Stowick)	⟨Wife⟩	£159	
W	1679/28	Greene, Bridget	Almondsbury	Spinster	£76	
W	1679/29	Greene, Elizabeth	Almondsbury	Widow	£33	
W	1611/33	Greene, Henry	⟨The Worthy⟩	Mariner	£177	
W	1618/27	Greene, John	Henbury	⟨Yeoman from will⟩	£118	
	1667/27	Greene, John	St. Nicholas	Upholsterer	£23	John or Joseph
	1676/16	Greene, John	Almondsbury	Yeoman	£26	
W	1678/18	Greene, Mark	St. Thomas	Glazier	£44	
	1678/76	Greene, Mark	St. Thomas	Glazier	£44	also 2nd copy account only
W	1639/40	Greene, Ralph	Olveston	Vicar of Olveston	£342	
W	1633/28	Greene, Thomas	SS. Philip & Jacob	Labourer	£3	

W	Ref	Name	Place	Occupation	Value
	1643/37	Greene, Thomas	SS. Philip & Jacob	Yeoman	£604
	1625/33	Greene, William	St. Mary, Redcliffe	Tiler	£19
W	1639/41	Greene, William	Almondsbury (The Worthy)	\<Yeoman\>	£248
W	1748/34	Greenfield, Mary	City of Bristol	Widow \<Single-woman in will\>	£6
W	1666/22	Greenfield, John	St. Mary, Redcliffe	Gent.	£34
W	1672/21	Greenfield, William	Westbury-on-Trym	\<Yeoman\>	£89
	1747/13	Greening, George	City of Bristol	Mariner	£6
W	1720/16	Greeted, Susanna	Horfield	Widow	£15
	1618/28	Gregorie, William	Winterbourne	Yeoman	£4
W	1643/40	Gregory, Ann	\<Mangotsfield\>	\<Spinster\>	£27
	1684/16a	Gregory, Francis	--	\<Mariner\>	£4
	1684/16b	Gregory, Francis	--	\<Mariner\>	£25
W	1732/26	Gregory, Richard	City of Bristol	Mariner	£19
W	1643/38	Gregory, William	Mangotsfield	--	£15
W	1733/36	Gregson, John	City of Bristol	Mariner	£14
	1682/21B	Gregson, Richard	City of Bristol	\<Upholsterer\>	£66
W	1747/14	Greison, Niels	City of Bristol	Mariner	£10
	1688/21	Grembary, Sarah	Temple	--	£9
W	1678/29	Grenvil, John	(see Barton)	--	
	1623/24B	Gribbell, John	St. Stephen	--	£3
	1695/17	Gribble, Isaiah	--	--	£7
	1623/24B	Gribble, John	(see Gribbell)	--	
	1757/7	Griffee, Jonathan (jnr)	City of Bristol	Mariner	£7
	1700/25	Griffen, William	St. James	--	£14
W	1660/26	Griffeth, Jane	St. Stephen	Widow	£18
	1609/31	Griffeth, John	St. Nicholas	Sailor	£9
	1675/29	Griffeth, Richard	St. John	--	£13
	1624/31	Griffeth, William	St. Nicholas	--	£10
W	1732/27	Griffey, William	City of Bristol	Mariner	£9
	1670/16	Griffin, Anthony	Temple	Mason	£14
W	1636/30	Griffin, Elizabeth	St. Augustine	\<Widow\>	£22

	Year ref.	Name	Parish or area	Occupation or status	Value	Notes
W	1665/17	Griffin, George	St. Nicholas	⟨Mariner⟩	£8	
	1669/33	Griffin, Joan	St. Augustine	Widow	£33	
W	1688/20	Griffin, John	St. Thomas	Sieve-maker	£14	
	1733/37	Griffin, John	City of Bristol	Mariner	£7	
W	1755/3	Griffin, John	City of Bristol	Tiler	£3	
	1698/14	Griffin, Martha	City of Bristol	Widow	£11	
	1695/16	Griffin, Richard	City of Bristol	Mariner	£27	
	1706/18	Griffin, Richard	City of Bristol	Tailor	£41	
	1690/17A	Griffin, Robert	City of Bristol	Seaman	£8	
	1690/30	Griffin, Roger	Compton Greenfield	--	£38	
	1718/15	Griffin, Timothy	City of Bristol	Mariner	£12	
	1664/17	Griffin, William	St. Stephen	Sail-maker	£10	
	1664/18	Griffin, William	St. Stephen	Sail-maker	--	an obligation
W	1733/38	Griffis, Abraham	City of Bristol	Mariner	£9	
	1689/18	Griffith, Christopher	City of Bristol	--	£838	
W	1731/39	Griffith, David	City of Bristol	Mariner	£10	
	1662/20	Griffith, Euan	St. James	--	£77	
	1687/30	Griffith, James	Westbury-on-Trym (Shirehampton)	Labourer	£14	
			(see Gryffeth)			
W	1611/34	Giffith, Joan	St. John	Widow	£25	
W	1666/18	Griffith, Joan	(see Griffyth)			
	1698/13	Griffith, John	City of Bristol	Mariner	£3	
W	1752/14	Griffith, John	(see Griffin)			
	1698/14	Griffith, Martha	St. Augustine	--	£4	
	1624/30	Griffith, Philip	Winterbourne	--	£53	
	1685/23	Griffith, Richard	All Saints	Goldsmith	£260	also 2nd copy
	1641/19	Griffith, Thomas	SS. Philip & Jacob	Tailor	£20	
	1678/27	Griffith, Thomas	Winterbourne	Yeoman	£7	
	1750/18	Griffiths, John	City of Bristol	Mariner	£3	
W	1742/25	Griffits, Thomas	St. Thomas	Farrier	£23	
W	1663/27	Grigg, Elias				

Reference	W	Name	Place	Occupation	Value	Notes
1643/39	w	Grigg, Thomas	St. Ewen	Soap-boiler	£63	also 2nd copy
1726/18	w	Grimes, James	City of Bristol	Mariner	£6	
1710/13	w	Grimes, Thomas	City of Bristol	Mariner	£8	
1712/21	w	Grimes, Thomas	City of Bristol	Mariner	£8	
1688/21		Grimsbary, Sarah	(see Grembary)			
1695/1		Grindall, John	(see Crendall)			
1694/27		Grindon, Susanna	--	Widow	£15	
1679/26		Grindon, Philip	St. Stephen	Mariner	£109	
1670/15		Grinfield, John	City of Bristol	--	£5	
1629/27		Grinman, Patrick	St. Stephen	--	£16	also 2nd copy
1741/23		Grinnill, Edward	City of Bristol	Mariner	£9	
1698/13		Griffyth, John	Winterbourne	Rector (Winterbourne)	£378	wife's will 1625
1625/34		Gromadge, Nicholas	Olveston	<Rough-mason>	£9	
1637/23	w	Grosse, Edmund	Christchurch	Merchant	£975	
1681/26	w	Grove, Cornelius	Henbury <Berwick>	Yeoman	£202	
1634/34	w	Grove, John	Henbury <Hallen>	<Yeoman>	£116	
1672/18		Grove, Joshua	Henbury	Yeoman	£140	
1738/10	w	Grover, John	City of Bristol	<Mariner>	£17	
1735/15	w	Groves, Henry	City of Bristol	House-carpenter	£10	died at sea
1729/15		Grownow, Sarah	St. Stephen	--	£6	
1683/17		Grubb, Phillip	City of Bristol	Smith	£4	
1679/81a		Grumwell, Elizabeth	Westbury-on-Trym (Shirehampton)	Widow	£297	appraised 1671
1679/81b		Grumwell, Elizabeth	Westbury-on-Trym (Shirehampton)	Widow	£297	account only
1611/34	w	Gryffeth, Joan	St. Nicholas	Widow	£83	
1680/22	w	Gueen, Margaret	Almondsbury	<Widow>	£169	
1623/20	w	Guggin, John	(alias Fill, which see)			
1617/19		Guie, Edward	--	--	£3	
1680/22	w	Gullock, James	City of Bristol	Cloth-worker	£97	
1693/11	w	Gullock, James	Temple	Cloth-worker	£106	
1664/16		Guning, Robert	SS. Philip & Jacob	--	£5	
1642/21		Guninge, Edward	(see Gonning)			

	Year ref.	Name	Parish or area	Occupation or status	Value	Notes
W	1642/22	Guninge, Elizabeth	Henbury <Charlton>	Widow	£135	
	1683/19	Gunter, Thomas	--	Inn-holder	£246	
	1720/17	Guppy, John	City of Bristol	Mariner	£9	
	1683/18	Gush, Israel	Henbury (Kingsweston)		£101	
	1670/13	Gush, John	Westbury-on-Trym	--	£234	
W	1696/15	Gush, Letitia	Westbury-on-Trym (Shirehampton)	--	£142	
W	1630/2	Gushe, Izable	Henbury	Widow	£82	
	1686/20	Gustwood, William	--	--	£23	
	1691/20	Gutheridge, Robert	St. Ewen	Barber	£12	
	1640/28	Guy, John	St. Leonard	Gent.	£1,174	
W	1698/18A	Gwilliam, John	<St. Nicholas>	Cooper	£46	
W	1617/21	Gwilliam, Thomas	Henbury (Redwick)	Yeoman	£263	
	1733/39	Gwilliams, Frances	Stapleton	Spinster	£1	
	1705/13	Gwillim, John	City of Bristol	Victualler	£355	
W	1745/12	Gwilly, John	City of Bristol	Mariner	£7	
	1629/28	Gwin, Jane	St. Mary-le-Port	Widow	£10	
	1634/35	Gwin, John	St. Leonard <died in captivity in Turkey> (see Guen)	--	£27	
W	1680/23	Gwin, Margaret	St. Mary-le-Port	Shoemaker	£82	
W	1611/35	Gwin, Philip	St. Mary-le-Port	--	£38	
	1635/35	Gwin, Philip	Compton Greenfield	<Husbandman>	£110	
W	1643/41	Gwin, Richard	City of Bristol	Mariner	£8	
	1736/15	Gwinn, Henry	--	--	£53	
	1684/15	Gwinn, Joan				rural type inv.
W	1663/28	Gwinn, Richard	Olveston	Husbandman	£287	
W	1620/43	Gyles, John	Almondsbury	Husbandman	£30	
W	1641/18	Gyles, John	Henbury (Aust)	Husbandman	£75	
	1706/15	Gyles, John	Dunster (Somerset)	Mariner	£13	
W	1618/29	Gyles, Thomas	Winterbourne	Husbandman	£67	

Ref	W	Name	Place	Occupation	Value	Notes
1753/15		Hackett, Richard	City of Bristol	Mariner	£9	
1750/19		Hackney, William	City of Bristol	Mariner	£17	
1639/42	w	Hackrell, Ann	St. John	<Widow>	£132	
1720/18	w	Hackworth, George	City of Bristol	Mariner	£9	
1716/27		Hacock, Thomas	City of Bristol	Mariner	£18	
1644/24		Hagfoard, Anne	St. James	Widow	£7	
1669/40		Haggett, Edward	St. Mary, Redcliffe	Cooper	£14	
1687/34		Haggett, Elianor	City of Bristol	Widow	£10	
1712/22		Hague, John	City of Bristol	Mariner	£13	
1625/35	w	Haines, Dominicke	<Almondsbury, Patchway>	--	£47	died at sea
1634/36	w	Haines, Edward	Henbury	<Yeoman>	£149	
1620/45	w	Haines, Elizabeth	<Lawrence Weston>	Widow	£60	
1734/20	w	Haines, George	Henbury	Surgeon	£9	
1670/22		Haines, John	City of Bristol	Husbandman	£64	
1709/20		Haines, John	Olveston	Yeoman	£18	
1689/25		Haines, Joseph	Mangotsfield	Mariner	£2	
1613/27		Haines, Marie	City of Bristol	--	£304	
1641/21		Haines, Maurice	St. Augustine	Yeoman	£78	
1641/22		Haines, Nicholas	Almondsbury	Miller	£71	
1623/27		Haines, Robert	Winterbourne (Hambrook)	Yeoman	£42	
1620/46	w	Haines, Thomas	Olveston <Ingst>	Husbandman	£95	
1625/36		Haines, Thomas	Henbury	Sailor	£18	
1640/31	w	Haines, Thomas	St. Stephen	Yeoman	£101	
1646/20	w	Haines, Thomas	Henbury (Northwick/Redwick)	<Schoolmaster>	£24	
1647/12		Haines, Thomas	Olveston	Yeoman	£42	
1625/38	w	Haines, Walter	Almondsbury	Husbandman	£64	
1623/28		Haines, William	Almondsbury	Sailor	£5	
1644/28	w	Haines, William	St. Stephen	Carpenter	£119	
1691/29	w	Haines, William	Olveston	Cutler	£49	

Year ref.	Name	Parish or area	Occupation or status	Value	Notes
W 1743/14A	Hale, Abraham	St. Peter (alias Hall, which see)	Cordwainer	£163	
1643/42	Hale, George	St. Stephen	Mariner	£30	
1665/28	Hale, George	Castle Precinct	--	£72	
1666/23	Hale, George	St. Peter (see Heale)	Soap-boiler	£32	
W 1670/17	Hale, Richard				
1677/23	Hale, Samuel				
1672/24	Hales, Richard	City of Bristol	Baker	£86	
W 1684/23	Hall, Alice	St. Thomas	Widow	£65	
1749/28	Hall, Clifford	City of Bristol	Gent.	£18	
1611/39	Hall, Edward	Almondsbury (Rednend)	Single-man	£3	
1635/36	Hall, Elizabeth	Almondsbury	Widow	£26	
1643/42	Hall, George	St. Stephen	--	£5	alias Hale
1609/32	Hall, John	Almondsbury (Rednend)	--	£28	
W 1620/44	Hall, John	Olveston <Woodhouse>		£60	
1623/29	Hall, John	St. Mary-le-Port	Shoemaker	£33	
1665/23	Hall, John	Clifton	Mariner	£12	
1669/38	Hall, John	City of Bristol	Brewer	£52	
1675/33A	Hall, John	Mangotsfield	--	£12	
1712/23	Hall, John	Mangotsfield	Coal-miner	£5	
1737/13	Hall, Joseph	City of Bristol <St. Peter ?>	Victualler	£125	inv. & account
W 1620/47	Hall, Margaret	Olveston	Widow	£26	
W 1694/30	Hall, Mary	City of Bristol	Spinster	£21	
W 1641/20	Hall, Richard	St. Stephen	Joiner	£129	
W 1618/31	Hall, Robert	Almondsbury (Hempton)	Husbandman	£105	
W 1611/38	Hall, Sibell	Almondsbury (Rednend)	<Widow>	£23	

Ref	W	Name	Place	Occupation	Value
1639/43a		Hall, Thomas	Henbury	--	£10
1639/43b	W	Hall, Thomas	(document concerning funeral charges)		
1644/25		Hall, Thomas	Clifton	--	£44
1705/14		Hall, Thomas	City of Bristol	Blacksmith	£195
1620/48		Hall, William	Stoke Gifford	Husbandman	£14
1670/24		Hall, William	St. Augustine	Yeoman	£3
1669/36		Hallett, Benjamin	St. Stephen	Mariner	£7
1726/19	W	Hallet, Stephen	City of Bristol	Mariner	£7
1644/26	W	Halling, Edward	St. James	<Chandler>	£21
1735/16		Hamilton, Powell	City of Bristol	Mariner	£11
1735/17		Hamilton, William	--	<Mariner>	£10
1647/13		Hamman, Edward	SS. Philip & Jacob	Weaver	£52
1688/23		Hammell, Henry	--	<Mariner>	£3
1628/31		Hammett, Pascall	(see Hamott)	--	
1748/37		Hammond, Elizabeth	City of Bristol	--	£12
1753/16		Hammonds, Jane	(see Hammonds, William)		
1730/25		Hammonds, Phillip	City of Bristol	Mariner	£13
1753/16		Hammonds, William	City of Bristol	Labourer	£9
1730/25		Hammons, Philip	(see Hammonds)		
1628/31		Hamott, Pascall	Landkey near Barnstaple, Devon	<Sailor>	£26
1740/22	W	Hanbury, Daniel	City of Bristol	Mariner	£8
1633/29a	W	Hancock, Annis or Agnes	Olveston (Ingst)	Widow	£215
1633/29b	W	Hancock, Annis	(document re administration)		
1611/41	W	Hancock, Edward	Almondsbury (Rednend)	--	£20
1668/28	W	Hancock, Elizabeth	Olveston <Ingst>	Widow	£113
1617/22		Hancock, Margaret	Almondsbury	Widow	£7
1668/30	W	Hancock, Maurice	Olveston <Ingst>	Yeoman	£161
1671/18		Hancock, John (snr)	Almondsbury	--	£355
1611/42		Hancock, Julian	Almondsbury	--	£80
1705/15		Hancock, Robert	Henbury (Charlton)	--	£111
1691/28		Hancock, Thomas	Henbury (Redwick)	--	£75

	Year ref.	Name	Parish or area	Occupation or status	Value	Notes
	1670/25	Hancock, William	Alveston	Yeoman	£504	
	1692/17	Hancock, William	--	--	£22	
W	1708/17	Hancock, William (snr)	Almondsbury	Blacksmith	£17	
W	1611/40	Hancocke, Agnes	<Almondsbury>		£57	
	1625/39	Hancocke, Anthony	St. Thomas	<Shearman>	£76	
W	1611/43	Hancocke, Thomas	Almondsbury (Almondsbury Hill)	--	£88	
	1628/32	Hancocke, Thomas	Almondsbury	--	£10	
	1642/23	Hancocke, William	--		£50	
	1749/29	Handlin, John	City of Bristol	Mariner	£8	
	1742/26	Handmore, John	City of Bristol	Baker	£18	
W	1628/33	Haneman, Hugh	Alveston (Earthcott)	<Yeoman>	£176	will: Thornbury
	1662/25	Hann, Ann	St. Michael	Widow	£217	
	1745/13	Harbert, Charles	(see Herber)			
W	1686/22	Harcom, Morgan	<Olveston>	Husbandman	£29	
	1694/22	Harcombe, Thomas	Olveston (Upper Hazel)	--	£168	
	1687/36	Hardeman, John	City of Bristol	Clothier	£58	
	1635/37	Harden, Alice	St. Thomas	--	£21	
W	1651/2	Harden, William	Stapleton	Yeoman	£182	
	1635/37	Harding, Alice	(see Harden)			
	1624/33	Harding, Edward	St. Thomas	Shearman	£30	
W	1731/40	Harding, Hanah	City of Bristol	<Widow>	£72	
	1744/7	Harding, Isaac	City of Bristol	Mariner	£10	
W	1716/28	Harding, John	City of Bristol	Glazier	£5	also a 1714 will
	1747/15	Harding, Mary	City of Bristol	(Widow)	£8	
	1746/21	Harding, Sarah	Almondsbury	--	£10	
	1681/38	Harding, Thomas	Stapleton		£105	
	1727/11	Harding, Thomas	Stapleton	Collier	£6	
	1635/38	Harding, William	St. Peter	--	£4	

	Reference	Name	Place	Occupation	Value	
W	1670/18	Hardwick, William	\<St. Nicholas\>	Cooper	£30	
W	1734/21	Hare, Abraham	\<SS. Philip & Jacob\>	Victualler	£157	
W	1731/41	Hare, Andrew	City of Bristol	Mariner	£8	
	1735/18	Hare, Edwards	City of Bristol	Mariner	£15	
	1713/20	Harfet, John	St. Nicholas	--	£11	
W	1692/16	Harford, George	--	Mariner	£8	
	1640/29	Harford, John	(see Harvord)			inv. & account
	1714/20	Harford, John	City of Bristol	Mariner	£14	
	1674/22	Harford, Richard	St. Peter	--	£5	
	1634/37	Harford, Robert	St. James	Yeoman	£19	
W	1684/21	Harford, Thomasina	City of Bristol	Widow	£42	
	1679/32	Harford, William	City of Bristol	Vintner	£44	
W	1702/10	Harford, William	Mangotsfield (Downend)	Baker \<Husbandman in will\>	£4	
W	1716/29	Harford, William	\<Westbury-on-Trym\> (Shirehampton)	Pilot	£331	
	1713/20	Harfot, John	(see Harfet)			
W	1640/30	Harison, Joan	St. Mary-le-Port	\<Widow\>	£27	
W	1686/22	Harkham, Morgan	(see Harcom)			
W	1714/21	Harkwood, Mary	City of Bristol	Widow	£15	
W	1699/15	Harman, Roger	(see Herman)			
W	1675/33B	Harper, Elizabeth	St. John	\<Widow\>	£65	
W	1618/32	Harries, Elizabeth	Henbury	Widow	£27	
W	1740/23	Harrington, Hester	City of Bristol	Widow	£5	
W	1678/30	Harris, Anne	Olveston (Tockington)	Widow	£115	
	1682/22	Harris, Christopher	Westbury-on-Trym (Shirehampton)	Yeoman	£118	
	1639/44	Harris, David	St. Augustine	--	£3	
	1722/7	Harris, David	City of Bristol	Mariner	£7	
W	1643/43	Harris, Edward	\<St. Nicholas\>	Cooper	£156	
	1761/14	Harris, Edward	City of Bristol	Mariner	£5	
	1737/14	Harris, Elias	City of Bristol	Mariner	£4	

Year ref.		Name	Parish or area	Occupation or status	Value	Notes
1673/15	W	Harris, Elizabeth	City of Bristol	Widow	£61	
1761/15	W	Harris, Hannah	City of Bristol	Widow	£10	
1745/14		Harris, Hector	City of Bristol	Mariner	£10	
1712/24		Harris, Henry	\<Henbury\> Aust	--	£29	
1730/26	W	Harris, Henry	City of Bristol	Mariner	£9	
1716/30	W	Harris, Howell	City of Bristol	Mariner	£10	
1609/33		Harris, John	St. Werburgh	--	£3	
1639/45a		Harris, John	St. James	Brewer	£12	
1639/45b		Harris, John	(list of goods, unvalued)			
1650/4		Harris, John	St. Stephen	Sailor	£18	
1686/23	W	Harris, John	City of Bristol	Trunk-maker	£543	
1687/35	W	Harris, John	\<City of Bristol\>	Cooper	£76	
1667/34		Harris, Lettice	St. Peter	Spinster	£13	
1758/13		Harris, Nathaniel	City of Bristol	Gent.	£56	plus goods, unvalued
1639/46		Harris, Nicholas	Westbury-on-Trym	--	£12	
1683/21		Harris, Philemon	Henbury (Charlton)	Day labourer	£17	
1683/23		Harris, Richard	--	--	£24	
1737/15		Harris, Richard	City of Bristol	Mariner	£11	
1664/20		Harris, Samuel	St. Mary-le-Port	Brewer	£10	
1684/22	W	Harris, Sarah	St. Michael	Widow	£49	
1669/37		Harris, Thomas	Henbury	Husbandman	£34	
1706/19		Harris, Thomas	Olveston	Butcher	£227	
1758/14	W	Harris, Thomas	City of Bristol	Mariner	£19	
1692/18	W	Harris, Walter	City of Bristol	Soapmaker	£4	
1623/30		Harris, William	St. Thomas	\<Inn-holder\>	£26	
1633/30	W	Harris, William	Henbury	\<Husbandman\>	£87	
1692/22	W	Harris, William	Henbury \<Stowick\>	Husbandman	£107	
1693/12	W	Harris, William	City of Bristol	Ironmonger	£144	
1740/24	W	Harris, William	SS. Philip & Jacob	Wool-comber	£5	
1729/16		Harrison, Christopher	City of Bristol	Mariner	£4	

W	Ref	Name	Place	Occupation	Value	Notes
W	1618/32	Harrison, Elizabeth	(see Harries)			
	1728/16	Harrison, George	City of Bristol	Mariner	£25	
	1748/38	Harrison, John	City of Bristol	Mariner	£10	
	1707/21	Harry, Thomas	City of Bristol	Mariner	£16	
	1633/31	Harsell, Edward	Christchurch	Goldsmith	£224	see Hassall 1633/33
	1629/29	Hart, Anne	St. John	Widow	£3	
W	1643/44	Hart, Edward	<St. Stephen>	--	£79	
	1732/28	Hart, Elizabeth	City of Bristol	Widow	£6	
	1623/31	Hart, Thomas	St. Peter	Cutler	£10	
	1677/22	Hartfordshire, Margaret	St. Stephen	--	£21	
	1678/78	Hartfordshire, Margaret	St. Stephen	Widow	£21	account only
	1676/22	Hartle, Thomas	--	--	£47	account only
	1678/73	Hartley, Thomas	St. James	--	£47	
	1732/29	Hartlidd, James	City of Bristol	Mariner	£2	
W	1749/30	Hartnell, William	City of Bristol	<Mariner>	£13	
W	1719/20	Hartt, Francis	City of Bristol	Mariner	£23	
	1683/20	Hartwell, Thomas	--	--	£42	
	1628/34	Harvart, William	St. Peter	Butcher	£5	
W	1702/10	Harverd, William	(see Harford)			
W	1625/40	Harvet, Job	(see Harvert)			
	1713/21	Harvey, Alexander	City of Bristol	Mariner	£7	
	1629/30	Harvey, Bassell	St. John	Joiner	£4	
	1692/19	Harvey, Henry	City of Bristol	Porter	£6	
	1665/26	Harvey, Michael	St. Peter	Victualler	£26	
W	1640/29	Harvord, John	Stapleton	Collier	£10	
	1613/28	Harvord, Simon	Portbury	--	£20	
W	1724/7	Harvy, John	City of Bristol	Mariner	£4	
	1719/21	Harvy, Samuel	City of Bristol	Mariner	£8	
W	1613/29	Harvye, Elizabeth	St. Peter	Widow	£35	
	1635/39	Hasellwood, Thomas	Temple	--	£4	
	1671/17	Haskins, Giles	City of Bristol	--	£22	
W	1649/14	Haskins, John	Mangotsfield	<Yeoman>	£164	
	1609/34	Haskins, Marie	(see Hoskins)			

Year ref.		Name	Parish or area	Occupation or status	Value	Notes
W	1689/26	Haskins, Nathaniel	Mangotsfield	⟨Yeoman⟩	£53	
	1639/47	Haskins, William	St. Stephen	--	£78	
W	1752/15	Haskins, William	SS. Philip & Jacob	⟨Cordwainer⟩	£57	
	1633/32	Hasler, Richard	St. James	--	£13	
	1733/40	Hasp, Robert	City of Bristol	Mariner	£15	
	1633/33	Hassail, Edward	Christchurch	Goldsmith	--	see Harsell 1633/31
	1667/33	Hassell, Robert	St. Augustine	--	--	
	1633/32	Haster, Richard	(see Hasler)			
	1667/33	Haswell, Robert	(see Hassell)			
W	1661/36	Hatch, Bridget	St. Michael	Widow	£104	
	1693/15	Hathaway, Jane	Mangotsfield	Widow	£51	
W	1749/31	Hathaway, John	City of Bristol	Mariner	£9	
W	1697/21	Hathaway, Josia	--	--	£30	
W	1729/17	Hathaway, Edward (jnr)	Winterbourne			
			⟨Frenchay⟩		£155	
W	1649/15	Hathway, Henry	Mangotsfield	Butcher	£173	
	1671/20	Hathway, Henry	Temple	Husbandman	£19	
	1651/3	Hatton, Thomas	St. Michael	--	£4	
W	1625/40	Havard, Job	(see Havert)	Gunsmith		
	1627/12	Havart, Gibbon	St. Mary, Redcliffe	Sawyer	£15	
W	1625/40	Havert, Job	St. Stephen	--	£21	
	1644/27	Havord, Edward	Christchurch	--	£70	
	1698/17	Hawkins, Amos	--	--	£4	
W	1664/23	Hawkins, John	St. Thomas	Cook	£91	
	1689/30	Hawkins, Nathaniel	St. Augustine	--	£31	
	1643/45	Hawkins, Robert	St. Mary, Redcliffe	--	£231	
	1697/20	Hawkins, Thomas	Christchurch	--	£22	
	1716/31	Hawkins, Thomas	Olveston	Mason	£11	
	1623/32	Hawkins, William	St. Nicholas	--	£2	
W	1731/42	Hawkins, William	City of Bristol	Mariner	£7	
W	1689/24	Hawkridge, Robert	City of Bristol	Mariner	£49	

Reference	W	Name	Place	Occupation	Value	Notes
1665/23		Hawll, John	(see Hall)		£70	inv. & account
1724/8		Hawstead, John	City of Bristol	Victualler	£27	inv. & account
1651/2	W	Hayarden, William	(see Harden) (Hayarden is on will only)			
1730/27	W	Hayden, Mary	<City of Bristol>	Spinster		
1697/22	W	Hayerdin, John	Mangotsfield (Berry Hill)	Husbandman		
1681/29	W	Hayes, Bryan	City of Bristol	Surgeon	£237	
1681/32	W	Hayes, James	St. Augustine	Merchant	£230	
1732/30		Hayes, Matthew	City of Bristol	Mariner	£62	
1620/50	W	Hayle, Robert	St. Nicholas	--	£4	
1679/31		Hayman, Anne	SS. Philip & Jacob	Widow	£15	
1673/14	W	Hayman, Dorothy	City of Bristol	Widow	£43	
1735/19		Hayman, George	City of Bristol	Mariner	£115	
1677/20	W	Hayman, Henry	<St. Augustine>	Baker	£8	
1646/21		Hayman, Thomas	St. James	Merchant	£301	
1676/19	W	Hayman, William	City of Bristol	Cooper	--	
1676/21		Hayman, William	(badly damaged version of above, 1676/19)	Cooper	£141	
1693/14		Hayman, William	City of Bristol	--	£39	
1623/25		Haynes, Edmund	Mangotsfield	<Yeoman>	£4	
1689/31	W	Haynes, Edward	Henbury (Kingsweston)		£128	
1648/9	W	Haynes, Joan	Olveston	Widow	£135	
1623/26		Haynes, John	Mangotsfield	--	£9	
1664/22	W	Haynes, Mary	Henbury	Widow	£204	
1618/30	W	Haynes, Maurice	Olveston	--	£257	
1664/21		Haynes, Maurice	Henbury	--	£83	
1672/25	W	Haynes, Richard	Henbury	Yeoman	£102	
1611/36		Haynes, Robert	Olveston	Blacksmith	£8	
1611/37	W	Haynes, Thomas <snr>	Olveston	--	£18	
1624/32	W	Haynes, Thomas	SS. Philip & Jacob	<Husbandman>	£9	
1647/14		Haynes, William	Christchurch	--	£100	
1668/32		Haynes, William	Stapleton	--	£79	
1680/27		Haynes, William	--	Blockmaker	£4	

	Year ref.	Name	Parish or area	Occupation or status	Value	Notes
W	1627/13	Hayord, John	St. Stephen	Shipwright	£13	also 2nd copy
W	1709/21	Hayter, George	--	Mariner	£18	
W	1639/48	Hayter, William	St. James	Milliner	£196	
	1665/25	Haytor, John	St. Mary, Redcliffe	Milliner	£30	
	1675/37	Hayward, Sarah	City of Bristol	Widow	£155	
W	1613/30A	Haywarden, Giles	Mangotsfield	Husbandman	£51	
W	1613/30B	Haywarden, Giles (jnr)	Mangotsfield	Tiler	£89	
W	1711/20	Hazard, Edward	City of Bristol	Tailor	£6	
	1627/11	Hazell, Richard	St. Mary, Redcliffe	--	£1	
	1726/20	Head, Anne	City of Bristol	Spinster	£3	
	1633/34	Head, John	St. Stephen	Shipwright	£3	
W	1713/22	Head, John	Clifton	Blacksmith	£56	
	1714/22	Head, Thomas	--	--	£20	
	1705/16	Heale, William	City of Bristol	Weaver	£8	
W	1646/22	Heale, John	St. Thomas	Butcher	£324	
	1689/27	Heale, John	St. Mary, Redcliffe	--	£162	
	1684/27	Heale, Richard	City of Bristol	Butcher	£6	
	1677/23	Heale, Samuel	St. Augustine	Mariner	£35	
	1629/31	Healing, Richard	Clifton	--	£23	
	1732/31	Heard, Henry	City of Bristol	--	£726	
W	1717/24	Heard, Susanna	<St. Stephen>	Widow	£62	
	1747/16	Heard, Timothy	City of Bristol	Mariner	£20	
	1702/11	Hearne, George	City of Bristol	Mariner	£52	
W	1668/29	Heath, Thomas	St. John	<Cooper>	£2	
	1669/43	Heath, Thomas	St. John	Cooper	£11	
	1683/25	Heathcott, Thomas	City of Bristol	Schoolmaster	£96	
	1669/41	Heavens, George	St. James	Mason	£124	
	1677/24	Heavens, George	St. James	Mason	£92	
W	1676/20	Heavens, Mary	<St. James>	Widow	£81	
	1710/14	Heavens, Philip	--	--	£6	
	1737/16	Hebb, Hannah	City of Bristol	Spinster	£17	

	Ref.	Name	Place	Occupation	Value	Notes
W	1629/32	Hedges, Edith	Stapleton	Widow	£4	also 2nd copy
	1633/35	Hedges, Richard	St. Stephen	<Carpenter>	£9	
	1642/24	Hedges, Roger	(see Hodges)			
W	1611/44	Hedges, Thomas	Stoke Gifford	--	£25	
	1628/36	Hedges, William	(see Heges)			
	1666/25A	Hedges, William	St. James	Carpenter	£21	also dated 1673
	1628/36	Heges, William	St. Mary, Redcliffe	--	£4	
W	1625/41	Helliar, Robert	(see Helliard)			
W	1625/41	Helliard, Robert	St. Mary, Redcliffe	Saltpetre-man	£46	
W	1719/22	Helliare, Mary	(see Hellier)			
	1714/23	Helliare, Simon	(see Hellier)			
	1646/23	Helliard, Thomas	(see Hilliord)			
W	1715/21	Hellier, Benjamin	City of Bristol	Hooper	£9	
	1676/24	Hellier, Christopher	City of Bristol	--	£27	
	1693/13	Hellier, Godfrey	--	--	£26	
W	1719/22	Hellier, Mary	Temple	Spinster	£21	
	1714/23	Hellier, Simon	Temple	Serge-weaver	£12	
W	1704/16	Helling, Jonathan	<City of Bristol>	<Mariner>	£17	
	1711/21	Hellman, Thomas	City of Bristol	Mariner	£14	
W	1639/49	Heminge, Christian	St. Stephen	Widow	£24	
W	1636/31	Hemings, William	Christchurch	Milliner	£483	
W	1681/30	Hemmings, Elizabeth	Barton Regis	--	£5	
	1663/33	Hemmings, George	Mangotsfield	Tailor	£22	
	1740/25	Hemmings, Robert	City of Bristol	Mariner	£19	
	1733/41	Hemptage, John	City of Bristol	Mariner	£1	
W	1734/22	Henderson, Isaac	City of Bristol	Mariner	£8	
	1730/28	Henderson, John	City of Bristol	Mariner	£5	
	1727/12	Henderson, William	City of Bristol	Mariner	£8	
	1623/33	Henly, Thomas	St. James	Scavenger	£30	
W	1751/8	Henry, William	City of Bristol	Mariner	£10	
W	1641/23	Hensman, Joan	St. Peter	<Widow>	£116	
	1729/18	Henten, David	City of Bristol	Mariner	£4	
W	1728/17	Herbelt, Christopher	City of Bristol	Mariner	£8	

	Year ref.	Name	Parish or area	Occupation or status	Value	Notes
W	1728/17	Herben, Christopher	(see Herbelt)			
	1745/13	Herber, Charles	City of Bristol	Mariner	£11	
	1665/22	Herbert, Edward	City of Bristol	Surgeon	£19	
	1635/40	Herbert, Moore	St. Stephen	Sail-maker	£24	
	1671/15	Herbert, Walter	St. James	--	£11	
W	1679/36	Herculis, John	City of Bristol	Cordwainer	£295	
W	1637/25	Hereford, Margaret	Christchurch	Widow	£169	
	1624/34	Hereford, Martin	Christchurch	Inn-holder	£124	
W	1699/15	Herman, Roger	City of Bristol	Tailor	£43	
W	1628/37	Hersse, Henry	Abbots Leigh	Mariner	£25	
	1698/19	Heughs, Ann	(see Huse)			
W	1729/19	Hewell, Joseph	<Henbury> (Redwick & Northwick)	Yeoman	£342	
	1644/31	Hewellyt, Richard	St. Mary, Redcliffe	--	£11	
	1660/4	Hewes, Lewis	(see Hughes)			
W	1729/19	Hewet, Joseph	(see Hewell)			
	1678/67	Hewett, Edward	City of Bristol	Carpenter	£2	inv. & account
	1768/CP	Hewett, John	Alveston	Victualler	£359	
	1710/15	Hewett, Thomas	City of Bristol	Mariner	£19	
	1672/22	Hewlin, Alexander	St. Nicholas	--	£9	
	1688/25	Hex, John	--	--	£1	
	1637/24	Heyman, James	St. Augustine	Merchant	£52	
	1676/21	Heyman, William	(see Hayman)			
W	1625/38	Heynes, Walter	(see Haines)			
	1623/34	Heywaye, Rafe	Henbury (Kingsweston)	--	£1	
	1730/2	Hiatt, Elizabeth	City of Bristol	Widow	£13	
	1681/37	Hibbert, Richard	City of Bristol	Inn-holder	£90	
W	1667/35	Hichens, Henry	(see Hitchings)			
W	1722/8	Hickes, Jacob	Mangotsfield	Cooper	£39	

	Ref.	Name	Place	Occupation	Value
W	1724/9	Hicks, Abraham	Almondsbury (Woodland)	<Yeoman>	£209
W	1644/29	Hicks, John	SS. Philip & Jacob	Inn-holder	£252
W	1712/25	Hicks, John	City of Bristol	Mariner	£8
	1646/24	Hicks, Roger	St. John	Milliner	£57
	1641/15	Hicks, Roger	(see Hix)		
W	1758/15	Hicks, Thomas	Littleton-on-Severn	Yeoman	£43
	1718/16	Hicks, William	City of Bristol	Tobacconist	£16
W	1742/27	Hicks, William	City of Bristol	Mariner	£5
W	1613/31	Hickman, Alice	Elberton	Widow	£14
	1609/35	Hickman, Maurice	--		£32
	1753/17	Hickman, Samuel	City of Bristol	Mariner	£10
W	1613/32	Hickman, William	Elberton	Tailor	£16
	1712/26	Hide, Robert	City of Bristol	Mariner	£47
W	1618/36	Hiett, Stephen	Westbury-on-Trym	Yeoman	£308
	1759/10	Higgins, Patrick	City of Bristol	Mariner	£15
	1641/24	Higgins, Phillip	St. Thomas	--	£48
W	1731/43	Higgins, William	City of Bristol	Mariner	£16
W	1634/38	Higgs, Gyles	Westbury-on-Trym (Southmead)	Weaver	£23
W	1617/23	Highway, Richard	Westbury-on-Trym (Shirehampton)	--	£57
	1623/34	Highway, Rafe	(see Heywaye)		
W	1714/24	Hignell, Edward	Winterbourne (Hambrook) <Marshfield in will>	Maltster	£133
W	1613/33	Hill, Agnes	Henbury	--	£29
	1665/21	Hill, Ann	Henbury	Spinster	£21
W	1691/27	Hill, Bridget	Castle Precincts	Widow	£22
	1688/24	Hill, Bridgett	City of Bristol	Widow	£20
	1640/32	Hill, Edith	Olveston <Cote>	Spinster	£13
W	1620/51	Hill, Edward	Olveston (Ingst)	Gent.	£662
W	1700/31	Hill, Edward	Almondsbury	--	£109
	1711/22	Hill, Edward	City of Bristol	Mariner	£4

Year ref.	Name	Parish or area	Occupation or status	Value	Notes
W 1684/19	Hill, George	Castle Precincts	Button-mould maker	£13	inv. & account
W 1635/41	Hill, Guy	St. Stephen	--	£6	
1684/24	Hill, Guy (snr)	St. Stephen	Joiner	£35	(see Hill 1684/19)
1699/13	Hill, Guy	--	--	£7	
W 1708/19	Hill, Joan	Winterbourne (Sturdon House)	Widow	£79	inv. & account
W 1625/42	Hill, John	Alveston <Earthcott>	Husbandman	£37	
W 1639/50	Hill, John	Almondsbury	--	£33	
W 1647/16	Hill, John	St. Peter (Castle)	Mould-maker	£34	
1660/3	Hill, John	City of Bristol	Baker	£147	
1737/17	Hill, John	SS. Philip & Jacob	Brickmaker	£51	
1743/14B	Hill, John	City of Bristol	Mariner	£15	
1685/27	Hill, Philip	--	Baker	£102	
1667/38	Hill, Richard	St. Stephen	--	£71	
1708/18	Hill, Robert	City of Bristol	Wine-cooper	£46	
1711/23	Hill, Samuel	City of Bristol	Mariner	£5	
1740/26	Hill, Samuel	City of Bristol	Mariner	£8	
1625/43	Hill, Thomas	St. Stephen	Mariner	£10	
1684/18	Hill, Thomas	Littleton-on-Severn	Yeoman	£59	
1691/6	Hill, Thomas	Winterbourne	Yeoman	£396	
1624/35	Hill, William	Henbury	Husbandman	£141	
1673/16	Hill, William	St. Mary, Redcliffe	Pauper	£1	
W 1624/36	Hillenes, Edward	Clifton	--	£16	also 2nd copy
1663/31	Hillery, Richard	St. Stephen	Mariner	£10	
1667/31	Hilliar, John	St. Peter	--	£2	
1634/39	Hillinge, Agnes	Clifton	--	£16	
1637/63	Hillinge, Ann	(see Watts)			alias Watts
W 1624/36	Hillinge, Edward	(see Hillenes)			
1646/23	Hilliord, Thomas	City of Bristol	--	£40	
W 1647/17	Hillman, Richard	City of Bristol	Salt-maker	£15	
1667/32	Hillman, Robert	St. Augustine	Mariner	£14	

W	Ref.	Name	Place	Occupation	Value	Notes
W	1639/49	Himinge, Christian	(see Heminge)			
	1732/32	Hinchellwood, George	(see Hinshellwood)			
	1691/25	Hind, Matthew	City of Bristol	Goldsmith	£30	
	1699/11	Hindes, John	--	--	£16	
W	1739/7	Hine, John	City of Bristol	Mariner	£10	died at sea
W	1640/33	Hine, John	St. Mary-le-Port	Yeoman	£117	alias Derby
W	1684/26	Hines, Cecilia	<City of Bristol>	Widow	£8	
	1760/12	Hinds, William	City of Bristol	Mariner	£10	
	1732/32	Hinshellwood, George	City of Bristol	Surgeon	£10	died at sea
	1695/18	Hipsley, Elizabeth	Temple	--	£15	
	1670/21	Hipsley, George	Temple	Dyer	£43	
	1640/34	Hiscocks, William	St. John	--	£9	
	1685/17	Hiscox, Joseph	City of Bristol	Surgeon	£80	
	1640/34	Hiscox, William	(see Hiscocks)			
	1716/32	Hisketh, John	City of Bristol	Mariner	£11	
	1684/20	Hiskins, William	Westbury-on-Trym (Shirehampton)	--	£133	
	1716/33	Hitchings, Anne	Elberton	Widow	£18	
W	1759/11	Hitchings, Hannah or Susannah	St. George (Co. Glos)	Spinster	£12	Bristol diocese
W	1667/35	Hitchings, Henry	St. Mary, Redcliffe	Merchant Tailor	£353	
	1689/23	Hitchings, Nathan	Henbury (Aust)	Yeoman	£329	
	1667/29	Hitchins, John	St. Thomas	Brewer	£7	
W	1650/5	Hitchins, Margaret	Elberton	Widow	£18	
W	1703/9	Hix, Arthur	Barton Regis	Coal-miner	£6	
	1688/25	Hix, John	(see Hex)			
	1647/15	Hix, Roger	St. Stephen	--	£2	
W	1665/29	Hixe, James	Compton Greenfield	<Husbandman>	£189	
	1609/36	Hixe, John (snr)	Olveston	--	£23	
W	1728/18	Hoar, Henry	City of Bristol	Tobacco-pipe maker	£20	
W	1679/34	Hobbs, Ann	Henbury (Stowick)	Widow	£87	
	1692/15	Hobbs, Arthur	Littleton-on-Severn	--	£26	
W	1689/22	Hobbs, Francis	Barton Regis	Cordwainer	£8	

Year ref.	Name	Parish or area	Occupation or status	Value	Notes
1714/25	Hobbs, Hester	Almondsbury (Hempton)	--	£96	
1649/16	Hobbs, James	St. James	--	£261	
1692/23	Hobbs, John	City of Bristol	Inn-holder	£95	
W 1662/22A	Hobbs, Joseph	St. Mary, Redcliffe	\<Felt-maker\>	£13	also 2nd copy
W 1637/26	Hobbs, Martha	Olveston	Widow	£72	
1643/46	Hobbs, Nicholas	St. Peter	--	£25	
W 1731/44	Hobbs, Stephen	Henbury	Yeoman	£197	
W 1661/38	Hobbs, Thomas	Littleton-on-Severn	\<Yeoman\>	£205	
W 1735/20	Hobbs, William	City of Bristol	Mariner	£9	
W 1661/39	Hoben, Walter	Stapleton	Collier	£83	
1699/14	Hobourne, William	City of Bristol	Carpenter	£2	
1687/32	Hobson, Thomas	City of Bristol	--	£21	
W 1731/45	Hockett, Joseph	City of Bristol	Mariner	£19	
W 1749/32	Hodder, Alexander	City of Bristol	Mariner	£4	
1676/23	Hodds, George	St. Thomas	Nailer	£6	
1696/16	Hodges, Charles	St. James	Mariner	£10	
W 1675/34	Hodges, Elizabeth	City of Bristol	Widow	£44	
1680/26	Hodges, Elizabeth	Clifton	Widow	£31	
W 1692/21	Hodges, Frances	St. Mary, Redcliffe	Widow	£61	
1667/30	Hodges, John	St. Thomas	Butcher	£13	
1668/31	Hodges, John	St. Stephen	--	£61	
W 1698/16	Hodges, John	St. James	Seaman	£11	\<Tobacconist in will\>
1723/11	Hodges, Joseph	City of Bristol	Tailor	£38	
1642/24	Hodges, Roger	Henbury	Yeoman	£85	
1699/16	Hodges, Samuel	--	--	£9	
1652/2	Hodges, Thomas	Henbury (Cribbs)	\<Carpenter\>	--	
1662/24	Hodges, Thomas	Henbury (Northwick & Redwick)	Yeoman	£694	
W 1701/13	Hodges, Thomas	SS. Philip & Jacob	Tailor	£54	

	Ref.	Name	Place	Occupation	Value	Notes
W	1717/25	Hodges, Thomas	City of Bristol	Mariner	£18	will: 1719 wills
W	1666/25B	Hodges, William <snr>	St. James	Carpenter	£218	
W	1749/33	Hogg, William	City of Bristol	Mariner	£16	
	1629/33	Hokes, John	St. Mary, Redcliffe	Felt-maker	£6	
W	1742/28	Hoking, John	City of Bristol	Mariner	£6	
	1709/22	Holbaraw, Mary	(see Holbrough)			
W	1698/18B	Holben, William	Barton Regis <Kingswood Chase>	Coal-miner	£176	
W	1687/38	Holbin, Thomas	(see Houlben)			
W	1721/12	Holbin, Thomas	City of Bristol	Butcher	£19	
W	1698/18B	Holbin, William	(see Holben)			
	1746/22	Holborow, John	City of Bristol	Cooper	£3	died at sea
	1699/14	Holbourne, William	(see Hobourne)			
W	1679/35	Holbrock, John	Henbury (Stowick)	Yeoman	£96	
	1636/32	Holbrooke, John	St. James	--	£6	
	1700/22	Holbrough, Mary	Stapleton	Spinster	£13	
W	1700/29	Holder, Samuel	Winterbourne	<Carpenter>	£162	
	1747/17	Holder, William	Mangotsfield	Blacksmith	£24	
	1740/27	Hollan, John	City of Bristol	Mariner	£7	
	1681/28	Holland, Frances	City of Bristol	(Mrs) Widow	£15	
W	1736/16	Holland, James	City of Bristol	Mariner	£10	
W	1737/18	Holland, Patrick	City of Bristol	Mariner	£11	
	1725/6	Holland, Thomas	City of Bristol	Mariner	£5	
	1637/27	Holland, Timothy	Compton Greenfield	Rector	£16	
W	1680/31	Holle, Thomas	(see Holly)			
W	1671/16	Hollester, Agnes	Compton Greenfield	Widow	£75	
W	1667/36	Hollester, Edward	<Compton Greenfield> Henbury	Yeoman <Gent.>	£104	Hollister 1677/25 is another copy
	1678/33	Hollester, Edward	Henbury (Compton Greenfield)	Yeoman	£46	
W	1642/25	Hollester, Elizabeth	Henbury (Compton Greenfield)	<Widow>	£255	
	1684/25	Hollester, Grace	Temple	Widow	£8	
	1700/26	Hollester, Hannah	Henbury (Northwick)	Spinster	£285	extra to next entry

	Year ref.	Name	Parish or area	Occupation or status	Value	Notes
	1700/27	Hollester, Hannah	Henbury (Northwick)	<Spinster>	£325	extra to above entry
w	1647/18	Hollester, John	City of Bristol	Yeoman	£4	--
w	1669/35	Hollester, Katherine	"Lewin's Mead"	Widow	--	
	1620/52	Hollester, Thomas	Henbury	Yeoman	£332	
w	1618/33	Holliday, John	St. Mary, Redcliffe	--	£19	
	1685/26	Holliday, Samuel	City of Bristol	Tobacco-cutter	£23	
	1666/24	Hollister, Edward	Henbury	--	£339	
	1677/25	Hollister, Edward	Henbury (Compton Greenfield)	Yeoman	£46	Hollester 1678/33 is another copy
	1680/66	Hollister, Edward	Compton Greenfield	--	£49	account only
	1697/19	Hollister, John	Henbury (Compton Greenfield)	--	£40	
w	1715/22	Hollister, John	City of Bristol	House-carpenter	£97	
	1717/26	Hollister, John	Almondsbury	Yeoman	£424	
w	1640/35	Hollister, Margery	St. Mary, Redcliffe	Single-woman	£23	
	1735/21	Hollister, Mark	Almondsbury	--	£406	
w	1662/21	Hollister, Mary	Henbury <Compton Greenfield>	Widow	£118	
	1687/33	Hollister, Nehemiah	-- (see Hollyester)	--	£21	
	1625/30	Hollister, Richard	Henbury (Kingsweston)	<Yeoman>		
w	1640/36	Hollister, Robert	Henbury (Kingsweston)	Yeoman	£388	also 2nd copy
w	1708/20	Hollister, Robert	Henbury (Compton Greenfield)	Yeoman	£155	
w	1729/20	Hollister, Stephen	Henbury (Northwick)	<Gent. in will>	£286	
	1680/64	Hollister, Thomas	Compton Greenfield	--	£234	account only
	1672/23	Hollister, William	Compton Greenfield	Yeoman	£145	
	1675/36	Hollister, William	City of Bristol	Inn-holder	£19	
w	1691/24	Hollister, William	Henbury (Crook's Marsh)	<Yeoman>	£192	

W	Reference	Name	Place	Occupation	inv.& account
	1715/23	Hollister, William	City of Bristol	House-carpenter	£10
	1678/31	Hollord, Nathaniel	City of Bristol	Mariner	£9
W	1741/24	Holloway, Jonathan	City of Bristol	Mariner	£12
W	1617/24	Holly, Joan	Compton	Widow	£91
	1701/14	Holly, John	Henbury	--	£409
W	1680/31	Holly, Thomas	Almondsbury (Cattybrook)	Yeoman	£188
W	1633/36	Hollye, John	Henbury	<Carpenter in will>	£137
	1625/30	Hollyester, Richard	Christchurch	Husbandman	£16
	1731/46	Holmes, Robert	City of Bristol	Fletcher	£10
W	1722/9	Holt, William	City of Bristol	Mariner	£6
	1734/23	Holton, Richard	City of Bristol	Mariner	£21
W	1669/44	Homead, Anne	St. Augustine	Widow	£21
	1663/32	Homead, Richard	Temple	Mariner	£112
	1721/13	Hone, John	City of Bristol	Mason	£8
	1681/36	Hooke, Elizabeth	St. James	Widow	£196
W	1624/39	Hoole, Thomas	Henbury <Lawrence Weston>	--	£25
	1670/23	Hoope, John	SS. Philip & Jacob	<Hatter>	£16
W	1694/29	Hooper, Edward	--	--	£2
	1727/14	Hooper, Ephraim	City of Bristol	Mariner	£13
	1727/13	Hooper, Gregory	City of Bristol	Mariner	£14
W	1731/47	Hooper, Henry	City of Bristol	Mariner	£6
W	1635/42	Hooper, John	Henbury (Aust)	Blacksmith	£44
W	1663/30	Hooper, Joseph	Olveston	Husbandman	£49
	1640/37	Hooper, Margaret	St. John	--	£5
	1617/25	Hooper, Ralph	SS. Philip & Jacob	Husbandman	£40
	1761/16	Hooper, Richard	City of Bristol	Mariner	£7
	1661/40	Hooper, Thomas	St. Werburgh	Tailor	£42
	1691/30	Hooper, William	St. Stephen	Mariner	£73
W	1617/26	Hopkins, Alexander	City of Bristol	Joiner	£55
	1739/8	Hopkins, Clement	City of Bristol	Victualler	£62
W	1687/9	Hopkins, John	City of Bristol	Tobacco-roller	£26

Year ref.	Name	Parish or area	Occupation or status	Value	Notes
W 1728/19	Hopkins, John	Westbury-on-Trym	Yeoman <Clerk, in will>	£16	<Parish Clerk>
W 1689/28	Hopkins, Mary	St. Peter	Widow	£16	
W 1740/28	Hopkins, Paul	City of Bristol	Mariner	£6	
W 1768/CP	Hopkins, Peter	Christchurch	Hatter	£17	inv. & account will 1762
1667/37	Hopkins, Richard	St. James	Yeoman	--	
W 1663/29	Hopkins, Thomas	Henbury	<Husbandman>	£44	
W 1683/24	Hopkins, Thomas	<Compton Greenfield>	<Salt-maker>	£90	
W 1685/25	Hopkins, Thomas	St. Peter	Hair-weaver	£254	
1706/20	Hopkins, Thomas	St. Mary, Redcliffe	Shipwright	£9	
1731/48	Hopper, Susannah	City of Bristol	Apothecary; widow	£857	details of 50 rooms
1717/27	Hopper, Thomas	City of Bristol	<Inn-keeper>	£331	
W 1681/34	Hopton, John	--	Gent.	£187	
1708/21	Hopwood, Stephen	Littleton-on-Severn	Brazier	£12	
W 1742/29	Hore, John	City of Bristol	Mariner	£3	
1748/39	Horgan, John	City of Bristol	Mariner	£11	
1740/29	Horn, Benjamin	City of Bristol	Mariner	£5	
1690/18	Hornby, Thomas	City of Bristol	--	£8	
1747/18	Horne, John	--	Yeoman	£20	
1644/30	Horne, Oliver	Olveston	Seaman	£4	
1720/19	Horne, Thomas	St. Stephen	<Mariner>	£19	
1736/17	Horner, James	City of Bristol	Mariner	£8	
1681/31	Horniblow, Thomas	City of Bristol	Cork-cutter	£12	
1628/38	Horrel, Ursula	St. John	--	£2	
W 1643/47	Horsam, John	St. Stephen	Ship-carpenter	£763	
W 1675/35	Horseman, Bridgett	Christchurch	Widow <Stocking-maker>	£54	
(w) 1740/30	Horseman, Walter	City of Bristol	Victualler	£55	

(a 1740 will of Walter Horseman, St. James, Saddler, exists)

W	Ref.	Name	Place	Occupation	Value	Notes
W	1643/47	Horsham, John	(see Horsam)			
	1649/17	Horsham, Richard	City of Bristol	Glover	£4	
	1677/58	Hort, Anthony	Westbury-on-Trym	--	£287	account only
W	1624/37	Hort, Edward	Olveston (Tockington)	Husbandman	£12	
	1763/5	Hort, James	City of Bristol	Mariner	£14	
W	1639/52	Hort, Joan	City of Bristol	Spinster	£23	
	1680/65	Hort, Joan	Almondsbury	--	£46	account only
	1714/26	Hort, John	Westbury-on-Trym	Gent.	£205	
	1620/53	Hort, Samuel	Mangotsfield	--	£1	
	1723/12	Hort, Samuel	City of Bristol	Mariner	£14	
W	1617/27	Hort, Thomas	Henbury (Compton Greenfield)	Yeoman	£11	
	1712/27	Hort, Thomas	City of Bristol	Mariner	£8	
W	1729/21	Hort, Thomas	<Henbury> (Kingsweston)	--	£302	inv. & account (1798 will)
W	1641/25	Horte, Agnes	Henbury	Widow	£57	
	1677/21	Horte, Joan	Almondsbury	Widow	£46	
W	1637/28	Horte, John	Olveston (Tockington)	Husbandman	£18	
W	1637/29	Horte, John	Westbury-on-Trym	Yeoman	£285	
W	1614/2	Horte, Julian	St. Mary-le-Port	Widow	£435	
	1639/51	Horte, Thomas	Henbury	Yeoman	£44	
W	1717/28	Horwood, Richard	Westbury-on-Trym	Slaughterman	£54	1716 will
	1609/34	Hoskins, Marie	Almondsbury (Over)	Widow	£77	
W	1717/29	Hoskins, Thomas	City of Bristol	Colourman	£10	
	1755/4	Hotching, John	City of Bristol	Tailor <Mariner>	£10	
	1708/22	Houghton, Richard	City of Bristol	Mariner	£10	
W	1687/38	Houlben, Thomas	City of Bristol	Tailor	£607	
	1635/43	Houlder, Joyce	St. Peter Castle Precinct	Single-woman	£2	
	1635/44	Hoult, Richard	City of Bristol	--	£45	
	1755/5	House, Joseph	City of Bristol	Mariner	£10	
	1660/5	House, Robert	Mangotsfield	--	£237	

Year ref.	Name	Parish or area	Occupation or status	Value	Notes
W 1639/53	Howall, Jerome	(see Howell)			
1670/20	Howard, Daniell	City of Bristol	Mariner	£45	
W 1637/30	Howell, Alice	Littleton-on-Severn	Widow	£140	
W 1662/22B	Howell, Clement	Mangotsfield	Yeoman	£45	
W 1690/17B	Howell, Francis	<City of Bristol>	<Haulier>	£57	
1705/17	Howell, Henry	St. Mary, Redcliffe	--	£3	
1708/23	Howard, Humphry	St. Stephen	Mariner	£25	
W 1703/10	Howell, James	Henbury (Lawrence Weston)	Yeoman	£175	also a 2nd copy
W 1639/53	Howell, Jerome	Mangotsfield	<Yeoman>	£200	
W 1639/54	Howell, John	Stoke Gifford	Yeoman	£54	
1678/32	Howell, John	St. Nicholas		£19	
1753/18	Howell, John	City of Bristol	Shipwright	£15	died at sea
1627/14	Howell, Katherine	St. James	--	£23	
1691/22	Howell, Margaret	St. John	Widow	£5	
1634/40	Howell, Maurice (Morris)	St. Nicholas	Sailor	£2	
W 1706/21	Howell, Robert	Temple	Haulier	£78	
W 1635/45	Howell, Thomas	St. Thomas	Saddler	£240	
1648/10	Howel, Thomas	'Stoke'	--	£168	
1721/14	Howell, Thomas	City of Bristol	Mariner	£2	
W 1734/24	Howell, Thomas	City of Bristol	Mariner	£10	
W 1646/25	Howell, Walter	St. Stephen	Cooper	£67	
1670/19	Howell, Walter	St. Thomas	Haulier	£13	
W 1680/30	Howell, Walter	St. John	Haulier	£98	
1618/34	Howell, William	St. Mary, Redcliffe	Tanner	£19	
W 1760/13	Howells, Anthony	City of Bristol	Mariner	£11	
W 1624/38	Howlet, Margaret	St. James	Widow	£11	
1609/37	Howlett, John	St. James	--	£22	
1620/54	Howlett, Morris	St. James	Brewer	£20	
1644/31	Howlett, Richard	(see Hewellyt)			
1748/40	Howragan, Michael	City of Bristol	Mariner	£5	

W	Ref.	Name	Place	Occupation	Value	Notes
W	1691/23	Hubberd, Moses	<St. George>	<Surgeon>	£16	
W	1683/26	Hudson, Alice	St. Augustine	Widow	£192	
	1709/23	Hudson, Hanah	(see Hutson)			
W	1689/29	Hudson, Joan	<City of Bristol>	<Widow>	£41	
W	1635/46	Hudson, Lancelot	St. Stephen	<Shipwright>	£28	
W	1740/31	Hudson, Luke	City of Bristol	Mariner	£5	
	1687/37	Hudson, Thomas	--	--	£21	
W	1700/28	Huggett, Mary	Westbury-on-Trym (Shirehampton)	Widow	£65	
	1712/28	Huggins, John	City of Bristol	Mariner	£20	
	1620/55	Hugh, Welthian	St. Peter	Servant	£9	
	1713/23	Hughes, Charles	City of Bristol	Mariner	£5	
W	1729/22	Hughes, Charles	City of Bristol	Mariner	£16	
	1609/38	Hughes, Henry	St. Nicholas	--	£54	
W	1661/37	Hughes, Henry	Stapleton	<Yeoman>	£256	
	1679/33	Hughes, Henry	SS. Philip & Jacob	--	£27	
	1692/20	Hughes, John	Abbots Leigh (St. George)	--	£22	
W	1730/30	Hughes, John	City of Bristol	Mariner	£7	
	1679/30	Hughes, Matthew	St. Thomas	--	£33	
	1724/10	Hughes, Matthew	City of Bristol	Mariner	£9	
	1660/4	Hughes, Lewis	St. Leonard	Cardmaker	£41	
W	1742/30	Hughes, Rice	City of Bristol	Mariner	£16	
	1688/26	Hughes, Richard	St. Stephen	Cooper	£1,092	
	1635/47	Hughes, Richard	St. Stephen	Shipwright	£15	
W	1629/34	Hughes, Thomas	City of Bristol	Mariner	£30	
	1680/29	Hughes, Thomas	City of Bristol	Brewer	£10	
W	1717/30	Hughes, Thomas	City of Bristol	Mariner	£11	
	1749/34	Hughes, Thomas	City of Bristol	House-carpenter	£15	
W	1748/41	Hughs, Thomas	City of Bristol	Mariner	£18	
W	1738/11	Hughson, George	City of Bristol	Mariner	£17	
	1768/CP	Huish, James	St. Mary, Redcliffe	Tobacconist	£470	
	1686/25	Hulbert, James	City of Bristol	Blockmaker	£25	also 2nd copy

	Year ref.	Name	Parish or area	Occupation or status	Value	Notes
	1672/22	Hulinge, Alexander	(see Hewlin)		£17	
W	1624/39	Hull, Thomas	(see Hoole)	Mariner	£11	
	1761/17	Humber, John	City of Bristol	Sailor	£697	
W	1705/18	Humphrey, Ralph	City of Bristol	Widow	£16	
W	1727/15	Humphreys, Rose	City of Bristol	Mariner	£24	
W	1748/42	Humphrys, James	⟨Bedminster⟩	--	£15	
W	1691/26	Hunbury, Katherine	St. Michael	--	£50	
W	1611/45	Hungerford, John	Alveston (Earthcott)	Husbandman		
W	1681/35	Hungerford, William	Alveston			
	1637/43	Hunt, Alice	(alias Nicholas, which see)		£41	
W	1690/19	Hunt, Christian	⟨Castle Precinct⟩	Widow	£192	
W	1672/26	Hunt, Flower	City of Bristol	Tobacco-pipe maker	£6	
W	1712/29	Hunt, James	City of Bristol	Mariner		
	1662/23	Hunt, John	(alias Estemed, which see)		--	
	1669/39	Hunt, Stephen	Temple			
W	1700/30	Hunt, Thomas	Stoke Gifford (Walls Court)	Yeoman	£488	
	1745/15	Hunt, William	City of Bristol	Mariner	£6	
	1719/23	Hunter, Abraham	City of Bristol	Shipwright	£12	
	1743/15	Hunter, James	City of Bristol	Mariner	£8	
	1738/12	Hunter, John	City of Bristol	Mariner	£8	
	1613/34	Hurcome, John	Mangotsfield	Yeoman	£22	
	1666/26	Hurden, Mary	(see Hurn)			
	1665/27	Hurle, John	St. Thomas	--	£6	
	1683/22	Hurles, Mary	--	Widow	£6	
	1706/22	Hurlestone, John	(see Hurrelstone)			
W	1719/24	Hurley, Anthony	Almondsbury	--	£131	
	1666/26	Hurn, Mary	Barton Regis	Widow	£76	
W	1628/39	Hurne, Joan	Abbots Leigh	Widow	£58	
W	1695/19	Hurne, John	City of Bristol	Joiner	£181	
W	1639/55	Hurne, Robert	Compton Greenfield	--	£59	

W	Ref	Name	Parish	Occupation	Value	Note
	1706/22	Hurrelstone, John	--	Cheesemonger	£14	
W	1677/19	Hurst, Marie	St. Peter	Widow	£54	
W	1671/19	Hurst, Nathaniel	St. Peter	Mariner	£27	
W	1633/37	Hurston, John	St. Stephen	<Victualler in will>	£207	
W	1740/32	Hurtt, Absolam	City of Bristol	Gent.	£13	died at sea
	1637/31	Hurtnall, Richard	(see Hurtnoll)			
	1623/35	Hurtnoll, John	St. Mary-le-Port	Shipwright	£29	
W	1686/24	Hurtnoll, John	City of Bristol	Butcher	£158	
	1637/31	Hurtnoll, Richard	St. Nicholas	Butcher	£26	
	1618/35	Hurtnoll, Thomas	St. Nicholas	<Butcher>	£17	
	1669/42	Hurtnoll, Thomas	St. Michael	Mariner	£8	
	1698/19	Huse, Ann	St. Thomas	Widow	£7	
W	1635/48	Hussey, Sampson	St. Augustine	Doctor <of Laws>	£21	
	1642/26	Hussey, Steven	<City of Bristol>	Captain	£24	
W	1713/24	Hutchings, Thomas	City of Bristol	Mariner	£8	
	1634/41	Hutchins, Katherine	Elberton	Widow	£81	
	1709/23	Hutson, Hannah	--	Widow	£62	
W	1743/16	Hutton, Stephen	City of Bristol	Mariner	£10	
	1699/12	Huttson, William	City of Bristol	Ropemaker	£2	
	1685/28	Hyde, Walter	--	--	£8	
	1639/56	Hyman, Thomas	St. Stephen	--	£47	
	1680/28	Hyman, Thomas	City of Bristol	Cooper	£11	
	1669/17	Hynam, Edward	City of Bristol	Cooper	£38	
W	1683/29	Iddy, Thomas	--	--	£5	
	1723/13	Ifeild, Thomas	City of Bristol	Mariner	£14	
W	1634/42	Iffe, Miles	Temple	Shearman	£17	
	1730/31	Imstrim, Magnes	City of Bristol	Mariner	£9	
	1698/24	Inan, John	--	Mariner	£9	
W	1669/45	Ingledon, William	(see Inkolden)			
	1640/38	Ingleton, Elizabeth	St. Stephen	Widow	£9	
	1618/37	Ingram, John	St. Thomas	Butcher	£12	

	Year ref.	Name	Parish or area	Occupation or status	Value	Notes
W	1669/45	Inkoldon, William	City of Bristol	Mariner	£274	
	1671/22	Inon, William	Westbury-on-Trym	--	£53	
	1746/23	Irwin, William	City of Bristol	Mariner	£9	
W	1662/26	Isbury, Phillip	Barton Regis	Shoemaker	£57	
	1644/32	Isgar, Paul	Stapleton	Vintner	£13	
	1667/42	Isger, Hannah	Abbots Leigh	--	£20	
W	1678/36	Ismede, Thomas	Almondsbury (Hempton)	<Mason>	£61	
	1721/15	Italian, Matthew	City of Bristol	Mariner	£4+	
	1643/48	Ithell, Robert	Temple	Weaver	--	
W	1749/35	Iveme, Charles	City of Bristol	Mariner	£16	
	1643/49	Ivey, George	St. Michael	Dyer	£46	
W	1707/22	Ivey, Thomas	City of Bristol	Gent.	£413	
W	1739/9	Jacks, Benjamin	City of Bristol	Mariner	£8	
	1712/30	Jackson, Arthur (snr)	City of Bristol	House-carpenter	£140	
W	1682/24	Jackson, Elizabeth	City of Bristol	Widow	£391	compare 1686/40B
W	1686/40B	Jackson, Elizabeth	City of Bristol	Widow	£466	see also 1682/24 and next entry
W	1686/CP	Jackson, Elizabeth	(formerly of Combehay, Somerset) <St. Augustine>	Widow	£466	acct: will 1681 inv. 1682/24
	1690/21	Jackson, John	St. Mary-le-Port	Butcher	£91	
	1698/22	Jackson, Thomas	--	--	£19	
	1642/27	Jackson, Thomas	St. Augustine	Shoemaker	£108	
W	1745/16	Jacob, Ann	<St. Stephen>	Spinster	£15	
	1642/28	Jacob, Edward	Christchurch	--	£40	
W	1716/34	Jacob, Mary	Mangotsfield	Spinster	£24	
	1710/16	Jacob, Richard	City of Bristol	Mariner	£14	
W	1726/21	Jacobs, Martha	City of Bristol	Widow	£18	<Spinster in will>

W	1783/CP	Jacques, Francis	City of Bristol	Baker	£1,250	inv. & account will 1779
W	1611/47	Jaine, Richard	Henbury	Husbandman	£130	
	1649/18	Jaine, Richard	City of Bristol	Shipwright	£2	
	1611/48	Jaines, John	Westbury-on-Trym	Mariner	£9	
	1687/43	James, Alexander (jnr)	St. Augustine	--	£118	
	1688/28	James, Alexander	City of Bristol	Yeoman	£141	
	1680/32	James, Benjamin (snr)	City of Bristol	Mariner	£932	
W	1672/29	James, Deborah	City of Bristol	Spinster	£421	
W	1639/57A	James, Dorothy	Mangotsfield	\<Widow\>	£6	
	1748/43	James, Francis	City of Bristol	Mariner	£18	
	1678/35	James, George	Mangotsfield	Cordwainer	£85	
	1691/31	James, Henry	--	--	£4	
	1620/56	James, Hugh	St. Nicholas	--	£33	
W	1613/35	James, John	St. Mary, Redcliffe	Cooper	£31	
	1662/28	James, John	St. Mary, Redcliffe	Cooper	£3	
W	1664/26	James, John	St. Leonard	Turner	£152	
	1753/19	James, John	--	Brewer	£1	
	1761/18	James, John	City of Bristol	Mariner	£4	
	1780/CP	James, John	City of Bristol	Butter merchant	£257	inv. & account
W	1647/9	James, Marie	Filton	Widow	£16	
	1708/24	James, Nathaniel	Henbury	Yeoman	£12	
W	1629/35	James, Reynold	Henbury (and Caldicott, Monmouth)	--		
W	1642/29	James, Richard	St. Thomas	Brewer	£2	
	1732/33	James, Richard	City of Bristol	Mariner	£62	
	1667/39	James, Robert	Henbury	Yeoman	£2	
	1690/22	James, Robert	City of Bristol	Shipwright	£61	
	1718/17	James, Robert	City of Bristol	Mariner	£7	
	1681/40	James, Samuel	Barton Regis	Carpenter	£8	
	1633/38	James, Thomas	St. James	Whitawer	£9	
W	1635/49	James, Thomas	City of Bristol	Esquire \<Gent.\>	£243	also 2nd copy
W	1639/57B	James, Thomas	Filton	--	£422	also 2nd copy
					£506	4 invs. & 1 a/c

	Year ref.	Name	Parish or area	Occupation or status	Value	Notes
	1728/20	James, Thomas	City of Bristol	Mariner	£13	
	1666/27	James, Tomsin	St. Mary, Redcliffe	--	£3	
	1635/50	James, William	Westbury-on-Trym	--	£139	
	1646/26	James, William	St. Nicholas	Cooper	£22	
w	1697/23	James, William	St. Michael	Cordwainer	£10	
w	1733/42	James, William	City of Bristol	Mariner	£12	
w	1733/43	Jameson, George	City of Bristol	Mariner	£8	
w	1731/49	Jameson, William	City of Bristol	Mariner	£10	
	1689/33	Jane, Edward	St. Stephen	Joiner	£131	
w	1749/36	Jane, John	City of Bristol	Mariner	£8	
w	1718/18	Jane, Peter	City of Bristol	Shipwright	£15	died at sea
	1735/22	Jane, Thomas	City of Bristol	Turner	£154	
w	1698/20	Janes, John	City of Bristol	Cooper	£17	
w	1661/47	Jaques, Henry	Mangotsfield	Husbandman	£39	
w	1663/34	Jarvice, Joan	Henbury	Widow	£84	
	1739/10	Jarvis, William	City of Bristol	Victualler	£996	
w	1712/31	Jayen, Ezekiel	(see Jayne)			
w	1697/25	Jayn, Mary	Henbury (Hallen)	Widow	£127	
	1773/CP	Jayne, Ann	Henbury	Widow	£144	inv. & account
	1701/15	Jayne, Edward	Westbury-on-Trym	Yeoman	£325	
	1633/39	Jayne, Elizabeth	Henbury	Widow	£42	
w	1712/31	Jayne, Ezekiel	Henbury (Compton Greenfield)	Carpenter	£77	
w	1690/20	Jayne, John	Henbury (Stowick)	Husbandman	£143	
	1737/19	Jayne, John	Almondsbury	Yeoman	£16	
	1752/16	Jayne, John	Almondsbury (and the account of Ann, late wife of John Jayne, deceased 1745)	Yeoman	£382	
	1672/27	Jayne, Michael	St. Thomas	Inn-holder	£88	
	1665/31	Jayne, Roger	Temple	Weaver	£3	
w	1707/23	Jayne, Susannah	Westbury-on-Trym (Stoke Bishop)	Widow	£103	

Ref	W	Name	Place	Occupation	Value	Notes
1715/24		Jayne, Thomas	SS. Philip & Jacob	Victualler	£67	
1666/28		Jayne, William	Henbury	Yeoman	£144	
1693/18		Jayne, William	--	Carpenter	£4	
1674/23		Jaynes, ----	--	Widow & Pauper	£1	
1716/35		Jeanes, Joseph	City of Bristol	Sail-maker	£2	
1723/14		Jeens, Joseph	City of Bristol	--	£9	
1662/27	W	Jefferies, Ann	St. James	Widow	£217	
1643/50		Jefferis, Elizabeth	(see Jeofferies)			
1745/17		Jefferis, John	City of Bristol	Mariner	£8	
1733/44		Jefferis, Samuel	City of Bristol	Mariner	£10	
1664/24		Jeffery, Sibilla	St. Mary-le-Port	Spinster	£15	
1694/33		Jefferys, Thomas	City of Bristol	Bookbinder	£13	
1685/29	W	Jefford, Bartholomew	City of Bristol	Mariner	£47	
1668/33	W	Jeffries, John	SS. Philip & Jacob	Victualler	£48	
1685/30		Jeffries, John	SS. Philip & Jacob	--	£103	
1641/26	W	Jeffris, Richard	SS. Philip & Jacob	<Husbandman>	£26	
1641/27		Jeffris, Thomas	St. James	Tailor	£248	
1679/37		Jeffryes, James	Castle Precincts	--	£17	
1731/50	W	Jellicut, Bushell	City of Bristol	Distiller	£115	
1694/31	W	Jelson, Joel	Barton Regis	<Grocer>	£409	
1611/48		Jenes, John	(see Jaines)			
1643/51		Jenkes, Edward	St. Mary-le-Port	<Cordwainer>	£69	
1628/35		Jenkin, Harry	Olveston (Ingst)	Husbandman	£76	
1717/31	W	Jenkins, Daniel	City of Bristol	Set-cooper	£22	
1685/31		Jenkins, Edward	City of Bristol	--	£1	
1728/21	W	Jenkins, Lewis	Almondsbury	<Labourer>	£77	
1696/17	W	Jenkins, Martha	City of Bristol	Widow	£80	
1676/25	W	Jenkins, Mary	<St. Nicholas>	Widow	£317	see also 1677/62
1684/29		Jenkins, Thomas	City of Bristol	Cordwainer	£112	
1702/12		Jenkins, Thomas	City of Bristol	--	£20	
1778/CP	W	Jenkins, Thomas	City of Bristol	Hooper	£677	account only will 1769
1675/38		Jenkins, William	St. Nicholas	Lighterman	£210	

Year ref.		Name	Parish or area	Occupation or status	Value	Notes
1677/62		Jenkins, William	St. Nicholas	Lighterman	£405	see also Mary Jenkins
			(document fragile & damaged: 26 page account of receipts & disbursements including inventory items)			
1694/34	W	Jenkins, William	St. Stephen	Mariner	£6	
1612/7		Jennings, Adam	(see Gennings)			
1620/38	W	Jennings, Mary	(see Gennings)			
1661/41		Jennings, Joan	Barton Regis	--	£22	
1641/28	W	Jennings, John	Westbury-on-Trym	Tailor	£32	
1733/45	W	Jennings, William	City of Bristol	Mariner <Hooper>	£7	
1643/50		Jeofferies, Elizabeth	St. Michael	--	£9	
1635/51	W	Jerrett, William (snr)	St. Mary, Redcliffe	<Mariner>	£3	
1684/28		Jinckes, Edward	City of Bristol	Tailor	£310	
1731/51	W	Jobe, William	<City of Bristol>	Mariner	£6	
1681/27	W	Jocelin, George	SS. Philip & Jacob	Butcher	£220	
1732/34	W	Jocham, James	City of Bristol	Mariner	£6	
1681/41		Jocham, Samuel	St. Stephen	Cooper	£73	
1620/57		Johnes, Humphrey	St. Stephen	--	£19	
1609/40		Johnes, John	(see Jones)			
1677/28		Johns, John	--	<Tailor>	£27	
1737/20	W	Johnson, Alexander	City of Bristol	Mariner	£5	
1661/45	W	Johnson, Anne	St. Stephen	Widow	£34	
1740/33		Johnson, Charles	City of Bristol	Mariner	£15	
1643/52	W	Johnson, Francis	St. Stephen	Merchant	£222	
1761/19		Johnson, Hindrick	City of Bristol	Mariner	£10	
1717/32	W	Johnson, John	City of Bristol	Mariner	£5	
1758/16	W	Johnson, Jonathan	St. Stephen	Mariner	£14	
1642/30A		Johnson, Peter	City of Bristol	Mariner	£41	
1727/16		Johnson, Peter	St. Nicholas	Mariner	£13	
1661/46	W	Johnson, Richard	St. Nicholas	<Musician>	£89	
1623/36		Johnsone, Thomas	(see Jonsone)			
1743/17	W	Johnston, Alexander	City of Bristol	Mariner	£7	

	Ref	Name	Place	Occupation	Value	Notes
W	1754/18B	Johnston, James	City of Bristol	Mariner	£6	
W	1722/10	Johnston, Robert	City of Bristol	Mariner	£5	
W	1722/10	Johntion, Robert	(see Johnston)			
	1752/17	Jollie, Thomas	City of Bristol	Mariner	£10	
	1699/17	Jones, Alice	St. Thomas	Widow	£8	
W	1701/16	Jones, Daniel	St. Thomas	⟨Yeoman⟩	£187	
	1609/39	Jones, David	St. Werburgh	Tailor	£17	
	1673/17A	Jones, David	St. Michael	--	£15	
	1695/20	Jones, David	City of Bristol	Mariner	£1	
	1720/20	Jones, David	City of Bristol	Mariner	£4	
	1733/46	Jones, David	City of Bristol	Mariner	£5	
	1661/42	Jones, Edmond	St. Mary, Redcliffe	Chapman	£18	
	1675/40	Jones, Edward	St. Mary, Redcliffe	Baker	£6	
	1676/27	Jones, Edward	Henbury	--	£63	
	1677/26	Jones, Edward	St. Stephen	⟨Joiner⟩	£18	
W	1688/29	Jones, Elinor	City of Bristol	Widow	£499	
	1628/40	Jones, Elizabeth	Elberton	Widow	£11	
	1679/38	Jones, Elizabeth	Barton Regis	Widow	£132	
	1687/39	Jones, Elizabeth	Clifton	Widow	£207	
W	1707/24	Jones, Elizabeth	SS. Philip & Jacob	Widow	£453	
W	1715/25	Jones, Evan	City of Bristol	Porter	£211	
	1683/28	Jones, Flewellin	--	--	£3	
	1661/43	Jones, Frances	St. Stephen	Spinster	£44	
	1732/35	Jones, Frances	City of Bristol	Widow	£17	
	1698/21	Jones, George	--	--	£62	
	1681/39	Jones, Giles	Winterbourne (Hambrook)	Husbandman	£7	
W	1637/32	Jones, Henry	Keevell (Wilts)	Gent.	£340	
	1713/25	Jones, Henry	City of Bristol	Mariner	£6	
	1728/22	Jones, Henry	City of Bristol	Shipwright	£6	died at sea
	1635/52	Jones, Hugh	St. Augustine	--	£3	
	1670/26	Jones, Hugh	St. Augustine	Mariner	£26	compare Margery Jones
	1620/57	Jones, Humphrey	(see Johnes)			

Year ref.		Name	Parish or area	Occupation or status	Value	Notes
1670/28		Jones, Humphry	Barton Regis	Nailer or Porter	£2	
1747/19	W	Jones, Jacob	City of Bristol	Mariner	£16	
1650/6	W	Jones, Jane	St. Nicholas	Widow	£79	
1609/40		Jones, John	Olveston (Hazel)	--	£40	
1611/49	W	Jones, John	St. Thomas	Shearman	£14	
1636/33	W	Jones, John	Clifton	<Tailor>	£100	also 2nd copy
1639/58		Jones, John	St. Stephen	--	£1	
1648/11	W	Jones, John	St. Augustine	Mariner	£4	
1664/25		Jones, John	St. Mary, Redcliffe		--	
1667/40		Jones, John	St. Augustine	Shipwright	--	
1677/29		Jones, John	SS. Philip & Jacob	'Sayer'	£173	
1684/30		Jones, John	St. Stephen	Anchor-smith	£80	
1688/27		Jones, John	City of Bristol	Ropemaker	£29	
1689/34		Jones, John	Elberton	--	£33	
1689/35		Jones, John	--	--	£8	
1695/21		Jones, John	--	--	£9	
1695/22	W	Jones, John	Westbury-on-Trym (Shirehampton)	Mariner	£22	
1697/24	W	Jones, John	City of Bristol	Mariner <Captain>	£8	
1710/17		Jones, John	City of Bristol	Mariner	£11	
1710/18		Jones, John	City of Bristol	Mariner	£10	
1716/36	(w)	Jones, John	City of Bristol	Mariner	£5	

(a 1716 will of John Jones, Verger at the Cathedral, exists)

Year ref.		Name	Parish or area	Occupation or status	Value	Notes
1716/37		Jones, John	City of Bristol	Mariner	£11	
1737/21		Jones, John	City of Bristol	Mariner	£6	
1740/34	W	Jones, John	City of Bristol	Mariner	£19	
1742/31	W	Jones, John	City of Bristol	Mariner	£10	
1746/24	W	Jones, John	<SS. Philip & Jacob>	White-smith	£17	
1748/44	W	Jones, John	City of Bristol	Mariner	£19	
1759/12		Jones, John Jenkin	City of Bristol	Mariner	£5	
1725/7		Jones, Joseph	City of Bristol	Mariner	£5	

Ref	Name	W	Place	Occupation	Value	Notes
1609/41	Jones, Katherine		St. Nicholas	—	£3	
1660/6	Jones, Lickeria		(alias Williams, which see)			
1670/27	Jones, Margery		<St. Augustine>	Wife	£31	wife of Hugh Jones
1667/41	Jones, Mary		St. James	Widow	£9	
1693/17	Jones, Mary		Castle Precincts	Widow	£7	
1708/27	Jones, Mary	W	<St. Stephen>	Widow	£23	
1727/18	Jones, Mary	W	St. Augustine	Widow	£511	
1681/42	Jones, Mathew		Henbury (Kingsweston)	Husbandman	£65	
1689/36	Jones, Matthew		St. Stephen	Shipwright	£8	
1694/32	Jones, Matthias		City of Bristol	Gunsmith	£93	
1727/17	Jones, Nathaniel		City of Bristol	Cooper	£5	died at sea
1640/39	Jones, Nicholas		St. Michael	—	£10	
1718/19	Jones, Philip		City of Bristol	Mariner	£4	
1609/42	Jones, Phillip		St. Augustine	Sailor	£3	
1702/13	Jones, Reece		Clifton	—	£42	
			(see Long)			
1637/33	Jones, Richard	W	St. James	<Brewer>	£13	
1641/29	Jones, Richard	W	City of Bristol	Mariner	£5	
1708/25	Jones, Richard	W	City of Bristol	Gunsmith	£459	inv. & account
1714/27	Jones, Richard		City of Bristol	Mariner	£10	
1754/19	Jones, Richard		St. Thomas	Inn-holder	£90	
1665/30	Jones, Robert		St. Peter	—	£30	
1675/39	Jones, Robert		(marked Robert Jones; but properly Samuel Harvy, which see)			
1719/21	Jones, Robert		City of Bristol	Mariner	£16	
1757/8	Jones, Robert	W	City of Bristol	<snuff-grinder, formerly mariner, in will>		
1711/24	Jones, Roger		Mangotsfield	—	£10	
1735/23	Jones, Samuel		City of Bristol	Hooper	£210	
1741/25	Jones, Samuel	W	<St. James>	Mariner	£5	
1706/23	Jones, Sarah	W	Henbury (Hallen)	<Widow>	£19	
1612/8	Jones, Teage	W	St. Mary, Redclife	Glover	£12	
1635/53	Jones, Thomas	W	St. Augustine	Tailor	£42	
1676/26	Jones, Thomas		SS. Phillip & Jacob	Husbandman	£12	
1708/26	Jones, Thomas		City of Bristol	Mariner	£10	

Year ref.	Name	Parish or area	Occupation or status	Value	Notes
1717/33	Jones, Thomas	City of Bristol	Butcher	£64	
1718/20	Jones, Thomas	Westbury-on-Trym	Potter	£8	
1732/36	Jones, Thomas	City of Bristol	Mariner	£4	
1747/20	Jones, Thomas	City of Bristol	Mariner	£18	
W 1776/CP	Jones, Thomas	⟨St. James⟩	Schoolmaster	£111	inv. & account will 1770
1661/44	Jones, Walter	St. Michael	Smith	£6	
1715/26	Jones, Walter	City of Bristol	Mason	£4	
W 1741/CP	Jones, Walter	St. James	Tailor	£27	
1713/26	Jones, Welthian	City of Bristol	Widow	£7	
1665/32	Jones, William	Temple	Cloth-worker	£21	
1689/32	Jones, William	-- (Lewins Mead)	--	£4	
1707/25	Jones, William	City of Bristol	Mariner	£10	
1709/24	Jones, William	--	⟨Mariner⟩	£9	
1720/21	Jones, William	City of Bristol	Mariner	£11	
1712/16	Jones, William	Westbury-on-Trym	⟨Mariner⟩	£6	
1732/37	Jones, William	City of Bristol	Glazier	£10	
1733/47	Jones, William	City of Bristol	Farrier	£7	
1742/32	Jones, William	City of Bristol	Mariner	£8	
1749/37	Jones, William	City of Bristol	Mariner	£10	
W 1624/40	Jonnes, John (jnr)	Filton	Yeoman	£113	
W 1698/23	Jonson, John	Elberton	Yeoman	£220	
W 1639/59	Jonsone, John	St. Mary, Redcliffe	--	£10	
1623/36	Jonsone, Thomas	St. Stephen	Sailor	£6	
1698/25	Jope, Elizabeth	--	--	£13	
W 1678/34	Jordan, Andrew	St. Thomas	Farrier	£37	
1740/35	Jordan, Charles	City of Bristol	Surgeon	£5	died at sea
1625/44	Jordan, John	St. Peter	⟨Cardmaker⟩	£10	
W 1677/27	Jordan, Richard	⟨City of Bristol⟩	Painter	£231	
1731/52	Jordan, Stephen	City of Bristol	Mariner	£10	
1643/53	Jordan, William	(see Jordon)			

W	Ref	Name	Parish	Occupation	Value	Notes
W	1629/36	Jorden, Andrew	St. Peter	Blacksmith	£104	also 2nd copy
	1628/41	Jorden, George	St. Thomas	--	£14	
	1672/28	Jorden, John	St. Thomas	Mariner	£3	
	1643/53	Jordon, William	--	Farrier	£26	
W	1681/21	Joslin, George	(see Jocelin)			
W	1727/19	Joyce, Martin	City of Bristol	Mariner	£5	
W	1703/11	Joyner, Joseph	Henbury (Kingsweston)			
	1682/23	Joyner, Lawrence	City of Bristol	--	£165	
W	1693/16	Joyner, Thomas	Henbury	Anchor-smith	£201	
	1671/21	Juings, James	St. Nicholas	--	£234	
	1628/41	Jurden, George	(see Jorden)	--	£30	
W	1740/36	Kates, Richard	City of Bristol	Mariner	£12	
W	1766/5	Kavnaugh, James	City of Bristol	Surgeon-mariner	£10	with wills
	1623/37	Kay, James	--	Mariner	--	
	1635/54	Keame, Edmund	St. Augustine	--	£4	
W	1725/8	Keare, Andrew	City of Bristol	Mariner	£8	
W	1668/34	Kearell, John	Henbury	Tailor	£42	
W	1668/34	Kearle, John	(see Kearell)			
	1779/CP	Keate, Benjamin	City of Bristol	Carpenter	£305	account only
W	1740/36	Keates, Richard	(see Kates)			
	1624/41	Kedgwin, Robert	All Saints	Cooper	£91	
W	1711/25	Kedgewin, Sturley	City of Bristol	Hooper	£6	died at sea
	1637/34	Keene, John	St. Stephen	--	£10	
W	1675/1	Keene, John	<St. Michael>	Anchor-smith	£616	a 7 ft. (210 cm.) roll
	1625/45	Keene, Nathan	St. Thomas	Pewterer	£5	
W	1684/32	Keene, Sarah	City of Bristol	Widow	£31	
	1663/35	Keech, Stephen	St. Stephen	--	£42	
W	1684/31	Keene, Thomas	City of Bristol	Sergeant-at-Mace	£32	
	1710/19	Keighley, John	City of Bristol	Mariner	£30	
W	1745/18	Keith, John	City of Bristol	Mariner	£12	
W	1742/33	Kelley, James	City of Bristol	Mariner	£7	

	Year ref.	Name	Parish or area	Occupation or status	Value	Notes
	1733/48	Kelley, John	City of Bristol	Mariner	£9	
W	1727/20	Kelly, Daniel	City of Bristol	Mariner	£3	
	1749/38	Kelly, Francis	City of Bristol	Mariner	—	
	1760/14	Kelly, Matthew	City of Bristol	Mariner	£12	
	1641/30	Kelly, Thomas	St. Augustine	Mariner	£4	
W	1748/45	Kelly, Thomas	City of Bristol	Mariner	£8	
	1732/38	Kelly, William	City of Bristol	Mariner	£5	
	1755/6	Kelson, James	City of Bristol	Cordwainer	£5	
W	1633/40	Kely, Anthony	All Saints	⟨Grocer⟩	£4,959	
	1635/55	Kely, Richard	St. Michael	Mariner	£2	
	1726/22	Kemmet, Charles	City of Bristol	Mariner	£6	
	1682/25	Kemp, John	St. Leonard	—	£181	
W	1702/14	Kendall, John	SS. Philip & Jacob	⟨Coal-driver⟩	£32	
	1668/35	Kenn, Christopher	St. James	—	£2	
	1667/44	Kenn, George	St. Michael	Smith	£2	
	1634/43	Kenne, Thomas	SS. Philip & Jacob	Glover	£4	
W	1730/32	Kenney, William	City of Bristol	Mariner	£6	
	1716/38	Kerby, George	City of Bristol	Tinman	£31	account only inv. 1716/38
	1717/34	Kerby, George	City of Bristol	Tin-plate worker	£36	
W	1742/34	Kerby, Philip	City of Bristol	Mariner	£6	
W	1731/53	Kerdiff, John	City of Bristol	Surgeon	£10	died at sea
W	1644/33	Kerswell, Alexander	St. Nicholas	Woollen-draper	£260	
	1758/17	Kerton, Daniel	City of Bristol	Mariner	£6	
	1715/27	Keting, David	City of Bristol	Mariner	£15	
W	1732/39	Kettleby, John	City of Bristol	Surgeon	£13	
W	1750/20	Kevish, William	City of Bristol	Mariner	£19	died at sea
	1611/51	Keynsam, John	(alias Kidwallider, which see)			
W	1661/48	Keynton, Edmond	(see Kineton)			
	1664/28	Keynton, Martha	(see Kineton)			
W	1751/9	Keys, Ann	City of Bristol	Widow	£14	

	Ref.	Name	Place	Occupation	Value	Notes
W	1611/46	Kibell, Joanne	Henbury (Stowick)	--	£3	
W	1611/50	Kible, Edward	Olveston	--	£20	
W	1620/58	Kible, Elizabeth	<Tockington> Olveston	Widow	£34	
W	1611/46	Kible, Joanne	(see Kibell)			
	1759/13	Kid, James	City of Bristol	Mariner	£11	
	1611/51	Kidwallider, John	--	--	£39	alias Keynsam
W	1692/24	Kight, Mary	(see Kite)			
W	1754/20	Kilvington, William	City of Bristol	Surgeon	£5	died at sea
	1681/45	Kimbar, John	City of Bristol	Coffee seller	£85	
	1683/30	Kimber, Ann	City of Bristol	Widow	£47	
W	1709/25	Kimble, John	(see Kimboll)			
W	1709/25	Kimboll, John	City of Bristol	Cordwainer	£6	
W	1661/48	Kineton, Edmond	Henbury	--	£352	
	1664/28	Kineton, Martha	Henbury	--	£124	
	1609/43	King, Arthur	Westbury-on-Trym (Shirehampton)	Vintner	£120	
	1673/17B	King, Anthony	Stapleton	Yeoman	£465	
	1681/43	King, Anthony	Stapleton	--	£270	
	1709/26	King, Edward	City of Bristol	Mariner	£10	
	1722/11	King, Elianor	Almondsbury	--	£4	
	1647/19	King, Henry	Westbury-on-Trym (Redland)	--	£34	
W	1681/44	King, Hester	Stapleton	Widow	£44	
	1719/25	King, James	City of Bristol	Mariner	£4	
W	1613/36	King, John	St. Thomas	Butcher	£48	alias Lovell
	1637/35	King, John	St. Mary, Redcliffe	Cooper	£35	
	1639/60	King, John	St. Mary, Redcliffe	--	£72	
W	1665/33	King, John	Stapleton	Yeoman	£97	
W	1701/17	King, Mary	St. Peter	Widow	£52	
	1683/31	King, Robert	City of Bristol (suburbs)	--	£2	
	1713/27	King, Samuel	City of Bristol	Mariner	£421	

Year ref.		Name	Parish or area	Occupation or status	Value	Notes
W	1736/18	King, Thomas	City of Bristol	Mariner	£7	
W	1747/21	King, Thomas	City of Bristol	Mariner	£5	
	1714/28	King, Walter	City of Bristol	Hot-presser	£36	
W	1672/31	King, William	St. Stephen	Tailor	£678	
	1690/23	King, William	City of Bristol	Turner	£4	
	1750/21	King, William	SS. Phillip & Jacob	Blacksmith	£10	
	1760/15	King, William	City of Bristol	Mariner	£13	
	1637/36	Kinge, Thomas	St. Mary, Redcliffe	Cooper	£36	2 other documents & see King 1637/35
	1729/23	Kingston, William	City of Bristol	Mariner	£9	
W	1732/40	Kingston, William	—	Surgeon	£9	died at sea
	1743/18	Kircum, William	City of Bristol	Mariner	£7	
W	1700/32	Kirke, Elizabeth	Westbury-on-Trym (Redland) (see Kircum)	Widow	£501	
	1743/18	Kirkeum, William	City of Bristol	Mariner	£14	
	1761/20	Kirkpatrick, Samuel	City of Bristol	Apothecary	£326	
W	1692/2	Kirwood, Richard	Westbury-on-Trym	Widow	£286	
	1671/23	Kiskins, Katherine	St. Nicholas	Mercer	£573	
W	1629/37	Kitchen, John	Christchurch	Single-woman	£462	
W	1672/30	Kitchen, Sarah	Alveston (Row Earthcott)	Widow	£22	
W	1692/24	Kite, Mary	City of Bristol	Mariner	£14	
	1738/13	Kittle, Henry	Stoke Gifford	Yeoman	£162	see Knapp 1700/8
W	1700/1	Knap, James	Stoke Gifford	Yeoman	£162	see Knap 1700/1
W	1700/8	Knapp, James	Stokes Gifford (Harry Stoke)			
W	1705/19	Knapp, John	Stoke Gifford (Harry Stoke)	Yeoman	£163	
W	1707/26	Knapp, Mary	Winterbourne	⟨Widow⟩	£97	
	1630/3	Knee, Thomas	—	--	£3	
	1611/52	Knight, Henry	—	--	£2	

W	Ref	Name	Parish/Place	Occupation	Value	Notes
	1702/15	Knight, James	City of Bristol	Cooper	£57	
W	1642/30B	Knight, Julian	St. Stephen	Widow	--	with wills
			(document in bad condition)			
W	1735/24	Knight, Martha	SS. Phillip & Jacob	Widow	£12	
	1702/16	Knight, Mary	City of Bristol	Widow	£133	
	1639/61	Knight, Richard	Temple	Vicar of Temple	£14	
W	1725/9	Knight, Thomas	Abbots Leigh	Yeoman	£19	
	1689/37	Knight, William	Alveston	--	£112	
W	1730/33	Knill, Robert	City of Bristol	Mariner	£5	
W	1720/22	Knowles, John	City of Bristol	Mariner	£14	
	1639/26	Kokye, Edward	(see Cockey)			
	1707/27	Kynaston, Richard	City of Bristol	Mariner	£18	
	1609/44	Kytchin, Susan	Temple	Widow (Shearman)	£35	
	1709/27	Lacy, William	--	<Mariner>	£14	
	1693/21	Ladwell, John	St. Peter	Butcher	£15	
	1693/22	Ladwell, William	--	--	£10	
	1618/38	Laine, John	(see Lane)			
W	1640/40	Lake, Alice	Henbury	--	£13	
	1743/19	Lamb, William	City of Bristol	Mariner	£11	
	1752/18	Lamphair, Thomas	<City of Bristol>	Mariner	£7	
	1662/30	Lancaster, Robert	<City of Bristol>	<Tailor>	£8	
	1617/28	Lanckston, Elinor	(see Langston)			
W	1710/20a	Landen, Walter	<St. Michael>	Maltman	£784	
W	1710/20b	Landen, Walter	(the account of Dorothy Landen, relict)		£20	
W	1733/49	Landers, Henry	City of Bristol	Mariner		
	1667/47	Landon, Lazarus	(see Langdon)			
W	1715/28	Landsdown, Anne	City of Bristol	Spinster	£6	
	1708/29	Landsdowne, Thomas	<St. Nicholas>	Barber-surgeon	£105	
	1683/34	Lane, Anne	City of Bristol	Widow	£210	
	1685/32	Lane, Anthony	St. Mary, Redcliffe	Mariner	£66	
W	1613/37	Lane, George	<St. Michael>	Merchant	£833	
	1618/38	Lane, John	SS. Phillip & Jacob	--	£8	also Laine

Year ref.	Name	Parish or area	Occupation or status	Value	Notes
W 1667/45	Lane, John	St. Stephen	Mariner	£798	
W 1708/28	Lane, John	Mangotsfield	Yeoman	£197	
1675/42	Lane, Michael	St. Thomas	Surgeon	£20	
1625/46	Lane, Phillipp	(see Leane)			
W 1618/40	Lanfier, Richard	St. Peter (The Castle)	Carpenter	£107	also Langfer
1709/28	Lang, Henry	City of Bristol	Serge-weaver	£5	
W 1710/20a	Langden, Walter	(see Landen)	Mariner	£14	
1757/9	Langdon, George	City of Bristol	Seaman	£2	
1667/47	Langdon, Lazarus	St. Stephen	Mason	£52	
1666/30	Langdon, William	St. James			
W 1618/40	Langfer, Richard	(see Lanfier)			
1691/32	Langford, Barbara	--	Widow	£20	
W 1759/14	Langford, George	City of Bristol	Mariner	£12	
1709/29	Langford, John	City of Bristol	Currier	£119	
W 1757/10	Langford, Joseph	<SS. Philip & Jacob>	Mariner	£7	
1755/7	Langford, Margit	Christchurch	--	£42	
W 1732/41	Langford, Thomas	City of Bristol	Mariner	£6	
W 1701/18	Langforde, Henry	Temple	--	£3	
W 1669/47	Langley, Edward	St. John	Merchant	£2,083	
1705/20	Langley, Hester	--	--	£18	
W 1620/59	Langley, John	St. John	Vintner	£70	
1624/42	Langlie, Thomas	St. John	Scrivener	£3	
W 1617/28	Langston, Elinor	Henbury (Aust)	Widow	£36	
1609/47	Langston, Joan	Henbury	Single-woman	£49	alias Nicholas
1613/38	Langston, John	Henbury (Aust)	--	£44	
1609/45	Langton, Richard	City of Bristol	Gent.	£7	
1676/28	Lanman, John	St. Thomas	Inn-holder	£113	1676/29 is a 2nd copy
1678/77	Lanman, John	St. Thomas	--	£113	account only
1715/28	Lansdown, Anne	(see Landsdown)			
1713/28	Lanston, William	City of Bristol	Mariner	£2	

W	Reference	Name	Parish	Occupation	Value
W	1677/32	Lardge, Christopher	City of Bristol	Gent.	£205
W	1637/37	Lardge, John	(see Large)		
W	1625/47	Lardge, St. John	St. Mark	Gent.	£12
W	1636/34	Lardge, Susan	St. Mark	Widow	£881
	1618/41	Large, Anne	St. Peter	Servant	£14
W	1609/46	Large, John	Westbury-on-Trym	<Yeoman>	£1,024
	1683/35	Large, William	Stoke Gifford	--	£64
	1750/22	Larkcombe, Thomas	Temple	Mariner	£9
W	1747/22	Larkin, Michael	<St. Michael>	Mariner	£8
	1717/35	Larny, John	City of Bristol	Mariner	£18
W	1637/38	Lascells, Henry	Barton Regis	Brickmaker	£42
	1625/48	Latchet, George	--	Clockmaker	£2
	1617/29	Lathburie, Robert	Stapleton	--	£38
	1754/21A	Lathbury, Leonard	Stapleton	--	£34
W	1738/14	Lathey, Richard	City of Bristol	Mariner	£6
W	1627/15	Laughton, Benjamin	City of Bristol	Mariner	£2
	1741/26	Lavasher, William	Christchurch	Musicianer	£13
	1618/39	Lavender, Boley	--	<Mariner>	£15
	1620/49	Law, William	Westbury-on-Trym	--	£2
	1679/39	Lawes, Alexander	St. Mary-le-Port	--	£5
	1633/41	Lawfell, John	St. Stephen	Shipwright	£4
W	1692/25	Lawfill, Anne	St. Stephen	<Widow>	£14
W	1669/48	Lawford, Christian	Stoke Gifford	Widow	£9
W	1680/34	Lawford, Dorothy	Stoke Gifford	Widow	£31
W	1681/48	Lawford, Rebekah	Stoke Gifford	Single-woman	£87
	1686/31	Lawford, Richard	Stoke Gifford	Yeoman	£99
W	1641/31	Lawford, Richard	Almondsbury	--	£66
W	1677/30	Lawford, Robert	Stoke Gifford	Yeoman	£929
W	1690/24	Lawford, Thomas	Stoke Gifford	Yeoman	£803
		Lawford, Thomas	(Little Stoke)		
W	1731/54	Lawford, William	City of Bristol	Yeoman	£345
	1681/47	Lawforde, Robert	St. Augustine	Mariner	£7
				Mercer	£8

	Year ref.	Name	Parish or area	Occupation or status	Value	Notes
	1747/23a	Lawley, Edward	SS. Philip & Jacob	Glassman	£11	see also 23b
	1747/23b	Lawley, Edward	SS. Philip & Jacob	Glass-maker	£9	extra to No. 23a
	1750/23a	Lawrance, John	City of Bristol	Mariner	£4	
	1750/23b	Lawrance, John	(sworn statement of debt of £3.16.10 owing from his estate)			
	1672/33	Lawrence, Edmond	City of Bristol	--	£27	
W	1752/19	Lawrence, Elizabeth	City of Bristol	Widow	£420	
	1696/18	Lawrence, Griffen			£149	
	1709/30	Lawrence, Henry	Almondsbury	Tailor	£4	
	1691/34	Lawrence, John	City of Bristol	Mariner	£6	
W	1712/32	Lawrence, John	City of Bristol	Mariner	£4	
W	1748/46	Lawrence, Nathaniel	City of Bristol	Mariner	£15	
	1672/36	Lawrence, Priscilla	City of Bristol	Widow	£5	
W	1729/24	Lawrence, Rowland	City of Bristol	Mariner	£10	
W	1714/29	Lawrence, William	Mangotsfield (Downend)	⟨Tanner⟩	£79	
	1718/21	Lawrence, William	Mangotsfield	Tanner	£3	
W	1732/42	Lawrence, William	City of Bristol	Mariner	£16	
	1752/20	Lawrence, William	City of Bristol	Mariner	£3	
W	1625/49	Lawton, William	Knolle, Co. Warwick ⟨Hampton-in-Arden⟩	Husbandman ⟨Yeoman⟩	£49	
W	1736/19	Leahy, James	City of Bristol	Mariner	£10	
W	1736/19	Leaky, James	(see Leahy)			
	1625/46	Leane, Phillipp	Christchurch	Pewterer	£14	also 2nd copy
W	1612/9	Leaper, John	(see Lepar)			
	1634/44	Leaper, Ann	Christchurch	Widow	£41	eleven documents
	1708/30	Leatch, John	City of Bristol	--	£56	
	1628/42	Leavasher, Thomas	--	--	£10	
	1747/24	Lee, Andrew	City of Bristol	Mariner	£16	
W	1766/6	Lee, James	City of Bristol	Mariner	£6	with wills
	1715/29	Lee, John	City of Bristol	Mariner	£18	
	1618/42	Leechgood, William	--	--	£1	

W	Ref	Name	Place	Status	Value	Notes
W	1687/41	Leeds, Clement	City of Bristol	Parchment-maker	£29	
	1624/43	Leeke, Alice	St. Thomas	Widow	£9	
W	1662/29	Leeke, Mary	St. Peter	<Spinster>	£12	
W	1640/41	Leeke, Thomas	St. John	Merchant	£192	
W	1730/34	Leen, Margaret	(see Leen, Samuel) (will of Margaret Leen, widow)			
W	1730/34	Leen, Samuel & Margaret	Olveston	--	£123	inv. & account
W	1752/CP	Leg, Grace	Henbury	Widow	£24	
	1643/54	Legg, Edward	Stapleton	Tailor	£29	
W	1686/32	Legg, Edward	Henbury (Kingsweston)	--	£114	
	1752/21	Legg, Grace	Henbury	Widow	£15	
	1665/34	Legg, Henry	Mangotsfield	Husbandman	£66	
	1721/17	Legg, Joan	<Temple>	Spinster	£15	
W	1668/36	Legg, John	Winterbourne	--	£28	
W	1681/46	Legg, Katherine	Almondsbury	Spinster	£28	
	1750/24	Legg, Martha	City of Bristol	--	£15	
	1718/22a	Legg, Richard	City of Bristol	Keeper of the gaol of Newgate	£12	dated 1713 (the account of Hannah Legg, widow.)
	1718/22b	Legg, Richard	<Winterbourne; Frenchay>	--	£43	
	1763/20	Legg, Richard	Almondsbury	--	£6	
W	1636/35	Legg, Robert	Henbury (King Road)	--	£87	
W	1708/32	Legg, Sarah	Henbury	Widow	£176	
	1726/23	Legg, Thomas	Henbury (King Road)	Yeoman	£160	
W	1708/31	Legg, William	Henbury	Yeoman	£171	
W	1660/8	Leggatt, Elizabeth	St. Thomas	Widow	£59	
	1750/25	Leggatt, John	City of Bristol	Victualler	£133	
W	1611/53	Legge, John	Henbury (Lawrence Weston)	--	£3	
W	1677/31	Legge, Katherine	Almondsbury	Widow	£19	
	1635/56	Legge, William	Henbury	--	£85	

Year ref.	Name	Parish or area	Occupation or status	Value	Notes
W 1734/25	Lennard, Peter	City of Bristol	Mariner	£1	
W 1612/9	Lepar, John	Christchurch	Baker	£121	
W 1713/29	Leslie, John	City of Bristol	Mariner	£8	
1734/26	Leslie, Thomas	City of Bristol	Mariner	£9	
1735/25	Letcher, James	City of Bristol	Mariner	£14	
W 1694/35	Levens, Thomas	Barton Regis	Coal-driver	£52	
1709/31	Levins, Richard	Barton Regis	Yeoman	£20	
W 1761/21	Lewden, John	City of Bristol	Mariner	£5	compare 1761/22
1761/22	Lewden, John	City of Bristol	Mariner	£14	alias Roe
1732/43	Lewellyn, John	Mangotsfield	Coal-miner	£5	
1680/33	Lewellin, Thomas	City of Bristol	Mariner	£5	
W 1665/35	Lewes, John	(see Lewis)			
1646/27	Lewes, Richard	--	--	£6	
1642/31	Lewes, Thomas	St. James	--	£5	
W 1639/62	Lewes, Thomas	Filton	--	£10	
W 1623/38	Lewes, William	St. Stephen	Shoemaker	£5	
W 1734/27	Lewis, Adam	City of Bristol	--	£19	
1675/41	Lewis, Ann	St. John	Widow	£10	
W 1757/11	Lewis, David	City of Bristol	Mariner	--	
1758/18	Lewis, David	City of Bristol	Mariner	£4	
1669/46	Lewis, Edmund	St. Nicholas	Cooper	£77	
1663/38	Lewis, Edward (jnr)	St. John	Haulier	£17	
1667/46	Lewis, Edward	St. John	Haulier	£142	
1757/12	Lewis, Edward	City of Bristol	Mariner	£19	
W 1701/19	Lewis, Elizabeth	(see Lowes)			
1704/17	Lewis, George	City of Bristol	Mariner	£64	
W 1734/28	Lewis, Henry	City of Bristol	Mariner	£8	
1673/20	Lewis, Hugh	St. Thomas	--	£77	
1686/29	Lewis, James	City of Bristol	Turner	£11	
W 1679/41	Lewis, Joan	St. Thomas	Widow	£56	
W 1665/35	Lewis, John	St. James	Brewer	£291	

W	Reference	Name	Place	Occupation	Value
	1673/21	Lewis, John	St. Werburgh	Mariner	£6
w	1679/40	Lewis, John	City of Bristol	Cooper	£122
	1709/32	Lewis, John	City of Bristol	Mariner	£9
	1754/21B	Lewis, John	City of Bristol	Cordwainer	£11
w	1728/23	Lewis, Joseph	City of Bristol	Mariner	£9
	1634/45	Lewis, Katherine	St. Leonard	—	£13
	1663/39	Lewis Matthew	Temple	Shearman	£7
w	1717/36	Lewis Morris	City of Bristol	Barber	£11
w	1679/42	Lewis, Oreana	City of Bristol	Widow	£62
w	1757/13	Lewis, Philip	City of Bristol	Mariner	£18
	1700/9	Lewis, Philip	—	—	£11
w	1774/CP	Lewis, Reece	City of Bristol	Fishmonger	£423
	1682/26	Lewis, Richard	Westbury-on-Trym (Shirehampton)		
w	1746/25	Lewis, Richard	City of Bristol	—	£53
w	1748/47	Lewis, Richard	City of Bristol	Mariner	£17
w	1673/18	Lewis, Sarah	Temple	Mariner	£5
	1624/44	Lewis, Thomas	—	Widow	£7
w	1702/17	Lewis, Thomas	St. Mary-le-Port	—	£17
w	1730/35	Lewis, Thomas	City of Bristol	Butcher	£12
	1735/26	Lewis, Thomas	City of Bristol	Mariner	£3
w	1696/19	Lewis, Walter	St. James	Mariner	£8
w	1697/26	Lewis, William	Almondsbury	Soap-boiler	£44
	1706/24	Lewis, William	—	Shoemaker	£82
w	1739/11	Lewis, William	City of Bristol	Victualler	£4
	1744/8	Lewis, William	City of Bristol	Mariner	£94
w	1623/38	Lews, William	(see Lewes)	Mariner	£7
	1749/39	Liberton, Thomas	City of Bristol (1749/39 is written on the back of a marriage allegation)	Mariner	£5
	1663/36	Liddell, John	St. Werburgh	—	—
	1719/26	Light, Abraham	—	—	£13
	1735/27	Light, John	City of Bristol	Mariner	£15
	1634/46	Light, Robert	St. James	Saltpetre-man	£1

W	Year ref.	Name	Parish or area	Occupation or status	Value	Notes
	1749/40	Lightbourne, Robert	--	Mariner	£6	
W	1735/28	Lillick, Richard	City of Bristol (will gives: of Bytheford, Devon)	Mariner	£4	
	1730/36	Limrick, William	City of Bristol	Mariner	£7	
	1664/30	Linard, Isaac	Winterbourne	--	£78	
	1735/29	Linch, Hugh	City of Bristol	Mariner	£11	
	1613/39	Linch, James	Henbury	--	£11	
W	1693/20	Linch, William	Winterbourne (Hambrook)	--	£16	
	1723/15	Line, William	Abbots Leigh		£10	
	1672/34	Ling, Matthew	St. Nicholas	Cooper	£37	
W	1629/38	Linge, John	St. Stephen	Cooper	£128	
	1698/26	Linging, Phillip	St. Thomas	--	£5	
W	1728/24	Link, Thomas	Almondsbury (Over) <Henbury> (Aust)	Yeoman	£29	
W	1623/39	Linke, Richard	City of Bristol	Tailor	£19	
	1741/30	Linn, Patrick	(see Linard)	Shipwright	£6	died at sea
	1664/30	Linnett, Isaac	Mangotsfield	Yeoman	£4	
	1730/37	Lipput, Aaron	Stapleton	Widow	£24	
W	1705/21	Lisiman, Sarah	City of Bristol	Saddler	£490	
W	1681/33	Little, Francis	St. Michael	--	£2	
	1663/40	Little, Robert	--	Saddler	£45	
	1658/33	Little, Thomas	City of Bristol	Mariner	£16	
	1741/27	Little, William	City of Bristol	Sail-maker	£3	died at sea
W	1718/23	Littlefaire, Thomas	City of Bristol	Mariner	£5	
	1753/20	Littleton, John	St. Mary, Redcliffe	<Widow>	£4	
W	1639/63	Lloyd, Edith	(see Floud)	Tidesman	£5	
	1682/30	Lloyd, Elizabeth	City of Bristol	Mariner	£16	
W	1740/41	Lloyd, James	City of Bristol	--	£290	inv. & account
W	1745/19	Lloyd, John	City of Bristol			
	1748/CP	Lloyd, Sarah	Mangotsfield (Downend)			

	Ref	Name	Place	Occupation	Value	Note
	1672/35	Lloyd, Thomas	City of Bristol	Haberdasher	£496	
	1709/34	Lloyd, Vincent	City of Bristol	Mariner	£2	
W	1624/46	Lloyde, Richard	Temple	Clothworker	£1,563	
W	1646/28	Lloyde, William	St. Thomas	Cardmaker	£30	
	1709/33	Llewellin, George	Mangotsfield	Horse-driver	£10	
W	1711/26	Llewellin, John (snr)	Mangotsfield	Coal-miner	£8	died at sea
	1703/12	Llewellin, Sarah	Mangotsfield	Wife	£19	
	1650/7	Llewellin, Simon	(see Lluellin)			
W	1678/39	Llewellin, William	Mangotsfield	Yeoman	£261	
	1650/7	Lluellin, Simon	St. Augustine	--	£14	
W	1639/64	Lock, Henry	St. Nicholas	Cook	£9	
	1739/12	Lock, Samuel	City of Bristol	Shipwright	£12	
	1740/37	Lockett, Richard	City of Bristol	Mariner	£16	
	1709/35	Lockier, Moses	City of Bristol	Mariner	£18	
W	1663/41	Lockston, Mary	(see Loxstone)			
W	1661/51	Lockstone, Edmond	Castle Precincts	Cordwainer	£123	
	1628/43	Lockstone, Thomas	Henbury	--	£19	
	1740/38	Loggin, Robert	City of Bristol	Mariner	£6	
	1740/39	Lombard, James	City of Bristol	Mariner	£9	
	1741/28	London, John	City of Bristol	Mariner	£9	
	1625/52	London, Mathew	Henbury	Baker	£16	
W	1740/40	Lone, Thomas	City of Bristol	Mariner	£8	
	1639/65	Long, Edward	Olveston	--	£454	
	1674/25	Long, Edward	Stapleton	Blacksmith	£7	
W	1728/25	Long, Edward	Henbury <Redwick>	Yeoman	£440	
W	1691/33	Long, Elizabeth	<City of Bristol>	Widow	£12	
	1636/36	Long, Henry	St. Mary-le-Port	<Blacksmith>	£59	
	1715/30	Long, Honour	Temple	Widow	£90	
	1728/26	Long, Jacob	City of Bristol	House-carpenter	£558	
W	1684/33	Long, James	Henbury	Yeoman	£199	
	1759/15	Long, James	City of Bristol	Mariner	£6	
W	1639/66	Long, John	Olveston	<Husbandman>	£106	
W	1662/32	Long, John	Winterbourne	Blacksmith	£21	

	Year ref.	Name	Parish or area	Occupation or status	Value	Notes
	1675/43	Long, John	Almondsbury (Compton)	Husbandman	£77	
	1686/27	Long, John	Olveston ('The Home')	Yeoman	£182	
	1687/42	Long, John	Henbury (Redwick)	--	£110	
	1730/38	Long, John	St. James	Surgeon	£51	
	1737/22	Long, John	City of Bristol	Mariner ⟨Hooper⟩	£5	
W	1686/26	Long, Margaret	Olveston	Widow	£161	compare 1686/27 above
W	1704/18	Long, Matthew	City of Bristol	Cooper	£54	
W	1617/30	Long, Michael	Almondsbury	--	£8	
W	1637/33	Long, Richard	St. Nicholas ⟨Christchurch in will⟩	--	£12	
	1688/30	Long, Richard	City of Bristol	--	£3	
W	1706/25	Long, Richard	City of Bristol	Mariner	£15	
W	1670/29	Long, Robert	Almondsbury (Compton)	Husbandman	£86	
	1675/45	Long, Robert	Stapleton	--	£5	
	1661/49	Long, Roger	Stapleton	Collier	£49	
	1681/49	Long, Roger	City of Bristol	Woollen-draper	£149	
W	1723/16	Longden, George	St. Mary, Redcliffe	Schoolmaster	£20	
W	1634/47	Longden, Thomas	St. Stephen	⟨Turner⟩	£65	
	1689/38	Longdon, Edward	St. Nicholas	Meal-man	£29	
	1674/24	Longdon, William	Stapleton	--	£31	
	1625/50	Longe, Mathew	--	Sailor	£7	
	1640/7	Longe, Maurice	Olveston	--	£26	
	1640/42	Looker, Thomas	Temple	Weaver	£6	
	1635/57	Lord, Richard	Castle Precinct	--	£11	
W	1634/48	Lord, Robert	SS. Phillip & Jacob	⟨Inn-holder⟩	£154	
	1683/32	Lord, Robert	--	--	£40	
	1742/CP	Lorring, John	Littleton-on-Severn	--	£170	
W	1750/26	Loscom, Benjamin	SS. Phillip & Jacob	Horse-driver	£19	
	1741/29	Loscombe, Thomas	SS. Phillip & Jacob	Coal-driver	£14	

Ref.	W	Name	Place	Occupation	Value	Notes
1617/31		Loue, John	St. Thomas	Merchant	£297	
1694/36		Loup, William	City of Bristol	Mariner	£15	
1662/31		Love, Ann	St. Stephen	Widow	£180	
1617/31		Love, John	(see Loue)			
1733/50	w	Lovejoy, Elizabeth	City of Bristol	Widow	£6	
1623/40		Lovelace, William	Clifton	--	£4	
1713/30		Lovell, Abraham	Mangotsfield	Coal-miner	£18	
1613/36	w	Lovell, John	Olveston <Pilning> (alias King, which see)	Husbandman	£239	
1620/60	w	Lovell, John	City of Bristol	Cordwainer	£20	
1709/36	w	Lovell, Thomas	Henbury (Charlton)	Yeoman	£174	
1698/27		Lovering, William	Henbury (Charlton)	Yeoman	£111	
1721/18	w	Lovering, William	Henbury (Charlton)	Yeoman	£111	
1644/34	w	Loveringe, James	Henbury (Charlton)	Yeoman	£105	
1643/55	w	Loveringe, Margaret	Henbury (Charlton)	Spinster	£250	
1629/39	w	Loveringe, Thomas	Henbury (Charlton)	Yeoman	£17	
1704/19		Lovewell, William	--	Tanner	£178	
1641/32		Lovringe, Margaret	Henbury (Charlton)	Widow	£6	
1732/44		Low, Anselm	City of Bristol	Mariner	£107	
1723/17		Lowden, William	City of Bristol	--	£84	
1633/42	w	Lowe, Ann	St. Stephen	Widow	£5	
1719/27	w	Lowe, Mary	Clifton	Widow	£8	
1756/10	w	Lowe, Thomas	City of Bristol	Weaver	—	soldier in will
1664/29		Lowering, Edward	St. Peter	Pewterer	£427	
1668/37	w	Lowering, Thomas (jnr)	Henbury <Charlton>	--	£58	
1701/19	w	Lowes, Elizabeth	Almondsbury	Widow	£10	
1751/10	w	Lowes, Joseph	City of Bristol	Mariner	£51	
1663/37		Lowle, John	Olveston	--	£55	
1686/30		Lownes, Elizabeth	SS. Philip & Jacob	Widow	£34	
1683/33	w	Lownes, John	SS. Philip & Jacob	Inn-keeper	£4	
1750/27		Lowns, Matthew	City of Bristol	Mariner	£162	
1663/41	w	Loxstone, Mary	St. Peter	Widow	£112	
1719/28		Lucas, George	Barton Regis	Inn-holder	£36	
1623/41		Lucas, Giles	St. Leonard	--		

	Year ref.	Name	Parish or area	Occupation or status	Value	Notes
W	1750/28	Lucas, John	City of Bristol	Mariner	£3	
	1644/35	Lucas, Owen	St. Thomas	--	£14	
W	1678/38	Luckock, Richard	City of Bristol	Cook	£26	
	1629/40	Luckott, Alice	St. Nicholas	Widow	£15	
W	1673/19	Ludbye, Elizabeth	Winterbourne	Widow	£51	
W	1722/12	Luffe, Jeremiah	City of Bristol	⟨Merchant⟩	£582	
	1666/29	Lugg, Edward	St. James	⟨Mariner⟩	£42	
W	1758/19	Lugg, Jane	City of Bristol	Widow	£2	
	1675/44	Lugg, Susanna	Elberton	Widow	£53	
	1693/19	Lugg, Thomas	--	--	£148	
	1705/22	Lugg, Thomas	City of Bristol	--	£57	
W	1749/41	Luggar, James	City of Bristol	Mariner	£10	
	1643/56	Lugge, James	Elberton	Butcher	£26	
			(see Lumsdon)			
W	1730/39	Lumsden, David	City of Bristol	Mariner	£12	
W	1730/39	Lumsdon, David	⟨City of Bristol⟩	⟨Wool-comber⟩	£183	
W	1691/35	Lux, Robert	--	--	£18	
	1672/32	Lux, Thomas				
	1742/35	Luxmore, Thomas	City of Bristol	Mariner	£3	
W	1763/6	Luxton, John	City of Bristol	Mariner	£9	
	1723/18	Lyddall, William	City of Bristol	Tidesman	£5	
	1628/44	Lyes, Edmond	Filton	Blacksmith	£40	
W	1678/37	Lyes, John (snr)	Barton Regis	⟨Victualler⟩	£41	
	1743/20	Lyell, Robert	City of Bristol	Mariner	£11	
	1678/37	Lyes, Thomas	(see Lyes, John)			
W	1648/12	Lymell, Elizabeth	Christchurch	Widow ⟨Soapmaker⟩	£122	
W	1644/36	Lymell, William	Christchurch	Soapmaker	£424	
W	1762/5	Lynch, Daniel	City of Bristol	Mariner	£7	
W	1686/28	Lynch, Jonathan	Olveston (Pilning)	Yeoman	£284	

W	Ref	Name	Place	Occupation	Value	Notes
	1758/4B	Lynch, Martin	City of Bristol	Mariner	£8	(this inventory, dated 1756, is on the back of that of John Brown, No. 1758/4A, which see.)
W	1613/40	Lynch, William	Henbury	Husbandman	£64	
W	1625/51	Lynche, George	Henbury	--	£50	
	1719/29	Lyncy, Archibald	City of Bristol	Mariner	£8	
	1624/45	Lyne, John	Almondsbury (Rednend)	Yeoman	£302	
W	1723/15	Lyne, William	(see Line)			
	1620/61	Lynge, John	St. Stephen	Cooper	£145	
	1741/30	Lynn, Patrick	(see Linn)			
W	1732/45	Lyse, Nathan	SS. Philip & Jacob	Butcher	£8	
W	1705/21	Lyssime, Sarah	(see Lisiman)			
W	1707/28	Lytten, Sarah	City of Bristol	Widow	£565	
	1685/62	Mabson, Henry	Olveston (Tockington)	--	£256	
W	1640/43	Mabson, Thomas	Henbury	--	£50	
	1754/22A	Mc Adam, Clements	City of Bristol	Mariner	£5	
W	1749/45	Mc Allister, John	<City of Bristol>	Mariner	£16	
W	1711/27	Macarty, Mary	(see Mecarte)			
W	1748/49	Mc Cahie, John	City of Bristol	Mariner	£15	
	1741/31	Mc Carty, Peter	City of Bristol	Mariner	£13	
	1726/24	Maccoy, Michael	City of Bristol	Mariner	£11	
W	1750/30	Mc Coy, James	City of Bristol	Mariner	£5	died at sea
	1760/20	Mc Curdy, Robert	City of Bristol	Shipwright	£14	
	1760/21	Mc Daniel, James	City of Bristol	Mariner	£8	
	1738/15	Mc Daniel, John	City of Bristol	Mariner	£9	
	1743/24A	Mc Donnell, John	City of Bristol	Mariner	£12	
	1750/31	Mc Dormitt, James	City of Bristol	Mariner	£5	
	1733/51	Mc Gregor, Robert	City of Bristol	Mariner	£11	
	1639/67	Machin, Henry	Badgworth, Glos.	Gent.	£381	
W	1618/43	Machin, James	Olveston	--	£33	
	1609/50	Machin, Joan	--	--	£10	

	Year ref.	Name	Parish or area	Occupation or status	Value	Notes
W	1676/30	Maching, William	(see Meachem)			
	1713/31	Mackbride, Daniel	City of Bristol	Mariner	£18	
	1713/32	Mackdaniel, Alexander	City of Bristol	Cordwainer	£18	
W	1731/55	Mackdannel, Robert	City of Bristol	Mariner	£3	
W	1725/10	Mackfaden, John	\<City of Bristol\>	\<Mariner\>	£6	(£6 – £8)
W	1747/25	Macklain, John	City of Bristol	Mariner	£12	
	1760/22	Mc Knight, Robert	City of Bristol	Mariner	£10	
	1733/52	Mc Laughlin, Neel	City of Bristol	Mariner	£10	
W	1748/50	Mc Master, Patrick	City of Bristol	Mariner	£10	
	1749/46	Mc Millian, Daniel	City of Bristol	Mariner	£7	
	1662/33	Maddassone, William	St. Nicholas	--	--	
W	1757/14	Maddley, Joseph	City of Bristol	Mariner	£17	
	1667/49	Maddocks, John	St. Leonard	Shipwright	£6	
W	1749/42	Maddocks, Thomas	Henbury	Mason	£10	

(1749/42 is written on back of a certificate of excommunication.)

	Year ref.	Name	Parish or area	Occupation or status	Value	Notes
W	1663/42	Maddockes, Joan	Westbury-on-Trym	Widow	£7	
	1670/32	Maddox, John	SS. Philip & Jacob	--	£21	
W	1706/26	Maddox, Thomas	St. James	Rough-pavier	£15	
	1740/42	Madgitt, Robert	City of Bristol	Mariner	£7	
W	1760/16	Madley, Joseph	City of Bristol	Mariner	£8	
	1764/CP	Maggs, John	\<St. Nicholas\>	Butcher	£83	inv. & account
	1695/26	Maggs, Samuel	Winterbourne	--	£29	
W	1734/29	Magnuss, William	City of Bristol	Mariner	£12	
	1711/28	Magraft, John	Barton Regis	Mariner	£10	
	1692/28	Magrath, James	Clifton	Planter	£54	
W	1743/21	Magree, James	City of Bristol	Mariner	£6	
W	1748/48	Maguire, Edward	City of Bristol	Mariner	£14	
	1690/28	Mahame, Roger	--	--	£16	
	1721/19	Mahany, Timothy	City of Bristol	Surgeon	£8	
W	1758/20	Mahoney, Michael	City of Bristol	Mariner	£6	died at sea
	1739/13	Mahony, Bartholomew	City of Bristol	Mariner	£4	

	Reference	Name	Place	Occupation	Value	Notes
W	1727/21	Mahony, Florence	City of Bristol	Surgeon	£19	died at sea
W	1687/44	Maid, Edward	City of Bristol	Haberdasher	£24	
	1628/48	Maiden, John	St. Peter	--	£2	died at sea
W	1755/8	Malcombe, William	SS. Philip & Jacob	Hooper	£14	
W	1755/8	Malcone, William	(see Malcombe)			
W	1641/33	Mallard, Joan	(see Mallet)			
W	1641/33	Mallet, Joan	Abbots Leigh	⟨Widow⟩	£9	
W	1729/25	Malowney, James	City of Bristol	Mariner	£3	
W	1735/31	Man, Mortickeo	(alias Oman, Mordecai, which see)			
	1758/21	Manders, Francis	City of Bristol	Mariner	£12	
	1708/33	Manley, William	(see Manly)			
	1739/14	Manly, James	SS. Philip & Jacob	Mason	£18	
	1708/33	Manly, William	SS. Philip & Jacob	Mason	£10	
	1743/22	Mann, Anne	City of Bristol	Widow	£6	
	1725/11	Mann, Elizabeth	City of Bristol	Widow	£20	
W	1714/30	Mann, John	⟨City of Bristol⟩	⟨Cork-cutter⟩	£304	
	1702/18	Manning, William	Bedminster	Clerk	£135	
			(Vicar of Bedminster, including St. Thomas & St. Mary, Redcliffe.)			
	1736/21	Mansell, John	City of Bristol	Haulier	£841	
	1666/32	Mansell, Thomas	Almondsbury	Yeoman	£129	
	1702/19	Manship, Edward	St. James	Mariner	£3	
	1760/17	Manuel, Charles	City of Bristol	Mariner	£7	
W	1750/29	Mapham, Edward	City of Bristol	Mariner	£4	
	1719/30	Mapson, John	Olveston (Tockington)	--	£239	
	1685/62	Mapson, Henry	(see Mabson)			
	1635/59	Marchant, John	Temple	Weaver	£24	
W	1749/43	Marcy, John	City of Bristol	Mariner	£10	
W	1620/63	Maricke, Agnes	Olveston	Widow	£9	
	1642/32	Markan, Leonard	St. Stephen	--	£51	
	1642/32	Markon, Leonard	(see Markan)			
W	1766/7	Marks, George	City of Bristol	Mariner	£5	with wills
W	1684/35	Marks, John	SS. Philip & Jacob	--	£1	

Year ref.	Name	Parish or area	Occupation or status	Value	Notes
1747/26	Marks, Joseph	City of Bristol	--	£49	inv. & account
1731/56	Marley, George	City of Bristol	Mariner	£6	
W 1732/46	Marlin, John	City of Bristol	Mariner	£10	
W 1634/49	Marlowe, Robert	City of Bristol	Gent.	£64	also 2nd copy and 2 other documents
1662/34	Marmaduke, John	St. Peter	Inn-holder	£32	
W 1652/1	Marshall, Lawrence	Mangotsfield	--	£88	
1754/22B	Marshall, Leonard	City of Bristol	Mariner	£7	
1609/48	Marshall, Thomas	Winterbourne	--	£40	
1660/11	Marshall, William	St. Stephen	Mariner	£13	
1623/42	Marshe, Nicholas	SS. Philip & Jacob	Mariner	£25	
1697/27	Marshell, Abraham	--	--	£6	
1643/57	Marston, Henry	St. Stephen	Parish Clerk	£32	
W 1624/47	Marten, John	Elberton	<Husbandman>	£90	
1618/44	Marten, Thomas	(see Martone)			
W 1651/4	Martenn, George	St. Thomas	Soapmaker	£15	
1666/34	Martimore, Johane	(see Mortimore)			
1709/37	Martin, Catherine	--	--	£8	
1731/57	Martin, Edward	City of Bristol	Mariner	£2	
W 1651/4	Martin, George	(see Martenn)			
W 1683/38	Martin, Henry	City of Bristol	Gent.	£2	
W 1613/41	Martin, Joan	Almondsbury <Gaunts Earthcott>	Widow	£61	
1679/44	Martin, John	St. Mary, Redcliffe	Sugar-baker	£20	
1708/34	Martin, John	City of Bristol	Mariner	£15	
1713/33	Martin, Roger	City of Bristol	Mariner	£7	
1730/40	Martin, Samuel	City of Bristol	Mariner	£5	
1692/26	Martin, Thomas	--	--	£10	
1720/23	Martin, William	City of Bristol	Cooper	£12	
1688/32	Martin, William	Henbury	Husbandman	£180	
W 1633/43	Martin, William	St. Nicholas	Joiner	£22	died at sea

Ref	W	Name	Place	Occupation	Value	Notes
1618/44		Martone, Thomas	Olveston	--	£5	
1665/37		Martyn, Roger	City of Bristol	Gent.	£18	
1609/49	W	Mascall, Richard	St. Peter	Butcher	£23	
1634/50	W	Mascall, Thomas	St. Stephen	Shipwright	£207	
1666/35		Mascall, William	Abbots Leigh	--	£716	
1678/40		Masey, Richard	City of Bristol	Soap-boiler	£18	
1724/11		Mashman, John	City of Bristol	Mariner	£8	
1690/25	W	Maskall, Joan	<Abotts Leigh>	<Widow>	£114	
1625/53		Maskall, Richard	St. Mary-le-Port	<Butcher>	£4	
1694/38	W	Maskell, Hugh	Westbury-on-Trym	--	£223	
1728/27		Mason, Edward	City of Bristol	Mariner	£8	
1635/60		Mason, John	St. Stephen	--	£98	
1650/8		Mason, John	St. James	Clerk	£84	
1687/43		Mason, John	City of Bristol	Blacksmith	£19	
1760/18		Mason, John	City of Bristol	Mariner	£8	
1735/30	W	Mason, Michael	City of Bristol	Mariner	£4	
1760/19		Mason, Thomas	City of Bristol	Surgeon	£10	died at sea
1687/45		Mason, William	--	-	£35	
1680/36		Massenger, Robert	City of Bristol	Milliner	£12	
1685/36	W	Massey, John	<St. Augustine>	Clerk	£59	
1682/27		Masters, Mary	City of Bristol	Widow	£44	
1689/39	W	Masters, Thomas	City of Bristol	Mariner	£200	
1672/37		Maszon, Thomas	St. Stephen	--	£15	
1731/58		Mathers, John	City of Bristol	Shipwright	£8	
1728/28	W	Mathes, Stephen	City of Bristol	Mariner	£8	died at sea
1627/16	W	Mathew, Anthony	Westbury-on-Trym (Shirehampton)	<Pilot>	£71	
1743/23		Mathews, John	SS. Philip & Jacob	Oatmeal-maker	£15	
1640/44		Mathews, William	Westbury-on-Trym (Shirehampton)	Mariner	£27	
1734/30		Matson, William	City of Bristol	Mariner	£4	
1611/54	W	Matte, Alice	Henbury (Aust)	<Widow>	£89	
1635/61		Matthewes, John	City of Bristol	--	£2	

	Year ref.	Name	Parish or area	Occupation or status	Value	Notes
	1749/44	Matthews, Ann	SS. Philip & Jacob	--	£6	
	1712/33	Matthews, Anne	City of Bristol	Spinster	£10	
w	1715/31	Matthews, Henry	City of Bristol	Mariner	£15	
w	1764/CP	Matthews, Jane	(see Matthews, Thomas)			
	1708/35	Matthews, John	City of Bristol	Cooper	£17	died at sea
w	1661/52	Matthews, Katherine	Westbury-on-Trym <Shirehampton>	Widow	£58	
w	1753/21	Matthews, Philip	City of Bristol	Mariner <Cooper>	£9	
w	1764/CP	Matthews, Thomas and Jane	<St. Mary, Redcliffe> / Henbury	Shipwright / Widow	£43 / £96	inv & account will 1757
	1620/62	Mattock, Agnes				
	1686/33	Mattock, William	Stoke Gifford (Little Stoke)	Yeoman	£62	
	1609/51	Mattocke, William	Westbury-on-Trym (Stoke Bishop)	--	£76	
	1758/21	Maunders, Francis	(see Manders)			
	1617/32	Mavox, Robert	St. Nicholas	Mariner	£4	
	1746/26	May, Philip	City of Bristol		£12	
w	1732/47	May, Thomas	City of Bristol	Surgeon	£10	died at sea
w	1642/32B	May, William	Olveston	Tailor	£58	alias Cooke with wills
	1647/20	Maye, Katheryn	Olveston (Ingst)	--	£86	
	1723/19	Mayes, Edward	SS. Philip & Jacob	Saddler	£106	
	1635/58	Mayes, Thomas	St. James (alias Clements, which see)	--	£4	
	1637/12	Maynard, Arthur	Henbury (Lawrence Weston)			
	1706/27	Maynard, John	SS. Philip & Jacob	Yeoman	£246	
	1754/22C	Maynard, Joseph	--	--	£8	
	1609/52	Maynard, William	Henbury (Lawrence Weston)	--	£25	
w	1692/29	Maynard, William		<Tailor>	£106	alias Cooke

	Ref.	Name	Place	Occupation	Value	Notes
	1573/1	Mayo, Henry	City of Bristol	Sailor	£42	alias Patche
W	1700/10	Mayo, Hester	Castle Precincts	<Widow>	£9	
W	1679/43	Mayo, Joyce	St. Mary-le-Port	--	£19	
W	1676/30	Meachem, William	Almondsbury (Hempton)	Yeoman	£80	
	1760/19	Measun, Thomas	(see Mason)			
W	1711/27	Mecarte, Mary	<City of Bristol>	<Widow>	£29	
	1692/28	Mecraft, James	(see Magrath)			
	1640/46	Medellton, Thomas	St. Thomas	--	£12	
W	1732/48	Meekison, Patrick	City of Bristol	Mariner	£9	
	1617/33	Megar, William	St. Nicholas	--	£25	
	1685/34	Mellsom, John	(see Milsum)			
	1694/37	Mentrume, Ann	(see Menturne)			
W	1694/37	Menturne, Ann	City of Bristol	Widow	£8	
W	1714/31	Mercer, Alexander	SS. Phillip & Jacob	Mariner	£143	
	1692/27	Mercer, Prudence	City of Bristol	Widow	£72	
	1678/42	Merchant, John	City of Bristol	Victualler	£30	
	1674/30	Meredith, Abel	Westbury-on-Trym	Gent.	£42	
W	1727/22	Meredith, Edward	Almondsbury (Patchway)	Yeoman	£146	
W	1727/23	Meredith, Elizabeth	Almondsbury (Patchway)	--	£121	
W	1749/47	Meredith, George	City of Bristol	Gent.	£17	
	1640/45	Meredith, John	St. Nicholas	Baker	£5	
	1671/26	Meredith, John	St. Mary-le-Port	--	£19	
	1677/34	Meredith, John	St. Mary-le-Port	Glazier	£249	
	1674/27	Meredith, Margery	Westbury-on-Trym	Widow	£131	
W	1681/51	Meredith, Mary	City of Bristol	Spinster	£69	
W	1639/68	Meredith, Nicholas	St. Ewen	Merchant	£865	City Chamberlain
W	1693/25	Merefield, William	City of Bristol	Victualler	£20	
	1646/29	Merete, Henry	St. Mary, Redcliffe	--	£11	
	1646/30	Merret, Richard	St. Thomas	Mason	£6	
	1646/29	Merrett, Henry	(see Merete)			

Year ref.		Name	Parish or area	Occupation or status	Value	Notes
W	1636/37	Merrick, Christopher	St. Peter	⟨Shearman⟩	£15	
W	1681/54	Merrick, Edward	Abbots Leigh	⟨Husbandman⟩	£6	
W	1639/69	Merrick, Robert	St. Peter	⟨Brewer⟩	£45	
	1709/38	Merricke, Edward	Almondsbury	Yeoman	£56	
	1679/45	Merritt, Alice	--	--	£8	
	1679/46	Merritt, John	Temple	Lime-burner	£76	
W	1679/47	Merry, Ann	City of Bristol	Widow	£145	
	1707/29	Merry, John	City of Bristol	Mariner	£9	
	1637/39	Merry, Richard	Christchurch	Maltster	£196	
	1675/52	Meryweather, John	City of Bristol	Gardener	£24	
	1683/41	Meryweather, John	Westbury-on-Trym	--	£52	
	1680/36	Messenger, Robert	(see Massenger)			
	1704/20	Metcalfe, Edward	--	--	£13	
	1702/20	Metcalfe, Joan	(see Midkife)			
W	1741/32	Metcalfe, William	City of Bristol	Mariner	£3	
W	1671/28	Mettes, John	⟨St. Augustine⟩	Mariner	£48	inv. & account
	1646/31	Middleton, James	St. Mary, Redcliffe	Silk-weaver	£37	
W	1617/34	Middleton, Thomas	Olveston	Yeoman	£88	
W	1695/24	Middleton, Thomas	Winterbourne	⟨Quarrier⟩	£18	
	1730/41	Middlewood, Mathias	City of Bristol	Mariner	£15	
	1674/32	Midford, William	Mangotsfield	--	£216	alias Powell
			(compare inventory of William Mitford, 1674/26)			
	1702/20	Midkife, Joan	St. James	--	£16	
	1704/20	Midkirff, Edward	(see Metcalfe)			
W	1618/45	Midleton, Eleanor	Olveston	Widow	£124	
	1640/46	Midleton, Thomas	(see Medellton)			
	1660/10	Mighen, Thomas	St. Peter	Fine-drawer	£8	
	1639/70a	Might, William	Temple	Brewer	£22	
	1639/70b	Might, William	(document concerning funeral charges)			
W	1746/27	Miles, Thomas	City of Bristol	Mariner	£15	
	1751/11	Miles, Thomas	SS. Philip & Jacob	Butcher	£320	

W	Ref.	Name	Place	Occupation	Value	Notes
	1629/41	Milkins, Francis	St. Mary-le-Port	--	£13	
	1739/15	Milkins, Richard	City of Bristol	--	£8	
W	1629/42	Mill, John	Henbury (Compton)	--	£124	
	1671/25B	Millard, Joan	Mangotsfield	Widow	£25	
	1688/33	Millard, Joan	City of Bristol	Widow	£20	2 similar invs.
	1665/38	Millard, John	St. Thomas	--	£67	
	1674/28	Millard, William	St. Mary-le-Port	Pewterer	£15	
W	1689/40	Millard, William	SS. Philip & Jacob	Castor-maker	£82	
W	1643/60	Miller, Anne	<All Saints>	Widow	£140	
W	1732/49	Miller, James	City of Bristol	Mariner	£5	
	1715/32	Miller, John	City of Bristol	Mariner	£6	
W	1731/59	Miller, John	City of Bristol	Mariner	£11	
	1747/27	Miller, John	City of Bristol	Mariner	£3	
W	1634/51a	Miller, Julian	St. Stephen	--	£30	

(also account of administration by Anne Millerd, 5lb)

W	Ref.	Name	Place	Occupation	Value	Notes
	1730/42	Miller, Laghlan or Langland	City of Bristol	Mariner	£11	
	1681/50	Miller, Nathan	Westbury-on-Trym (Redland)			

W	Ref.	Name	Place	Occupation	Value	Notes
W	1643/58	Miller, Thomas	St. Augustine	<Inn-keeper>	£108	
	1643/59	Miller, Thomas	All Saints	Linen-draper	£320	also 2nd copy
	1715/33	Miller, William	City of Bristol	Merchant	£43	
W	1732/50	Miller, William	City of Bristol	Surgeon	£12	
	1618/46	Millerd, Christopher	Mangotsfield	<Mariner>	£5	
W	1664/33	Millerd, David	St. James	--	£8	
	1665/36	Millerd, Elizabeth	St. James	<Miller>	£52	
	1663/44	Millerd, Henry	Mangotsfield	Widow	£66	inv. & account
	1727/24	Millet, Isaac	Stoke Gifford	--	£7	
W	1699/18	Millet, William	Stoke Gifford	<Yeoman>	£188	
W	1696/20	Millett, Ellenor	Mangotsfield	Widow	£690	
W	1694/39	Millett, Jacob	Filton	Yeoman	£71	
	1748/51	Millett, Mary	City of Bristol	<married>	£380	
W	1684/36	Millett, Thomas	Mangotsfield	Yeoman	£16	
				Yeoman	£130	

	Year ref.	Name	Parish or area	Occupation or status	Value	Notes
	1661/50	Millington, Robert	St. Mary, Redcliffe	--	£9	
	1741/33	Millman, Edward	City of Bristol	Mariner	£4	
W	1685/38	Mills, Edith	Winterbourne	Spinster	£43	
	1611/57	Mills, Elizabeth	St. Stephen	Widow	£10	
	1625/54	Mills, Elizabeth	Henbury	Widow	£117	
W	1684/39	Mills, Elizabeth	Henbury	<Widow>	£62	
	1731/60	Mills, Elizabeth	City of Bristol	Widow	£83	
	1746/28	Mills, Francis	City of Bristol	<Mariner>	£16	
W	1711/29	Mills, George	City of Bristol	Mariner	£15	
	1667/50	Mills, John	SS. Phillip & Jacob	--	£24	
	1685/37	Mills, John	Winterbourne	--	£101	
	1699/19	Mills, John	City of Bristol	Wine-cooper	£3	
	1729/26	Mills, Joseph	City of Bristol	Baker	£83	inv. & account
	1637/40	Mills, Richard	Henbury (Compton Greenfield)	--	£210	
	1677/33	Mills, Richard	Henbury	Husbandman	£43	
W	1639/71	Mills, Thomas	(see Mylles)			
	1675/46	Mills, Thomas	Henbury	--	£71	
	1714/32	Mills, Thomas	Henbury (Hallen)	Husbandman	£316	
W	1673/22	Mills, William	Olveston	Husbandman	£124	
W	1649/19	Millsom, Nicholas	Almondsbury (Hempton)	--	£201	
W	1690/26	Milner, Elizabeth	<City of Bristol>	Yeoman	£228	
W	1628/49	Milsom, Edward	SS. Phillip & Jacob	<Widow>	£27	
W	1705/23	Milsom, John	Stapleton	Coal-miner	£26	also 2nd copy
	1734/31	Milsom, John	City of Bristol	Carver	£18	
	1682/29	Milsom, Richard	Stapleton	Coal-miner	£44	
	1762/CP	Milsome, Jacob	Temple	Victualler	£88	
	1685/34	Milsum, John	SS. Phillip & Jacob	Victualler	£15	
	1620/64	Milton, Thomas	Christchurch	Tiler	£4	
	1709/39	Milward, Edward	City of Bristol	Mariner	£6	inv. & account

Ref.	W	Name	Place	Occupation	Value	Notes
1644/38	W	Minard, Elias	St. Michael	Joiner	£2	
1706/28		Minchinton William	St. Thomas	<Victualler>	£32	
1640/47		Minnes, John	St. James	Mariner	£17	
1750/33		Mint, John	City of Bristol	Mariner	£18	
1702/20		Mitcalfe, Joan	(see Midkife)			
1745/20	W	Mitchell, John	City of Bristol	Mariner	£8	
1667/48	W	Mitchell, Richard	Henbury	Yeoman	£62	
1748/52	W	Mitchell, Richard	City of Bristol	Mariner	£10	
1682/28	W	Mitchell, Thomas	City of Bristol	Mariner	£20	
1633/44		Mitchell, William	St. Thomas	Butcher	£43	
1644/37	W	Mitford, William	Mangotsfield	--	£162	alias Powell
1674/26		Mitford, William	Mangotsfield	--	£229	alias Powell
		(compare inventory of William Midford 1674/32)				
1683/37		Mittford, George	Mangotsfield	Yeoman	£176	
1681/53		Mockredge, Peter	Temple	Weaver	£30	
1640/48	W	Moges, Peter	SS. Philip & Jacob	Gardener	£88	
1708/36	W	Moggs, Gabriel	City of Bristol	Gent.	£11	
1671/27	W	Moggs, James	SS. Philip & Jacob	Gardener	£248	
1673/25		Moggs, John	SS. Philip & Jacob	--	£21	
1684/38	W	Moggs, John	SS. Philp & Jacob	Gardener	£106	
1687/46		Moggs, John	City of Bristol	Gardener	£5	
1640/48	W	Moggs, Peter	(see Moges)			
1718/24		Moggs, Sarah	SS. Philip & Jacob	Widow	£33	
1675/50		Moggs, Thomas	Christchurch	Embroiderer	£378	dated 1713
1678/71		Moggs, Thomas	Christchurch	--	£325	account only
1704/21		Moggs, Walter	Barton Regis	Yeoman	£147	
1678/41		Monck, Richard	(alias Mount, which see)			
1717/37	W	Moncrieffe, William	City of Bristol	Surgeon	£23	
1633/45		Mongomery, Roberda	St. Mark	--	£21	
1618/49	W	Montaine, John	SS. Philip & Jacob	Carrier	£134	
1717/38	W	Montgomery, John	<City of Bristol>	Mariner	£9	
1620/91		Monyan, John	(see Teague)			
1683/40	W	Mooddy, Edward	--	--	£5	died at sea

Year ref.	W	Name	Parish or area	Occupation or status	Value	Notes
1719/31		Moody, Joseph	City of Bristol	Mariner	£10	
1706/29		Moody, Robert	Watford, Ireland	Mariner	£10	2 documents
1639/72	W	Moody, Thomas	St. Leonard	Cooper	£125	
1684/41		Moone, Dennis	St. Augustine	Mariner	£13	
1664/31		Moone, Joan	St. Peter	Widow	£84	
1669/51		Moone, John	St. James	--	£203	
1623/43		Moone, Margery	Almondsbury (Patchway)	--	£3	
1611/56		Moone, Marie	Abbots Leigh (& Tewkesbury)	Single-woman	£20	
1611/59	W	Moone, Nicholas	Almondsbury	Husbandman	£32	
1741/34		Moor, Charles	City of Bristol	Mariner	£4	
1749/48		Moore, David	City of Bristol	Mariner	£13	
1629/43		Moore, Edward	St. Nicholas	--	£7	
1609/53		Moore, Elizabeth	Almondsbury	--	£20	
1684/40		Moore, Elizabeth	City of Bristol	Widow	£30	
1643/61	W	Moore, George	St. Stephen	Gent.	£401	
1669/50		Moore, Gilbert	St. Ewen	Surgeon	£234	
1635/-		Moore, Herbert	(see Herbert, M., 1635/40)			
1750/32	W	Moore, Isaac	City of Bristol	Mariner	£6	
1625/55		Moore, Joan	(see More)			
1618/47	W	Moore, Johan	St. Mary, Redcliffe	Widow	£18	
1681/52	W	Moore, Joseph	SS. Philip & Jacob	<Felt-maker>	£63	
1747/28	W	Moore, Robert	City of Bristol	Mariner	£15	
1732/51		Moore, Stephen	City of Bristol	Victualler	£4	
1666/31		Moore, Symon	St. Mary, Redcliffe	--	£4	
1636/38		Moore, Walter	SS. Philip & Jacob	--	£5	
1636/39		Moore, William	(see More)			
1617/35		Mooreman, Walter	St. Mary-le-Port	--	£35	
1675/48		Motes, Margaret	<City of Bristol>	--	£27	
1727/25	W	Moran, Thomas	City of Bristol	Cooper	£12	died at sea

	Ref	Name	Place	Occupation	Value	Notes
	1719/32	Morce, Evan	City of Bristol	Mariner	£16	
	1625/55	More, Joan	Almondsbury	--	£91	
W	1635/62	More, John	Stapleton	Single-man	£84	
	1636/39	More, William	Stapleton	Yeoman	£66	
W	1613/42	Moreman, Walter	Elberton	--	£75	
	1680/35	Morfell, Michael	'London'	--	£6	formerly of Bristol
	1676/31	Morgan, --	--	Widow	£10	(document states 'Richard Morgan' on outside) (alias Thomas, which see)
W	1629/57	Morgan, Ann	Clifton	Widow	£17	alias Thomas
W	1695/23	Morgan, Ann	Westbury-on-Trym (Redland)	Widow		see also 1629/57
W	1627/17	Morgan, Anne	City of Bristol	Widow	£132	died at sea
	1749/49	Morgan, David	City of Bristol	Cordwainer	£4	
	1753/22	Morgan, Elizabeth	City of Bristol	Single-woman	£5	
	1706/30	Morgan, George	City of Bristol	Mariner	£7	
	1731/61	Morgan, George		Cooper	£19	
	1720/25	Morgan, Grace	--	Widow	£5	
W	1637/41	Morgan, Henry	St. Leonard	Sailor	£73	
W	1669/49	Morgan, Henry	SS. Philip & Jacob	Gardener	£55	
W	1737/23	Morgan, Isaac	City of Bristol	Mariner	£10	
W	1744/9	Morgan, James	--	<Inn-holder>	--	(document regarding administration)
W	1624/48	Morgan, Joan	Henbury	--	£30	
W	1675/51	Morgan, John	St. Nicholas	<Mariner>	£18	
	1718/25	Morgan, John	City of Bristol	Porter	£11	
	1720/24	Morgan, John	Westbury-on-Trym (Shirehampton)	Mariner	£10	
	1733/53	Morgan, John	City of Bristol	Mariner	£2	
	1741/35	Morgan, John	City of Bristol	Mariner	£12	
W	1748/53	Morgan, John	City of Bristol	Mariner	£19	
	1761/23	Morgan, Joseph	City of Bristol	Mariner	£3	
W	1617/36	Morgan, Margaret	St. Mark	--	£16	
	1635/63	Morgan, Mathew	Temple	Architector	£86	also 2nd copy

Year ref.	Name		Parish or area	Occupation or status	Value	Notes
1728/29	Morgan,	Patrick	City of Bristol	Mariner	£4	
1639/73	Morgan,	Richard	St. Stephen	Mariner	£62	
1752/22	Morgan,	Stephen	SS. Philip & Jacob	Yeoman	£5	
1620/65	Morgan,	Thomas	St. John	--	£12	
1635/64	Morgan,	Thomas	St. John	Tailor	£19	
1636/40	Morgan,	Thomas	St. John	<Haulier>	£14	
1725/12	Morgan,	Thomas	City of Bristol	Victualler	£111	
1706/31	Morgan,	Walter	SS. Philip & Jacob	--	£142	
1663/43	Morgan,	William	St. Nicholas	--	£14	
W 1684/34	Morgan,	William (snr.)	Olveston			
			<Tockington>	Yeoman	£49	
W 1685/39	Morgan,	William	SS. Philip & Jacob	Gardener	£12	
1688/31	Morgan,	William	City of Bristol	Tobacco-roller	£49	
1702/21	Morgan,	William	Olveston			
			(Tockington)	--	£20	
1779/CP	Morgan,	William	City of Bristol	Corn-factor	£518	account only
1757/15	Morley,	Edward	City of Bristol	Miller	£19	
W 1709/40	Morley,	John	City of Bristol	Mariner	£18	
W 1740/44	Morrey,	John	City of Bristol	Mariner	£10	
W 1618/48	Morrice,	Edward	(see Morris)			
1625/56	Morrice,	George	Westbury-on-Trym			
			(Shirehampton)	Mariner	£58	
1690/27	Morris,	Edmund	City of Bristol	Merchant	£24	
W 1618/48	Morris,	Edward	St. Werburgh	Widow	£219	
1693/24	Morris,	Elizabeth	Temple	Yeoman	£36	
1643/62	Morris,	John	Almondsbury	--	£81	
1664/32	Morris,	John	St. Mary, Redcliffe	Tobacconist	£6	
1693/23	Morris,	John	Temple	Mariner	£36	
1740/43	Morris,	Jonathan	City of Bristol	Buckle-maker	£8	
1628/45	Morris,	Richard	St. James	Mariner	£2	
1748/54	Morris,	Robert	--		£6	

		Name	Place	Occupation	Value	Notes
W	1726/25	Morris, Stephen	City of Bristol	Mariner	£10	
	1624/49	Morris, William	St. Stephen	Hooper	£112	alias Snacknall
W	1703/13	Morris, William	Barton Regis	Inn-holder	£89	
W	1746/29	Morris, William	City of Bristol	Mariner	£8	
W	1758/22	Morrisson, Charles	City of Bristol	Mariner	£10	
W	1726/26	Morrisson, William	--	<Mariner>	£13	
	1609/54	Morse, John	--	--	£3	
W	1637/42	Morse, Richard	Almondsbury	<Husbandman>	£3	
W	1629/44	Morse, Sara	St. Michael		£44	
	1640/49	Morse, William	St. Mary, Redcliffe	Husbandman	£18	
	1709/41	Morse, William	City of Bristol	Mariner	£5	
	1666/34	Mortimer, Johane	Almondsbury	Widow	£8	see also 1666/33 Mortimer, Thomas
	1620/66	Mortimer, John	Henbury	Husbandman	£101	
W	1670/31	Mortimer, John	Olveston <Tockington>	Yeoman	£209	
	1666/33	Mortimer, Thomas	Almondsbury	--	£77	see also 1666/34 Mortimer, Johane
	1673/24	Mortimer, George	Almondsbury	--	£201	
W	1669/52	Morton, Mary	City of Bristol	Widow	£45	will 1668
	1675/49	Moseley, Benjamin	St. Stephen	Cooper	£12	
	1683/36	Mosely, John	City of Bristol	Cooper	£86	
	1731/62	Moss, Josiah	City of Bristol	Mariner	£6	
	1742/36	Mote, Charles	City of Bristol	Cordwainer	£7	
	1674/29	Motes, John	--	--	£28	
W	1747/29	Mott, Abraham	City of Bristol	Mariner	£16	
W	1729/27	Mould, William	City of Bristol	Mariner	£4	
W	1739/16	Mounsher, Richard	City of Bristol	Mariner	£10	
W	1678/41	Mount, Richard	St. James	--	£7	alias Monck
	1709/42a	Mountain, Arthur	Barton Regis	Yeoman	£57	
	1709/42b	Mountain, Arthur	(the account of Mary Mountain, alias Cribb)			
W	1693/26	Mountaine, Elizabeth	Barton Regis	Widow	£102	
W	1684/37	Mountaine, Francis	SS. Philip & Jacob	Gardener	£221	

	Year ref.	Name	Parish or area	Occupation or status	Value	Notes
W	1618/49	Mountaine, John	(see Montaine)			
	1671/25A	Mountaine, John	SS. Philip & Jacob	Yeoman	£26	
W	1672/38	Mountaine, John	SS. Philip & Jacob	Yeoman	£26	
W	1682/32	Mountaine, John	Barton Regis	Coal-miner	£12	
W	1709/43	Mountaine, Richard	Barton Regis	Coal-miner	£12	
	1618/44	Mourton, Thomas	(see Martone)			
W	1773/CP	Moxham, Thomas	SS. Philip & Jacob	Grocer	£34	inv. & account will 1768
	1685/35	Muggleworth, Mary	City of Bristol	Widow	£100	
	1750/33	Muit, John	(see Mint)			
	1695/25	Mulgrove, John	--	--	£3	
W	1732/52	Mullen, Thomas	City of Bristol	Mariner	£5	
W	1749/50	Mullett, Thomas	City of Bristol	Mariner	£5	
W	1679/48	Mullins, George	City of Bristol	Shipwright	£16	
	1738/16	Mullins, Nicholas	City of Bristol	Mariner	£8	
W	1731/63	Mullineux, Nicholas	City of Bristol	Mariner	£5	
	1682/31	Munday, Elizabeth	City of Bristol	Widow	£46	
	1660/9	Munday, Thomas	Temple	Mariner	£61	
W	1730/43	Murfey, John	City of Bristol	Mariner	£9	
	1743/24B	Murphey, James	City of Bristol	Mariner	£3	
	1727/26	Murphy, Bartholomew	City of Bristol	Mariner	£6	
W	1737/24	Murphy, John	City of Bristol	Mariner	£16	
W	1732/53	Murphy, Patrick	City of Bristol	Mariner	£8	
	1741/36	Murphey, James	City of Bristol	Mariner	£10	
W	1730/43	Murphey, John	(see Murfey)			
	1742/37	Murphey, Thomas	City of Bristol	\<Mariner\>	£6	
	1721/20	Murr, John	(see Morrey)		£19	
W	1740/44	Murray, John	City of Bristol	--	£7	
W	1742/38	Murray, John	City of Bristol	Mariner	£5	
W	1742/39	Murray, Peter	City of Bristol	Mariner	£5	
W	1740/45	Murrey, Darby	City of Bristol	Mariner		

Ref		Name	Place	Occupation	Value	Notes
1683/39	w	Mursevant, William	St. James	Seaman	£10	
1701/20		Muttley, George	Littleton-on-Severn	Yeoman	£466	
1739/51		Myatt, Joseph	City of Bristol	Victualler	£31	
1639/71	w	Mylles, Thomas	Henbury	--	£125	
1673/23		Mynard, Robert	Temple	--	£72	
1611/58		Naish, Alice	(see Nash)			
1623/44		Naishe, Francis	(see Nash)			
1689/41	w	Naish, Thomas	City of Bristol	Organ maker	£30	
1712/34		Nanfon, Thomas	City of Bristol	Mariner	£9	
1746/30		Nappy, William	City of Bristol	Mariner	£10	
1611/58		Nash, Alice	Abbots Leigh	--	£15	
1641/34	w	Nash, Bartholomew	Almondsbury	--	£15	
1623/44		Nash, Francis	Henbury	--	£27	
1694/40	w	Nash, James	Henbury	Yeoman	£102	
1748/55	w	Nash, John	City of Bristol	Mariner	£10	
1742/40	w	Nash, Samuel	City of Bristol	Mariner	£12	
1704/22		Nash, Thomas	--	--	£10	
1642/33	w	Nashe, Emmanuel	St. Stephen	⟨Draper⟩	£8	
1679/50	w	Neads, John	St. Stephen	⟨Joiner⟩	£37	
1748/CP	w	Neady, Margaret	City of Bristol	Widow	£2	
1751/12		Neal, Felix	City of Bristol	Mariner	£5	
1711/30	w	Neale, Mary	City of Bristol	Widow	£13	
1716/39		Neale, John	City of Bristol	Mariner	£11	
1672/40	w	Neason, Jonas	⟨City of Bristol⟩	Cooper	£126	inv. & account
1629/45		Neason, Phillip	(see Nesonn)			
1700/11		Neast, Thomas	SS. Philip & Jacob	--	£98	
1733/54		Neast, William	City of Bristol	Brass-founder	£102	
1628/46		Neave, Thomas	St. Leonard	Joiner	£4	
1722/13		Neck, Anthony	City of Bristol	Mariner	£3	
1723/20	w	Neck, Katharine Frances	Almondsbury (Over)	Spinster	£222	
1711/31	w	Neck, William	Almondsbury	Clothier (alias farmer)	£259	
1668/41	w	Neeve, James	St. Mary, Redcliffe	Glover	£51	

	Year ref.	Name	Parish or area	Occupation or status	Value	Notes
W	1668/40	Neeve, John	Temple	Tobacco-roller	£226	
W	1618/51	Nelme, Marie	Henbury	Widow	£94	
W	1623/45	Nelmes, Edward	\<Lawrence Weston\> Westbury-on-Trym	--	£8	
	1609/56	Nelmes, Robert	Portbury (Ham Green)	--	£20	
	1634/52	Nelmes, Thomas	Portbury	--	£11	
W	1618/50	Nelmes, William	\<St. John\>	Grocer	£75	
W	1640/50	Nelson, Edward	Henbury (Lawrence Weston)	Husbandman	£62	
	1665/39	Nelson, Edward	Temple	\<Shearman\>	£97	
	1686/35	Nelson, Edward	St. Thomas	Baker	£126	
	1727/27	Nelson, Henry	St. Stephen	Baker	£4	
	1721/21	Nelson, John	City of Bristol	Mariner	£14	
W	1692/30	Nelson, Robert	City of Bristol	Victualler	£112	
W	1749/52	Nesbitt, John	City of Bristol	Ship-carpenter	£81	
	1647/21	Nesen, Robert	City of Bristol	Mariner	£6	
	1647/21	Neson, Robert	(see Nesen)	Mariner	£3	
W	1684/43	Nesonn, Jonas	City of Bristol	Button-maker	£42	
	1629/45	Nesonn, Phillip	St. Mary, Redcliffe	--	£49	
	1728/30	Nett, Cornelius	--	--	£46	
	1733/55	Netten, Langworthy	City of Bristol	Mariner	£1	
	1671/29	Neves, Thomas	St. Michael	--	£22	
	1741/37	Newland, William	City of Bristol	Mariner	£11	
W	1743/25	Newman, John	City of Bristol	Mariner \<Hooper\>	£10	
	1679/49	Newman, Richard	Clifton	Haberdasher	£68	
	1752/23	Newman, Robert	City of Bristol	Mariner	£8	
W	1657/1	Neworke, John (snr)	City of Bristol	Soap-boiler	£36	
W	1747/30	Newton, James	City of Bristol	Mariner	£10	
	1646/32	Newton, John	St. James	--	£44	
	1641/35	Newton, Richard	St. Peter	--	£3	

W	Ref	Name	Place	Occupation	Value	Notes
W	1637/43	Nicholas, Alice	Almondsbury <Woodland> (alias Langston, which see)	Single-woman	£21	alias Hunt
	1609/47	Nicholas, Joan	City of Bristol	Mariner	£18	
	1712/35	Nicholas, John	St. Augustine	Mariner	£3	
	1892/3	Nicholas, Phillip	City of Bristol	Mariner	£15	
	1748/56	Nicholas, Robert	(see Nicholas, William)			
	1642/34	Nicholas, Susan	St. Mary, Redcliffe	--	£4	
	1625/57	Nicholas, Thomas	Temple	<Shearman>	£66	
	1642/34	Nicholas, William & Susan	City of Bristol	Widow	£24	inv. & account
	1723/21	Nicholls, Alice	City of Bristol	Shipwright	£10	
	1749/53	Nicholls, Charles	City of Bristol	Mariner	£7	
	1719/33	Nicholls, Joseph	St. Ewen	Mariner	£677	
W	1661/54	Nicholls, John	St. Ewen	Widow	£110	
	1663/46	Nicholls, John	Henbury	Merchant	£183	
W	1685/40	Nicholls, Margerie	Westbury-on-Trym	Mariner	£270	
W	1698/28	Nicholls, Samuel	Westbury-on-Trym	Cordwainer	£33	
	1686/36	Nicholls, Samuel	City of Bristol	Mariner	£3	
	1737/25	Nicholls, William	City of Bristol	Spinster	£10	
W	1749/54	Nicholls, William	<SS. Philip & Jacob>	Mariner	£19	
	1664/35	Nicholson, Grace	(see Nicholls)			
	1664/34	Nickcolls, John	(see Nickins)			
	1664/34	Nickens, John	St. Ewen	Trunk-maker	£20	
W	1733/56	Nickins, John	Portbury (Ham Green)	Shipwright	£9	died at sea
	1700/12	Nicklass, Richard (William)	--	--	£5	
	1700/12	Nickles, William	Castle Precincts	Surgeon	£112	
W	1733/56	Nicklus, William	(see Nickles)			
	1733/57	Nickolas, William	(see Nicklass, Richard)			
	1701/21	Nickolass, William	Stoke Gifford	Yeoman	£90	
	1639/74	Nickolls, Thomas	SS. Philip & Jacob	Maltster	£34	
	1639/74	Nisbee, Agnes	Almondsbury	--	£5	
		Nisbie, Agnes	(see Nisbee)			
	1742/41	Noads, Samuel	City of Bristol	Surgeon	£712	

	Year ref.	Name	Parish or area	Occupation or status	Value	Notes
W	1695/27	Noakes, Robert	City of Bristol	Baker	£196	
W	1679/51	Noble, Agnes	City of Bristol	Widow	£41	also 2nd copy
	1625/58	Noble, John	--	--	£13	
	1674/31	Noble, Katherine	--	Widow	£5	
	1666/36	Noble, Margaret	Winterbourne	Widow	£7	
	1753/23	Noble, Simon	City of Bristol	Mariner	£4	
W	1697/1	Noble, Thomas	Winterbourne (Hambrook)	Husbandman	£16	
	1620/67	Node, Richard	Almondsbury	--	£4	
W	1618/52	Norden, Edward	St. Leonard	Point-maker	£4	
	1678/43	Noke, Anthony	City of Bristol	Barber-surgeon	£40	
	1646/33	Nokes, John	Temple	Cloth-worker	£134	
	1752/24	Noot, Ann	Clifton	Widow	£15	
W	1686/34	Noote, Robert	Almondsbury (Over)	Yeoman	£230	
W	1733/58	Norcombe, Thomas	City of Bristol	Mariner	£14	
W	1682/33	Norcott, Elizabeth	SS. Philip & Jacob	Widow	£51	
W	1661/53	Norgrove, Elizabeth	Stapleton	Widow	£24	
W	1620/68	Norman, Joan	Christchurch	Saddle-maker <Widow>	£19	
	1717/39	Norman, Nicholas	City of Bristol	Mariner	£7	
	1667/52	Norman, Thomas	St. Stephen	Seaman	£6	
W	1633/46	North, John	<Henbury> (Aust)	<Labourer>	£10	
W	1624/50	North, Robert	St. Thomas	Blacksmith	£275	
W	1673/26A	Northall, Henry	City of Bristol	Whitawer	£20	
W	1681/55	Northall, Hester	St. Peter	Widow	£21	
	1617/37	Northall, James	SS. Philip & Jacob	--	£29	
W	1672/41	Northall, Joan	St. Mary, Redcliffe	Bone-lace weaver	£90	
W	1628/47	Northall, John	SS. Philip & Jacob	<Gent.>	£79	
	1641/36	Northall, Robert	St. Mary, Redcliffe	Sea-faring man	£2	
	1650/9	Northall, Susanna	SS. Philip & Jacob	Widow	£22	
	1663/45	Northall, Thomas	St. Thomas	<Tobacco dealer>	£22	

W	Ref	Name	Place	Occupation	Value	Notes
	1670/33	Northern, Thomas	City of Bristol			(an obligation; now with wills)
W	1672/39	Northerne, Marjory	City of Bristol	Widow	£116	
W	1611/60	Northie, William	Almondsbury	--	£5	
	1667/51	Northover, George	Clifton	--	£95	
	1680/37	Norton, Josias	Henbury	Husbandman	£48	
	1709/44	Norton, Samuel	City of Bristol	Ropemaker	£4	
W	1707/30	Norton, William	Henbury	Yeoman	£141	
W	1730/44	Norvil, Hanah	City of Bristol	Widow	£11	
W	1749/55	Nott, James	City of Bristol	Mariner	£10	
	1612/10	Nottingham, John	St. John	Haulier	£7	
	1684/42	Nottingham, Samuel	SS. Philip & Jacob	--	£33	
W	1618/53	Nowell, Annis (or Agnes)	Winterbourne	Widow	£17	
W	1617/38	Nowell, Henry	Winterbourne	Weaver	£3	
	1754/23A	Nox, Andrew	City of Bristol	Mariner	£5	
	1694/41	Nuckle, William	--	--	£2	
W	1716/40	Nurse, Giles	Henbury	Butcher	£14	
	1644/39	Nurse, Richard	St. Stephen	Ship-carpenter	£21	
	1682/34	Nutt, John	City of Bristol	Cordwainer	£22	
W	1717/40	Nutt, Richard	SS. Philip & Jacob	--	£83	
	1762/CP	Nutt, Thomas	SS. Philip & Jacob	Butcher	£43	inv. & account
W	1759/16	Nyland, Peter	City of Bristol	Mariner	£12	
	1646/33	Oackes, John	(see Nokes)	Whitawer	£186	
	1635/65	Oakelie, Edmond	St. Peter	<Mariner>	£12	also 2nd copy
	1710/21	Oakley, John	--	Locksmith	£17	2nd copy on will
W	1620/69	Oatley, Barnard	St. Michael	Mariner	£9	
	1712/36	Oatway, John	City of Bristol	Mariner	£12	
W	1744/10	O'Brian, Morgan	City of Bristol	Mariner	£5	
	1738/17	Obrian, Henry	City of Bristol	Yeoman	£80	formerly of Jamaica
	1731/64	Obrien, Timothy	City of Bristol	Mariner	£7	
W	1730/45	Odam, George	City of Bristol	Mariner		

Year ref.		Name	Parish or area	Occupation or status	Value	Notes
1758/23		Ogleby, William	City of Bristol	Mariner	£9	
1760/23		Oglevy, John	City of Bristol	Mariner	£18	
1696/21		Okley, John	--	--	£19	
1690/29		Old, John	Clifton	--	£3	
1750/34	W	Old, William	City of Bristol	Mariner	£5	
1698/1	W	Oldbury, Mary	Castle Precinct	<Spinster>	£18	
1636/41	W	Oldfield, David	St. Stephen	Parish Clerk		
1623/46	W	Oldfield, John	St. Nicholas	<Merchant>	£11	
1728/31		Oldis, John	Keynsham	<Hosier>	£84	
1675/54	W	Oldland, Richard	Henbury (Redwick)	Brass-worker	£15	
1688/34	W	Oldland, William	Henbury (Charlton)	Yeoman	£93	
1749/56	W	Oldrieff, John	City of Bristol	Yeoman	£83	
1678/44		Oliver, Abraham	St. James	Mariner	£16	
1635/66	W	Oliver, Frances	St. Werburgh	Mariner	£2	
1717/41		Olliffe, Sarah	City of Bristol	Widow	£106	
1625/59		Olliver, Henry	St. Werburgh	Widow	£85	
1731/65	W	Olsen, William	(see Ossen)	--	£13	
1715/34	W	Olver, Anthony	City of Bristol	Mariner	£45	
1735/31	W	Oman, Mordecai	City of Bristol	Mariner	£10	alias Man
1609/57		Ombewell, Nevell	St. Peter	--	£7	
1746/31	W	Oneile, Con	City of Bristol	Mariner	£9	
1670/11		Onion, Katherin	(see Eoynion)			
1726/27	W	Onion, Jonathan	Olveston			
1732/54	W	Orange, William	(Tockington)	Yeoman	£66	
1641/37		Orchard, Agnes	City of Bristol	Mariner	£6	
1617/39		Orchard, Alice	Littleton-on-Severn	Widow	£113	
1639/75	W	Orchard, Alice	St. Peter	--	£12	
1662/35		Orchard, Alice	Henbury (Kingsweston)	Widow	£43	
			Henbury	Spinster	£17	

	Ref	Name	Place	Occupation	Value	Notes
W	1661/55	Orchard, Dorothy	Henbury ⟨Compton⟩	Spinster	£123	
	1661/57	Orchard, Elizabeth	Henbury	Spinster	£87	
	1608/1	Orchard, John	Henbury (Kingsweston)	--	£16	
	1646/34	Orchard, John	Henbury	Husbandman	£17	
W	1688/35	Orchard, John	Almondsbury	Yeoman	£197	
	1689/49	Orchard, Maurice	St. Peter	Soapmaker	£27	
	1657/2	Orchard, Richard	City of Bristol	Notary Public	£187	also marked 'Allchurch'
	1687/3	Orchard, Richard	SS. Philip & Jacob		£1	
W	1689/42	Orchard, Richard	Henbury ⟨Redwick⟩	Yeoman	£501	
	1723/22	Orchard, Richard	City of Bristol	Mariner	£11	
	1623/47	Orchard, Thomas	St. James	--	£10	
W	1739/17	Ord, William	City of Bristol	Surgeon	£14	died at sea
W	1742/42	Osborn, John	City of Bristol	Apothecary	£6	died at sea
W	1704/23	Osborne, Elizabeth	⟨Castle Precincts⟩	Widow	£76	
W	1623/48	Osborne, Robert	Horfield	⟨Yeoman⟩	£55	'Olsen' on will
W	1731/65	Ossen, William	SS. Philip & Jacob (see Austin)	Glass-bottle maker	£8	
W	1746/32	Ostings, John				
	1673/26B	Ouldbury, John	City of Bristol	Mariner	£37	
	1671/30	Ouldston, Roger	Castle Precinct	--	£170	
	1679/52	Overton, Thomas	SS. Philip & Jacob	Gardener	£4	
	1750/35	Overton, John	City of Bristol	House-carpenter	£5	2 documents
	1706/32	Owen, Charles	City of Bristol	Cordwainer	£1	
W	1729/28	Owen, David	Abbots Leigh	Yeoman	£195	
W	1733/60	Owen, Edward	City of Bristol	Mariner	£6	
W	1634/53	Owen, Elizabeth	Mangotsfield	⟨Widow⟩	£8	also 2nd copy
	1773/59	Owen, Griffin	City of Bristol	Mariner	£12	
	1763/CP	Owen, James	City of Bristol	Mariner	£281	
W	1683/42	Owen, Jane	St. Leonard	Widow	£36	
W	1639/76	Owen, John	Mangotsfield	⟨Yeoman⟩	£8	
	1664/36	Owen, John	St. Mary-le-Port	Sheargrinder	£9	
	1675/53	Owen, John	Mangotsfield	--	£44	
W	1723/23	Owen, John	City of Bristol	⟨Victualler⟩	£100	

	Year ref.	Name	Parish or area	Occupation or status	Value	Notes
	1648/13	Owen, Nicholas	Mangotsfield	--	£21	
W	1639/77	Owen, Richard	Filton	⟨Yeoman⟩	£73	
	1643/63	Owen, Richard	Mangotsfield	--	£28	
	1712/37	Owen, Robert	City of Bristol	Mariner	£5	
	1650/10	Owen, Thomas	St. James	Mariner	£2	
	1684/44	Owen, Thomas	Temple	Mariner	£8	
	1704/24	Owen, Thomas	St. Thomas	Tobacco-pipe maker	£202	
	1715/35	Owen, William	City of Bristol	Mariner	£9	
	1704/24	Owin, Thomas	(see Owen)			
W	1643/64	Owldfield, Avis	St. Thomas	Widow	£60	
W	1662/36	Owldland, Arthur	Olveston	--	£169	2 documents
W	1613/43	Owldland, Margaret	Henbury (Northwick)	Widow	£50	
	1686/37	Oxford, Edward	Westbury-on-Trym	Butcher	£32	alias Robinson
	1715/36	Pack, William	City of Bristol	Shipwright	£12	died at sea
W	1625/60	Packer, Elizabeth	St. James	Widow	£156	
W	1683/43	Packer, George	Stapleton	⟨Gent.⟩	£12	
W	1675/58	Packer, Hannah	--	Widow	£63	
	1627/18	Packer, Joan	St. James	Widow	£65	also 2nd copy
	1669/55	Packer, Thomas	Stapleton	Gent.	£18	
	1706/33	Packer, Thomas	City of Bristol	Victualler	£249	
W	1669/54	Pacock, Mary	Westbury-on-Trym ⟨Shirehampton⟩			
W	1678/45	Pacy, Edith	Temple	Widow	£32	
W	1669/53	Pacy, Percival	Temple	⟨Widow⟩	£138	
	1684/48	Padfield, Thomas	St. Mary, Redcliffe	Weaver	£185	
W	1740/46	Page, Abraham (snr)	SS. Philip & Jacob	Wool-comber	£2	
	1705/24	Page, Francis	--	⟨House-carpenter⟩	£91	
	1738/18	Page, Francis	City of Bristol	House-carpenter	£30	
W	1731/66	Paglar, Jeremiah	City of Bristol	Gent.	£6	
W	1731/66	Pagler, Jeremiah	(see Paglar)	⟨Mariner⟩	£11	

Ref.	Name	Place	Occupation	Value	Notes
1670/36	Paicker, John	--	--	£2	
1617/40	Paine, Marie	St. Stephen	--	£40	
W 1642/35	Paine, Richard	St. Stephen	Mariner	£239	
1731/67	Paine, Richard	City of Bristol	Mariner	£5	
1664/38	Paine, Thomas	(see Payne)			
1710/22	Paine, Timothy	City of Bristol	Mariner	£92	
1628/53	Painter, Humfrey	St. Thomas	--	£5	
W 1613/44	Palmer, Agnes	Stoke Gifford	Widow	£9	
1617/41	Palmer, Edward	--	--	£2,382	
1683/45	Palmer, Joan	Stoke Gifford (Stoke Harris)	Spinster	£19	
W 1734/32	Palmer, John	City of Bristol	Mariner	£9	<Tailor, in will>
W 1736/22	Palmer, Mary	Westbury-on-Trym (Shirehampton)	Spinster	£15	
1639/78	Palmer, Thomas	St. Mary, Redcliffe	Vicar	£190	Vicar of Redcliffe with St. Thomas
1710/23	Palmer, Walter	City of Bristol	Victualler	£209	
W 1733/61	Pape, Thomas	City of Bristol	Mariner	£5	
1719/34	Paradise, Stephen	City of Bristol	Cooper	£13	
W 1618/54	Paramore, Walter	(see Partamore)			
1639/79	Parfitt, Joyce	(see Parfyte)			
1639/79	Parfyte, Joyce	St. Mary, Redcliffe	--	£9	
1700/13	Parimon, John	(see Perryman)			
1671/31	Parincheife, Samuel	St. John	Victualler	£22	
1716/41	Parish, George	City of Bristol	Mariner	£7	
1633/47a	Parker, Alice	St. Stephen	Widow	£31	
1633/47b	Parker, Alice	(guardian's caveat)			
1634/54	Parker, Alice	St. Stephen	Widow	£31	
W 1722/14	Parker, Ara	Littleton-on-Severn	Spinster	£198	
1737/26	Parker, George	City of Bristol	--	£9	
W 1650/11	Parker, Henry	Mangotsfield <Downend>	Husbandman	£51	

Year ref.	Name	Parish or area	Occupation or status	Value	Notes
1672/44	Parker, John	SS. Philip & Jacob	Gardener	£25	
1693/27	Parker, John	St. James	--	£32	
1629/46	Parker, Margery	Henbury (Charlton)	--	£36	
W 1667/53	Parker, Mary	Westbury-on-Trym <Shirehampton>	Widow	£117	
W 1676/32	Parker, Thomas	Henbury (Charlton)	--	£348	
W 1639/80	Parker, William	Westbury-on-Trym	<Husbandman>	£37	
1644/40	Parker, William	Henbury (Charlton)	Yeoman	£164	
W 1661/56	Parker, William	Westbury-on-Trym <Shirehampton>	Yeoman	£233	
1690/33	Parker, William	Westbury-on-Trym (Shirehampton)	Mariner	£13	
W 1711/32	Parker, William <snr>	Littleton-on-Severn	Yeoman	£225	
1722/15	Parker, William	Winterbourne	--	£80	
1697/28	Parlour, James	Henbury (Aust)	--	£100	
W 1620/70	Parminter, Thomas	Winterbourne	Yeoman	£3	
1689/52	Parminter, Thomas	City of Bristol	--	£3	
W 1628/50	Parnell, Alice	Almondsbury (Compton)	Widow	£37	
1701/22	Parnell, Jane	St. Stephen	Widow	£33	
W 1684/45	Parnell, Nicholas	Alveston <Earthcott>	--	£83	also 2nd copy
1712/38	Parnell, Nicholas	Almondsbury (Hempton)	Yeoman	£134	
1697/29	Parnell, William	St. Stephen	--	£39	
1620/71	Parphet, Hugh	All Saints	--	£19	
W 1633/49	Parphett, Edmond (or Edward)	St. Mary, Redcliffe	<Carpenter>	£39	

	Ref	Name	Place	Occupation	Value	Notes
	1677/36	Parphey, William	St. Mary, Redcliffe	--	£15	also 2nd copy
W	1618/54	Parramore, Walter	St. Stephen	Mariner	£26	
	1713/34a	Parrett, Samuel	(see Parrott)			
W	1725/13	Parris, Joan	City of Bristol	Widow	£19	
	1713/34a	Parrot, Samuel	St. James	Tin-plate maker	£12	
	1713/34b	Parrott, Samuel	(the account of Mary Parrott, relict)			
W	1664/41	Parry, Hugh	St. John	Blacksmith	£112	
	1713/35	Parry, John	City of Bristol	Mariner	£16	
	1620/72	Parry, Judith	St. Leonard	Widow	£7	alias Roberts
	1716/42	Parry, Thomas	City of Bristol	--	£10	
W	1749/57	Parry, Thomas	--	Mariner	£14	
			(written at foot of an account of an incident on a slave trader)			
W	1739/18	Parsloe, Nathaniel	City of Bristol	Mariner	£18	
	1717/42	Parsons, Benjamin	City of Bristol	Mariner	£14	
W	1675/57	Parsons, Christian	<Stapleton>	<Widow>	£22	
	1674/34	Parsons, Francis	SS. Philip & Jacob	Mariner	£6	
W	1746/33	Parsons, George	City of Bristol	Victualler	£5	
	1694/44	Parsons, Hugh	--	--	£6	
	1671/6	Parsons, Hugh	Abbots Leigh	--	£13	
W	1695/30	Parsons, John	<City of Bristol>	Mariner	£13	
W	1618/55	Parsons, Katherine	SS. Philip & Jacob	Widow	£9	
	1611/62	Parsons, Mary	St. Peter	--	£1	
W	1731/68	Parsons, Richard	City of Bristol	Mariner	£15	
W	1641/38	Parsons, Richard	Abbots Leigh	Mariner	£109	
	1692/31	Parsons, William	St. Peter	Victualler	£103	
	1665/40	Partridge, George	St. Nicholas	--	£142	
	1679/54	Partridge, Joan	St. James	Widow	£6	
	1633/48	Partridge, Walter	St. Mary, Redcliffe	--	£91	
	1749/48	Passey, Philip	--	<Mariner>	£4	
	1640/51	Patch, Joan	St. James	Widow	£12	
	1624/51	Patch, John	St. Peter	--	£3	
	1573/1	Patche, Henry	(alias Mayo, which see)			
	1667/57	Patience, Alexander	SS. Philip & Jacob	Mariner	--	

	Year ref.	Name	Parish or area	Occupation or status	Value	Notes
	1690/32	Patrick, John	St. James	Gardener	£11	
	1644/44	Patteson, Henry	St. Peter	Translator <i.e. cobbler>		
	1715/37	Paul, Elizabeth	City of Bristol	Spinster	£26	
	1670/35	Paul, Henry	St. Augustine	Surgeon	£20	
	1701/23	Paule, Mary	(see Paull)		£41	
	1644/23	Paull, Mary	--	--		
	1729/29	Pavey, Charles (jnr)	Silley, Glam.	Mariner	£11	
W	1692/33	Pavey, Sarah	Elberton	Spinster	£11	
W	1687/47	Payne, Anne	City of Bristol	Widow	£96	
	1660/27	Payne, Elizabeth	St. Peter	Widow	£41	
	1644/41	Payne, George	St. Peter	--	£29	
W	1689/51	Payne, George	St. Nicholas	<Joiner>	£282	
W	1611/61	Payne, John	Abbots Leigh	Husbandman	£75	
	1685/42	Payne, Nicholas	St. James	Cordwainer	£5	
W	1732/55	Payne, Sarah	City of Bristol	Widow	£59	
	1664/38	Payne, Thomas	Henbury	--	£13	
	1707/31	Payne, Timothy	City of Bristol	Mariner	£31	
W	1660/24	Payton, Alice	Henbury	Spinster	£975	
	1634/55	Payton, John	Westbury-on-Trym	--	£93	
W	1666/40	Payton, John	St. John	<Hauler>	£1	
	1723/24	Payton, Samuel	City of Bristol	Sawyer	£60	
	1636/42	Payton, Thomas	St. Augustine	--	£5	
W	1667/58	Peacocke, Christopher	Westbury-on-Trym <Shirehampton>	<Pilot>	£8	
	1689/54	Pear, Ann	(alias Probin, which see)		£1155	
W	1792/1	Pearce, Ann	Christchurch	Spinster	--	
W	1681/58	Pearce, Anne	Abbots Leigh	Widow	£26	
	1664/37	Pearce, Anthony	St. Mark	--	£19	
W	1733/62	Pearce, Blaney	City of Bristol	Mariner	£10	
	1644/42	Pearce, Elinor	(see Pearse)			

W	Ref.	Name	Place	Occupation	Value	Notes
	1650/12	Pearce, George	Christchurch	Inn-holder	£125	
	1695/29	Pearce, Henry	--	--	£4	
W	1731/69	Pearce, James	City of Bristol	Mariner	£8	
W	1665/43	Pearce, Joan	St. James	Widow	£100	
W	1618/56	Pearce, John	Almondsbury (Woodland)	Weaver	£84	
	1620/73	Pearce, John	Harry Stoke	--	£46	
	1636/43	Pearce, John	Westbury-on-Trym (Shirehampton)	--	£1	2 documents
W	1641/39	Pearce, John	Henbury	Husbandman	£40	
W	1641/40	Pearce, Richard	Almondsbury	<Husbandman>	£72	
	1667/56	Pearce, Richard	Henbury	--	£39	compare 1668/42A
W	1668/42A	Pearce, Richard	Henbury	--	£39	compare 1667/56
	1617/42	Pearce, Thomas	Stapleton	Haulier	£34	
	1643/65	Pearce, Thomas	St. James	Blacksmith	£15	
	1660/12	Pearce, Thomas	Mangotsfield	Mariner	£29	
	1663/47	Pearce, Thomas	City of Bristol	Mariner	£215	
	1676/34	Pearce, Thomas	City of Bristol	Weaver	£25	
	1712/39	Pearce, Thomas	City of Bristol	Mariner	£10	
	1667/54	Peard, Christopher	St. Stephen	Mariner	£196	
	1708/38	Peare, Robert	City of Bristol	Mariner	£15	
	1644/42	Pearse, Elinor	Henbury <Almondsbury>	Widow	£16	
W	1628/51	Pearse, John	Redend	--	£37	
		(see Pearce)				
W	1641/39	Pearse, John	City of Bristol	Mariner	£5	
W	1729/30	Pearson, Henry	City of Bristol	<Baker>	£43	
	1640/52	Pearson, John	St. Thomas	--	£94	
	1683/44	Pearson, John	--		£22	
	1662/37	Pearson, Margaret	St. Augustine	Widow		
		(see Pesely)				
	1620/74	Peaselie, John				
W	1640/53	Peasley, John	Henbury (Aust)	Yeoman	£317	
W	1609/58	Peasly, Alice	Almondsbury	Widow	£41	
W	1713/36	Pedler, Christopher	City of Bristol	Mariner	£15	

	Year ref.	Name	Parish or area	Occupation or status	Value	Notes
	1733/63	Pedven, James	City of Bristol	Mariner	£2	
	1706/34	Peeke, John	City of Bristol	Baker	£18	
	1661/60	Peele, Anthony	St. Stephen	Shipwright	£9	
	1694/45	Pegler, John	--	--	£3	
	1690/34	Pegler, William	--	--	£3	
W	1678/46	Peirce, Hugh	SS. Philip & Jacob	Tiler	£10	
W	1665/43	Peirce, Joan	(see Pearce)			
	1612/11	Peirce, William	Westbury-on-Trym (Lawrence Weston)			
W	1749/59	Peircey, Joseph	City of Bristol	--	£18	
	1736/23	Peirs, John, Matravers		Mariner	£10	
	1695/32	Peirson, John	City of Bristol	Soapmaker	£10	
	1662/37	Peirson, Margaret	(see Pearson)	Surgeon	£315	
	1781/CP	Pell, John	Castle Precinct	Lighterman	--	'no goods to hand'
	1719/35	Penberthy, Katherine	City of Bristol	Widow	£35	
	1709/54	Pence, Lawrence	(alias Spence, which see)			
	1667/55	Pendas, John	(see Pidas)			
	1691/37	Pendry, Thomas	St. James	--	£62	
	1691/36	Penington, John		--	£53	
	1675/56	Pennington, Robert	Christchurch	Inn-holder	£223	
	1685/41	Penrose, Bartholomew	City of Bristol	Shipwright	£16	
	1624/52	Pentegrace, Robert	St. Nicholas	--	£5	
	1623/50	Pentegrace, Robert	(see Pentygreace)			
	1623/50	Pentygreace, Robert	St. Nicholas	--	£9	
W	1681/57	Pepwall, John	Mangotsfieldd	Gent.	£26	
	1673/27	Pepwell, Bridget	City of Bristol	Mistress	£30	
W	1639/81	Pereman, William	Henbury	--	£80	
W	!633/49	Perfitt, Edmond	(see Parphett)			
W	1671/32	Periman, William (snr)	Henbury	⟨Yeoman⟩	£96	
	1671/31	Perincheife, Samuel	(see Parincheife)			

	Reference	Name	Place	Occupation	Value	Notes
	1719/36	Perkins, James	SS. Philip & Jacob	Yeoman	£28	
W	1715/38	Perkins, Joan	City of Bristol	Widow	£68	
	1690/31	Perkins, Peter	St. James	--	£10	
	1699/21	Perks, Thomas	Mangotsfield	Gunsmith	£6	
	1635/67	Perrie, John	(see Pirrie)			
	1644/43	Perrie, William	St. Stephen	Seafarer	£26	
	1726/28	Perriman, Abigail	Almondsbury	--	£270	
W	1648/14	Perriman, Edward	St. Stephen	<Mariner>	£45	
	1688/37	Perriman, Robert	Henbury	Fishman	£19	
W	1722/16	Perriman, Thomas	Olveston (Tockington)	Yeoman	£486	
W	1639/81	Perriman, William	(see Pereman)			
	1628/54	Perrin, Anthony	Henbury	--	£5	
	1716/43	Perrot, George	City of Bristol	Mariner	£9	
W	1686/40A	Perry, Samuel	Winterbourne	Gent.	£390	
	1700/13	Perryman, John	--	--	£3	
W	1713/37	Perryman, Thomas	<Henbury> (Aust)	Yeoman	£409	
W	1633/50	Perye, Thomas	St. Mary, Redcliffe	--	£6	
	1642/36	Peryman, Thomas	Littleton-on-Severn	Yeoman	£103	
W	1620/74	Pesely, John	Elberton	--	£61	
W	1643/66	Peter, Henry	Henbury (Charlton)	Yeoman	£5	
	1640/54	Peters, Elinor	Henbury (Charlton)	Widow	£26	
	1623/49	Peters, George	(see Petters)			
W	1735/32	Peterson, Hans	City of Bristol	Mariner	£8	
W	1665/41	Peterson, John (snr)	St. Nicholas	--	£1,825	
W	1743/26	Peterson, John	City of Bristol	Mariner	£4	
	1666/37	Peterson, Peter	St. Stephen	Mariner	£37	
	1749/60	Peterson, Peter	--	<Mariner>	£17	
W	1613/45a	Petipace, Walter	St. James	Brewer	£16	alias Baker
W	1613/45b	Petipace, Walter	St. James	Brewer	--	this inv. with will
	1643/66	Petre, Henry	(see Peter)			
	1661/58	Pett, Robert	St. Stephen	Shipwright	--	
	1661/59	Pett, Robert	St. Stephen	Shipwright	£3	compare 1661/58

Year ref.		Name	Parish or area	Occupation or status	Value	Notes
1623/49		Petters, George	St. Stephen	–	£8	
1644/44		Petteson, Henry	St. Peter	Translator <i.e. Cobbler>	£26	
1620/75		Pettingale, Margaret	All Saints	Widow	£101	
1731/70		Petty, William	City of Bristol	Mariner	£10	
1644/44		Pettyson, Henry	(see Patteson)			
1713/38		Peuryfy, William	City of Bristol	Mariner	£15	
1664/40	W	Peverell, John	St. Mary-le-Port	<Vintner>	£367	
1609/59		Pewe, Thomas	–	Shipwright	£19	
1760/24	W	Phelan, Pagett	City of Bristol	Mariner	£12	
1643/67		Phelps, Alice	St. Stephen	–	£5	
1717/43		Phelps, Charles	City of Bristol	Ship-carpenter	£10	died at sea
1643/68	W	Phelps, Elizabeth	St. James	Widow	£196	
1625/64	W	Phelps, George	Almondsbury	–	£53	
1695/28	W	Phelps, Jennette	SS. Philip & Jacob	Widow	£37	
1646/35		Phelps, John	Abbots Leigh	Mariner	£38	2 documents
1723/26	W	Phelps, John	City of Bristol	<Shipwright>	£138	
1624/53	W	Phelps, Thomas	St. James	<Yeoman>	£2	
1640/56		Phelps, Thomas	St. James	House-carpenter	£323	
1640/57		Phelps, Walter	St. Thomas	–	£34	3 documents
1694/47		Phelps, William	SS. Philip & Jacob	Victualler	£126	
1646/35		Phelpes, John	(see Phelps)			
1690/35		Phelpes, David	St. Peter	Tobacco-roller	£56	
1634/56	W	Phelpes, Israel	Almondsbury	<Single-woman>	£9	
1633/51		Phelpes, Joan	(see Felpes)			
1640/55	W	Phelpes, Lettis	St. Thomas	Widow	£31	
1643/69		Phelpes, Thomas	St. Nicholas	–	£5	
1666/38		Phelpes, William	St. Mary, Redcliffe	Mariner	£820	
1637/44		Philbridge, James	St. Mary, Redcliffe	–	£1	
1736/24		Phillips, David	City of Bristol	Mariner	£5	
1750/36		Phillips, Elizabeth	City of Bristol	Widow	£10	

	Ref.	Name	Place	Occupation	Value	Notes
(w)	1752/25	Phillips, James	City of Bristol	Cooper	--	no values given
	1726/29	Phillips, John	City of Bristol	Mariner	£17	
		Phillips,	<a 1726 will of John Phillips, SS. Philip & Jacob, Gardener, exists>				
W	1749/62	Phillips, John	City of Bristol	Mariner	£6	
W	1755/9	Phillips, Joseph	City of Bristol	--	£5	
W	1709/45	Philkins, Thomas (jnr)	St. Owland, Co. Mon.	Mariner	£7	
W	1665/42	Phillipps, John	Filton	Wheelwright	£59	
W	1766/8	Phillips, Allen	City of Bristol	Mariner	£2	with wills
W	1700/6	Phillips, Ann	City of Bristol	Spinster	£59	
W	1624/54	Phillips, Edward & Jane				
W	1674/33	Phillips, Elizabeth	St. John	Spinster	£4	
W	1670/34	Phillips, George	City of Bristol	<Brazier>	£28	
W	1749/61	Phillips, James	St. Mary, Redcliffe	Mariner	£29	
	1625/62	Phillips, John	City of Bristol	--	£10	
W	1627/19	Phillips, John	Filton	Husbandman	£71	
	1734/33	Phillips, John	SS. Philip & Jacob	Cooper	£40	
W	1671/34	Phillips, Katherine	City of Bristol Westbury-on-Trym <Shirehampton>	--	£19	died at sea also 2nd copy
	1731/72	Phillips, Michael	City of Bristol	Widow	£75	
	1710/24	Phillips, Richard	City of Bristol	Ship-carpenter	£10	
	1716/44	Phillips, Richard	City of Bristol	Mariner	£12	
	1731/71	Phillips, Richard	City of Bristol	Mariner	£5	
W	1634/57	Phillips, Robert	St. Peter	Mariner	£5	
	1719/37	Phillips, Robert	City of Bristol	<Tailor>	£30	
W	1749/63	Phillips, Robert	City of Bristol	Mariner	£7	
	1634/58	Phillips, Roger	Christchurch	Mariner	£19	
W	1705/29	Phillips, Thomas	(see Stephens, Thomas)	--	£2	
	1740/47	Phillips, Thomas	City of Bristol	Mariner	£15	
W	1672/43	Phillips, William	Winterbourne	Husbandman	£125	
	1715/39	Phillips, William	City of Bristol	Mariner	£16	
	1709/46	Phillpot, William	Temple	Mariner	£4	
	1636/44	Philpot, James	St. Michael	--	£3	also Filpot

	Year	Name	Parish or area	Occupation or status	Value	Notes
W	1677/35	Philpott, Elizabeth	<SS. Philip & Jacob>	Widow	£67	
	1693/9	Philpott, George	--	--	£96	
W	1696/28	Philpott, Hannah	City of Bristol	Widow	£28	
	1609/5	Philpott, Margaret	(alias Bass, which see)			
	1643/70	Philpott, William	St. John	<Cooper>	£6	
	1682/54	Phippen, Hercules		Glazier	£60	
W	1711/33	Phippes, Edward	<St. James>	<Tobacco-cutter>	£18	
W	1613/46	Phippes, Elizabeth	Mangotsfield	Widow	£9	
	1748/57	Phippin, Joseph	City of Bristol	Baker	£53	
	1758/24	Phipps, Abraham	--	--	£15	
(w)	1767/CP	Phipps, Abraham	St. George	Coal-miner	£2	widow's will
W	1613/47	Phipps, George	Mangotsfield	--	£12	
W	1679/53	Phipps, George	City of Bristol (Castle St.)			
W	1707/32	Phipps, Richard	<Barton Regis>	Maltster	£445	
	1747/31	Phipps, Richard	City of Bristol	<Horse-driver>	£20	
	1680/38	Phipps, William	SS. Philip & Jacob	Mariner	£14	
W	1742/43	Phipps, William	City of Bristol	--	£20	
W	1708/39	Phips, Thomas	Barton Regis	Mariner	£18	
W	1652/3	Piccatt, Thomas	St. Nicholas	Yeoman	£237	
	1620/76	Pickarell, Joan	(see Pickrell)	<Shipwright>	£88	
	1731/73	Pickett, Adam	City of Bristol	Mariner	£11	
W	1652/3	Pickett, Thomas	(see Piccatt)			
W	1680/39	Pickett, William	City of Bristol	Soapmaker	£47	
	1609/60	Pickmere, Judith	--	--	£5	
W	1617/43	Pickrell, Edward	St. Michael	Blacksmith	£33	
	1620/76	Pickrell, Joan	St. Michael	Widow	£52	
	1667/55	Pidas, John	Barton Regis	Yeoman	£20	
W	1756/11	Piggott, Francis	City of Bristol	Mariner	£15	
	1756/12	Pigott, Ann	City of Bristol	--	£15	compare also Ann Pigott, 1756/12 alias Primmer

Ref.		Name	Place	Occupation	Amount	
1742/44		Piguenit, Francis	City of Bristol	Mariner	£12	
1666/39	W	Pill, Humphrey <snr>	St. Thomas	<Felt-maker>	£7	
1713/39	W	Pillorne, Mary	Winterbourne	Widow, <Mercer of small wares>	£33	
		Pillourn, Mary	(see Pillorne)			
1713/39	W	Pichback, William	City of Bristol	Mariner	£7	
1728/32	W	Pinder, Thomas	City of Bristol	Mariner	£5	
1735/33	W	Pinny, Alexander	City of Bristol	Mariner	£524	
1707/33		Piper, Joseph	City of Bristol	Mariner	£2	
1731/74	W	Pirkins, Anne	St. Mary, Redcliffe	Widow	£5	
1690/30		Pirrie, John	St. Stephen	Mariner	£22	
1635/67		Pitcher, Mary	Barton Regis	Widow	£31	
1687/48	W	Pitcher, Robert	Barton Regis	Cordwainer	£31	
1687/49		Pitching, Pascall	City of Bristol	Mariner	£16	
1761/24		Pitman, George	Henbury (Charlton)	--	£92	
1696/27		Pitt, Alice	St. Thomas	Widow	£79	
1672/42	W	Pitt, John	City of Bristol	Mariner	£9	
1686/38		Pitt, Robert	St. Peter	Grocer	£60	
1664/39	W	Pitts, Katherine	St. Nicholas	Widow	£78	
1642/37	W	Plaisteed, Anthony	St. Leonard	Single-man	£4	
1633/52		Platt, John	City of Bristol	Mariner	£18	
1734/34		Player, Edward	Henbury	--	£43	
1672/45		Player, Simon	Winterbourne	Smith	£64	
1732/56	W	Player, Thomas	Henbury	--	£108	
1668/44		Player, William	City of Bristol	Mariner	£10	
1689/53	W	Pleari, Joseph	--	<Hatter>	£3	
1702/22		Pleary, Joseph (jnr)	(see Pleari)			
1705/25		Plomer, Samuel (jnr)	City of Bristol	Plumber	£78	
1724/12		Plomer, Sarah	City of Bristol	Spinster	£326	inv. & account
1673/28		Plomley, Thomas	St. Augustine	--	£38	
1734/35	W	Plowman, William	City of Bristol	Victualler	£8	
1710/25		Plumley, George (jnr)	City of Bristol	Mariner	£12	
1674/35	W	Plumley, John	City of Bristol	Clothier	£27	

	Year	Name	Parish or area	Occupation or status	Value	Notes
	1694/42	Plumley, John	City of Bristol	Glazier	£5	
W	1694/48	Plumley, John	(duplicate of 1694/42, above)			
W	1673/28	Plumly, Thomas	(see Plomley)			
	1625/63	Plummer, Thomas	--	--	£4	
W	1696/25	Pockridge, Thomas	City of Bristol	Inn-holder	£208	
W	1722/17	Pollard, John	City of Bristol	Mariner	£11	
	1632/57	Pollock, John	City of Bristol	Mariner	£17	
	1692/32	Pomeroy, Robert	--	--	£40	
	1633/53	Ponten, Joan	Winterbourne	--	£3	
W	1731/75	Pontin, Richard	SS. Phillip & Jacob	--	£171	
	1633/53	Ponting, Joan	(see Ponten)			
	1688/36	Pontyn, Peter	St. Peter	Tanner	£126	
W	1646/36	Poole, Ann	(see Poole, Thomas)			
W	1671/33	Poole, Anne	St. Stephen	Widow	£51	
	1756/13	Poole, Henry	City of Bristol	Wheelwright	£213	inv. & account
W	1695/31	Poole, Jane	SS. Phillip & Jacob	Widow	£40	
(w)	1734/36	Poole, Jane	City of Bristol	Widow	£15	
	1711/34	Poole, John	City of Bristol	Plasterer	£42	
	1617/44	Poole, Maurice	St. James	Carpenter	£6	
	1662/38	Poole, Richard	Mangotsfield	Husbandman	£34	
	1643/71	Poole, Thomas	St. James	Point-maker	£43	
W	1646/36	Poole, Thomas & Ann	St. James	Whitawer	£215	
W	1717/44	Poole, Thomas	City of Bristol	Merchant	£79	
W	1778/CP	Poole, William	SS. Phillip & Jacob	Maltster	£1,447	inv. & account
	1634/59	Poope, William	(see Pope)			
	1663/49	Poope, Thomas	(see Pope)			
	1604/1	Poore, Maurice	Almondsbury	--	£47	
W	1623/51	Poore, Nicholas	Almondsbury (Over)	--	£28	compare 1625/61
W	1625/61	Poore, Nicholas	Almondsbury (Over)	--	£26	compare 1623/51
W	1628/55	Pope, Elizabeth	St. Peter	Widow	£9	

W	Ref	Name	Place	Occupation	Value	Notes
W	1711/35	Pope, Guy	Almondsbury	Yeoman	£431	
W	1663/50	Pope, James	Henbury	<Yeoman>	£179	
	1620/77	Pope, John	<Lawrence Weston>	--	£35	
	1637/45	Pope, John	St. Ewen	Pin-maker	£1	
W	1634/69	Pope, Margery,	St. Thomas	--	£30	
	1688/38	Pope, Nicholas	(alias Strange, which see)			
	1663/49	Pope, Thomas	City of Bristol	House-carpenter	£102	
	1675/55	Pope, Thomas	Henbury	Maltster	£21	
	1734/37	Pope, Thomas	St. John	Cooper	£4	
	1634/59	Pope, William	Mangotsfield	Mariner	£3	
	1757/16	Pope, William	St. Nicholas	Cooper	£4	
W	1683/46	Poplee, William	City of Bristol	Mariner	£14	
	1710/26	Porch, William	St. Peter	Widow	£18	
	1678/9	Porter, Alice	City of Bristol	<Widow>	£143	
W	1773/CP	Porter, Ann	(alias Baker, which see)			
W	1625/65	Porter, Katherine	Abbot's Leigh	Mariner	£60	
	1732/58	Porter, Peter	<City of Bristol>	-	£13	
	1682/35	Porter, Richard	City of Bristol	Rough-mason	£34	
	1663/48	Porter, Anthony	Abbots Leigh	Surgeon	£8	
W	1720/26	Porter, David	St. Augustine	<Inn keeper>	£609	inv. of an Inn 5 ft. (150 cm) long
	1658/1	Potter, John	City of Bristol	<Cooper>	£314	
	1698/29	Potter, Nicholas	City of Bristol	--	£2	
W	1633/54	Potter, Robert	--	Clerk	£106	
W	1758/25	Potter, Thomas	Almondsbury	Mariner	£12	
	1741/38	Potts, John	City of Bristol	-	£18	
	1684/47	Pound, William	St. John	--	£91	
W	1765/2	Povey, Thomas	Abbots Leigh	Mariner (Cooper)	£10	with wills
W	1746/34	Pow, Francis	City of Bristol	Mariner	£8	with wills
	1624/55	Powell, Agnes	Henbury	Widow	£37	account only
	1635/68	Powell, Agnes	Henbury	Widow	£37	2 documents

	Year	Name	Parish or area	Occupation or status	Value	Notes
	1696/24	Powell, Ann	SS. Phillp & Jacob	--	£2	
W	1647/22	Powell, Elizabeth	St. Michael	Widow	£340	
W	1661/61	Powell, Elizabeth	St. Peter	<Widow>	£69	
	1741/39	Powell, Elizabeth	City of Bristol	Widow	£9	
	1709/47	Powell, Evan	--	<Mariner>	£10	
	1683/37	Powell, George	(alias Mittford, which see)			
W	1763/7A	Powell, Hannah	City of Bristol	Widow	£12	with 1765 wills
	1663/52	Powell, Humphrey	City of Bristol	--	£22	alias Wall
	1636/45	Powell, John	St. Michael	Parson	£5	<rector 1615 to 1633>
	1727/28	Powell, John	Almondsbury	Yeoman	£62	
	1748/58	Powell, John	--	Mariner	£12	
	1718/26	Powell, Mary	City of Bristol	Widow	£18	
	1639/82	Powell, Richard	--	--	£4	
	1676/35	Powell, Richard	--	Mariner	£7	
W	1748/59	Powell, Samuel	--	<Mariner>	£17	
W	1639/83	Powell, Susan	St. Nicholas	Widow	£15	
W	1611/63	Powell, Thomas	Temple	Cloth-worker	£20	
	1646/37	Powell, Thomas	St. Michael	Seaman	£1	also marked St. Nicholas
	1717/45	Powell, Thomas	City of Bristol	Shipwright	£17	died at sea
W	1723/25	Powell, Thomas	City of Bristol	Shipwright	£14	died at sea
	1752/26	Powell, Thomas	City of Bristol	Mariner	£10	
	1713/40	Powell, Walter	City of Bristol	Mariner	£8	
W	1623/72	Powell, William	(alias Whitney, which see)			
	1674/26	Powell, William	(alias Mitford, which see)			
	1674/32	Powell, William	(alias Midford, which see)			
W	1681/56	Pownoll, William	St. Augustine	Gardener	£110	
	1644/45	Pownoll, Israell	St. Augustine	Gent.	£116	
	1670/37	Poyte, John	St. Peter	Cooper	£15	
	1699/20	Pranne, Aaron	--	--	£4	
	1761/26	Pratt, George	City of Bristol	Victualler	£205	inv. & account

	Ref.	Name	Place	Occupation	Value
W	1722/18	Pratt, William	City of Bristol	Yeoman	£117
W	1761/25	Pratt, William	City of Bristol	Mariner	£8
	1725/14	Pratten, William	City of Bristol	Mariner	£20
	1623/52	Prendergast, Margery	St. Stephen	Widow	£21
W	1625/78	Prentice, William	(alias Thorne, which see)		
	1733/64	Presbury, Nathaniel	(see Prisbury)		
	1739/19	Prescott, William	City of Bristol	Mariner	£16
	1721/22	Preston, John	City of Bristol	Mariner	£5
	1689/50	Prestwich, Edward	City of Bristol	Victualler	£13
	1740/48	Prewet, Mary	(document re administration)		
W	1640/58	Prewett, Anthony	St. Mary, Redcliffe	Woollen-draper	£389
	1696/22	Prewett, Henry	Barton Regis	Carrier	£51
	1696/23	Prewett, Mary	Barton Regis	Widow	£36
	1702/23	Prewett, Suzanna	Mangotsfield (Downend)	Widow	£67
	1694/43	Prewett, Thomas	City of Bristol	Cooper	£12
	1646/39	Price, Ann	Temple	Widow	£1
	1729/32	Price, Anne	City of Bristol	Widow	£377
	1618/57	Price, Bridget	City of Bristol	Widow	—
	1706/35	Price, Charles	—	—	£75
	1692/34	Price, David	Christchurch	—	£3
W	1628/52	Price, Elizabeth	Hampton-in-Arden Co. Warwick	Widow	£21
	1711/36	Price, Elizabeth	City of Bristol	Widow	£18
	1752/27A	Price, Elizabeth	City of Bristol	Widow	£12
W	1710/27	Price, Esther	Almondsbury	Widow	£70
W	1735/34	Price, Evan	City of Bristol	Mariner	£6
	1686/39	Price, Francis	City of Bristol	Tailor	£7
	1633/55	Price, John	Westbury-on-Trym	Mariner	£11
W	1636/46	Price, John	St. Thomas	<Apothecary>	£61
	1715/40	Price, John	City of Bristol	Surgeon	£337
	1730/46	Price, John	City of Bristol	Mariner	£10

Year	Name	Parish or area	Occupation or status	Value	Notes
W 1628/56B	Price, Margery	Olveston (Tockington)	Widow	£48	
1729/31	Price, Martha	Henbury	Widow	£63	
1628/57	Price, Peter	City of Bristol	Basket-maker	£6	
1684/46	Price, Reece	St. Mary, Redcliffe	Potter	£1	
W 1679/55	Price, Thomas	City of Bristol	Serjeant-at-Mace	£182	
W 1628/56A	Price, William	Olveston (Tockington)	Tailor	£36	
W 1709/48	Price, William	City of Bristol	Mariner	£3	
W 1710/28	Price, William	Westbury-on-Trym (Stoke Bishop)	<Husbandman>	£11	
1713/41	Price, William	City of Bristol	--	£15	
1714/33	Price, William	Henbury	Yeoman	£217	
W 1732/59	Price, William	City of Bristol	Mariner	£3	
1678/47	Prichard, Lewis	Temple	Porter	£41	
W 1703/14	Prichard, Richard	Westbury-on-Trym (Shirehampton)	<Yeoman>	£55	
W 1694/46	Prickett, John	City of Bristol	Tobacco-cutter	£78	
1640/59	Priddy, George	Stapleton	--	£1	
1627/20	Prigg, John	Filton	Yeoman	£55	
W 1624/56	Prigg, Thomas	Henbury	--	£18	
1714/34	Priggs, Thomas	Winterbourne (see Pigott)	Felt-maker	£75	
1756/12	Primmer, Ann	City of Bristol	Merchant	£2	
1609/61	Prince, Robert	Christchurch	Lay Clerk (Cath.)	£69	
W 1634/60	Prince, Thomas	Olveston	Spinster	£9	
W 1613/48	Prior, Alice	City of Bristol	Mariner	£7	
W 1751/13	Prior, James	Westbury-on-Trym (Shirehampton)	Yeoman	£27	
1624/57	Prior, John	St. Thomas	Widow	£22	
W 1640/60	Prior, Judith	City of Bristol	Shipwright	£13	died at sea
1733/64	Prisbury, Nathaniel				

W	Ref	Name	Place	Occupation	Value	Notes
	1718/27	Pristone, William	Westbury-on-Trym	Mariner	£5	
W	1682/36	Pritchard, Edward	Olveston	Parish Clerk	£16	
W	1663/51	Pritchard, Robert	St. Peter	Rector	£104	
	1732/60	Pritchard, Thomas	City of Bristol	Brewer	£4	
W	1680/40	Pritchet, Thomas	Olveston (Ingst)	--	£103	3 documents
W	1640/61	Pritchett, Elinor	Olveston	--	£9	alias Pear
	1689/54	Probin, Ann	St. Stephen	Widow	£8	
W	1680/41	Probin, Thomas	St.Stephen	Widow	£26	
W	1636/49	Prosser, William	(alias Rosser, which see)	Mariner		
	1674/36	Prosser, William	St. Stephen	--	£12	
	1718/28	Prosser, Thomas	City of Bristol	--	£27	
W	1733/65	Prout, Elianor	Henbury	Widow	£4	
	1647/23	Prout, Henry	Olveston	Yeoman	£35	
	1696/26	Prout, Jonathan	Henbury	--	£133	
W	1633/56	Proutt, Samuel	Olveston	Husbandman	£29	
W	1649/20	Provice, John	Almondsbury	Yeoman	£167	
	1687/50	Provinder, Richard	SS. Philip & Jacob	Yeoman	£15	
	1666/41	Prowse, Charles	Alveston	--	£206	
W	1646/38	Prowse, Mary	Almondsbury	Widow	£48	
W	1729/33	Pruett, Edmund	late of Kingston, Jamaica	--	£996	inv. & account
			(see Prigg)			
W	1624/56	Pryg, Thomas	St. Nicholas	Mariner	£5	also Pryme
	1634/61	Prynne, George	Henbury (Northwick)			
	1624/58	Pryor, William				
	1642/38	Puddie, Richard	St. Mary, Redcliffe	Yeoman	£43	
	1709/49	Pugsley, John	City of Bristol	Felt-maker	£26	
	1687/51	Pugsley, Richard	City of Bristol	Mariner	£8	
	1628/58	Pullen, James	Olveston (Hazel)	Tailor	£26	
	1753/24	Pullen, James	(see Pullin)	Yeoman	£185	
W	1618/58	Pullen, John	Olveston (Upper Hazel)	Yeoman	£27	
	1748/60	Pullen, Thomas	City of Bristol	Mariner	£10	

Year		Name	Parish or area	Occupation or status	Value	Notes
1753/24		Pullin, James	Clifton	--	£8	
1700/33	w	Pullin, Joan	Almondsbury (Cattybrook)	Widow	£56	
1668/42B	w	Pullin John	Mangotsfield	Tanner	£320	
1701/24	w	Pullin, John	Almondsbury	Tailor	£279	
1701/24	w	Pulling, John	(see Pullin)			
1676/33		Pumrey, Elizabeth	City of Bristol	Widow	£6	
1678/48		Punfield, William	St. Stephen	--	£47	
1709/50		Purchis, Joseph	City of Bristol	Mariner	£10	
1735/14		Purlong, Charles	(alias Furlong, which see)			
1642/39		Purnell, John	St. Michael	--	£7	
1719/38		Purnell, John	<City of Bristol>	Ironmonger	£311	
1734/38		Puslow, Samuel	SS. Philip & Jacob	Tanner	£109	
1760/25		Putham, George	City of Bristol	Mariner	£10	
1763/CP		Putham, Mary	City of Bristol	Widow	£747	inv. & account
1643/72	w	Puxton, Alice	St. Thomas	<Widow>	£82	
1668/43	w	Puxton, Michael	St. Mary, Redcliffe	Soap-boiler	£293	
1746/35		Pyke, Thomas	City of Bristol	Mariner	£10	
1706/36	w	Quarman, Cornelius	City of Bristol	Mariner	£15	
1721/23		Quarryman, Thomas	SS. Philip & Jacob	Tailor	£16	
1747/32		Quested, Alexander	City of Bristol	Mariner	£4	
1740/26		Quin, Ennis	City of Bristol	Mariner	£10	
1740/49		Quin, Patrick	City of Bristol	Mariner	£6	
1635/69	w	Quindram, Mary	St. Werburgh	Widow	£15	
1618/59		Quinterne, Francis	(see Quintril)			
1618/59		Quintril, Francis	St. Michael	--	£2	
1704/25		Radford, James	SS. Philip & Jacob	--	£4	
1642/40		Radman, Henry	St. Michael	--	£4	
1643/73		Ragland, Thomas	St. Stephen	<Cooper>	£69	

	Ref.	Name	Place	Occupation	Value	Notes
W	1629/56	Rainstorpe, Joan	(alias Tailer, which see)			
W	1634/62	Raishley, Alice	St. Nicholas	Widow	£29	
	1748/61	Raker, John	City of Bristol	Mariner	£10	
W	1703/15	Ramsden, Jeffrey	City of Bristol	<Exciseman>	£99	inv. & account
	1677/38	Randall, Henry	St. James	--	£11	
	1735/35	Randall, Joseph	City of Bristol	Bell founder	£88	<brass founder>
W	1613/49	Randall, Moses	Olveston	--	£32	
W	1723/27	Ranger, Rose	City of Bristol	Widow	£6	
	1633/57	Rannoles, Anne	Westbury-on-Trym	Widow	£8	
	1730/47	Raoul, Daniel	--	Mariner	£5	
	1742/45	Rawle, John	City of Bristol	Mariner	£10	
W	1739/20	Rayly, Michael	City of Bristol	Mariner	£7	
	1749/64	Rayment, Joseph	City of Bristol	Mariner	£10	
	1629/47	Rayne, Haulfe	St. Nicholas	Cooper	£4	
	1633/57	Raynolds, Anne	(see Rannoles)			
	1760/27	Raynolds, John	Stapleton	Cordwainer	£5	
W	1667/60	Read, Edward	SS. Philip & Jacob	--	£41	
W	1643/74	Read, James	City of Bristol	Brewer	£290	
W	1675/59	Read, James	<St. Augustine the less>			
W	1634/63	Read, Lydia	St. Ewen	Clerk	£552	
	1637/46	Read, Nicholas	St. Michael	Spinster	£106	
	1716/46	Read, Samuel	City of Bristol	--	£27	
	1647/24	Read, Thomas	St. Mary, Redcliffe	Surgeon	£5	
	1690/36	Read, William	--	--	£3	
	1639/84	Reade, Henry	Stapleton	--	£12	
	1640/62	Reade, Henry	Stapleton	--	£3	
W	1641/41	Reade, Mary	Christchurch	--	£3	
	1636/47	Reade, Richard	St. Thomas	Soapmaker	£284	
	1625/66	Reade, Thomas	--	Shearman	£53	
	1732/61	Reain, John	City of Bristol	--	£9	also 2nd copy
	1628/59	Rece, Mathew	(see Reece)	Mariner	£11	
W	1733/67	Rechey, William	City of Bristol	Mariner	£10	

	Year	Name	Parish or area	Occupation or status	Value	Notes
	1666/42	Record, John	St. Stephen	Mariner	£4	
	1629/48	Reddiford, John	St. Stephen	Joiner	£4	
W	1624/59a	Redman, William	SS. Philip & Jacob	--	£7	copy of 59a with additions 1630
W	1624/59b	Redman, William	SS. Philip & Jacob	--	£31	
W	1640/63	Redman, William	SS. Philip & Jacob (the valuation of an Inn & its grounds only)	--	£6	
W	1746/36	Redmond, James	City of Bristol	Mariner	£11	
	1708/40	Redwood, Henry	City of Bristol	Tobacconist	£91	
	1736/25	Redwood, Philip	City of Bristol	Shipwright	£9	
W	1725/15	Redy, Peter	City of Bristol	Mariner	£9	died at sea
	1635/70	Reece, Ann	St. Nicholas	Widow	£3	
	1640/64	Reece, Anne	St. Leonard	Widow	£48	
	1666/43	Reece, David	St. Augustine	Yeoman	£42	
	1639/85	Reece, Jenkin	(see Rese)			
W	1690/37	Reece, Joyce	City of Bristol	Widow	£9	
	1628/59	Reece, Mathew	St. Leonard	--	£9	
	1690/38	Reece, William	City of Bristol	Cooper	£11	
	1718/29	Reece, William	City of Bristol	Mariner	£3	
	1711/37	Reed, John	City of Bristol	Mariner	£17	
	1684/51	Reed, Lewis	City of Bristol	Tanner	£12	
W	1690/39	Reed, Sarah	St. Augustine	Widow	£8	
	1690/36	Reed, William	(see Read)			
	1639/84	Reede, Henry	(see Reade)			
W	1637/47	Reeks, Margaret	(see Rickes)			
	1746/37	Rees, William	City of Bristol	Mariner	£14	
	1635/70	Reese, Ann	(see Reece)			
	1744/11	Reese, Charles	City of Bristol	Mariner	£16	
W	1685/43	Reeve, Edmond	Horfield	Yeoman	£49	
	1728/33	Reeves, John	City of Bristol	Mariner	£10	
W	1636/48	Reeves, William	Abbots Leigh	--	£14	

W	Ref.	Name	Place	Occupation	Value
W	1747/33	Renalls, George	City of Bristol	Mariner	£15
	1687/52	Rendall, Edward	City of Bristol	Pipe-maker	£118
	1735/35	Rendall, Joseph	(see Randall)		
	1730/49	Rennolds, Jonathan	City of Bristol	Mariner	£10
	1639/85	Rese, Jenkyn	St. Mary, Redcliffe	--	£6
	1730/48	Revan, John	City of Bristol	Mariner	£12
W	1617/49	Reve, George	(see Ryve)		
W	1752/28	Reymer, John	(see Raymore)		
W	1742/46	Reymore, John	City of Bristol	Mariner	£20
W	1662/39	Reynell, Benjamin	City of Bristol	Mariner	£3
	1669/56	Reynolds, Elizabeth	St. Mary, Redcliffe	Widow	£51
	1730/49	Reynolds, John	Temple	--	£11
	1748/62	Reynolds, Jonathan	(see Rennolds)		
W	1623/53	Reynolds, Nathan	City of Bristol	Labourer	£6
W	1695/33	Reynolds, Richard	Westbury-on-Trym (Stoke Bishop)	Husbandman	£26
	1691/38	Reynolds, Robert	City of Bristol	Inn-holder	£192
	1715/41	Reynolds, Thomas	--	--	£14
W	1730/50	Reynolds, William	City of Bristol	Mariner	£5
	1639/85	Rhodes, John	City of Bristol	Mariner	£17
W	1729/34	Rice, Jenkin	(see Rese)		
W	1730/51	Rich, Henry	<Almondsbury> (Over)	Yeoman	£8
	1705/26	Richards, Henry	City of Bristol	<Mariner>	£19
	1733/66	Richards, Jane	Henbury (Charlton)	Spinster	£135
W	1741/40	Richards, John	City of Bristol	Baker	£100
	1734/39	Richards, John	City of Bristol	Mariner	£6
	1718/30	Richards, Joseph	City of Bristol	Mariner	£4
	1715/42	Richards, Mary	City of Bristol	Widow	£5
	1714/35	Richards, Richard	City of Bristol	Mariner	£6
W	1642/41	Richards, Symon	City of Bristol	Yeoman	£138
W	1755/10	Richards, Thomas	Filton	<Yeoman>	£139
W	1721/24	Richards, Thomas	City of Bristol	Carpenter	£19
		Richards, William	Henbury	<Yeoman>	£217

Year	Name	Parish or area	Occupation or status	Value	Notes
1729/35	Richards, William	City of Bristol	Mariner	£5	
W 1741/41a	Richards, William	City of Bristol	Mariner	£7	
W 1741/41b	Richards, William	City of Bristol	Mariner	£10	
1751/14	Richards, William	City of Bristol	Mariner	£5	
1752/27B	Richardson, William	City of Bristol	Mariner	£7	
W 1733/67	Richey, William	(see Rechey)			
W 1613/50	Richman, Richard	Henbury (Kingsweston)	Husbandman	£140	
1761/27	Rickards, Robert	City of Bristol	Mariner	£7	
W 1637/47	Rickes, Margaret	Westbury-on-Trym (Shirehampton)	--	£20	
1751/15	Ricketts, James	City of Bristol	Mariner	£5	
1637/50	Rider, John	SS. Phillip & Jacob	Haberdasher	£2	
1661/63	Rider, John	St. Mary, Redcliffe	--	£3	
1661/62	Rider, Robert	St. Mary, Redcliffe	--	£8	
1700/14	Ridley, Giles	City of Bristol	Tailor	£18	
W 1643/75	Ridley, Richard	Olveston (Tockington)	⟨Yeoman⟩	£183	
W 1643/75	Ridlye, Richard	(see Ridley)			
W 1644/46	Rieve, Roger	Olveston (Tockington)	Husbandman	£245	
1608/2	Riffes, John	--	--	--	
		(details of fittings in house let to John Riffes)			
1643/79	Rimer, Thomas	St. Nicholas	⟨Butcher⟩	£50	
1804/CP	Ring, Joseph	Temple	Potter	£887	inv. & account
W 1691/39	Risdell, Bridget	⟨City of Bristol⟩	⟨Widow⟩	£3	
1750/41B	Rishton, John	City of Bristol	Mariner	--	a 1740 inv., reused for Sevell 1750/41A
1729/36	Rishton, Thomas	City of Bristol	Linen-draper	£2,083	
W 1738/19	Ritch, George	City of Bristol	Mariner	£3	
1667/59	Rive, John	St. Stephen	Mariner	£55	

	Reference	Name	Parish/Place	Occupation	Value	inv. & account
	1684/49	Rivers, John	City of Bristol	Cooper	£8	
	1686/1	Roach, Daniel	St. Stephen	Soapmaker	£66	
W	1674/37	Roach, Edward	Abbots Leigh	Shipwright	£105	
	1676/36	Roach, Elizabeth	Castle Precinct	Widow	£14	
W	1669/60	Roach, Hugh	Abbots Leigh	Shipwright	£33	
W	1712/40	Roach, Hugh	Abbots Leigh	Shipwright	£100	
	1746/38	Roach, Israel	City of Bristol	Mariner	£12	
	1679/56	Roach, Morgan	St. Nicholas	Victualler	£12	
W	1623/54	Roach, Thomas	Abbots Leigh	Husbandman	£68	
	1673/29	Roach, Thomas	Almondsbury	Husbandman	£69	
	1685/44	Roach, Thomas	St. Mary, Redcliffe	Felt-maker	£1	
	1609/62	Roach, William	(see Roche)			
	1623/55	Roach, William	St. John	Surgeon-barber	£13	
	1738/20	Roach, William	St. John	Haulier	£1061	
	1743/27	Roads, Jacob	City of Bristol	Mariner	£12	
	1750/38	Roades, Henry	SS. Philip & Jacob	--	£10	
W	1643/76	Robbins, Agatha	(see Robbins, Robert)			
	1714/36	Robbins, John	Almondsbury	--	£160	
	1750/37	Robbins, Richard	City of Bristol	Victualler	£10	
W	1643/76	Robbins, Robert & Agatha	St. Mary-le-Port	Shoemaker	£92	
	1733/68	Robbins, Thomas	City of Bristol	Mariner	£14	
	1756/14	Robbinson, Richard	City of Bristol	Mariner	£7	
	1714/36	Robens, John	(see Robbins)			
	1643/77	Robes, John	St. James	--	£124	
	1758/26	Robert, John	City of Bristol	Mariner	£9	
	1668/45	Roberts, George	St. Stephen	Mariner	£8	
	1611/64	Roberts, Henry	St. Peter	--	£5	
	1714/37	Roberts, Isaac	City of Bristol	Mariner	£59	
	1719/39	Roberts, Joan	City of Bristol	Spinster	£15	
W	1741/42	Roberts, John	City of Bristol	Mariner	£10	
	1620/72	Roberts, Judith	(alias Parry, which see)			
W	1617/45	Roberts, Mary	St. Peter	Widow	£13	
W	1665/44	Roberts, Phillip	St. Thomas	Mariner	£14	

	Year	Name	Parish or area	Occupation or status	Value	Notes
	1730/52	Roberts, Richard	City of Bristol	Mariner	£6	
W	1623/56a	Roberts, Walter	St. John	--	£4	
	1623/56b	Roberts, Walter & Margaret	St. John	--	£8	
	1696/29	Roberts, William	--	--	£19	
W	1763/7B	Robertson, Benjamin	City of Bristol	Mariner	£17	
W	1731/76	Robertson, James	City of Bristol	Mariner	£6	
W	1749/65	Robertson, Robert	City of Bristol	Mariner	£19	
W	1727/29	Robins, Gabriel	City of Bristol	Tiler	£9	
W	1688/40A	Robins, John	Stoke Gifford (Little Stoke)	Yeoman	£242	
	1734/40	Robins, John	City of Bristol	Mason	£18	
W	1694/49	Robins, Samuel	Westbury-on-Trym (Shirehampton)	Yeoman	£60	
	1748/63	Robins, Samuel	City of Bristol (alias Oxford, which see)	Mariner	£15	
W	1686/37	Robinson, Edward	City of Bristol	Physician	£7	
	1709/51	Robinson, Edward	City of Bristol	Mariner	£7	
	1743/28	Robinson, George	Abbots Leigh	--	£40	
	1672/46	Robinson, John	--	--	£3	
	1692/36	Robinson, John	City of Bristol	Mariner	£7	
	1733/69	Robinson, John	City of Bristol	Mariner	£7	
W	1733/70	Robinson, John	(see Robbinson)			
	1756/14	Robinson, Richard	Abbots Leigh		£69	
W	1687/53	Robinson, Ruth	Abbots Leigh	Widow	£127	
W	1674/37	Roch, Edward	(see Roach)			
W	1618/60	Roche, Henry	Abbots Leigh	Yeoman	£10	
	1676/36	Roche, Elizabeth	(see Roach)			
	1609/62	Roche, William	Olveston	Single-man	£56	also Roach
W	1695/CP	Rocke, Richard	<City of Bristol>	<Cordwainer>	£59	will 1692
W	1620/78	Rockwell, Thomas	St. Stephen	Mariner	£254	
W	1623/57	Rockwell, Walter	St. James	Mariner	£20	
W	1676/37	Rodman, Elizabeth	--	--		

W	Reference	Name	Place	Occupation	Value	Notes
W	1693/28	Rodman, Henry	Alveston (Earthcott)	Yeoman	£265	
	1677/39	Roe, Anne	SS. Philip & Jacob	Widow	£20	
	1681/59	Roe, Dennis	Barton Regis	Yeoman	£87	
	1700/15	Roe, Hugh	St. Stephen	--	£16	
W	1669/59	Roe, John	Barton Regis	--	£66	
	1686/41	Roe, John	--	Butcher	£7	
W	1713/42	Roe, John	SS. Philip & Jacob	Smith	£18	
	1761/21	Roe, John	(alias Lewdon, which see)			
	1625/67	Roe, Margaret	SS. Philip & Jacob	Almswoman	£2	
	1692/35	Roe, Mathew	(see Rowe)			
W	1733/71	Roe, Philip	City of Bristol	Mariner	£5	
	1639/86	Roe, William	(see Rowe)			
W	1683/47	Rogers, Ann	City of Bristol	Widow	£38	
W	1641/42	Rogers, Anne	St. Nicholas	Single-woman	£48	also 2nd copy
W	1604/2	Rogers, Anthony	Stapleton	<Yeoman>	£8	on back of will
	1755/11	Rogers, Edmund	Clifton	--	£19	
W	1706/37	Rogers, Edward	Westbury-on-Trym	--	£163	
	1771/1	Rogers, Elizabeth	--	--	£28	
	1637/48	Rogers, John	St. Augustine	--	£3	
	1642/42	Rogers, John	Temple	Shearman	--	
	1682/38	Rogers, John	City of Bristol	--	£5	
	1609/63	Rogers, Owen	Temple	Shearman	£12	
	1764/CP	Rogers, Stephen	St. Stephen	Mariner	£74	inv. & account
W	1682/37	Rogers, Thomas	City of Bristol	Baker	£61	
W	1708/41	Rogers, Thomas	Westbury-on-Trym (Hung Road)	Mariner	£4	
W	1759/17	Rogers, William	City of Bristol	<Mariner>	£16	
	1752/29	Rolph, Thomas	City of Bristol	Pump-maker	£132	inv. & account
	1628/60	Rome, John	SS. Philip & Jacob	--	3s 0d	
	1635/71	Rome, John (snr)	St. James	Carpenter	£2	
	1665/45	Rome, Mary	(see Roome)			
	1648/15	Rome, William	Westbury-on-Trym (Shirehampton)	Husbandman	£107	
W	1623/54	Rooch, Thomas	(see Roach)			
	1673/29	Rooch, Thomas	(see Roach)			

Year ref.	Name	Parish or area	Occupation or status	Value	Notes
W 1674/38	Rooke, Elizabeth	Temple	Widow	£19	
W 1665/45	Roome, Mary	Westbury-on-Trym ⟨Shirehampton⟩			
W 1620/79	Roome, William	Henbury	Widow	£148	
1713/43	Roots, Ann	City of Bristol	Yeoman	£179	
1756/15	Rose, Ann	City of Bristol	Widow	£167	
1730/53	Rose, Thomas	City of Bristol	Widow	£19	
1675/62	Roseworme, John	City of Bristol	Mariner	£5	
1711/38	Rose, Samuel	Barton Regis	Painter (Artist)	£48	
1746/39	Ross, Thomas	City of Bristol	Victualler	£176	
W 1720/27	Rosse, David	City of Bristol	Mariner	£5	
W 1718/31	Rosser, Joseph	City of Bristol	Mariner	£5	
			House-carpenter	£305	inv. and will dated 1715 alias Prosser
W 1636/49	Rosser, William	St. Nicholas	⟨Salter⟩	£96	
1708/42	Rosser, William	Westbury-on-Trym	Yeoman	£19	
1711/39	Rosser, Morgan	City of Bristol	Mariner	£16	
1688/40B	Rossiter, Henry	--	--	£51	account only
1677/55	Rossworm, --	--	Colonel	£47	
1681/60	Roswell, George	Winterbourne	--	£3	
1671/36	Rouche, Nathaniel	Almondsbury	Husbandman	£266	
W 1710/29	Roulston, George	(see Rowlston)			
1728/34	Rouse, Edward	City of Bristol	Mariner	£12	
1755/12	Rouse, Jonas	City of Bristol	Mariner	£7	
1755/12	Rouse, Thomas	(see Rouse, Jonas)			
W 1617/46	Rousell, Elizabeth	St. Nicholas	Widow	£6	
1677/37	Rousell, Prudence	City of Bristol	Spinster	£4	
1618/61	Row, David	St. Stephen	--	£38	
1663/55	Row, Thomas	Barton Regis	--	£19	
1721/25	Rowe, Israel	City of Bristol	--	£10	
1692/35	Rowe, Mathew	--	--	£3	
W 1639/87	Rowe, Thomas	SS. Philip & Jacob	--	£71	

W	Ref	Name	Place	Occupation	Amount
	1639/86	Rowe, William	St. Michael	--	£2+
W	1675/60	Rowell, Hannah	St. James	Widow : Pauper	£1
W	1643/78	Rowland, Katherine	St. Mary, Redcliffe	Spinster	£180
W	1732/62	Rowland, Richard	City of Bristol	Mariner	£7
W	1710/29	Rowlston, George	Henbury <Aust>	Yeoman	£184
W	1716/45	Rowlstone, Mary	<Henbury> (Aust)	Widow	£73
W	1697/30	Roworth, John <snr>	City of Bristol	Cordwainer	£200
	1644/41	Royall, William	St. James	Mariner	£4
	1637/49	Royden, Thomas	Brislington	--	£169
	1663/54	Roynion, Clement	(see Roynon)		
	1663/54	Roynon, Clement	St. Nicholas	--	£72
	1669/57	Roynon, John	--	--	£31
W	1715/43	Rudge, Ann	--	Widow	£243
	1767/CP	Rudge, John	City of Bristol	Presser & Packer	£56
	1739/21	Rudge, Thomas	City of Bristol	Butcher	£13
	1740/50	Rudgway, Richard	City of Bristol	Mariner	£10
W	1757/17	Rugg, Thomas	City of Bristol	Mariner	
	1747/34	Rummin, John (jnr)	City of Bristol	Mariner	£15
	1611/65	Rumney, Edward	Westbury-on-Trym	--	£12
	1671/35	Rumney, Hugh	Henbury	Yeoman	£63
	1669/58	Rumney, Jane	Westbury-on-Trym	Widow	£10
W	1663/53	Rumney, William	Westbury-on-Trym	<Husbandman>	£27
	1617/47	Rumny, Edmond	St. Mary, Redcliffe	Felt-maker	£77
	1761/28	Rumsey, Patrick	<City of Bristol>	Mariner	£22
W	1729/37	Runcorne, Richard	Christchurch	<Mariner>	£9
	1642/43A	Runninger, Anthony	City of Bristol	Bodice-maker	£10
W	1727/30	Runny, Thomas	<City of Bristol>	Mariner	£5
W	1721/26	Runwa, Francis	Littleton-on-Severn	<Mariner>	£5
W	1715/44	Russell, Nathaniel	Littleton-on-Severn	Yeoman	£142
W	1671/38	Russell, George	Littleton-on-Severn	Husbandman	£188
W	1684/50	Russell, George	Olveston (Pilning)	Husbandman	£279
W	1694/15	Russell, Isaac		--	£187

	Year ref.	Name	Parish or area	Occupation or status	Value	Notes
W	1761/29	Russell, James	City of Bristol	Mariner	£2	
	1625/68	Russell, John	Olveston (Ingst)	Labourer	£2	
W	1708/43	Russell, Jonathan	Littleton-on-Severn	\<Yeoman\>	£183	
W	1639/88	Russell, Katherine	Littleton-on-Severn	Widow	£27	
W	1647/25	Russell, Richard	Littleton-on-Severn	Yeoman	£224	died at sea
W	1760/28	Russell, Robert	City of Bristol	Stone-carver	£12	
W	1745/21	Ruttinburge, William	City of Bristol	Mariner	£13	
W	1754/23B	Ryan, Charles	City of Bristol	\<Hooper\>	£366	
W	1740/51	Ryan, Edward	City of Bristol	Mariner \<Hooper\>	£15	
	1636/50	Ryder, Ralphe	Christchurch	Yeoman	£56	
W	1617/48	Ryman, John	St. Peter	Smith	£63	
	1643/79	Rymer, Thomas	(see Rimer)			
W	1617/49	Ryve, George	Christchurch	Inn-holder	£170	
	1640/68	Sachfield, Martin	St. Augustine	Mariner	£25	
	1743/29	Sadbury, Francis	City of Bristol	Mariner	£18	
W	1727/31	Sadler, William	City of Bristol	Mariner	£20	
	1633/58	Sage, Thomas	--	--	£27	
W	1665/56	Sage, William	Compton Greenfield	Yeoman	£17	
W	1749/66	Saires, James	City of Bristol	Mariner	£12	
	1748/64	Salcombe, John	City of Bristol	Mariner	£6	
	1689/57	Salisbury, Sarah	St. Stephen	--	£20	
W	1624/60	Sallway, Edward	Almondsbury	--	£51	
	1683/50	Salmon, Samuel	SS. Philip & Jacob	--	£4	
	1641/43	Salmon, Thomas	St. Stephen	Mariner	£15	
	1675/67	Salmon, Thomas	St. John	--	£2	
	1684/59	Salmon, William	Almondsbury (Hempton)	Yeoman	£56	
	1721/27	Salter, Edward	Barton Regis	Victualler	£86	
	1637/51	Salterne, George	St. James	Esquire	£188	
W	1711/40	Sam, Daniel	City of Bristol	Mariner	£18	

	Reference	Name	Place	Occupation	Value	Notes
	1625/69	Sam, Daniel	St. Thomas	--	£5	
	1667/69	Samborne, Joseph	St. Thomas	--	£7	2 other documents
	1625/69	Samm, Daniel	(see Sam)			
	1636/51	Samme, Avis	Temple	--	£11	
	1678/49	Sampson, Daniel	Almondsbury	--	£307	
	1716/48	Sampson, Jane	City of Bristol	Baker	£404	3 documents
W	1676/40	Sampson, Joan	<City of Bristol>	<Widow>	£85	
	1639/89	Sampson, John	(see Samson)			
W	1679/57	Sampson, John	Henbury (Charlton)	Gent.	£375	
W	1689/56	Sampson, Martha	Henbury (Charlton)	Widow	£266	
	1716/47	Sampson, Phillip	City of Bristol	Baker	£522	
	1729/38	Samson, Samuel	City of Bristol	Mariner	£7	
W	1622/1	Samuell, John	Mangotsfield	Carpenter	£23	
W	1620/81	Sanders, Antony	Abbots Leigh	--	£8	
W	1719/40	Sanders, Hannah	(see Saunders)			
	1643/80	Sanders, Henry	(see Saunders)			
W	1665/51	Sanders, Henry	Abbots Leigh	<Shipwright>	£75	
	1625/70	Sanders, John	Almondsbury	--	£51	
	1628/61	Sanders, John	Henbury	Husbandman	£15	
W	1684/58	Sanders, John	St. Mary, Redcliffe	--	£13	
W	1687/55	Sanders, John	Abbots Leigh	Shipwright	£55	
W	1665/53	Sanders, Phillip	Abbots Leigh	<Mariner>	£15	
W	1742/47	Sanders, Richard	City of Bristol	Cordwainer	£191	
	1617/50	Sanders, Samuel	Christchurch	--	£12	
	1692/37	Sanders, Samuel	City of Bristol	Milliner	£51	
	1653/3	Sanders, William	St. Michael	<Blacksmith>	£2	
	1719/41	Sanders, William	Almondsbury	Yeoman	£283	
	1639/90	Sandford, Edward	(see Sanford)			
W	1739/22	Sandford, Elizabeth	City of Bristol	Spinster	£8	
	1687/54	Sandford, Richard	City of Bristol	Merchant Tailor	£19	
	1708/44	Sandford, Richard	<St. Ewen>	Surgeon	£133	
W	1677/40	Sandford, Samuel	Westbury-on-Trym	Inn-holder	£216	
	1736/26	Sandford, William	City of Bristol	Mariner	£7	

	Year ref.	Name	Parish or area	Occupation or status	Value	Notes
	1746/40	Sandoe, Henry	City of Bristol	Mariner	£10	
	1642/43B	Sandy, Edward	St. Nicholas	--	£122	bond due
W	1639/90	Sanford, Edward	Henbury	--	£21	
	1739/22	Sanford, Elizabeth	(see Sandford)			
W	1722/19	Sanger, Deborah	City of Bristol	<Widow>	£67	
W	1661/71	Sankey, Margaret	St. Mary, Redcliffe	<Widow>	£7	
	1641/44	Sankye, William	St. Mary, Redcliffe	--	£7	
	1639/89	Sansom, John	Westbury-on-Trym	--	£29	
W	1680/42	Sansom, Robert	<St. Nicholas>	Labourer	£20	alias Atkins
W	1611/66	Sansome, Joane	Henbury (Charlton)	Single-woman	£51	
	1611/67	Sansome, Joanne	Henbury	Widow	£15	
W	1669/67	Sargant, Joan	Westbury-on-Trym	Widow	£81	
W	1633/59	Satchfield, John	(see Serchfield)			
W	1656/1	Satchfield, Mary	Long Ashton, Som.	Widow	£11	
	1620/80	Sattiford, William	St. James	Mariner	£9	
W	1666/57	Saulle, John	St. Augustine	Soapmaker	£121	
W	1710/30	Saunders, Abraham	Westbury-on-Trym (Shirehampton)	Mariner	£66	
W	1710/31	Saunders, Anne	City of Bristol	Widow	£4	
W	1620/81	Saunders, Antony	(see Sanders)			
W	1669/65	Saunders, Elizabeth	<Abbots Leigh>	Widow	£19	
W	1719/40	Saunders, Hannah	Abbots Leigh	Spinster	£8	
	1643/80	Saunders, Henry	St. Stephen	Cook	£46	
W	1665/51	Saunders, Henry	(see Sanders)			
	1625/70	Saunders, John	(see Sanders)			
	1680/45	Saunders, John	Almondsbury	Husbandman	£137	
	1758/30	Saunders, John	City of Bristol	Currier	£3	
	1783/CP	Saunders, John	City of Bristol	Victualler	£97	inv. & account
W	1727/32	Saunders, Joseph	Stapleton	Clerk	£193	
	1679/65	Saunders, Matthew	St. Nicholas	--	£4	
W	1665/53	Saunders, Phillip	(see Sanders)			

	Reference	Name	Place	Occupation	Value	Note
	1629/49	Saunders, Richard	St. Mary, Redcliffe	Plumber	£6	
	1617/50	Saunders, Samuel	(see Sanders)			
	1611/68	Saunders, Thomas	St. Michael	Sailor	£7	
	1613/51	Saunders, Thomas	Christchurch	Pinker	£15	also 2nd copy
	1747/35	Saunders, Thomas	City of Bristol	Mariner	£15	
	1653/3	Saunders, William	(see Sanders)			
W	1709/52	Saunders, William	Olveston (Pilning)	Yeoman	£417	
	1717/46	Saunders, William	Almondsbury	Yeoman	£285	
	1719/41	Saunders, William	(see Sanders)			
	1633/60	Savadge, Thomas	St. Werburgh	--	£4	
	1684/52	Savage, Anne	Stoke Gifford	Widow	£78	
W	1745/22	Savage, James	SS. Philip & Jacob	Gunsmith	£15	
W	1668/46	Savage, John	Stoke Gifford	Husbandman	£102	
W	1633/61	Savage, Mathew	(see Savige)			
	1756/16	Savage, Thomas	City of Bristol	Victualler	£19	
W	1695/36	Savedge, Joan	Abbots Leigh	Widow	£39	
W	1691/41	Savedge, John	Abbots Leigh	<Shipwright>	£345	
W	1633/61	Savige, Mathew	Almondsbury	Yeoman	£174	
W	1624/61	Savydge, Joan	Abbots Leigh	<Widow>	£32	
W	1617/51	Saw, William	St. Mary, Redcliffe	Dyer	£6	
	1678/68	Sawyer, Elizabeth	St. John	--	£90	account only
W	1753/25	Sawyer, Francis	City of Bristol	Mariner	£10	
	1743/30	Sayer, Charles	City of Bristol	Mariner	£18	
W	1749/66	Sayers, James	(see Saires)			
	1623/58	Scampe, John	St. Stephen	Almsman	£4	
	1667/2	Scarlett, Humphrey	(alias Austin, which see)			
	1623/58	Schampe, John	(see Scampe)			
W	1740/52	Schmiedel, Godfrey	City of Bristol	Mariner	£12	
	1723/28	Scolfield, James	City of Bristol	Broker	£10	
	1640/65	Scooler, Edith	Henbury	Widow	£22	
	1676/42	Scoper, Henry	(see Skoper)			
W	1637/52	Scorie, Margaret	Mangotsfield	<Widow>	£18	
W	1682/42	Scott, John	St. Stephen	--	£34	

	Year ref.	Name	Parish or area	Occupation or status	Value	Notes
W	1717/47	Scott, John	City of Bristol	Mariner	£18	
W	1750/39	Scott, John	City of Bristol	Mariner	£4	
W	1684/53	Scott, Mary	City of Bristol	Widow	£21	
W	1731/77	Scott, Richard	City of Bristol	Mariner	£20	
W	1750/40	Scott, Thomas	City of Bristol	Cordwainer	£19	
W	1625/71	Scoulter, Alexander	Henbury	--	£113	
	1624/62	Scoulter, Catherine	Henbury	--	£53	
	1625/72	Scoulter, Edith	Henbury	--	£42	
W	1731/78	Scouly, Thomas	City of Bristol	Mariner	£3	
W	1641/45	Screene, John	Almondsbury	Husbandman	£138	
	1640/66	Scriven, Arthur	Elberton	--	£39	
	1754/24A	Scriven, Benjamin	City of Bristol	Mariner	£5	
W	1669/68	Scriven, John	Elberton	<Husbandman>	£58	
W	1694/55A	Scriven, John	Olveston	Husbandman	£231	
	1717/48	Scrivin, William	Almondsbury	Yeoman	£359	
W	1738/21	Scudder, George	City of Bristol	Mariner	£12	
	1733/73	Sculk, Anne	City of Bristol	Widow	£16	
	1668/52A	Sculke, Rowland	St. Augustine	Hauler	£103	
	1683/53	Scuse, Elizabeth	St. Michael	Widow	£34	
	1660/16	Scuse, George	(see Skuse)			
	1725/16	Seaborne, Nicholas	City of Bristol	Mariner	£125	inv. & account
	1768/CP	Seabrook, James	City of Bristol	Silversmith	£17	
W	1683/55	Seacomb, Elizabeth	City of Bristol	Widow	£61	
W	1675/26	Seager, Agnes	Almondsbury (Over)	Widow	£302	
			(document marked 'Fishpoole' on the outside)			
W	1676/38	Seager, Bridget	Elberton	Widow	£28	
W	1640/67	Seager, James	Elberton	Yeoman	£244	
W	1633/62	Seager, John	Almondsbury (Over)	Yeoman	£295	
W	1646/40	Seager, John	Alveston <Hazel>	<Yeoman>	£172	
	1650/13	Seager, John	Almondsbury (Over)	--	£105	
	1668/51	Seager, John	St. Peter	Tanner	£150	

	Reference	Name	Place	Occupation	Value
W	1679/61	Seager, John	Almondsbury	Yeoman	£363
W	1633/63	Seager, Robert	Olveston	<Husbandman>	£24
	1699/24	Seager, Samuel	Almondsbury (Easter Compton)	Yeoman	£1,023
W	1611/69	Seager, Thomas	Elberton	<Yeoman>	£260
W	1637/53	Seager, Thomas	Olveston (Hazel)	<Yeoman>	£182
W	1663/63	Seager, Thomas	Olveston	Yeoman	£50
W	1721/28	Seager, Thomas	Henbury <Compton Greenfield>	Yeoman	£174
W	1679/68	Seager, William	St. James	Mason	£16
	1673/37	Seakam, John	St. Stephen	Shipwright	£29
	1683/48	Seale, Robert	St. Thomas	Inn-holder	£18
	1717/49	Sealy, Amos	City of Bristol	Apothecary	£8
W	1664/45	Seaman, Edward	St. Stephen	Barber-surgeon	£31
W	1727/33	Search, William	Olveston	<Inn-holder>	£133
	1633/64	Seargant, Thomas	Westbury-on-Trym	<Husbandman>	£44
	1609/64	Seargaunte, Alice	(see Sergeant)		
	1761/30	Searle, George	City of Bristol	Mariner	£11
W	1627/21	Seavall, Edward	(see Sevell)		
W	1613/52	Seavall, John	Almondsbury	Husbandman	£91
	1617/52	Seavall, Robert	Almondsbury	--	£13
W	1691/40	Seavell, Edward	Henbury (Aust)	Yeoman	£42
W	1639/91	Seavell, Elizabeth	Henbury (Aust)	Widow	£23
W	1668/47	Seavell, Mary	Henbury	Single-woman	£50
W	1697/34	Seavell, Thomas	Littleton-on-Severn	Yeoman	£65
W	1633/65	Seavell, William	<Henbury> (Aust)	Husbandman	£141
W	1660/15	Seavill, William	Compton Greenfield	<Husbandman>	£331
W	1668/47	Seawell, Mary	(see Seavell)		
W	1643/81	Segar, John <snr>	Olveston (Hazel)	Yeoman	£1018
W	1637/53	Segar, Thomas	(see Seager)		
W	1670/39	Selcock, Anthony <snr>	Winterbourne	Yeoman	£174
	1618/62	Seldon, Jonas	City of Bristol	Wire-drawer	£12
W	1694/53	Selfe, Jane	Westbury-on-Trym	Widow	£57

Year ref.	Name	Parish or area	Occupation or status	Value	Notes
1661/66	Selfe, John	Temple	Clothworker	£69	
W 1679/69	Selfe, William	Temple	--	£60	
1744/12	Sellwood, Caleb	City of Bristol	Mariner	£7	
W 1689/60	Selman, Edward	--	Cooper	£11	
1689/2	Selway, Richard	Henbury	--	£59+	
1668/50	Selwin, Nathaniel	St. Mary, Redcliffe	Surgeon	£89	
1634/64	Serchfeild, John	Clifton	--	£281	
W 1633/59	Serchfield, John	Clifton	Yeoman	£89	
1609/64	Sergeant, Alice	Westbury-on-Trym	Widow	£11	
1743/31	Sergeant, Thomas	City of Bristol	Mariner	£5	
1694/54	Serjant, Robert	City of Bristol	Glazier	£20	
1752/30	Serle, John	City of Bristol	Mariner	£10	
1662/13	Seshell, Richard (jnr)	(see Cissell)			
W 1711/41	Sessell, Richard	City of Bristol	Victualler	£19	
1640/68	Setchfield, Martin	(see Sachfield)			
W 1625/73	Sevall, Jane	Henbury (Aust)	Widow	£198	
W 1633/65	Sevall, William	(see Seavell)			
1686/43	Sevel, John	(see Sevill)			
W 1627/21	Sevell, Edward	Almondsbury (Hempton)	Yeoman	£305	
1750/41A	Sevell, William	Henbury	Yeoman	£3	
1686/43	Sevill, John	Compton Greenfield	Husbandman	£256	
1705/27	Seward, Edith	City of Bristol	Widow	£40	
1672/49	Sewell, Elizabeth	Henbury	Single-woman	£51	
1718/32	Seymour, Walter	⟨Christchurch⟩	Basket-maker	£74	excluding debts, see also 1719/42
1719/42	Seymour, Walter	⟨Christchurch⟩ (the account of Sarah Seymour, relict)	Basket-maker	£116	
1639/92	Shaddocke, John	St. Nicholas	Gunner	£6	
1672/47	Shanan, Thomas	St. Stephen	--	£3	
1666/49	Shaparo, John	(see Shepheard)			

Ref.	W	Name	Location	Occupation	Value	Notes
1646/41		Shapeley, William	(see Shapley)			
1646/41		Shapley, William	City of Bristol	Mariner	£10	
1747/36		Sharp, Alexander	City of Bristol	Mariner	£6	
1723/29		Sharp, George	City of Bristol	Cooper	£18	
1635/72	W	Sharpe, John	St. Stephen	Mariner	£1,995	
1674/40	W	Shatford, William	St. Mary-le-Port	--	£21	
1692/40		Shaugh, Thomas	City of Bristol	Cooper	£17	
1734/41		Shaw, Cornelius	City of Bristol	Mariner	£4	
1611/70	W	Shaw, Daniel	St. Michael	⟨Tucker⟩	£8	
1711/42	W	Shawe, George	City of Bristol	Mariner	£117	
1732/63	W	Shaw, James	City of Bristol	Mariner	£9	
1635/73		Sheapard, Andrew	(see Sheapewarde)			
1635/73		Sheapewarde, Andrew	St. Stephen	⟨Mariner⟩	£11	also 2nd copy
1644/48	W	Sheapheard, Anthony	Horfield	--	£50	
1674/41		Shearman, Alexander	Temple	Shearman	£16	
1667/72		Sheate, Ambrose	Stapleton	--	£80	
1746/41		Sheile, Richard	--	⟨Mariner⟩	£8	
1721/29		Shelbery, John	City of Bristol	Gent.	£41	
1635/74		Shepard, William	SS. Philip & Jacob	Butcher	£2	
1628/62		Sheperde, Andrewe	SS. Philip & Jacob	--	£1	
1617/53		Shephard, David	St. Mary-le-Port	--	£25	
1620/82		Shepheard, Edward	(see Sherrod)			
1609/65		Shepheard, John (snr)	Clifton	--	£36	
1666/49		Shepheard, John	Stapleton	Husbandman	£1	
1663/56		Shepherd, John	St. Mary, Redcliffe	Felt-maker	£15	
1773/CP	W	Shepherd, Joseph	City of Bristol	Saddler	£230	inv. & account will 1770
1742/48		Shepherd, Mary	--	Widow	£12	
1753/26		Shepherd, William	Henbury (Northwick)	--		
1715/45		Sheppard, Abraham	City of Bristol	--	£271	
1609/65		Sheppard, John	(see Shepheard)	Mariner	£19	

Year ref.	Name	Parish or area	Occupation or status	Value	Notes
W 1709/53	Sheppard, John	City of Bristol	Mariner \<Gunsmith in will\>	£12	
W 1744/13	Sheppard, John	City of Bristol	Mariner	£14	
1666/45	Sheppard, William	SS. Phillip & Jacob	\<Butcher\>	£3	
1684/54	Sheppard, William	City of Bristol	Mariner	£4	
1718/33	Sheppard, William	SS. Phillip & Jacob	Mariner	£11	
1746/42	Sheppard, William	Henbury	Yeoman	£203	
W 1734/42	Shepperd, Elianor	City of Bristol	Widow	£1	
1628/63	Shepperd, Robert	St. Stephen	Sailor	£4	
1690/40	Shepperd, Joan	--	--	£6	
1690/40	Shepward, Joan	(see Shepperd)			
1620/82	Sherewood, Edward	(see Sherrod)			
W 1750/42	Sheriff, James	City of Bristol	Mariner	£4	
W 1718/34	Sherman, Emanuell	SS. Phillip & Jacob	Mariner	£13	
W 1771/CP	Sherman, Thomas	Stapleton	Yeoman	£4	inv. & account
W 1620/83	Sheron, Susan	St. Werburgh	Widow	£71	
W 1750/42	Sherriff, James	(see Sheriff)			
1620/82	Sherrod, Edward	St. James	--	£4	
W 1620/83	Sherwood, Susan	(see Sheron)			
W 1682/40	Shinkle, Mary	(alias Skinker, which see)			
1740/53	Shinnig, John	City of Bristol	Mariner	£10	
1682/43	Shinstone, Jeremiah	Barton Regis	--	£1	
W 1662/40	Shiply, Margery	Mangotsfield	Widow	£22	
1620/84	Shipman, Richard	Henbury	Yeoman	£2	
1649/21	Shipman, William	--	--	£14	
W 1745/23	Shipton, Richard	City of Bristol	Mariner	£8	
1745/24	Shipton, William	City of Bristol	Mariner	£8	
W 1634/65	Shipway, John	St. Mary-le-Port	\<Cordwainer\>	£224	
W 1679/63	Shipway, John	Henbury	\<Husbandman\>	£60	
1684/57	Shires, Isaac	City of Bristol	Mariner	£20	
1664/44	Shore, Alice	St. James	--	£427	

Ref.		Name	Place	Occupation	Value	Notes
1678/50		Short, John	St. Stephen	Tailor	£71	
1745/25	W	Short, Samuel	⟨St. Thomas⟩	⟨Cordwainer⟩	£13	inv. & account
1758/27		Short, Walton	St. Stephen	Painter	£76	
1666/47		Shorte, Thomas	Horfield	--	£4	
1669/63		Shough, Walter	St. James	Cooper	£84	
1688/41		Showell, Arnold	--	--	£29	
1712/41	W	Showell, Mary	City of Bristol	Widow	£209	
1673/33		Shurte, John	City of Bristol	Mariner	£16	
1670/41		Shute, John	City of Bristol	Blacksmith	£32	
1724/13	W	Shute, John	City of Bristol	Yeoman	£87	
1730/55	W	Shute, John	City of Bristol	Surgeon	£11	
1635/75		Shute, Walter	St. John	--	£6	
1648/16	W	Shuter, Julian	City of Bristol	Widow	£301	
1682/44	W	Shuter, Mary	⟨St. Mary, Redcliffe⟩	Widow	£14	
1667/65		Shuter, Nicholas	St. Mary, Redcliffe	⟨Tanner⟩	£2	
1637/54		Shuter, Richard	St. Thomas	Haberdasher	£508	
1643/82		Shutter, William	City of Bristol	Haberdasher	£280	
1679/64		Silcock, Henry	Stapleton	--	£61	
1682/41	W	Silcock, Henry	Stapleton	⟨Yeoman⟩	£250	
1690/44		Silcock, Thomas	Stapleton	Yeoman	£242	
1861/62	W	Silcock, William	Almondsbury (Hempton)			3 documents
1714/38	W	Silcox, Joseph	City of Bristol	Tailor	£34	
1698/31	W	Silke, Edward	City of Bristol	Sugar-baker	£108	
1672/48		Sillcocke, Richard (snr)	St. Stephen	Baker	£11	
1716/51		Sillivent, Robert	City of Bristol	Yeoman	£20	
1733/72		Silly, Henry	City of Bristol	Mariner	£13	
1673/36	W	Simes, William	SS. Philip & Jacob	Mariner	£5	
1640/69	W	Simkins, Nicholas	St. Augustine	Blacksmith	£204	
1663/62	W	Simkins, William	Temple	Cloth-worker	£4	
1717/50	W	Simmons, John	Winterbourne	⟨Yeoman⟩	£17	
	W	Simmons, Mary	Winterbourne	Widow	£71	
			(Hambrook)	Widow	£217	

	Year ref.	Name	Parish or area	Occupation or status	Value	Notes
	1667/68	Simmons, Joseph	Stoke Gifford	Yeoman	£175	
	1727/34	Simmons, Peter	City of Bristol	Sail-maker	£15	died at sea
	1671/37	Simons, Ann	St. Augustine	Widow	£39	alias Atkins
	1698/30	Simons, Elizabeth	St. Thomas	Widow	£295	
		Simpkins, Nicholas	(see Simkins)			
w	1640/69	Simpkins, William	City of Bristol	Mariner	£10	
w	1749/67	Sims, Grace	SS. Phillip & Jacob	Widow	£109	
	1679/58	Sims, John	SS. Phillip & Jacob	Farrier	£21	
	1687/57	Sims, John	City of Bristol	Mariner	£5	
w	1731/79	Sims, Robert	SS. Phillip & Jacob	Farrier	£38	
	1675/61	Sims, Walter	(see Symonds)			
w	1679/62	Sims, William	Barton Regis	<Blacksmith>	£108	
	1677/43	Simson, John	City of Bristol	Mariner	£12	
	1729/39	Sinclair, William	City of Bristol	Mariner	£5	
w	1735/36	Sinclera, Robert	City of Bristol	Mariner	£13	
	1710/32	Sinderling, Edmond	—	—	£2	
w	1699/23	Singer, John	St. Michael	Surgeon	£35	also 2nd copy
w	1633/66	Sinnock, Nigell	City of Bristol	Mariner	£8	
	1747/37	Sinot, Lawrence	City of Bristol	Mariner	£7	
w	1720/28	Siscell, Richard	City of Bristol	Tiler	£33	
	1710/33	Sisell, Hester	City of Bristol	Spinster	£63	
	1718/35	Sisell, Peter	(see Cecill)			
	1695/11	Sisile, Richard	(see Cecile)			
	1706/6	Sissell, David	(see Cissell)			
	1635/15	Skeech, William	St. Nicholas	Mariner	£11	
	1664/27	Skeedmore, Deborah	St. Peter	—	£5	
	1643/83	Skeets, Thomas	City of Bristol	Mariner	£16	
	1748/65	Skeuse, John	Mangotsfield	—	£201	
w	1668/48	Skinker, Mary	City of Bristol	Spinster	£24	alias Shinkle
	1682/40	Skinker, Thomas	City of Bristol	Mariner	£11	
w	1722/20	Skinner, Barnaby	City of Bristol	Whitawer	£45	
	1697/32					

W	Ref.	Name	Place	Occupation	Value
	1635/76	Skone, Joan	St. Stephen	Wife	£5
	1676/42	Skoper, Henry	St. John	--	£8
W	1694/52	Skrine, Phillip	City of Bristol	Mariner	£6
W	1721/30	Skriven, Arthur	Olveston (Pilning)	Yeoman	£291
	1733/73	Skulk, Anne	(see Sculk)		
	1660/16	Skuse, George	--	⟨Blacksmith⟩	£17
W	1639/93	Slacke, William	--	Mariner	£2
	1623/59	Slade, Ann	St. James	⟨Single-woman⟩	£23
	1692/39	Slade, John	St. Nicholas	Serge-weaver	£1
W	1705/28	Slade, Nicholas	City of Bristol	Cow keeper	£133
	1692/43	Slade, Richard	Almondsbury	--	£2
	1639/94a	Slade, Roger	--	Cook	£175
	1639/94b	Slade, Roger	St. Michael	(obligation concerning his goods)	
W	1741/43	Sladen, John	City of Bristol	Mariner	£12
	1665/49	Slane, Elizabeth	St. James	Widow	£57
W	1710/34	Slater, James	(see Slatter)		
W	1710/34	Slatter, James	Barton Regis	Gardener	£68
	1618/64	Slayne, Simon	St. James	--	£16
	1737/27	Slead, Isaac	City of Bristol	Gent.	£12
	1734/43	Slond, Hannah	City of Bristol	Spinster	£10
W	1662/42	Slond, John	Alveston	Smith	£85
	1625/74	Slye, Marie	St. Thomas	--	£31
	1618/64	Slyne, Simon	(see Slayne)		
W	1612/2	Smale, John	(alias Cheshire, which see)		
W	1748/66	Small, James	City of Bristol	Mariner	£10
	1749/68	Small, James	City of Bristol	Mariner	£10
	1663/59	Small, John	St. Werburgh	Cloth-worker	£15
	1691/42	Small, John	Almondsbury (The Worthy)	--	£13
W	1629/12	Smalle, Joan	(alias Chisheere, which see)		
W	1750/43	Smart, Alexander	City of Bristol	Mariner	£10
W	1648/17	Smart, Anselm	St. John	Glazier	£150

	Year ref.	Name	Parish or area	Occupation or status	Value	Notes
	1627/22	Smarte, Robert	Stoke Gifford	Yeoman	£3	
	1691/42	Smeale, John	(see Small)			
W	1670/38	Smether, James	Westbury-on-Trym <Shirehampton>			
	1722/21	Smether, John	City of Bristol	Mariner	£401	
W	1679/60	Smith, Agnes	Henbury (Northwick)	Distiller	£20	
	1624/63	Smith, Alice	Henbury	Widow	£80	
	1671/43	Smith, Anne	Stoke Gifford	Widow	£2	
W	1694/56	Smith, Anne	St. John	Widow	£228	
W	1664/46	Smith, Anthony	Stoke Gifford	Yeoman	£132	
	1678/52	Smith, Anthony	St. Nicholas	Cooper	£235	
W	1708/45	Smith, Anthony	City of Bristol	Mariner	£12	
W	1730/54	Smith, Archibald	City of Bristol	Mariner	£7	
W	1745/26	Smith, Benjamin	City of Bristol	Mariner	£7	
	1671/41	Smith, Bridget	Elberton	Widow	£12	
	1639/95	Smith, Edmund	Mangotsfield	--	£10	
	1634/66	Smith, Edward	Henbury	Mariner	£12	
	1712/43	Smith, Edward	City of Bristol	Latten-plate worker	£75	
W	1679/59	Smith, Elinor	Elberton	<Spinster>	£4	
	1675/65	Smith, Elizabeth	Henbury	Widow	£99	
W	1761/31	Smith, Elizabeth	City of Bristol	Widow	£14	
	1740/54	Smith, Ezekial	City of Bristol	Mariner	£18	
	1742/49	Smith, Francis	City of Bristol	Mariner	£8	
	1760/29	Smith, Francis	City of Bristol	Mariner	£3	
	1669/61	Smith, George	St. Mary, Redcliffe	Brewer	£13	
W	1665/52	Smith, Henry	City of Bristol	Shipwright	£63	
W	1665/54	Smith, Henry	Henbury <Northwick>	<Yeoman>	£12	
	1671/42	Smith, Henry	Elberton	Yeoman	£43	
W	1641/47	Smith, Isabel	Olveston	Widow	£125	

W	Reference	Name	Place	Status/Occupation	Value	Notes
	1707/34	Smith, James	City of Bristol	Blockmaker	£24	
	1618/65	Smith, Joan	(see Smythe)			
W	1640/70	Smith, Joan	SS. Philip & Jacob	--	£10	
W	1641/46	Smith, Joan	Alveston (Earthcott)	Widow	£102	
W	1617/54	Smith, Johanne	Elberton	Widow	£34	
	1618/66	Smith, John	(see Smythe)			
	1628/65	Smith, John	St. Thomas	--	£12	
W	1661/70	Smith, John	Olveston	<Husbandman>	£147	
	1669/69	Smith, John	Westbury-on-Trym	--	£24	
W	1669/70	Smith, John	Westbury-on-Trym <Shirehampton>	--	£147	
	1673/31	Smith, John	Castle Precinct	Pilot	£147	
	1683/51	Smith, John	SS. Philip & Jacob	Mariner	£44	
	1707/35	Smith, John	City of Bristol	--	£3	
W	1714/39	Smith, John	Henbury (Northwick)	Mariner	£16	
W	1729/40	Smith, John	City of Bristol	Yeoman	£137	
W	1734/44	Smith, John	City of Bristol	Mariner	£14	
	1755/13	Smith, John	City of Bristol	Mariner	£5	
W	1641/48	Smith, Joseph	Olveston (Pilning)	--	£114	
	1728/35	Smith, Joseph	City of Bristol	--	£261	
	1724/15	Smith, Judith	Horfield	Mariner	£14	
W	1700/34	Smith, Lancelott	Stapleton	Widow	£19	alias Allen
	1639/96	Smith, Margaret	Westbury-on-Trym (Shirehampton)	Husbandman	£53	
W	1633/68	Smith, Martin	Horfield	Widow	£156	
	1722/22a	Smith, Mary	City of Bristol	<Husbandman>	£82	
	1722/22b	Smith, Mary	(printed form re administration by her mother Elizabeth)	Spinster	£20	
	1731/80	Smith, Mary	Mangotsfield	Widow	£4	
	1737/28	Smith, Mary	SS. Philip & Jacob	Spinster	£6	
W	1766/CP	Smith, Mary	(see Smith, Samuel & Mary)			

Year ref.	Name	Parish or area	Occupation or status	Value	Notes
1629/50	Smith, Maurice	St. Augustine	Shoemaker	£4	
1628/64	Smith, Paul	St. Peter	Butcher	£4	
W 1627/23	Smith, Richard	⟨Henbury⟩ (Northwick)		—	fragment only
W 1675/66	Smith, Richard	Henbury	⟨Yeoman⟩	£101	
1736/27	Smith, Richard	City of Bristol	Husbandman	£15	
1635/77	Smith, Robert	St. Nicholas	Mariner	£80	
W 1667/64	Smith, Robert	St. Thomas	Cooper	£76	
W 1684/61	Smith, Robert	Henbury (Stowick)	⟨Baker⟩	£205	
W 1759/18	Smith, Robert	SS. Philip & Jacob	Rough-mason	£18	
1670/42	Smith, Samuel	Frenchay	Mariner	£25	
W 1776/CP	Smith, Samuel & Mary	City of Bristol	Rough-mason	£1,718+	Mary's will 1775
1760/30	Smith, Stephen	City of Bristol	—	£10	
W 1731/81	Smith, Susanna	City of Bristol	Mariner	£14	
W 1613/53	Smith, Thomas	Westbury-on-Trym (Shirehampton)	Widow		
W 1617/55	Smith, Thomas	SS. Philip & Jacob	Yeoman	£259	
W 1633/71	Smith, Thomas	Mangotsfield	Husbandman	£28	
W 1643/84	Smith, Thomas	Olveston (Hazel)	—	£24	
W 1643/85	Smith, Thomas (snr)	Henbury (Aust)	Yeoman	£251	
W 1664/49	Smith, Thomas	Elberton	Yeoman	£139+	damaged
1666/44	Smith, Thomas	Henbury	⟨Yeoman⟩	£730	
W 1683/52	Smith, Thomas	Almondsbury (Earthcott)	Yeoman	£480	
W 1684/56	Smith, Thomas	Henbury ⟨Lawrence Weston⟩	Clothier	£655	
W 1696/30	Smith, Thomas	Henbury (Northwick)	⟨Husbandman⟩	£76	
1698/7	Smith, Thomas	City of Bristol	Yeoman	£162	
1712/42	Smith, Thomas	City of Bristol	Mariner	£31	
W 1722/23	Smith, Thomas	Almondsbury	Mariner	£10	
			Yeoman	£380	

	Reference	Name	Place	Occupation	with wills	inv. & account
W	1740/55	Smith, Thomas	<City of Bristol>	<Mariner>	£17	
	1748/67	Smith, Thomas	City of Bristol	Mariner	£9	
	1750/44	Smith, Thomas	--	--	£19	
W	1764/3	Smith, Thomas	Temple	Mariner	£5	
W	1773/CP	Smith, Thomas	<St. Augustine>	Mariner	£57	
	1665/50	Smith, Walter	Westbury-on-Trym	Husbandman	£3	
W	1644/49	Smith, William	Mangotsfield	Carpenter	£8	
W	1666/52	Smith, William	St. Mary-le-Port	Butcher	£71	
W	1678/54	Smith, William	Henbury	<Yeoman>	£203	
	1688/42	Smith, william	Winterbourne	Yeoman	£24	
	1692/44	Smith, William	--	Cordwainer	£16	
	1721/31	Smith, William	Olveston (Sheepcombe)		£19	
W	1740/56	Smith, William	City of Bristol	Mariner <Cooper>	£7	
W	1633/70	Smithe, John	Olveston	Yeoman	£110	
W	1741/44	Smiths, Samuel	City of Bristol	Mariner	£14	
	1678/56	Smyth, Anne	Olveston	Widow	£170	
W	1704/27	Smyth, Elizabeth	Almondsbury (Over)	Widow	£103	
W	1724/14	Smyth, Giles	SS. Philip & Jacob	Horse-driver	£17	
	1676/39	Smyth, Henry	Henbury	--	£18	
W	1704/26	Smyth, Joan	Almondsbury (Ellinghurste)	Widow	£273	
W	1704/28	Smyth, John	<St. John>	--	£19	
W	1633/69	Smyth, John	Olveston (Tockington)	Yeoman	£363	
	1609/66	Smyth, Katherine	Henbury	--	£149	
	1641/49a	Smyth, Lewis	St. Mary-le-Port	--	£40	
	1641/49b	Smyth, Lewis	(list of debts & additions to inventory)			
W	1628/66	Smyth, Margaret	Olveston <Ingst>	Spinster	£19	
W	1613/54	Smyth, Robert	Almondsbury	--	£39	
W	1724/16	Smyth, Robert (snr)	Henbury (Berwick)	<Yeoman>	£160	
W	1611/73	Smyth, Thomas <snr>	Olveston	Husbandman	£9	
	1667/66	Smyth, Thomas	Olveston	Yeoman	£238	

Year ref.		Name	Parish or area	Occupation or status	Value	Notes
W	1666/50	Smyth, William	Henbury <Aust>	Yeoman	£61	
	1686/42	Smyth, William	St. Thomas	Victualler	£57	
	1611/72	Smythe, Isabell	Elberton	Widow	£73	
	1618/65	Smythe, Joan	St. Peter	Widow	£37	
	1618/66	Smythe, John	St. Stephen	Shipwright	£47	also Smith
	1694/55B	Smythe, Richard	Olveston			
			(Upper Hazell)			
	1609/67	Smythe, William	City of Bristol	Yeoman	£45	
W	1634/67	Snacknaile, Elizabeth	St. Stephen	Hooper	£5	
	1642/45	Snacknaile, Marie	St. Stephen	Widow	£30	
	1642/44	Snacknaile, Thomas	St. Stephen	Widow	£7	
	1624/49	Snacknall, William	(alias Morris, which see)	Hooper	£25	
	1686/44	Snailham, William		--		
W	1634/67	Snaknaille, Elizabeth	(see Snacknaile)			
	1729/41	Snapp, William	City of Bristol	Mariner	£8	
	1642/44	Snecknell, Thomas	(see Snacknaile)			
W	1636/52	Snell, Mary	Castle Precincts	Widow	£556	
W	1661/69	Snell, James	St. Mary, Redcliffe	--	£53	
	1673/35	Snooke, Robert	Clifton	--	£84	
W	1687/56	Snooke, Edith	Clifton	Widow	£18	
	1673/35	Snouk, Robert	(see Snoake)			
	1673/34	Snow, Andrew	SS. Philip & Jacob	<Nailer>	£115	
	1727/35	Snowball, John	City of Bristol	Mariner	£7	
	1740/57	Soaper, John	City of Bristol	Mariner	£4	
	1729/42	Somerell, Samuel	(see Sumerell)			
W	1670/40	Somers, Joan	Mangotsfield	Widow	£170	
	1689/59	Somers, Thomas	Mangotsfield	--	£22	
	1613/55	Somers, William	Henbury			
			(Redwick)			
	1629/51	Somersett, Margaret	(see Somersyte)	Tailor	£7	
	1629/51	Somersyte, Margaret	St. Mary, Redcliffe	--	£3	

Ref	W	Name	Place	Occupation	Value	Notes
1712/45	W	Sommerhill, Edward	(see Sumerhill)			
1753/27	W	Sommers, Abraham	City of Bristol	Mariner	£7	
1664/48	W	Sommers, Henry	Mangotsfield	Yeoman	£141	
1643/87		Sommers, John	City of Bristol	Brewer	£151	
1683/56		Sommers, Thomas	St. Thomas	Inn-holder	£102	
1648/20		Souch, Welthian	City of Bristol	Widow	£3	
1747/38	W	Southall, George	City of Bristol	Mariner	£10	
1690/45	W	Southell, Sarah	City of Bristol	<Widow>	£27	
1667/70	W	Sowle, Andrew	St. Leonard	Painter-stainer	£18	
1671/40	W	Sparke, Elizabeth	Abbots Leigh	Widow	£100	
1692/38	W	Sparkes, Hugh	Abbots Leigh	--	£169	
1640/72		Sparkes, John	St. Augustine	--	£5	
1640/71		Sparkes, Thomas	St. Augustine	Sailor	£30	
1666/51	W	Sparkes, Thomas	St. Augustine	Mariner	£27	
1726/30		Sparkes, William	Abbots Leigh	Shipwright	£15	died at sea
1674/39	W	Sparrow, Elizabeth	Abbots Leigh	Widow	£91	
1628/68		Sparrow, George	St. Leonard	--	—	
1672/52	W	Sparrow, Henry	Abbots Leigh	Husbandman	£115	
1636/53		Sparrow, Jacob	St. Augustine	--	£15	
1639/97	W	Sparrowe, Joan & Elizabeth	Alveston (Earthcott)		£14	
1618/67	W	Sparrowe, Richard	Abbots Leigh	--	£18	
1685/50		Speed, Thomas	City of Bristol	--	£22	
1709/54		Spence, Lawrence	--	Mariner	£19	
1754/24B		Spencer, John	City of Bristol	Mariner	£3	alias Pence
1620/85	W	Spencer, Rebecca	Olveston	Widow	£11	
1678/55	W	Spencer, Susanna	<St. Michael>	Widow	£30	
1760/31		Spencer, Thomas	City of Bristol	Mariner	£10	
1663/61	W	Spencer, William	St. Michael	Mariner	£109	
1635/78	W	Sperin, Christopher	St. Peter	<Inn-holder>	£242	
1691/43		Sperrin, John	SS. Phillip & Jacob	Weaver	£177	
1732/64		Spicer, John	City of Bristol	Mariner	£10	
1716/49		Spooner, Henry	City of Bristol	Ship-carpenter	£18	

Year ref.	Name	Parish or area	Occupation or status	Value	Notes
W 1703/16	Spooner, John	City of Bristol	Brass-founder	£163	
W 1623/60	Spranger, James	Henbury (Northwick)	Husbandman	£215	
1709/55	Spratt, Dowell	--	<Mariner>	£14	
1617/56	Springall, Edward	Winterbourne (Hambrook)	--	£15	
1617/56	Springhall, Edward	(see Springall)			
1680/43	Spurgin, Martha	St. Mary, Redcliffe	Widow	£183	
1613/56	Spurlock, Joan	St. Mary, Redcliffe	Widow	£18	
1677/42	Squire, John	Westbury-on-Trym (Shirehampton)	Inn-holder	£62	
W 1716/50	Squire, Robert	Almondsbury (Compton)	Husbandman <Servant in will>	£31	
W 1672/53	Squire, William	<St. Michael>	Merchant	£63	
1676/41	Squibb, Thomas	--	--	£11	
1620/86	Stackes, Henry	(see Stakes)			
1624/64	Stacy, Nicholas	St. Mary, Redcliffe	Felt-maker	£7	
W 1690/42	Stainer, Jane	Abbots Leigh <Ham Green>	Widow	£243	
W 1611/74	Stainred, William	St. Thomas	Barber	£6	
1620/86	Stakes, Henry	St. Thomas	Mariner	£1	
1749/69	Stalaway, John	City of Bristol	Victualler	£18	
1760/32	Stalker, John	City of Bristol	Mariner	£10	
W 1689/58	Stallard, John	Henbury	Husbandman	£164	
W 1620/87	Stamborne, Edith	Winterbourne	Single-woman	£15	
W 1628/67	Stamborne, Joan	(see Stamburne)			
W 1633/72	Stamborne, Margery	Henbury <Compton Greenfield>	Widow	£41	
W 1613/57	Stambourne, Nicholas	Henbury	--	£37	
1628/67	Stamburne, Joan	Winterbourne	--	£6	
W 1727/36	Stamp, George	City of Bristol	Mariner	£12	

	Ref.	Name	Place	Occupation	Value	Notes
W	1667/73	Standfast, Johanna	Christchurch	Wife	£104	
W	1611/74	Standred, William	(see Stainred)		—	alias Tilladam
	1624/65	Stanfast, Edmond	St. Leonard		£93	
	1663/57	Stanford, Henry	SS. Philip & Jacob	Serge-weaver	£34	
	1643/86	Stanton, John	—	Currier		
	1663/24	Starke, Anne	(alias Gibbons, which see)			
W	1623/64	Stayndred, William	St. Ewen	Barber	£43	
	1641/50	Stayner, William	Abbots Leigh	Shipwright	£77	
W	1671/39	Stearte, George	City of Bristol	Surgeon	£40	
W	1648/18	Steavens, Elizabeth	City of Bristol	<Widow>	£57	
	1754/24C	Steel, James	City of Bristol	Surgeon	£12	ship's surgeon
W	1731/82	Steel, John	City of Bristol	Mariner	£5	
	1752/31	Steel, Richard	City of Bristol	Mariner	£3	
W	1618/68	Steell, Ann	St. Peter	Widow	£8	
W	1686/45	Steer, Richard	City of Bristol	Bridle-cutter	£132	
	1664/47	Steevens, Alice	(see Stevens)			
	1685/45	Steevens, John	Christchurch	Tinman	£67	
	1660/13	Stephen, William	—	Shipwright	£176	
	1641/51	Stephens, Aron	St. Thomas	Cloth-worker	£8	
W	1648/18	Stephens, Elizabeth	(see Steavens)			
W	1680/44	Stephens, Frances	Henbury (Hallen)	Spinster	£90	
W	1708/47	Stephens, James	City of Bristol	Wine-cooper	£8	died at sea
	1748/68	Stephens, James	Winterbourne	Schoolmaster	£7	inv. & account
W	1669/66	Stephens, John	Henbury <Kingsweston>	Yeoman	£204	
	1673/32	Stephens, John	St. Mary, Redcliffe	—	£57	
	1680/46	Stephens, John	Almondsbury	—	£28	
W	1708/46	Stephens, John	Littleton-on-Severn	Yeoman	£261	
	1712/46	Stephens, John	(see Stevens)			
	1731/83	Stephens, John	City of Bristol	<Patten-maker>	£18	
	1737/29	Stephens, John	(see Stevens)			
	1706/38	Stephens, Joyce	Almondsbury	Cow keeper (Widow)	£52	

Year ref.		Name	Parish or area	Occupation or status	Value	Notes
W	1715/46	Stephens, Katherine	Littleton-on-Severn	Widow	£241	
W	1666/56	Stephens, Mary	St. John	Widow	£171	
W	1662/41	Stephens, Robert	Stoke Gifford	Clerk	£86	
	1668/52B	Stephens, Susana	City of Bristol	(Mrs) Widow	£75	dated 1658 outside
	1693/29	Stephens, Thomas	City of Bristol	Soap-boiler	£25	
W	1695/34	Stephens, Thomas (snr)	Almondsbury (The Worthy)	Yeoman	£597	
W	1705/29	Stephens, Thomas	Almondsbury (The Worthy)	<Yeoman>	£150	
	1663/60	Stephens, William	St. John	Distiller	£48	
	1749/70	Steres, Thomas	City of Bristol	Mariner	£6	
	1629/52	Sterrie, James	St. Stephen	Sail-maker	£23	
	1669/64	Sterry, Thomas	St. Stephen	Mariner	£27	
W	1732/65	Stevans, Thomas	City of Bristol	Mariner	£11	
W	1664/47	Stevans, Alice	Stoke Gifford	Widow	£63	
W	1667/63	Stevens, Cicely	St. Thomas	Widow	£7	
	1672/51	Stevens, Edward	(administrator of the estate of John Blackbourne, which see)			
	1617/57	Stevens, John	City of Bristol	Shoemaker	£1	
	1679/66	Stevens, John	St. John	Mariner	£3	
	1685/46	Stevens, John	St. Mary-le-Port	Cook	£23	
	1694/51	Stevens, John	City of Bristol	--	£55	
	1712/46	Stevens, John	City of Bristol	Hooper	£15	died at sea
	1737/29	Stevens, John	City of Bristol	--	£39	
W	1681/61	Stevens, Richard	Stoke Gifford (Great Stoke) (alias Westley, which see)	Yeoman	£292	
	1640/81	Stevens, Roger	Olveston (Tockington)	Weaver	£11	
	1699/25	Stevens, Thomas	Temple	Yeoman	£58	
	1637/55	Stevens, Walter	Temple	Weaver	£11	
W	1625/75	Stevens, William	St. John	Merchant	£172	
W	1634/68	Stevens, William	Clifton	Husbandman	£46	alias Tombs

W	Ref.	Name	Place	Occupation	Value	Notes
W	1667/67	Stevens, William	St. Stephen	Linen-draper	£29	
W	1683/49	Stevens, William	Westbury-on-Trym (Sneyd Park)	\<Yeoman\>	£351	
	1661/64	Steward, Hercules	Temple	Cloth-worker	£48	
W	1661/65	Steward, Joan	Temple	Widow	£56	
	1647/26	Stibbens, Judith	St. Thomas	Widow	£30	
	1666/46	Stibbins, Henry	Henbury	Tailor	£6	
W	1643/35	Stibbins, John	City of Bristol	Soapmaker	£28	
	1613/58	Stile, John	St. Peter	--	£4	
	1668/49	Stile, Leonard	St. Thomas	Cutler	£10	
	1628/70	Stinchcombe, John	Winterbourne	--	£34	
	1685/48	Stinchcombe, Nathaniel	Mangotsfield (Downing)	Tanner	£58	
	1713/44	Stirling, William	City of Bristol	Mariner	£5	
W	1636/55	Stirredge, William	St. Werburgh	Skinner	£70	
	1662/44	Stoakes, Edward	Henbury	Yeoman	£343	
	1684/CP	Stoakes, George	St. Stephen	--	£223	account only
W	1685/47	Stoakes, Henry	Henbury (Charlton)	Yeoman	£536	
	1609/68	Stoakes, John	(see Stokes)			
W	1660/14	Stoakes, John	Henbury	Yeoman	£225	
	1682/55	Stoakes, John	\<Stowick\>			
W	1667/62	Stoakes, Katherine	(see Stokes)			
W	1697/31	Stoakes, Margaret	Henbury \<Kingsweston\>	\<Widow\>	£229	
	1690/41	Stoakes, Sarah	Westbury-on-Trym (Shirehampton)	Widow	£232	
	1639/99	Stoakes, Simon	Westbury-on-Trym (Shirehampton)	--	£40	
W	1718/36	Stoakes, Simon	St. Nicholas	Cloth-worker	--	
	1634/54	Stoaks, Robert	City of Bristol	Mariner	£18	
W	1708/48	Stockes, William	Henbury (see Stokes)	--	£14	3 documents

Year ref.	Name	Parish or area	Occupation or status	Value	Notes
1624/66	Stockman, Richard	St. Thomas	⟨Shearman⟩	£6	
1678/51	Stockman, Thomas	St. James	Carpenter	£69	
1620/88	Stoddin, Peter	St. Stephen	Sailor	£35	
1623/61	Stoke, John	St. Stephen	Seafaring man	£4	
1639/98	Stokes, Alice	Henbury	Widow	£18	
1740/58	Stokes, Charles	City of Bristol	Gent	£20	
1661/67	Stokes, Edward	Henbury	—	£102	
1675/63	Stokes, George	St. Stephen	Cooper	£223	
W 1667/61	Stokes, Joan	Henbury ⟨Hallen⟩	—	£44	
1609/68	Stokes, John	Westbury-on-Trym (Stoke Bishop)	Husbandman	£41	also Stoakes
1664/43	Stokes, John	Westbury-on-Trym	Yeoman	£140	
1682/55a	Stokes, John	Henbury	Husbandman	£50	not exhib.
1682/55b	Stokes, John	Henbury	Husbandman	£50	exhibited copy
W 1675/64	Stokes, Sarah	Westbury-on-Trym (Shirehampton)	Widow	£142	
W 1612/12	Stokes, William	Henbury (Hallen)	Husbandman	£159	
W 1708/48	Stokes, William	⟨City of Bristol⟩	⟨Inn-holder⟩	£12	
W 1628/69	Stone, Antonie	Temple	⟨Painter⟩	£41	
1661/68	Stone, Bartholomew and Margery	St. Thomas	Inn-holder	£23	
1697/33	Stone, Francis	City of Bristol	Victualler	£11	
1751/16	Stone, Henry	City of Bristol	Mariner	£15	
1680/47	Stone, Mary	City of Bristol	Widow	£56	
1726/31	Stone, Mary	Olveston	Widow	£41	
W 1611/75	Stone, Maude	Temple	Widow	£5	
W 1730/56	Stone, John	City of Bristol	Mariner	£3	
W 1647/27	Stone, Phillip	St. Stephen	Mariner	£9	
1692/42	Stone, Samuel	—	—	£32	

	Reference	Name	Place	Occupation	Value	Notes
W	1733/74	Stoneman, John	City of Bristol	Mariner	£13	
W	1733/75	Storey, James	City of Bristol	Mariner	£8	
W	1743/32	Storie, James	City of Bristol	Mariner	£7	
W	1633/73	Storie, John	(see Storry)			
W	1633/73	Storry, John	St. Stephen	--	£250	
	1732/66	Stout, John	City of Bristol	Tailor	£7	
	1739/23	Stout, William	City of Bristol	Mariner	£11	
	1678/53	Stoute, Robert	City of Bristol	Cordwainer	£33	alias Pope
	1639/100	Strange, Arthur	SS. Philip & Jacob	Husbandman	£110	
W	1634/69	Strange, Margery	Winterbourne	Single-woman	£10	
W	1662/43	Strange, Richard	Stoke Gifford	Yeoman	£96	
W	1640/73	Strange, Robert	Mangotsfield	Yeoman	£33	
W	1692/41	Stratton, Ann	Stapleton	<Widow>	£64	
W	1620/89	Streate, William	City of Bristol	--	£63	
W	1709/56	Street, John	Almondsbury	Mariner	£3	
W	1673/30	Street, Walter	Henbury <Charlton>	Husbandman	£81	
W	1635/79	Streete, Joan	<Henbury>	<Widow>	£3	
W	1634/70	Streete, Owen	St. Peter	--	£28	
W	1620/89	Streete, William	(see Streate)			
W	1629/53	Strenger, Edmond	Olveston (Tockington)	Husbandman	£6	
	1729/43	Stretch, Daniel	City of Bristol	Mariner	£8	
W	1714/40	Stretton, John	Henbury (Compton Greenfield)	Yeoman	£183	
	1637/56	Stringer, Christian	Stapleton	--	£72	
W	1633/74	Stringer, Frances	St. Peter	Widow	£48	
W	1685/49	Stringer, Jane	Henbury	--	£124	
W	1635/80	Stringer, Michael	St. Peter	<Whitawer>	£302	
W	1725/17	Stringer, Robert	City of Bristol	Mariner	£8	
	1630/4	Stringer, Thomas	St. Peter	Whitawer	£121	
W	1677/41	Stringer, Thomas	Henbury	Husbandman	£84	
W	1702/24	Stringer, William	Henbury	Husbandman	£186	

Year ref.	Name	Parish or area	Occupation or status	Value	Notes
W 1740/59	Strong, Thomas	City of Bristol	Mariner	£4	
1743/33	Stroud, John	City of Bristol	Mariner	£6	
1647/28	Strugnell, John	City of Bristol	Pin-maker	£10	
W 1748/69	Stubbs, James	City of Bristol	Mariner	£20	
1721/32	Sture, Philip	City of Bristol	Victualler	£10	
1705/30	Sturge, Thomas	Winterbourne (Frenchay)	--	£48	
W 1617/58	Sturges, Joan	Stoke Gifford	Widow	£115	
1699/22	Stutely, Charles	--	--	£9	
W 1618/68	Style, Ann	(see Steell)			
W 1715/47	Subbern, John	City of Bristol	Mariner	£11	
1715/48	Sulevan, Timothy	St. Augustine	Ale-draper	£74	
W 1731/84	Sullivane, Jeremiah	City of Bristol	Mariner	£5	
1738/22	Sullivan, Daniel	City of Bristol	Mariner	£3	
1740/60	Sullivan, Daniel	City of Bristol	Mariner	£7	
1746/43	Sullivan, John	City of Bristol	Mariner	£10	
1716/51	Sullivent, Robert	(see Sillivent)			
1729/42	Sumerell, Samuel	Henbury (Kingsweston)	--	£373	
W 1712/45	Sumerhill, Edward	Henbury (Kingsweston)	--		
W 1682/39	Sumers, Edward	<St. Mary-le-Port>	Yeoman	£146	
W 1664/48	Sumers, Henry	(see Sommers)	Butcher	£235	
1717/51	Summers, Benjamin	SS. Philip & Jacob	Butcher	£36	
1739/24	Summers, Charles	City of Bristol	Scrivener	£5	
1667/71	Summers, Henry	SS. Philip & Jacob	--	--	
W 1670/40	Summers, Joan	(see Somers)			
1642/46	Summers, John	St. Stephen	Mariner	£23	
1663/58	Surman, Thomas	St. Mary, Redcliffe	--	£22	
1756/17	Surman, William	City of Bristol	Brush-maker	£54	inv. & account
1629/54	Sutton, Richard	St. Peter	Vintner (servant)	£2	

	1732/67	Sutton, Ruth	Mangotsfield	Widow	£8
	1640/74	Swallow, John	Almondsbury	—	£17
	1623/62	Swanly, William	St. Stephen	<Seafaring man>	8s 6d
	1733/76	Swanson, George	City of Bristol	Mariner	£7
	1706/39	Sweet, George	City of Bristol	House-carpenter	£14
	1690/43	Sweet, Joseph	City of Bristol	Bookseller	£13
W	1665/55	Sweete, Anne	St. Nicholas	Widow	£19
	1672/50	Sweete, Henry	City of Bristol	Surgeon	£43
	1665/47	Sweete, Richard	St. Nicholas	—	£27
	1683/54	Sweeper, Edward	City of Bristol	Brazier	£187
W	1694/57	Sweeper, Henry	—	Brazier	£29
	1666/48	Sweeper, John	St. James	—	£137
W	1684/60	Swetman, William	Temple	<Rough-mason>	£35
W	1627/24	Swetnam, Lawrence	St. Mary, Redcliffe	Merchant	£9
W	1628/71	Swifte, Annis (Agnes)	<Henbury> (Aust)	Widow	£113
	1618/63	Sydner, Richard	Westbury-on-Trym	—	£3
	1618/63	Sydnor, Richard	(see Sydner)		
	1694/50	Syfere, Richard	St. Werburgh	Joiner	£34
W	1742/50	Sylevan, Timothy	(see Sylivan)		
W	1742/50	Sylivan, Timothy	City of Bristol	Mariner	£6
W	1707/36	Symbs, Charles	Barton Regis	Yeoman	
				<Cordwainer in will>	
W	1707/37	Symbs, Jane	Barton Regis	Widow	£54
W	1753/28	Symes, Hannah	City of Bristol	Widow	£12
W	1753/28	Symes, Robert	(see Symes, Hannah)		£98　inv. & account
	1703/17	Symonds, Charles	—	—	£3
	1609/69	Symonds, John	Henbury	—	£116
W	1611/71	Symonds, Raphe	Filton	Husbandman	£87
	1644/50	Symonds, Robert	St. James	Rough-mason	£3
W	1679/62	Symonds, Walter	City of Bristol	Saddler	£46
	1665/46	Symons, Lucie	Filton	Widow	£25
	1629/55	Symons, Richard	Henbury	—	£4
	1617/59	Symons, Thomas	St. Peter	—	£28

	Year ref.	Name	Parish or area	Occupation or status	Value	Notes
	1624/67	Symons, William	St. Leonard	Mariner	£14	
	1665/48	Symons, William	City of Bristol	Mariner	£199	
	1633/67	Sympkins, William	Alveston	Carpenter	£5	
	1695/35	Syms, William	Barton Regis	Yeoman	£130	
	1601/1	Sypher, Thomas	Henbury	<Blacksmith>	£9	
	1720/29	Tagg, Richard	Stapleton	Miller	£17	
W	1629/56	Tailer, Joan	St. James	Widow	£101	
	1727/37	Toker, John	City of Bristol	Mariner	£10	
	1761/32	Talant, Bartholomew	City of Bristol	Mariner	£12	alias Rainstorpe
W	1725/18	Talbot, Peter	City of Bristol	Mariner	£20	
W	1742/51	Tallack, Robert	City of Bristol	Mariner	£10	
	1633/76	Tamsin, Elizabeth	St. Stephen	Widow	£3	
	1699/26	Tandy, Bryan	City of Bristol	Cooper	£47	
	1739/25	Tannat, Robert	City of Bristol	Mariner	£16	inv. & account
	1731/85	Tanner, Benjamin	City of Bristol	Gent.	£18	
	1689/64	Tanner, John	Henbury	Husbandman	£62	
W	1722/24	Tanner, Robert	City of Bristol	Mariner (Hooper)	£8	
W	1861/63	Tanner, Robert	Almondsbury (Over)	Yeoman	£61	
	1731/86	Tanner, William	City of Bristol	Mariner	£12	
	1697/35	Tanton, Walter	Stapleton	Haulier	£12	
	1699/28	Taplen, John	Stapleton	Husbandman	£18	
	1704/29	Tarr, Benjamin	City of Bristol	Cooper	£16	died at sea
	1673/38	Taunton, Robert	St. Augustine	Organ maker	£32	
	1735/37	Taviner, James	City of Bristol	Shoemaker	£6	
W	1724/17	Taylard, Elizabeth	City of Bristol	<Widow>	£19	
W	1704/31	Tayler, Ann	City of Bristol	Widow	£413	
W	1635/81	Tayler, Charles	St. Nicholas	Cooper	£36	2 documents
	1697/4	Tayler, George	City of Bristol	Haulier	£215	
W	1642/47	Tayler, Joan	Westbury-on-Trym (Shirehampton)	<Widow>	£5	

	Ref.	Name	Location	Occupation	Value	Notes
W	1613/59	Tayler, John	Alveston (Veels End)	Yeoman	£78	
W	1628/74	Tayler, John	<St. Werburgh>	--	£5	
W	1704/30	Tayler, Josiah	City of Bristol	Shipwright	£9	
	1665/57	Tayler, Nathaniel	(see Taylor)			
	1627/25	Tayler, Richard	St. Mary, Redcliffe	Cooper	£2	
	1634/71	Tayler, Richard	Henbury	--	£3	
W	1662/46	Tayler, Richard	Winterbourne	Husbandman	£166	
	1618/69	Tayler, Thomas	St. Nicholas	Cooper	£24	
	1686/46	Tayler, William	City of Bristol	Haulier	£74	
W	1672/54	Tayler, Arthur (snr)	St. Peter	Felt-maker	£14	
W	1733/77	Tayler, Charles	City of Bristol	Mariner	£4	
	1679/70	Tayler, Daniel	Henbury (Kingsweston)	Gent.	£182	
	1680/52	Tayler, Edmund	St. Stephen	Cooper	£4	
	1668/57	Tayler, Elizabeth	St. Augustine	Widow	£9	
	1740/61	Tayler, Francis	--	Mariner	£10	
	1740/62	Tayler, Francis	Mangotsfield	Mariner	£8	
W	1646/42	Tayler, George	St. Stephen	Cooper	£54	
W	1690/46	Tayler, George	(see Tylar)			
	1737/30B	Tayler, Giles	City of Bristol	Mariner	£10	
	1710/35	Tayler, Henry	City of Bristol	Surgeon	£10	
W	1731/87	Tayler, James	City of Bristol	Mariner	£7	died at sea
W	1633/75	Tayler, John	SS. Phillip & Jacob	Blacksmith	£52	
W	1717/52	Tayler, John	City of Bristol	House-carpenter	£66	
W	1720/30	Tayler, John	<City of Bristol>	<Tailor>	£179	
W	1737/30A	Tayler, John	City of Bristol	Mariner	£2	
W	1663/65	Tayler, Mary	Winterbourne <Hambrook>	Widow	£75	
W	1675/68	Tayler, Morgan	St. Leonard	<Mariner>	£309	also 2nd copy
	1665/57	Tayler, Nathaniel	St. John	Mariner	£11	
W	1620/90	Tayler, Richard	Henbury	Bachelor	£6	
W	1748/70	Tayler, Richard	City of Bristol	Mariner	£15	
W	1748/71	Tayler, Richard	City of Bristol	Mariner	£5	

	Year ref.	Name	Parish or area	Occupation or status	Value	Notes
	1744/14	Taylor, Samuel	City of Bristol	Mariner	£5	
	1705/31	Taylor, Thomas	City of Bristol	Cordwainer	£19	
	1711/43	Taylor, Thomas	City of Bristol	Mariner	£79	
W	1668/56	Taylor, William	St. Stephen	--	--	
	1728/36	Taylor, William	City of Bristol	Mariner	£12	
W	1733/78	Taylor, William	City of Bristol	Mariner	£2	
	1661/74	Taynton, John	Henbury <Compton Greenfield>	<Yeoman>	£37	
W	1625/76	Taynton, William	Henbury		£222	
	1756/18	Taynton, William	City of Bristol	Hooper	£9	died at sea
	1635/82a	Tayte, William	St. Stephen	Mariner	£12	
	1635/82b	Tayte, William	(the account of Anne Tayte, relict)			
	1646/43	Teague, George	St. Stephen	Mariner	£44	also 2nd copy
	1620/91	Teague, John	St. Stephen	--	£200	alias Monyan
	1730/57	Teast, Anne	City of Bristol	Widow	£68	
	1669/71	Teast, John	St. Nicholas	Mariner	£3	
	1635/83	Teaste, Thomas	Henbury	--	£322	
W	1641/52	Tempest, Ann	St. Peter	Widow	£176	
	1713/45	Temple, Mary	Temple	--	£34	
W	1688/44	Temple, William	City of Bristol	Tobacco-cutter	£84	
W	1668/53	Terrett, Thomas <snr>	SS. Philip & Jacob	Blacksmith	£45	
	1692/45	Terrill, Edith	SS. Philip & Jacob	Widow	£80	
	1712/44	Terrill, Edith	(the account of Ann Spooner, exeutrix: see inv. 1692/45)			
	1640/75	Terrill, Thomas	Almondsbury	Husbandman	£104	
	1728/37	Terrill, William	City of Bristol	Mariner	£6	
W	1723/30	Teyler, Philip	(see Tyler)			
	1661/72	Teyler, Robert & Joan	(see Tyler)			
	1761/33	Thair, John	City of Bristol	Mariner	£11	
	1694/60	Theed, James	City of Bristol	Mariner	£5	
	1728/38	Thomas, Abraham	City of Bristol	Skinner	£6	

W	Reference	Name	Place	Occupation	Value	Notes
	1629/57	Thomas, Ann	Westbury-on-Trym (Redland) (alias Morgan, which see)	--	£15	alias Morgan see also 1627/17
W	1627/17	Thomas, Anne	--	Widow	£47	
	1685/53	Thomas, Athalia	City of Bristol	Spinster	£2	
	1678/57	Thomas, Bartholomew	City of Bristol	Mariner	£9	
W	1711/44	Thomas, Bridget	St. Thomas	Brewer	£12	
W	1625/77	Thomas, Edward	Olveston	--		
	1753/29	Thomas, Elenor	<Tockington>	Widow	£6	
W	1626/2	Thomas, Elizabeth	St. Thomas	Widow	£13	
	1686/48	Thomas, Elizabeth	Horfield	--	£26	
	1747/39	Thomas, Elizabeth	--	Widow	£20	
W	1749/71	Thomas, George	City of Bristol	Mariner	£15	
W	1643/88	Thomas, Griffith	St. Mary, Redcliffe	Brewer	£48	
W	1752/32	Thomas, Griffith	City of Bristol	Mariner	£5	
	1690/47	Thomas, Henry	St. Thomas	Cooper	£98	
	1739/26	Thomas, Henry	City of Bristol	Mariner	£10	
	1724/18	Thomas, Hugh	City of Bristol	Mariner	£11	
W	1726/33	Thomas, Isaac	Compton	--	£320	Almondsbury, in will
W	1716/52	Thomas, James	Winterbourne (Frenchay)	Quarrier	£23	
	1618/70	Thomas, John	St. Stephen	Shipwright	£16	
W	1684/64	Thomas, John	Westbury-on-Trym (Shirehampton)	--	£135	inv. & account
	1707/38	Thomas, John	St. James	Cooper	£30	
W	1718/37	Thomas, John	City of Bristol	Mariner	£9	
	1742/52	Thomas, John	City of Bristol	<Victualler in will>	£5	
	1751/17	Thomas, John	City of Bristol	Mariner	£1	
	1752/33	Thomas, John	City of Bristol	Merchant Tailor	£10	
W	1746/44	Thomas, Joseph	City of Bristol	Mariner	£11	
W	1748/72	Thomas, Joseph	<City of Bristol>	Mariner	£13	
	1679/72	Thomas, Lewis	SS. Philip & Jacob	--	£9	

Year ref.	Name	Parish or area	Occupation or status	Value	Notes
1735/38	Thomas, Mary	City of Bristol	Spinster	£15	
1712/47	Thomas, Matthew	City of Bristol	Mariner	£8	
1685/52	Thomas, Melliner	City of Bristol	Widow	£33	
1685/CP	Thomas, Mellinie	City of Bristol	Widow	£33	account only
1712/48	Thomas, Michael	City of Bristol	Mariner	£12	
1716/53	Thomas, Nathaniel	City of Bristol	Mariner	£14	
W 1699/27	Thomas, Phillip	Temple	--	£19	
1627/26	Thomas,Phillipp and Joan				
		Christchurch	--	£28	
1714/41	Thomas, Richard	City of Bristol	Cordwainer	£8	
		(the account of Richard Davis, administrator)			
W 1742/53	Thomas, Robert	City of Bristol	Mariner	£8	
W 1757/18	Thomas, Robert	City of Bristol	Mariner	£18	
1694/58	Thomas, Roger	St. James	--	£20	
(w) 1707/39	Thomas, Thomas	City of Bristol	Lime-burner	£80	
		(a 1707 will of Thomas Thomas, Alveston, Yeoman, exists)			
W 1624/68	Thomas, Thomas	Chrstchurch		£26	
W 1731/88	Thomas, Thomas	City of Bristol	Mariner	£4	
1758/28	Thomas, Thomas	City of Bristol	Mariner	£4	
1618/71	Thomas, William	SS. Philip & Jacob	--	£33	
W 1721/33	Thomas, William	Westbury-on-Trym	Inn-holder	£143	
W 1736/28	Thomas, William	City of Bristol	Mariner	£14	
W 1746/45	Thomas, William	City of Bristol	Mariner	£10	
W 1735/40	Thomkins, Thomas	City of Bristol	Mariner	£4	
1747/40	Thompson, George	City of Bristol	Mariner	£18	
1748/74	Thompson, Hendrick	City of Bristol	Mariner	£10	
W 1734/45	Thompson, James	City of Bristol	Mariner	£17	
1743/34	Thompson, James	City of Bristol	Mariner	£5	
1691/44	Thompson, John	--	--	£5	
W 1748/73	Thoms, John	City of Bristol	Mariner	£16	
1633/76	Thomsine, Elizabeth	(see Tamsin)			

	Ref	Name	Place	Occupation	Value	Notes
W	1670/44	Thomson, Margery	--	<Widow>	£130	<Broad Street>
W	1725/19	Thomson, Samuel	City of Bristol	Mariner	£9	
W	1761/34	Thorn, John	<St. Mary, Redcliffe>	Cabinet-maker	£19	died at sea
	1745/27	Thorne, Anthony	City of Bristol	Mariner	£7	
	1611/76	Thorne, Edith	Winterbourne	Widow	£4	
W	1745/29	Thorne, Henry	City of Bristol	Mariner	£7	
W	1618/72	Thorne, Thomas	St. Werburgh	Tailor	£45	
W	1625/78	Thorne, William	Henbury (Northwick)	<Husbandman>	£48	alias Prentice
	1710/36	Thorp, Edward	City of Bristol	Mariner	£17	
W	1712/49	Thorp, Mary	<Castle Precincts>	Widow	£12	
	1708/49	Thorpe, Thomas	City of Bristol	Mariner	£6	
W	1737/31	Thrall, Abraham	Temple	Tiler	£17	
W	1733/79	Thrall, Isaac	City of Bristol	--	£5	
W	1718/38	Thrall, Samuel	<City of Bristol>	<Tiler & Plasterer>	£19	
	1623/63	Threlkelle, Michael	All Saints	Hosier	£118	
W	1745/28	Thresher, John	City of Bristol	Mariner	£11	
	1609/18	Throme, Christopher	(see Drome)			
	1617/60	Thrupp, John	City of Bristol	Vintner	£2,004	parchment roll 6 ft (180 cm) long
	1620/92	Thrupp, William	St. Thomas (see Thurstone)	--	£5	
W	1613/60	Thruston, John	All Saints	Cordwainer	£35	
(w)	1689/63	Thurkild, Edward	(a 1689 will of Edward Thirkeld, Cook, All Saints, exists)			
W	1747/41	Thurman, Edward	City of Bristol	Mariner	£20	
W	1613/61	Thurner, John	Almondsbury	Husbandman	£66	
W	1680/48	Thurner, John	Almondsbury (Over)	<Yeoman>	£41	see 1680/51 & 69
W	1680/51	Thurner, John	Almondsbury (Over)	Yeoman	£68	see 1680/48 & 69
W	1680/69	Thurner, John	Almondsbury (Over)	<Yeoman>	£22	see 1680/48 & 51
	1672/55	Thurner, John (snr)	Almondsbury	Yeoman	£96	
W	1724/19	Thurston Edward (jnr)	City of Bristol	Apothecary	£13	died at sea
	1635/84	Thurston, George	Christchurch	Shoemaker	£23	
	1660/18	Thurston, Jonathan	Elberton	--	£55	

Year ref.	Name	Parish or area	Occupation or status	Value	Notes
W 1613/60	Thurstone, John	Littleton-on-Severn	--	£128	
1633/77a	Thydall, Thomas	Temple	Lime-burner	£6	
1633/77b	Thydall, Thomas	(document re administration)			
1720/31	Tibbes, John	City of Bristol	Mariner	£19	
W 1686/51	Tibott, Joan	Winterbourne	Widow	£106	
1688/45	Tibbot, Samuel	Temple	Brewer	£53	
1671/46	Tiler, Edward	Stapleton	Coal-miner	£11	
1671/45	Tiler, William	Stapleton	Horse-driver	£46	
W 1686/47	Tiley, Thomas	City of Bristol	Cooper	£429	
1618/73	Tilladams, Marie	--	<Lime-burner>	£13	
1742/54	Tillard, Thomas	St. Peter		£17	
1613/62	Tillat, Joan	--	--	£4	
1618/1	Tilledge, John	(alias Adams, which see)			
W 1760/33	Tillesley, Daniel	SS. Philip & Jacob	Shag-weaver	£8	
W 1670/43	Tillett, William	Stoke Gifford	Yeoman	£294	
1625/80	Tillie, Gillian	<Abbots> Leigh	--	--	
W 1682/45	Tillie, John	Barton Regis	Yeoman	£138	
W 1743/35	Tilling, William	City of Bristol	Glazier	£16	
1664/50	Tillis, John	St. Nicholas	Butcher	£29	alias Adams
W 1625/79	Tilly, Edward	SS. Philip & Jacob <out parish>	--	£125	
W 1685/51	Tilly, John	City of Bristol	Whitawer	£2	
1629/59	Tilly, Nicholas	SS. Philip & Jacob	--	£113	
1620/94	Tilye, Thomas	St. Michael	--	£1	
W 1714/42	Timberman, Samuel	City of Bristol	Serge-weaver	£9	
1730/58	Tinkard, Richard	City of Bristol	Mariner	£3	
W 1735/39	Tinker, Margaret	City of Bristol	Widow	£10	
W 1734/46	Tinker, Samuel	City of Bristol	Mariner	£11	
1639/101a	Tinson, George	St. Michael	--	£4	
1639/101b	Tinson, George	(a note of his goods, no values)			
W 1694/59	Tipper, Giles	Mangotsfield	Tanner	£20	

W	Name	Reference	Place	Occupation	Value	Notes
W	Tipper, Richard	1698/33	Winterbourne	Husbandman	£16	
	Tirke, Edward	1643/90	(see Tirke)			
	Tirkle, Edward	1643/90	City of Bristol	Cook	£32	
W	Tisdell, Polow	1720/32	City of Bristol	Mariner	£4	
	Tobee, Thomas	1733/80	City of Bristol	Mariner	£9	
	Tobey, John	1680/49	St. Mary, Redcliffe	--	£4	
	Tobey, John	1705/32	--	--	£504	
	Tobin, John	1751/18	City of Bristol	Cooper	£7	
W	Tock, William	1758/29	Westbury-on-Trym	Yeoman	£166	
	Todd, Alexander	1626/32	City of Bristol	Mariner	£11	
	Toghill, William	1767/2	SS. Philip & Jacob	Butcher	£180	
	Told, Matthew	1715/49	City of Bristol	Surgeon	£10	died at sea
	Tolson, Edward	1643/89	Temple	Clothworker	£272	
	Tombs, Edward	1722/25	Westbury-on-Trym (Shirehampton)	Yeoman	£280	
	Tombs, Thomas	1715/50	City of Bristol	Surgeon	£13	died at sea
W	Tombs, William	1634/68	(alias Stevens, which see)			
	Tombes, Daniel	1742/55A	Temple	Mariner	£50	4 documents
	Tomblinson, Edmond	1636/56	St. Mark	Merchant	£26	
W	Tomes, Mary	1663/64	St. Mary, Redcliffe	--	£39	
	Tomkins, John	1662/48	(see Thomkins)			
W	Tomkins, Thomas	1635/40	St. Michael	Chapman	£66	
	Tomkins, William	1628/72	Temple	<Blacksmith>	£150	appraised 1674
	Tomlinson, Joan	1679/71	City of Bristol	Widow	£253	
	Tomlinson, John	1708/50	(see Tomkins)			
	Tompkins, William	1628/72	City of Bristol	Mariner	£10	
	Tompson, Thomas	1628/73	Abbots Leigh	Tailor	£37	
W	Toms, Francis	1625/81	City of Bristol	<Husbandman>	£13	
W	Tool, Patrick	1732/68	St. Werburgh	Mariner	£9	
	Toose, Edward	1611/77	City of Bristol	Clerk	£34	
	Tope, John	1736/29	<City of Bristol>	Mariner	£7	
W	Topping, James	1732/69	City of Bristol	<Mariner>	£7	
W	Totherway, Richard	1766/9	City of Bristol	Mariner	£7	with wills

	Year ref.	Name	Parish or area	Occupation or status	Value	Notes
W	1768/CP	Touffi, William	SS. Philip & Jacob	Millwright	£265	
	1684/63	Tovey, Ann	St. Stephens	Widow	£22	
W	1674/42	Tovey, Edith	Stapleton	Widow	£23	
W	1694/61	Tovey, Edith	Almondsbury	Widow	£326	
	1728/39	Tovey, John	Almondsbury	--	£138	
W	1668/54	Tovey, Margery	Alveston ⟨Rough Earthcott⟩	⟨Widow⟩	£58	
W	1660/17	Tovey, Robert	Alveston ⟨Earthcott⟩	⟨Carpenter⟩	£114	
	1704/32	Tovey, Samuel	City of Bristol	Baker	£11	
	1709/57	Tovey, Samuel	Olveston (Tockington)		£118	
W	1729/44	Tovey, Thomas ⟨snr⟩	Almondsbury	Yeoman	£138	
	1678/58	Tovey, Thomas	Almondsbury	⟨Yeoman⟩	£141	
	1680/67	Tovey, Thomas	Almondsbury (Rednend)	--		account only
W	1661/73	Tovey, William	Olveston ⟨Awkley⟩	Yeoman	£141	
W	1709/58	Tovey, William	Horfield	Yeoman	£93	
W	1741/45	Tovey, William	City of Bristol	Mariner	£63	
W	1688/43	Tovie, John	Christchurch	Soapmaker	£7	
W	1650/14	Tovy, John	Olveston (Tockington)		£33	
	1609/70	Toyye, Agnes	Olveston	--	£14	
W	1633/78	Towenson, Phillip	Temple	Widow	£9	
	1733/81	Towie, Patrick	City of Bristol	⟨Shearman⟩	£84	
W	1633/78	Townsend, Phillip	(see Towenson)	Mariner	£8	
	1662/47	Townsend, Andrew	SS. Philip & Jacob	Baker	£41	
W	1745/30	Townsend, James	City of Bristol	Mariner	£3	
W	1663/66	Townsend, John	Temple	Shearman	£33	
W	1725/20	Townsend, John	SS. Philip & Jacob	Tailor	£54	will 1723
W	1683/57	Townsend, Richard	St. Werburgh	--	£21	

	Ref.	Name	Place	Occupation	Value	Notes
W	1635/85	Townsend, Sarah	St. Augustine	Widow	£27	
	1629/60	Trapnell, Thomas	Christchurch	--	£5	
	1700/16	Treago, James	St. Stephen	--	£13	
	1620/93	Treckell, Robert	--	<Button-maker>	£1	
	1686/49	Trego, William	--	Mariner	£7	
	1703/18a	Tregoe, James		Mariner	£69	
	1703/18b	Tregoe, James	(the account of Ann Tregoe, relict)			
	1713/46	Tregoe, John	City of Bristol	Mariner	£7	
	1675/69	Trepet, Thomas	St. Nicholas	<Cooper>	£29	
W	1748/75	Trested, Thomas	City of Bristol	Mariner	£16	
	1635/86	Trewman, John	St. Mary, Redcliffe	<Hatter>	£168	also a 2nd copy
	1734/47	Trickey, John	City of Bristol	Peruke-maker	£14	
	1675/69	Tripett, Thomas	(see Trepet)			
W	1633/79	Trippet, Elizabeth	St. Stephen	Widow	£13	
W	1743/36	Tristram, Stephen	City of Bristol	Gent.	£23	
W	1724/20	Trivet, Richard	St. Thomas	<Corn-chandler>	£218	will 1723
	1609/71	Trivilyan, Thomas	St. Stephen	Clerk	£17	
	1741/46	Trotman, John		Saddle-tree maker	£42	
	1754/24D	Trotman, Thomas	City of Bristol	--	£18	
	1707/40	Trotten, Thomas		Mariner	£15	
	1737/32	Trotter, Bartholomew	City of Bristol	Mariner	£6	
	1683/58	Trotter, John	St. James	-	£15	
	1635/86	Trueman, John	(see Trewman)			
	1644/51	Trueman, Thomas	St. James	--	£64	
W	1636/57	Trumper, Christopher	Westbury-on-Trym	Curate	£15	
W	1636/58	Trumper, Katherine	Westbury-on-Trym	Widow	£11	
W	1748/75	Trusted, Thomas	(see Trested)			
	1748/76	Tucker, Ann	City of Bristol	--	£10	(inventory also marked 'John Weston')
W	1687/58	Tucker, Benjamin	Mangotsfield	Coal-miner	£125	
	1704/33	Tucker, Benjamin	Winterbourne	Yeoman	£211	
W	1682/46	Tucker, Edmund	Mangotsfield	Yeoman	£44	
W	1689/61	Tucker, Edmund	<City of Bristol>	<Carpenter>	£369	

Year ref.		Name	Parish or area	Occupation or status	Value	Notes
1609/72		Tucker, Edward	St. Michael	Mariner	£24	
1609/73		Tucker, Henry	Stapleton	--	£28	inv. & account
1611/78	W	Tucker, Henry	St. Thomas	Smith	£36	
1674/43		Tucker, James	St. James	--	£6	
1689/62		Tucker, John	--	Pipe-maker	£60	
1724/21	W	Tucker, John	City of Bristol	Mariner	£18	
1746/46a		Tucker, John	City of Bristol	Yeoman	£8	died at sea
1746/46b		Tucker, John	(document re debts owed to James Tunbridge, Gent.)			
1696/31	W	Tucker, Mary	Mangotsfield	Widow	£13	
1686/50	W	Tucker, Obadiah	Mangotsfield	Carpenter	£68	
1748/77	W	Tucker, Peter	City of Bristol	Mariner	£5	
1722/26	W	Tucker, Robert	Winterbourne	<Yeoman>	£109	
1750/45	W	Tucker, Samuel	City of Bristol	Gent.	£15	
1736/30	W	Tucker, Richard	City of Bristol	Mariner	£5	
1732/70	W	Tuckey, Samuel (jnr)	City of Bristol	Meal-man	£866	
1725/21		Turberville, Charles	City of Bristol	Mariner	£4	
1639/102	W	Turke, Joan	SS. Philip & Jacob	<Widow>	£427	
1624/69	W	Turke, Robert	SS. Philip & Jacob	<Miller>	£128	
1639/103A	W	Turner, Benjamin	St. Thomas	Physician	£251	
1698/32	W	Turner, Hester	Winterbourne	--	£99	
1688/46		Turner, James	St. Nicholas	--	£5	
1729/45	W	Turner, James	<City of Bristol>	--	£9	
1729/46	W	Turner, Joseph	Winterbourne	Yeoman	£176	
1684/62		Turner, William	St. Nicholas	--	£4	
1691/45	W	Turner, William	Winterbourne	Yeoman	£104	
1736/31	W	Turner, William	City of Bristol	Mariner	£3	
1727/38		Turnpenny, John	City of Bristol	Mariner	£18	
1710/37		Turpin, Robert	City of Bristol	Mariner	£27	
1680/50		Tuther, Maudlin	(alias Brooks, which see)			
1671/44		Tutt, John	Temple	Cordwainer	£10	
1695/37	W	Tuttey, Hester	SS. Philip & Jacob	Widow	£8	

W	Ref	Name	Place	Occupation	Value	Notes
	1701/25	Tutton, John	--	Mariner	£9	
W	1716/54	Tweelvetree, John	City of Bristol	Mariner	£10	
W	1629/58	Tylie, Edward	Henbury (Aust)	Husbandman	£75	
W	1690/46	Tylar, George	Barton Regis	Gardener	£406	
W	1664/51	Tyler, Edward	Stapleton	Collier	£39	
W	1644/52	Tyler, Elioner	St. Augustine	Widow	£6	
W	1690/46	Tyler, George	(see Tylar)			
W	1617/61	Tyler, Isabelle	Stapleton	Widow	£36	
W	1662/45	Tyler, Joan	Almondsbury	Widow	£82	
W	1668/16	Tyler, John	Elberton	Yeoman	£56	alias Clarke 1670 will
	1677/44	Tyler, John	St. Peter	--	£27	
W	1734/48	Tyler, John	City of Bristol	Brewer	£20	
W	1723/30	Tyler, Philip	<SS. Philip & Jacob>	<Skinner>	£18	
W	1611/79	Tyler, Robert	Stapleton	<Husbandman>	£39	
	1661/72	Tyler, Robert and Joan	Mangotsfield	Mariner	£8	
W	1732/71	Tyler, Samuel	City of Bristol	<Victualler, in will>	£3	
			--	--	£8	
W	1693/30	Tyler, Thomas	Alveston (Groveling)	Husbandman	£17	
W	1611/80	Tyler, William	St. Stephen	--	£17	
W	1629/61	Tyler, William	St. Augustine	--	£2	also a 2nd copy
W	1635/87	Tyler, William	City of Bristol	Tiler	£9	
W	1741/47	Tyley, John	(see Tilye)			
W	1620/94	Tyley, Thomas	(see Tyllye)			
	1644/53	Tylie, William	St. Augustine	<Joiner>	£38	
W	1628/75	Tyller, Nicholas	Henbury	<Blacksmith>	£60	
W	1640/77	Tyller, Phillip	(alias Adams, which see)			
W	1667/1	Tyllis, Joyce	St. Mary-le-Port	<Butcher>	£99	alias Adams
W	1640/76	Tyllis, Richard	St. Mary, Redcliffe	<Hatter>	£11	
	1644/53	Tyllye, William	SS. Philip & Jacob	Carrier	£364	
W	1668/55	Tylton, John				

	Year ref.	Name	Parish or area	Occupation or status	Value	Notes
	1756/19	Tyndale, Nathaniel	City of Bristol	Musician	£20	
	1682/47	Tyson, John	St. Augustine	--	£21	
W	1737/33	Udey, John	City of Bristol	Mariner	£4	
W	1635/88	Ufford, Alice	(see Wooford)			
W	1703/19	Unckles, John <snr>	<Barton Regis>	<Carrier>	£60	
W	1695/38	Unkles, John	SS. Philip & Jacob (out parish)	Yeoman	£162	
W	1703/19	Unkles, John	(see Unckles)			
W	1704/34	Upcote, John	Abbots Leigh	--	£102	
W	1732/72	Upiom, James	City of Bristol	Mariner	£3	
W	1732/72	Upjohn, James	(see Upiom)			
W	1732/72	Upjom, James	(see Upiom)			
W	1661/75	Usher, James	Almondsbury	Yeoman	£22	
	1609/74	Usher, Thomas	St. Thomas	--	£3	
W	1665/58	Usher, Thomas	St. James	<Haberdasher of small wares>	£115	
	1646/44	Ussell, Elizabeth	City of Bristol	--	£32	
W	1643/91	Ussell, Richard	Almondsbury	<Husbandman>	£82	
	1680/53	Uzell, Edward	Henbury	Husbandman	£202	
W	1643/91	Uzwell, Richard	(see Ussell)			
	1680/53	Uzzell, Edward	(see Uzell)			
W	1634/72	Uzzell, John	St. Mary, Redcliffe	--	£42	
W	1672/56	Uzzell, John	<City of Bristol>	--	£129	
	1723/31	Vain, George	(see Venn)			
W	1726/34	Varah, John	City of Bristol	Mariner	£7	of Whitehaven Cumberlan
	1725/22	Vaughan, Hugh	City of Bristol	Mariner	£19	
W	1762/6	Vaughan, James	City of Bristol	Mariner	£8	
	1667/74	Vaughan, John	(see Vaughn)			

	Ref.	Name	Place	Occupation	Value	Notes
	1737/34	Vaughan, John	SS. Philip & Jacob	Victualler	£15	
W	1742/55B	Vaughan, John	City of Bristol	Mariner	£10	
W	1694/62	Vaughan, Katherine	City of Bristol	Widow	£37	
W	1732/73	Vaughan, Robert	Henbury			
W	1728/40	Vaughan, Thomas	<Westbury, in will>	Yeoman	£12	
	1667/74	Vaughn, John	City of Bristol	Mariner	£5	
	1709/59	Veale, Thomas	St. Stephen	--	£2	
	1683/59	Veck, Stephen	City of Bristol	Mariner	£18	
	1683/59	Veke, Stephen	(see Veke)	--		
W	1640/78	Ven, Giles	Westbury-on-Trym (Shirehampton)	--	£1	badly written
	1750/46	Venables, William	City of Bristol	Mariner	£9	
	1761/35	Venables, William	City of Bristol	Butcher	£10	
W	1635/89	Venman, Prudence	St. Stephen	Widow	£10	
	1723/31	Venn, George	City of Bristol	Wine-cooper	£138	
	1756/20	Venn, Thomas	City of Bristol	Mariner	£66	
W	1640/79	Veratt, Elizabeth	Henbury	Widow	£6	
W	1639/103B	Verett, Edward	Henbury	Husbandman	£48	
W	1640/79	Verrett, Elizabeth	(see Veratt)			
	1623/65	Verruck, William	St. Nicholas	Sailor	£74	
	1693/31	Vey, William	City of Bristol	--	£3	
W	1708/51	Viccary, William	--	Mariner	£20	
W	1712/50	Vidler, Izabell	Winterbourne	Widow	£19	
W	1642/48	Vidler, John	Stoke Gifford	Husbandman	£6	
W	1668/58	Vidler, Thomas	Stoke Gifford	<Yeoman>	£147	
	1662/55	Vimpany, Richard	Henbury	Yeoman	£879	
	1689/65	Vimpany, William	Henbury (Compton Greenfield)		£62	
W	1760/34	Vinables, Elizabeth	City of Bristol	Yeoman	£68	
	1677/45	Vizard, Arthur	City of Bristol	Widow	£10	
	1678/75	Vizard, Arthur	St. John	Maltster	£37	
	1683/59	Voke, Stephen	(see Veke)	Maltster	£37	account only

Year ref.	Name	Parish or area	Occupation or status	Value	Notes
W 1716/55	Voules, Samuel	Winterbourne (Hambrook)	Inn-holder	£71	
1671/50	Vowel, Wethyon	--	\<Widow\>	£25	\<Welthian?\>
1640/80	Vowell, David	St. Nicholas	--	£6	
1609/75	Wade, Anthony	St. Nicholas	\<Haulier\>	£13	
1679/79	Wade, Anthony	City of Bristol	Victualler	£32	
W 1707/41	Wade, Elizabeth	City of Bristol	Widow	£211	
1623/66	Wade, Francis	Stoke Gifford	--	£22	
1697/38	Wade, Jane	--	--	£6	inv. & account
W 1637/57	Wade, John	Almondsbury	Husbandman	£140	
1644/54	Wade, John	St. Leonard	Joiner	£8	
W 1664/59	Wade, John	Almondsbury	Yeoman	£110	
1633/80	Wade, Nicholas	Almondsbury	Husbandman	£89	
1667/82	Wade, Roger	Westbury-on-Trym	Mariner	£7	
1705/33	Wade, Sarah	Filton	Widow	£4	
1611/81	Wade, Thomas	St. Stephen	Shipwright	£23	
W 1629/62	Wade, Thomas	Filton	Husbandman	£128	
1679/80	Wade, Thomas (snr)	Filton	Yeoman	£104	
W 1680/56	Wade, Thomas (snr)	Filton	Yeoman	£105	
1716/56	Wade, Thomas	City of Bristol	Mariner	£5	
W 1613/63	Wade, William	Filton	Husbandman	£17	
1677/52	Wade, William	--	--	£12	
1678/74	Wade, William	St. James	Nailer	£18	account only
1733/82	Wade, William	City of Bristol	Mariner	£10	
W 1750/47	Wadman, Walter	\<City of Bristol\>	\<Mariner\>	£14	
W 1618/74	Wager, Cuthbert	Almondsbury (Over)	--	£33	
1742/56	Wagget, John	City of Bristol	Cooper	£6	died at sea
1756/21	Waggit, Richard	City of Bristol	Mariner	£15	
1629/63	Wakeleye, Mathew	St. James	Whitawer	£1	
W 1633/81	Wakelie, Elizabeth	(see Wakly)			

	Ref	Name	Place	Occupation	Value	Notes
W	1628/76	Wakelie, John	Temple	Shearman	£35	
W	1710/38	Wakely, John	Mangotsfield	Yeoman	£84	
W	1743/37	Wakem, Abraham	City of Bristol	Mariner	£8	
W	1633/81	Wakly, Elizabeth	Temple	Widow	£9	
	1663/71	Wale, John	St. Werburgh	Mercer	£139	
W	1679/73	Walker, Abraham	City of Bristol	Clothier	£44	
W	1741/48	Walker, Anthony	City of Bristol	Mariner	£10	
W	1637/58	Walker, Barbara	St. Nicholas	Widow	£296	
	1617/62	Walker, Edward	--	--	£8	
	1625/82	Walker, Elizabeth	Almondsbury	--	£4	
	1772/CP	Walker, George	<St. Mary, Redcliffe>	Mariner (Master)	£767	inv. & account
	1637/59	Walker, Henry	Littleton-on-Severn	Bachelor	£30	
	1747/42	Walker, James	City of Bristol	Mariner	£4	
	1617/63	Walker, John	Olveston	--	£39	
W	1634/73	Walker, John	St. James	<Rough-mason>	£11	
	1662/50	Walker, John	Temple	Baker	£7	
W	1682/48	Walker, John	Henbury (Kingsweston)	Yeoman	£185	
	1637/60	Walker, Joseph	St. Michael	Mariner	£37	
	1624/70	Walker, Phillipp	St. Thomas	Mariner	£67	
W	1634/74	Walker, Thomas	Horfield	Husbandman	£73	
W	1739/27	Walker, Thomas	City of Bristol	Cordwainer	£92	inv. & account
W	1723/32	Walker, Weeks	City of Bristol	Mariner	£8	
W	1636/59	Walker, William	St. Nicholas	Yeoman	£260	
	1684/77	Walker, William	--	--	£20	
W	1746/47	Walker, William	<St. Stephen> (alias Powell, which see)	Rigger of ships	£8	died at sea
W	1663/52	Wall, Humphrey	SS. Philip & Jacob	Skinner	£33	
W	1677/47	Wall, Humphry	St. James	Widow		
W	1661/76	Wall, Jane		<Tobacco-pipe maker>	£55	
	1708/52	Wall, John	City of Bristol	Mariner	£3	
	1708/53	Wall, Mary	City of Bristol	Spinster	£10	
W	1687/65	Wall, Maurice	City of Bristol	Cordwainer	£157	

	Year ref.	Name	Parish or area	Occupation or status	Value	Notes
W	1618/75	Wall, Thomas	Christchurch	Pewterer	£4	
W	1749/72	Walldron, George	City of Bristol	⟨Mariner⟩	£16	
W	1617/64	Walle, Maurice	Olveston	Yeoman	£128	
	1686/2	Wallen, Michael	City of Bristol	Butcher		
				⟨Victualler in will⟩	£217	
	1691/47	Walline, John	St. Thomas	--	£1	
	1721/34	Walling, Thomas	City of Bristol	Mariner	£4	
	1667/80	Wallington, John	SS. Phillip & Jacob	--	£22	
W	1669/75	Wallis, Sarah	Olveston	⟨Single-woman⟩	£127	
W	1669/74	Wallis, Thomas	Henbury	--	£75	
	1684/75	Wallis, Thomas	Henbury	--	£51	
	1690/49	Wallis, Thomas	St. Nicholas	--	£3	
W	1717/53	Wallis, Thomas	Henbury	Carpenter	£97	
W	1678/61	Wallis, William	SS. Philip & Jacob	Yeoman	£25	
	1715/51	Wallwinn, Thomas	(alias Warren, which see)			
W	1742/57	Walsh, James	City of Bristol	Mariner	£14	
W	1702/25	Walter, Henry	SS. Philip & Jacob	Inn-holder	£221	
	1700/17	Walter, James	Clifton	--	£6	
	1716/57	Walter, Jeptha	City of Bristol	Mariner	£8	
	1729/47	Walter, John	Mangotsfield	Tailor	£15	
W	1639/104	Walter, Margery	St. Mark (Gaunts)	⟨Widow⟩	£296	
	1670/47	Walter, Robert	City of Bristol	Mariner	£10	
W	1634/75	Walter, Thomas	Almondsbury	Weaver	£34	
	1704/35	Walter, Thomas	Mangotsfield	--	£3	
	1708/54	Wanfogt, John	City of Bristol	Mariner	£6	
	1643/92	Warburton, John	St. Peter	Blacksmith	£35	
	1613/64	Ward, Dennis	--	--	£16	
	1711/45	Ward, James	City of Bristol	Mariner	£16	
W	1704/36	Ward, John	City of Bristol	Gallipot maker	£41	
W	1748/78	Ward, Thomas	City of Bristol	Mariner	£10	
W	1625/83	Warden, Elizabeth	St. Werburgh	Widow	£23	

W	1624/71	Warden, John	St. Stephen	Tailor	£31	
	1660/19	Warden John	Temple	Mariner	£12	
W	1665/60	Warden, Phillip	St. Stephen	Shipwright	£44	
	1694/65	Warden, Samuel	City of Bristol	Mariner	£30	
	1684/76	Warden, Thomas	St. Nicholas	Joiner	£16	
	1618/76	Ware, John	St. Ewen	Merchant	£120	
	1687/64	Ware, John	Castle Precinct	Silk-weaver	£132	
	1625/84	Ware, Katherine	St. Ewen	Single-woman	£297	
	1712/51	Ware, Samuel	City of Bristol	Scrivener	£71	
W	1611/82	Warne, Edith	SS. Philip & Jacob	<Spinster>	£7	
W	1637/61	Warne, John	SS. Philip & Jacob	<Husbandman>	£31	
W	1637/61	Warne, Thomas	(see Warne, John)			
W	1711/46	Warneford, John	Almondsbury	Yeoman	£78	
W	1698/34	Warner, John	Mangotsfield	Tailor	£66	
	1639/105	Warr, Robert	St. Augustine	Ropemaker	£7	
W	1734/49	Warrander, John	City of Bristol	Mariner	£2	
W	1676/45	Warren, Ann	—	<Widow>	£371	fragile; damaged
W	1685/59	Warren, Ann	City of Bristol	Widow	£7	
W	1688/51	Warren, Ann	City of Bristol	Widow	£147	
	1687/66	Warren, George	City of Bristol	Shipwright	£11	
	1663/67	Warren, Henry	St. Thomas	Cordwainer	£191	
	1623/67	Warren, Humphrey	St. Mary, Redcliffe	Plate-maker	–	
W	1609/76	Warren, John	SS. Philip & Jacob	Almsman	£2	
W	1620/95	Warren, John	St. Mary, Redcliffe	Cloth-worker	£26	
	1635/90	Warren, John	St. Mary, Redcliffe	Soapmaker	£17	
	1731/89	Warren, Nathaniel	City of Bristol	Hosier	£362	
W	1664/57	Warren, Thomas	Temple	<Clothier>	£64	
	1715/51	Warren, Thomas	City of Bristol	Mariner	£17	
W	1691/48	Warren, William	Mangotsfield	Yeoman	£61	
W	1705/34	Warrett, William	(see Werrat)			
	1639/106	Warrington, Richard	St. Mary-le-Port	Butcher	£97	alias Wallwinn
W	1667/80	Warrington, John	(see Wallington)			

Year ref.		Name	Parish or area	Occupation or status	Value	Notes
1668/64		Warrington, John	SS. Philip & Jacob (the account of Barbara Warrington, relict)	Yeoman	£22	
1611/83	W	Wasboroughe, Marie	Henbury	Widow	£6	
1679/74		Wasborow, Charity	Westbury-on-Trym (Shirehampton)	Widow	£105	
1711/47		Wasborow, Henry	City of Bristol	Gent.	£17	
1623/68	W	Wasborow, John	Westbury-on-Trym	--	£452	
1751/19		Wasborow, Sarah	Henbury	Widow	£16	
1706/40		Wasborow, William	Westbury-on-Trym	Yeoman	£18	
1613/65	W	Wasborowe, William	Henbury	Husbandman	£209	
1671/51		Wasbrow, Alice	Henbury	Widow	£50	
1617/65		Wasbrow, John	Henbury	Single-man	£26	
1646/47	W	Wasbrow, Margaret	<Henbury, Kingsweston>	--	£43	
1699/32	W	Wasbrow, Thomas	Westbury-on-Trym (Sea Mills)	Yeoman	£110	
1647/29		Wasbrowe, Joan	Henbury	--	£181	
1718/39		Waterford, Elizabeth	City of Bristol	Widow	£18	
1664/56		Waterford, Henry	Christchurch	--	£46	
1677/46	W	Waterford, John	SS. Philip & Jacob	Carpenter	£39	
1666/54	W	Waterford, Thomas	SS. Philip & Jacob	--	£41	
1772/CP		Waters, James	St. George (Glos)	Millwright	£179	
1751/20		Waters, Margaret	City of Bristol	Widow	£8	
1749/73	W	Waters, Richard	City of Bristol	Victualler	£18	
1736/32		Waters, Thomas	City of Bristol	Mariner	£7	
1643/93		Waters, William	St. Mary, Redcliffe	--	£67	
1675/72		Waters, William	St. Peter	Dyer	£31	
1677/56	W	Waters, William	St. Peter	--	£33	account only
1730/59		Wathen, Francis	City of Bristol	Mariner	£9	
1642/49		Wathen, Gyles	Olveston (Woodhouse)	--	£10	

	Ref	Name	Place	Occupation	Value
	1643/94	Wathen, James	St. John	\<Cordwainer\>	£265
W	1683/63	Wathen, James \<snr\>	Almondsbury	Inn-keeper	£57
W	1676/46	Wathen, Philip	City of Bristol	Cordwainer	£73
(w)	1758/31	Watkeys, William	City of Bristol	Mariner	£6
			(a 1758 will of William Watkins, C of B, Victualler, exists)		
W	1635/91	Watkin, Katherine	St. Werburgh	Widow	£38
	1692/49	Watkins, Agnes	Olveston (Coate)	Widow	£196
W	1671/48	Watkins, Daniel	\<SS. Philip & Jacob\>	Gent.	
				\<Schoolmaster in will\>	£33
	1636/60	Watkins, Edmond	St. Nicholas	Sailor	£2
W	1740/63	Watkins, Henry	City of Bristol	Mariner	
			\<Clifton\>	\<Yeoman, in will\>	
	1617/66	Watkins, Hugh	St. Thomas	Dyer	£4
W	1620/96	Watkins, James	St. John	--	£30+
W	1637/62	Watkins, John	Clifton	--	£192
	1683/60	Watkins, John	St. Mary, Redcliffe	--	£55
	1759/19	Watkins, John	City of Bristol	Tobacconist	£2
W	1693/34	Watkins, Joseph	SS. Philip & Jacob	Soapmaker	£113
	1709/60	Watkins, Luke	--	Mariner	£621
	1675/71	Watkins, Philip	--	\<Weaver\>	£16
	1623/69	Watkins, Robert	St. Mark	Servant	£7
W	1618/77	Watkins, Thomas	St. Peter	Cooper	£14
W	1662/52	Watkins, Thomas	St. John	Barber-surgeon	£12
W	1676/43	Watkins, Thomas	-- (Wine Street)	Set-cooper	£98
	1689/68	Watkins, Thomas	St. Mary, Redcliffe	--	£24
	1684/65	Watkins, Walter	City of Bristol	--	£2
W	1629/64	Watkins, William	St. James	Yeoman	£3
	1680/62	Watkins, William	Olveston (Coate)	--	£21
W	1687/62	Watkins, William	Henbury (Kingsweston)	Yeoman	£272
	1687/63	Watkins, William	--	Husbandman	£150
W	1699/31	Watkins, William	Henbury (Stowick)	--	£4
	1730/60	Watkins, William	City of Bristol	Yeoman	£183
				Mariner	£16

2 documents

	Year ref.	Name	Parish or area	Occupation or status	Value	Notes
	1609/80	Webb, Richard	Westbury-on-Trym	Husbandman	£25	
W	1667/81	Webb, Robert	St. Peter	Cordwainer	£21	
	1733/83	Webb, Sarah	City of Bristol	Widow	£104	
W	1618/78	Webb, Thomas	St. James	--	£32	
	1664/52	Webb, Thomas	St. Thomas	--	£18	
	1737/35	Webb, Thomas	City of Bristol	--	£2	
W	1634/76	Webb, Walter	Elberton	⟨Yeoman⟩	£178	
W	1644/55	Webb, Walter	Elberton	Husbandman	£41	
	1734/50	Webb, Walter	SS. Philip & Jacob	Tanner	£72	
	1743/38	Webb, Walter	City of Bristol	Mariner	£8	
	1629/66	Webb, William	Christchurch	--	£7	
W	1639/109	Webley, John	(see Weblie)			
	1692/48	Webley, John	Stoke Gifford	Yeoman	£16	
W	1641/53	Weblie, Ann	Winterbourne (Hambrook)	Widow	£150	
W	1639/109	Weblie, John	Winterbourne ⟨Hambrook⟩	Husbandman	£182	
W	1733/84	Weddell, Elizabeth	City of Bristol	Widow	£14	
	1739/28	Wederhead, George	(see Weaderhead)			
W	1706/41	Wedmore, Thomas	City of Bristol	Butcher	£141	
W	1688/50	Wedmore, William	City of Bristol	Butcher	£52	acct: will 1688/50 inv. 1688/50
W	1692/CP	Wedmore, William	City of Bristol	Butcher	£52	acct: will 1688/50 inv. 1688/50
W	1695/CP	Wedmore, William	City of Bristol	Butcher	£52	
	1660/23	Weekeham, Thomas	(see Wickham)			
	1736/33	Weeks, James	Westbury-on-Trym (Stoke Bishop)	Cordwainer	£18	
	1731/90	Weeks, John	City of Bristol	Mariner	£4	
	1674/47	Weeks, John & Mary	Barton Regis	--	£64	
W	1715/52	Weeks, William	Alveston	--	£98	

	W	Name	Place	Occupation	Value	Notes
1684/73		Weight, William	(see White)			
1634/77	W	Welch, Edmund	St. Stephen	<Shipwright>	£36	
1734/51		Welch, John	City of Bristol	Hooper	£14	died at sea
1744/16		Welch, Matthew	City of Bristol	Cooper	£10	died at sea
1721/35	W	Welch, Peter	City of Bristol	Mariner	£6	
1736/34		Welch, Robert	City of Bristol	Mariner	£4	
1742/58		Welch, Sylvester	(see Welsh)			
1738/23		Welch, Walter	City of Bristol	Cooper	£8	died at sea
1759/20	W	Weller, William	City of Bristol	Mariner	£5	
1635/92		Wellis, Kathren	Henbury (Kingsweston)	–	£99	
1633/83	W	Wells, Edmond	St. Mary, Redcliffe	Baker	£19	
1758/32	W	Wells, John	City of Bristol	Mariner	£19	
1637/65A	W	Welsh, Joan	St. Stephen	Widow	£49	
1721/35		Welsh, Peter	(see Welch)			
1742/58		Welsh, Sylvester	City of Bristol	Mariner	–	
1633/82	W	Welsh, William	St. Stephen	Shipwright	£15	
1660/22		Welsteed, Roger	St. Stephen	Seaman	£30	
1663/70		Welsteede, William	St. Mary-le-Port	–	–	
1637/70		Wenne, Thomas	(see Winn)			
1683/61		Werat, Richard	(see Werrett)			
1705/34	W	Werrat, William	<Almondsbury>	<Husbandman>	£8	
1712/52	W	Werratt, Joseph	Henbury (Charlton)	Labourer	£54	
1683/61	W	Werrett, Richard <jnr>	Almondsbury	Husbandman	£57	
1685/58		Werrett, Sarah	Alveston	Spinster	£129	
1750/48		Wesley, Ann	City of Bristol	Widow	£2	
1678/59		West, Edward	Elberton	Husbandman	£13	
1611/85		West, George	St. John	–	£2	
1684/66	W	West, Henry	Almondsbury <Over>	Husbandman	£188	
1671/52	W	West, John	St. James	<Felt-maker>	£22	
1694/63	W	West, John	Almondsbury (Over)	Yeoman	£94	
1729/49		West, John	Almondsbury	–	£58	

	Year ref.	Name	Parish or area	Occupation or status	Value	Notes
	1744/15	Watkins, William	City of Bristol	Mariner	£7	
W	1730/61	Watkon, John	City of Bristol	Mariner	£4	
W	1762/7	Watson, David	City of Bristol	Mariner	£14	
W	1728/41	Watson, James	‹City of Bristol›	Ship-carpenter	£7	died at sea
	1613/66	Watson, Marie	St. Mark	Widow	£200	
	1611/84	Wattes, Thomas	SS. Philip & Jacob	Butcher	£8	
	1699/29	Wattkins, Elizabeth	SS. Philip & Jacob	Widow		
	1701/26	Watts, Aaron	Temple	Tallow-chandler	£338	
	1634/39	Watts, Agnes	(alias Hillinge, which see)	Blacksmith	£19	
	1637/63	Watts, Ann	(see Watts, Edmond)			
W	1682/53	Watts, Edith	City of Bristol	—	£121	
	1637/63	Watts, Edmond	Clifton	—	£14	2 other documents
W	1761/36	Watts, Jane	‹St. Michael›	Spinster	£10	
	1677/49	Watts, John	St. Mary, Redcliffe	Cutler	£21	
	1680/59	Watts, John	—	—	£15	
W	1703/20	Watts, John	City of Bristol	Victualler	£70	
	1716/58	Watts, John	City of Bristol	Gent.	£8	
	1727/39	Watts, John	City of Bristol	—	£7	
W	1682/51	Watts, Michael	St. Nicholas	‹Mariner›	£59	
	1710/39	Watts, Owen	—	‹Mariner›	£8	
	1639/107	Watts, Robert	St. Stephen	—	£12	
	1677/50	Watts, Samuel	St. Werburgh	Joiner	£72	
	1707/42	Watts, William	City of Bristol	Victualler	£14	
	1609/77	Waye, Henry	Henbury	Husbandman	£57	
	1739/28	Weaderhead, George	City of Bristol	Mariner	£8	
	1639/108	Weale, Alice	St. Thomas	Widow	£334	
	1620/97	Weale, Robert	—	—	£77	
	1687/64	Wear, John	(see Ware)			
	1609/78	Weare, John	Westbury-on-Trym	Weaver	£7	
	1664/53	Weare, Robert	St. Stephen	—	£11	

	Ref.	Name	Place	Occupation	Value
W	1719/43	Weare, Ruth	Temple (see Ware)	—	£7
	1712/51	Weare, Samuel	(see Ware)		
	1646/46	Weare, William	St. Michael	Joiner	£32
	1630/5	Wears, Richard	Winterbourne	—	£10
	1739/28	Weatherhead, George	(see Weaderhead)		
W	1637/64	Weaver, Henry	St. Mary, Redcliffe	Mariner	£176
	1692/46	Weaver, Henry	Westbury-on-Trym (Stoke Bishop)		
W	1725/23	Weaver, John	City of Bristol	Husbandman	£108
W	1636/61	Webb, Agnes	Elberton	Mariner	£209
W	1747/43	Webb, Alexander	City of Bristol	<Widow>	£26
W	1699/30	Webb, Andrew	Henbury (Berwick)	Mariner	£12
	1625/85	Webb, Christopher	St. Nicholas	Yeoman	£153
	1674/48	Webb, Elisha	—	Merchant	£10
W	1664/58	Webb, Elizabeth	St. Thomas	—	£30
	1676/50	Webb, Francis	—	Widow	£20
	1703/21	Webb, George	City of Bristol	—	£4
W	1726/35	Webb, George	Mangotsfield	—	£3
W	1729/48	Webb, George	St. Thomas	Clothier	£10
	1700/18	Webb, Hezekiah	Alveston <Earthcott>	Glazier	£5
W	1673/44	Webb, Joan	Mangotsfield	—	£3
	1663/73	Webb, John	St. Michael	Widow	£34
	1679/77	Webb, John	City of Bristol	Broadweaver	£42
	1705/35	Webb, John	City of Bristol	Blacksmith	£5
	1716/59	Webb, John	<SS. Philip & Jacob>	Surgeon	£243
W	1745/31	Webb, John	City of Bristol	Mariner	£3
(w)	1749/74	Webb, John		<Mariner?>	£17
				Mariner	£15
			(a 1749 will of John Webb, Alveston, Butcher, exists)		
W	1629/65	Webb, Joseph	Mangotsfield	Spinster	£192
W	1686/55	Webb, Joyce	<St. Nicholas>	Widow	£8
	1609/79	Webb, Katherine	Westbury-on-Trym	Widow	£15
	1679/76	Webb, Margaret	St. Leonard	Widow	£14
	1686/52	Webb, Mary	St. James	Widow	£13

Year ref.	Name	Parish or area	Occupation or status	Value	Notes
W 1613/67	West, Margerie	Henbury (Kingsweston)	Widow	£57	
1618/79	West, Mary	Henbury	Widow	£11	
W 1677/48	West, Richard	St. Mary, Redcliffe	Felt-maker	£12	
W 1611/86	West, Thomas	Henbury (Kingsweston)	--	£54	
W 1639/110	West, Thomas	Olveston (Woodhouse)	Husbandman	£83	
1712/53	West, Timothy	--	Mason	£11	
1707/43	West, William	City of Bristol	Mariner	£10	
W 1714/43	Westcoat, Thomas	(see Westcott)			
1772/CP	Westcott, Samuel	City of Bristol	Collar-maker	£41	inv. & account
1714/43	Westcott, Thomas	City of Bristol	Mariner	£19	
1734/52a	Westell, Thomas	City of Bristol	Brazier & Broker	£707	inv. (1729) & account
1734/52b	Westell, Thomas	(document appointing a guardian for his daughter Anne)			
W 1712/54	Westerberry, Andrew	City of Bristol	Mariner	£10	
1749/75	Westicott, John	City of Bristol	Mariner	£10	
1640/81	Westley, Roger	Temple	<Mariner>	£18	
1701/27	Westley, Robert	--	Mariner	£32	alias Stevens
W 1742/59	Westmore, George	City of Bristol	Mariner	--	
1628/77	Weston, Edward	St. Mary, Redcliffe	--	£6	
W 1637/65B	Weston, George	St. Mary, Redcliffe	<Mariner>	--	with 1637 wills
		(a note of his goods on the 'Prudence', trading to the Barbadoes; and a covering letter to his wife.)			
1640/82	Weston, George	St. Mary-le-Port	Victualler	£54	
W 1625/86	Weston, Joan	Temple	Widow	£8	
1748/76	Weston, John	(see Tucker, Ann)			
W 1633/84	Weston, Nicholas	St. Mary, Redcliffe	<Husbandman>	£23	3 documents
1617/67	Westone, John	Temple	Gardener	£3	
1635/93	Westwood, Richard	St. James	--	£2	
1756/22	Whale, Elizabeth	City of Bristol	Widow	£16	

W	Reference	Name	Place	Occupation	Value	Notes
W	1668/66	Whale, Mary	St. Nicholas	Widow	£30	
	1641/54	Whatly, John	St. James	Yeoman	£48	
W	1629/67	Wheadden, Solomon	(see Wheddon)			
	1761/37	Wheatcraft, Henry	Clifton	—	—	
	1620/99	Wheaton, Edward	St. Michael	Sailor	£2	
	1722/27	Wheaton, John	City of Bristol	Mariner	£6	
W	1629/67	Wheddon, Solomon	St. Nicholas	Sailor	£45	
	1736/35	Wheeler, George	Clifton	Victualler	£15	
	1629/69	Wheeler, John	(alias Wilkes, which see)			
	1699/34	Wheeler, Thomas	—	—	£15	
W	1642/16	Wheeler, William	(alias Dowlsworth, which see)			
	1741/49	Wheeler, William	City of Bristol	Mariner	£5	
W	1629/68	Wheler, Elizabeth	St. John	<Widow>	£11	
	1681/65	Whichchurch, Richard (jnr)	City of Bristol	Butcher	£6	
	1637/66	Whinge, Lawrence	Winterbourne	—	£24	
	1716/60	Whippey, Thomas	City of Bristol	Mariner	£3	
	1636/62	Whippie, John	Abbots Leigh	Ship-carpenter	£22	& a caveat, 1636/62b
	1643/95	Whitakre, Ellinor	City of Bristol	Widow	£12	
	1681/65	Whitchurch, Richard (jnr)	(see Whichchurch)			
	1631/91	White, Andrew	City of Bristol	Mariner	£7	
W	1657/33	White, Ann	Westbury-on-Trym	Widow	£37	
	1686/54	White, Ansell	City of Bristol	Mariner	£3	
W	1688/49	White, Arthur	Henbury (Lawrence Weston)	<Yeoman>	£225	
W	1715/53	White, Edward	City of Bristol	Mariner <Cooper>	£5	
W	1719/44	White, Edward	City of Bristol	Mariner	£379	
	1639/111	White, George	St. Stephen	<Shipwright>	£89	
W	1678/62	White, George	City of Bristol	Shipwright	£7	
W	1747/44	White, George	City of Bristol	Mariner	£10	
	1729/50	White, Giles	City of Bristol	Mariner	£7	
	1625/87	White, Henry	City of Bristol	Victualler	£14	
W	1679/75	White, James (snr)	Olveston (Tockington)	Shoemaker	£83	

	Year ref.	Name	Parish or area	Occupation or status	Value	Notes
W	1763/8	White, Jesse	City of Bristol	Cooper	£19	died at sea
	1624/72	White, John	St. Mary, Redcliffe	Tailor	£5	
W	1636/64	White, John	St. Thomas	Cordwainer	£34	
	1685/54	White, John	St. Michael	Tiler & Plasterer	£2	
	1717/54	White, John	City of Bristol	Mariner	£207	
W	1732/74	White, John	City of Bristol	Mariner	£5	
	1637/67	White, Joyce	St. Mary, Redcliffe	Widow	£5	
	1691/46	White, Katherine	Henbury	Widow	£34	
	1697/36	White, Mathew	Henbury	Yeoman	£118	
	1623/70	White, Nicholas	St. Werburgh	Joiner	£25	
	1670/45	White, Nicholas	--	--	£2	inv. & account
			(drowned:- includes note on Coroner's charges etc.)			
	1678/60	White, Patience	St. Michael	Widow	£54	
W	1675/74	White, Richard	Henbury <Lawrence Weston>	Yeoman	£283	
	1695/39	White, Richard	Henbury (Stowick)	Yeoman	£171	
W	1629/70	White, Robert	Westbury-on-Trym (Cote)	<Yeoman>	£268	
W	1665/59	White, Robert	Almondsbury <Patchway>	Yeoman	£80	2 documents
W	1674/45	White, Robert	Westbury-on-Trym	Yeoman	£379	
	1760/35	White, Simon	City of Bristol	Mariner	£7	
	1761/38	White, Simon	City of Bristol	Mariner	£21	inv. & account
	1762/8	White, Simon	City of Bristol	Mariner	£16	compare 1761/38
	1733/85	White, Stephen	City of Bristol	Mariner	£7	
W	1636/69	White, Susanna	St. Mary, Redcliffe	Widow	£43	
	1636/65	White, Thomas	St. Nicholas	Draper	£20	
W	1693/33	White, Thomas	Olveston (Tockington)	Cordwainer	£84	

W	Reference	Name	Location (City of Bristol)	Occupation	Value
	1682/52	White, William	City of Bristol	Tanner	£95
	1684/73	White, William	St. Stephen	Sergeant-at-Mace	£15
	1687/61	White, William	St. Stephen	Mariner	£16
W	1684/72	Whitehood, Alice	(see Whitwood)		
	1675/70	Whitechurch, Anthony	St. Thomas	Cooper	£10
	1664/55	Whiteing, John	St. Thomas	Butcher	£82
	1668/61	Whiteing, John	Temple	Weaver	£220
	1620/98	Whitehead, Thomas	(see Whitfield)		
	1617/68	Whitehouse, William	Abbots Leigh	House-carpenter	£2
W	1690/48	Whitfield, Elizabeth	Elberton	Widow	£80
	1661/78	Whitfield, Richard	Elberton	Yeoman	£519
	1620/98	Whitfield, Thomas	St. Stephen	--	£4
W	1671/54	Whitfield, Thomas	Elberton	<Yeoman>	£60
W	1731/92	Whitfield, Thomas	City of Bristol	Mariner	£3
W	1680/55	Whithood, Richard	Almondsbury <Over>	--	£67
W	1749/76	Whiting, Harley	City of Bristol	Barber-surgeon	£8
	1705/36	Whiting, John	City of Bristol	Grocer	£1,691
	1623/71	Whiting, Thomas	Westbury-on-Trym	--	£88
W	1623/72	Whitney, William	St. Mary, Redcliffe	<Merchant Tailor>	£30
	1746/48	Whitstrong, Charles	City of Bristol	Mariner	£9
	1639/111	Whitt, George	City of Bristol	--	£5
	1676/48	Whitt, Matthew	(see Whyte)		
	1745/32	Whittingham, George	City of Bristol	Tide-waiter	£48
W	1684/72	Whitwood, Alice	Almondsbury (Over)	Widow	£40
W	1624/73	Whitwood, John	Stapleton	Miller	£5
	1676/48	Whyte, Matthew	(see White)		
	1630/6	Wickham, Christian	(see Wyckcom)		
W	1662/53	Wickham, Edward	Henbury <Charlton>	Shipwright	£100
W	1709/61	Wickham, Grace	Almondsbury	Widow	£47
	1717/55	Wickham, Jane	Clifton	Widow	£12

Year ref.	Name	Parish or area	Occupation or status	Value	Notes
W 1624/74	Williams, Henry	Winterbourne (Hambrook)	--	£37	
1643/97	Williams, Henry	St. Mary-le-Port	--	£5	
1671/49	Williams, Hercules	--	--	£7	
W 1759/22	Williams, Isaac	City of Bristol	Mariner	£16	
1666/55	Williams, James, Isack & Mary				
1692/47	Williams, Jane	Olveston	--	£40	
W 1713/47	Williams, Jarvis	Clifton	Widow	£12	
1640/84	Williams, Joan	City of Bristol	--	£8	
W 1641/55	Williams, John	St. Stephen	Widow	£6	
1675/73	Williams, John	SS. Philip & Jacob	--	£11	
1680/60	Williams, John	City of Bristol	--	£17	
		Westbury-on-Trym (Shirehampton)			
1685/57	Williams, John	City of Bristol	--	£43	
1689/67	Williams, John	City of Bristol	--	£5	
1692/50	Williams, John	City of Bristol	Mariner	£28	
1695/40	Williams, John	St. James	--	£38	
1708/56	Williams, John	City of Bristol	Mariner	£14	
W 1713/48	Williams, John	City of Bristol	Mariner	£10	
1724/22	Williams, John	City of Bristol	Mariner	£7	
W 1735/41	Williams, John	City of Bristol	Mariner	£6	
1740/64	Williams, John	City of Bristol	Mariner	£3	
1741/50	Williams, John	City of Bristol	Mariner	£10	
1742/60	Williams, John	--	Yeoman	£7	
W 1746/49	Williams, John	City of Bristol	Mariner	£18	
1747/47	Williams, John	City of Bristol	Mariner	£5	
1757/19	Williams, John	City of Bristol	Mariner	£5	
W 1760/36	Williams, John	City of Bristol	Mariner	£5	
		City of Bristol	Mariner	£16	
		(will states: landsman from Lydney, Glos.)			
1742/61	Williams, Jonathan	City of Bristol	Victualler	£657	

	Ref.	Name	Place	Occupation	Value	Notes
W	1687/59	Williams, Joseph	Henbury (Billsom)	Yeoman	£528	
W	1701/28	Williams, Joseph	Henbury (Northwick)	Yeoman	£750	
	1708/57	Williams, Joseph	City of Bristol	<Mariner>	£10	
W	1743/39	Williams, Joseph	<Westbury-on-Trym>	Mariner	£6	
	1729/51	Williams, Lawrence	City of Bristol	Mariner	£10	
W	1758/33	Williams, Lewis	City of Bristol	Mariner	£14	
	1660/6	Williams, Lickeria	--	Widow	£7	
	1664/54	Williams, Margaret	St. Michael	--	£29	
	1686/56	Williams, Margaret	Henbury	--	£97	alias Jones
W	1617/70	Williams, Mary	(see Williams, Thomas & Mary)		£53	
W	1669/76	Williams, Mary	St. Leonard	Widow	£16	
	1735/42	Williams, Mary	City of Bristol	Widow	£49	
	1667/78	Williams, Matthew	St. Stephen	Widow	£72	
	1669/73	Williams, Matthew	St. Mary, Redcliffe	--	£3	
	1685/56B	Williams, Michael	--	--	£210	
	1668/63	Williams, Morgan	Almondsbury	--	£210	account only
	1680/68	Williams, Morgan	Almondsbury	--	£23	
	1677/51	Williams, Morgan	Westbury-on-Trym	--	£22	
	1705/37	Williams, Morris	--	Mason	£49	
W	1719/45	Williams, Moses	Almondsbury <Patchway>	<Yeoman in will>	£74	
W	1662/54	Williams, Nicholas	Olveston	Shoemaker	£4	
W	1748/79	Williams, Oliver	City of Bristol	Mariner	£28	
	1667/75	Williams, Pascus	St. Peter	--	£12	
	1672/57	Williams, Paul	City of Bristol	Barber-surgeon	£261	
	1727/40	Williams, Peter	Henbury	Yeoman	£95	
	1754/25	Williams, Philip	Littleton-on-Severn	Yeoman	£6	
	1709/62	Williams, Phillip	--	<Mariner>	£5	
	1731/93	Williams, Reese	City of Bristol	Mariner	£48	
W	1618/81	Williams, Richard	Almondsbury	--	£11	
W	1635/95	Williams, Richard	St. Mary-le-Port	Butcher	£224	
	1648/19	Williams, Richard	Olveston	--	£3	
	1649/22	Williams, Richard	St. Mary, Redcliffe	--		

Year ref.	Name	Parish or area	Occupation or status	Value	Notes
W 1611/87	Wickham, John	Henbury (Charlton)	Husbandman	£40	
W 1643/96	Wickham, John	St. Michael	Shoemaker	£47	
1666/53	Wickham, John	St. Mary, Redcliffe	--	--	
W 1700/35	Wickham, Mary	Almondsbury	Widow	£66	
1706/42	Wickham, Nicholas	City of Bristol	Mariner	£17	
1660/23	Wickham, Thomas	St. Stephen	--	£16	
1667/76	Wickham, William	Almondsbury	Yeoman	£74	
1684/67	Wickham, William	Stoke Gifford	Yeoman	£130	
1627/27	Wicks, John	St. James	--	£4	
W 1647/30	Wickwick, John (snr)	Mangotsfield	⟨Coal-miner⟩	£40	
W 1668/67	Widlake, Godfrey	St. Peter	⟨Barber-surgeon⟩	£261	will 1667
W 1646/48	Widlake, John	Christchurch	⟨Barber-surgeon⟩	£85	
W 1640/83	Widlake, William	Stapleton	--	£2	
W 1747/45	Wilcher, Henery	City of Bristol	Mariner	£3	
1667/83	Wilcox, John	St. James	Brewer	£26	
1732/75	Wilcox, Samuel	City of Bristol	Mariner	£4	
1730/62	Wilcox, William	City of Bristol	Gardener	£6	
W 1747/46	Wilde, Edward	City of Bristol	Mariner	£8	
1680/57	Wilden, William	SS. Philip & Jacob	--	£2	
W 1646/49	Wilkes, Bridgett	⟨City of Bristol⟩	Widow ⟨Glover⟩	£120	
W 1684/74	Wilkes, Henry	City of Bristol	Barber-surgeon	£12	
1686/53	Wilkey, William	--	--	£15	
1683/62	Wilkins, George	Temple	Yeoman	£24	
1673/39	Wilkins, Susanna	Temple	Widow	£18	
1699/33	Wilkinson, George	--	--	£4	
1629/69	Wilks, John	St. Mary, Redcliffe	Mariner	£13	
1609/81	Wilcox, Christopher	Westbury-on-Trym (Shirehampton)	--	£138	alias Wheeler
1609/82	Willcox, Henry	Temple	Shearman	£14	
1711/48	Willcox, Joan	City of Bristol	Widow	£20	

	Reference	Name	Place	Occupation	Value
	1728/42	Willcox, Richard	City of Bristol	Corn-chandler	£115
W	1620/100	Willcoxe, Martha	Temple	Widow	£14
W	1685/61	Willet, Blanch	City of Bristol	Widow	£11
	1623/73	Willet, Thomas	St. Stephen	Cooper	9s 10d
	1639/112	Willett, Abraham	SS. Philip & Jacob	--	£10
	1637/68	Willett, Alice	St. Ewen	Widow	£35
	1649/13	Williams, Alice	(alias Goode, which see)		
W	1716/61	Williams, Andrew	Elberton	Yeoman	£337
W	1696/33	Williams, Ann	City of Bristol	Spinster	£33
W	1629/72	Williams, Anne	City of Bristol	Widow	£13
W	1693/32	Williams, Anne	Henbury (Stowick)	Widow	£33
	1697/37	Williams, Arthur	--	--	£13
	1661/77	Williams, Bartholomew	St. Nicholas	Butcher	£16
	1680/58	Williams, Charles	SS. Philip & Jacob	--	£1
	1717/56	Williams, Charles (jnr)	Henbury	Yeoman	£186
	1680/61	Williams, Cornelias	Henbury	--	£79
W	1629/73	Williams, David	City of Bristol	Joiner	£71
	1708/55	Williams, David	City of Bristol	Mariner	£9
W	1732/76	Williams, David	City of Bristol	Mariner	£5
	1635/94	Williams, Edmond	St. Nicholas	Cooper	£43
	1618/80	Williams, Edward	St. Mary-le-Port	Victualler	£5
	1737/36	Williams, Edward	City of Bristol	Mariner	£16
W	1665/61	Williams, Elizabeth	St. Nicholas	Widow	£35
W	1706/43	Williams, Elizabeth	St. Stephen	<Widow>	£156
W	1710/42	Williams, Elizabeth	City of Bristol	Widow	£35
W	1751/21	Williams, Elizabeth	City of Bristol	Widow	£19
	1623/74	Williams, Ellie (Eliza)	SS. Philip & Jacob	--	£5
	1643/98	Williams, Elnor	--	--	£2
	1668/62	Williams, George	SS. Philip & Jacob	Button-maker	£8
	1759/21	Williams, George	City of Bristol	Mariner	£5
	1710/40	Williams, Gibbion	City of Bristol	Maltster	£100
	1688/47	Williams, Hannah	--	Widow	£11

Year ref.	Name	Parish or area	Occupation or status	Value	Notes
W 1738/24	Williams, Richard	City of Bristol	Mariner	£7	
W 1757/20	Williams, Richard	City of Bristol	Mariner	£19	
1711/49	Williams, Robert	City of Bristol	Mariner	£4	
W 1721/36	Williams, Robert	City of Bristol	Mariner	£6	
W 1635/96	Williams, Roger	Westbury-on-Trym	Inn-holder	£50	
1729/52	Williams, Sarah	Henbury	--	£223	
W 1639/113	Williams, Sybil	St. John	\<Widow\>	£6	
1617/69	Williams, Thomas	St. James	--	£11	
W 1617/70	Williams, Thomas & Mary	St. James	--	£26	
1624/75	Williams, Thomas	St. Stephen	Merchant	£18	
W 1628/78	Williams, Thomas \<snr\>	SS. Philip & Jacob	\<Hooper\>	£5	
	Williams, Thomas	St. Thomas	--	£6	
W 1700/36	Williams, Thomas	City of Bristol	Cooper	£59	
W 1707/44	Williams, Thomas	City of Bristol	Mariner	£11	
1710/41	Williams, Thomas	City of Bristol	Joiner	£10	
1732/77	Williams, Thomas	City of Bristol	Mariner	£5	
1749/77	Williams, Thomas	City of Bristol	Mariner	£8	
1625/88	Williams, Walter	St. James	--	£4	
1682/50	Williams, Walter	St. Mary, Redcliffe	--	£3	
1637/69	Williams, William	St. Stephen	Merchant	£14	
1748/80	Williams, William	City of Bristol	Mariner	£5	alias Devascote
W 1750/49	Williams, William	\<St. Nicholas\>	Yeoman	£10	
1676/49	Williams, William	Temple	Cooper	£223	
1681/64	Williams, William	St. James	--	£4	
W 1685/60	Williams, William	Henbury	Yeoman	£324	
1713/49	Williams, William	City of Bristol	Mariner	£5	
1732/78	Williams, William	City of Bristol	--	£44	
W 1747/48	Williams, William	City of Bristol	Cooper	£12	
W 1685/56A	Williamson, George	City of Bristol	Clerk	£448	died at sea
1749/78	Williamson, Hugh	City of Bristol	Mariner	£8	
1695/5	Williamson, John	City of Bristol	Mariner	£4	

	Ref.	Name	Place	Occupation	Value	Notes
	1663/72	Willie, William	St. Augustine	Cooper	£18	
	1680/54	Willington, Priscilla	City of Bristol	Widow	£38	
W	1668/59	Willington, Richard	Westbury-on-Trym <Shirehampton>	<Yeoman>	£52	
	1609/83	Willington, Robert	Westbury-on-Trym	--	£135	
	1667/79	Willington, Thomas	Westbury-on-Trym	Husbandman	£17	
W	1706/44	Willis, Alice	City of Bristol	Widow	£3	
W	1736/36	Willis, Edward	SS. Philip & Jacob	Coal-miner	£38	1735 will
	1646/50	Willis, Francis	--	--	£3	
	1617/71	Willis, Joan	(see Willis, Robert & Joan)			
	1720/33	Willis, John	Westbury-on-Trym (Shirehampton)	Pilot	£73	compare with 1728/43 version
			(the account of Christopher Smith, administrator)			
	1728/43	Willis, John	Westbury-on-Trym (Shirehampton)	Pilot	£73	list of goods sold
W	1694/64	Willis, Nicholas	Barton Regis	Yeoman	£361	
	1627/28	Willis, Richard	<Henbury> (Aust)	Waterman	£29	
	1617/71	Willis, Robert & Joan	Henbury (Kingsweston)	--	£4	
	1729/53	Willis, Sarah	Mangotsfield	Widow	£37	
W	1696/32	Willis, Susanna	Westbury-on-Trym (Shirehampton)	Widow	£106	
	1669/72	Willis, Thomas	Westbury-on-Trym	--	£113	
W	1674/46	Wills, Simon	St. Stephen	Mariner	£61	
W	1698/35	Wills, Richard	City of Bristol	Pin-maker	£15	
	1706/45	Wills, John	--	--	£109	
W	1759/23	Wills, Robert	City of Bristol	Ship-carpenter	£4	
	1639/115	Willsheare, Robert	St. John	Tailor	£126	compare 1640/85
W	1640/85	Willsheare, Robert	St. John	Tailor	£126	compare 1639/115
	1636/66	Willsheere, John	(see Wilshire)			
W	1640/85	Willshire, Robert	(see Willsheare)			
	1732/79	Willson, James	City of Bristol	Mariner	£6	
	1629/71	Willson, Joseph	Temple	Journey-man brewer	£1	
W	1732/80	Willson, Thomas	City of Bristol	Gunsmith	£3	died at sea

Year ref.	Name	Parish or area	Occupation or status	Value	Notes
1749/79	Willson, Thomas	City of Bristol	Horner	£19	
1758/34	Wilmott, William	City of Bristol	Mariner	£6	
W 1673/45	Wilsheare, Richard	(see Wiltshire)			
1636/66	Wilshire, John	St. Augustine	--	£16	
1737/37	Wilson, Alexander	City of Bristol	Mariner	£14	
1743/40	Wilson, Henry	City of Bristol	Mariner	£8	
1639/114	Wilson, John	Temple	Sea-faring man	--	
1706/46	Wilson, John	--	Mariner	£10	
W 1720/34	Wilson, John	City of Bristol	Mariner	£7	
1634/78	Wilson, Lawrence	St. Mary, Redcliffe	<Tailor>	£16	
W 1731/94	Wilson, Matthew	City of Bristol	Mariner	£16	
W 1742/62	Wilson, Richard	City of Bristol	Mariner	£14	
1738/25	Wilson, Thomas	City of Bristol	Mariner	£16	
1731/95	Wilson, Vincent	City of Bristol	Farrier	£12	
1746/50	Wilson, William	City of Bristol	Mariner	£6	
W 1663/68	Wilton, William	Olveston	Yeoman	£132	
W 1673/45	Wiltshire, Richard	St. Nicholas	<Cooper>	£41	
W 1740/65	Winbow, William	City of Bristol	Maltster	£178	1739 will
1605/1	Wimbowe, William	Henbury	Yeoman	£98	
1751/CP	Windburn, Close	City of Bristol	Mariner	£6	
W 1617/72	Window, Scholastica	St. Peter	Widow	£13	
W 1722/28	Windsworth, Samuel	<City of York>	Mariner	£6	
W 1757/21	Winmill, Richard	City of Bristol	Mariner	£10	
W 1730/63	Winn, Ralph	City of Bristol	Mariner	£5	
1637/70	Winn, Thomas	St. Mary, Redcliffe	--	£16	
1647/31	Winne, Margaret	St. Mary, Redcliffe	Widow	£22	
1623/76	Winnold, Nicholas	St. John	--	£6	
W 1641/56	Winscombe, Morgan	Temple	Cloth-worker	£22	
W 1687/60	Winston, Richard	SS. Philip & Jacob	Victualler <Butcher in will>		
W 1722/28	Winsworth, Samuel	(see Windsworth)		£215	

Reference	W	Name	Place	Occupation	Value
1674/49		Wintell, John	St. Nicholas	--	£8
1757/22		Winter, John	City of Bristol	Mariner	£12
1636/67		Winter, Thomas	St. James	Joiner	£8
1670/46		Wise, Christopher	St. James	Skinner	£11
1728/44		Witchell, Daniel	Olveston	Yeoman	£295
1611/55		Witchell, Elizabeth	(see Wychill)		
1676/44		Witchell, Joan	Mangotsfield	Widow	£171
1674/44	W	Witchell, Richard	Mangotsfield	Yeoman	£174
1684/70		Wither, Phillip	Henbury (Northwick)	Yeoman	£160
1673/46		Wither, Richard	Henbury	Yeoman	£316
1712/55		Wither, Richard	<Henbury> Northwick		
1624/76	W	Witherlie, Elizabeth	Stapleton	--	£48
1673/42		Witherly, Richard	Henbury	<Widow>	£60
1641/57		Witherly, Thomas	Almondsbury	--	£97
1671/47		Witherly, Thomas	(alias Brookes, which see)	Husbandman	£50
1660/20		Witherly, William	Winterbourne	Yeoman	£10
1684/68	W	Withers, Edward	Almondsbury (Over)	<Yeoman>	£43
1673/40		Withers, John	Winterbourne	Yeoman	£26
1711/50	W	Withers, Thomas	Olveston (Ingst)	Yeoman	£125
1712/56		Withers, Thomas	Olveston (Ingst)	Yeoman	£165
1750/50	W	Withey, Willilam	City of Bristol	Victualler	£48
1715/54		Witts, Edmond	City of Bristol	Mariner	£14
1760/37		Woadham, Edmond (jnr)	City of Bristol	Mariner	£16
1623/78		Wodham, William	(see Woodam)		
1628/82	W	Wodshall, John	Henbury	<Tailor>	£52
1716/62	W	Woes, Thomas	City of Bristol	Mariner	£6
1623/77	W	Wolfaite, John	Almondsbury	--	
1635/98		Wolfe, Isaac	<Compton> Christchurch	<Yeoman>	£296
1632/1		Wolley, Edmund	Mangotsfield	Cutler	£118
1624/77	W	Wollie, John	(see Woolley)	--	£112
1636/69	W	Wollie, John	(see Woolly)		

Year ref.		Name	Parish or area	Occupation or status	Value	Notes
1617/73	W	Wollvin, Edward	(see Woolvin)			
1734/53		Wood, Angell	City of Bristol	Mariner	£7	
1625/89		Wood, John	Henbury	—	£27	
1716/63	W	Wood, John	City of Bristol	Mariner	£4	
1737/38		Wood Robert	Clifton	Tiler	£11	
1628/81	W	Wood, Thomas	Almondsbury <Easter Compton>	—	£50	
1660/21		Wood, Thomas	Temple	Weaver	£98	
1623/78		Woodam, William	Westbury-on-Trym	—	£9	
1637/71	W	Woodcock, Gyles	St. Mary, Redcliffe	<Schoolmaster>	£6	
1609/84		Woodford, Robert	—	—	£16	
1743/41	W	Woodman, William	<SS. Philip & Jacob>	Mariner	£4	
1628/82	W	Woodshall, John	(see Wodshall)			
1625/90		Woodson, John	City of Bristol	—	£4	
1625/91		Woodson, Richard	St.Thomas	Surgeon	£35	
1668/60		Woodstock, John	SS. Philip & Jacob	Gardener	£116	
1667/77		Woodward, Phillip	St. James	—	£43	
1635/97	W	Woodward, Robert	St. Michael	—	£51	
1689/66	W	Woodward, Thomas	City of Bristol	Mariner	£5	
1692/51		Woodward, Thomas	City of Bristol	Woollen-draper	£40	
1636/68		Woodward, William	Christchurch	<Tailor>	£17	2 documents and compare 1637/72
1637/72		Woodward, William	Christchurch	Tailor	—	compare 1636/68
1709/63	W	Woodward, William	City of Bristol	Tailor	£17	
1721/37		Woodward, William	City of Bristol	<Mariner>	£8	
1671/53	W	Woodyard, Tobias	City of Bristol	<Victualler>	£12	
1635/88	W	Wooford, Alice	St. Peter	Widow <Ale seller>	£24	
1628/80		Woolcocke, George	St. Peter	Sailor	£3	
1662/49		Wooley, Edmund	Winterbourne	Miller	£128	
1628/79		Woolfe, Wilmote	St. James	Widow	£6	
1726/36	W	Woollam, Robert	Westbury-on-Trym	Yeoman	£146	

		Name	Location	Occupation	Value	Notes
W	1632/1	Woolley, Edmund	(see Wolley)		£16	
	1624/77	Woolley, John <jnr>	Stapleton	--	£17	
W	1629/74	Woolls, Anselm	St. Augustine	--	£10	
W	1636/69	Woolly, John	St. Thomas	Shoemaker	£37	also Woullven
W	1617/73	Woolvin, Edward	St. Augustine	Lacemaker	£36	
W	1617/74	Woolvin, Katherine	St. Augustine	Widow	£29	relict of Edward
W	1633/85	Wooly, Cicely	Mangotsfield	Widow	£56	
	1673/41	Woory, John	Castle Precinct	Tobacco-roller	£23	
	1688/48	Wootten, William	--	--	£124	
W	1628/83	Worgan, Christopher	St. Stephen	Cooper	£41	
	1682/49	Worgan, Edward	St. Mary, Redcliffe	Tobacco-roller	£6	
	1676/47	Worgan, Elizabeth	St. Stephen	--	£116	
W	1660/29	Worgan, John	St. John	Vintner	£36	
W	1673/43	Worgan, Susanna	St. Stephen	Widow	£7	
	1640/86	Workman, Henry	St. Peter	--	£28	
	1668/65	Workman, Richard	--	--	£33	
	1646/51	Worldley, Christopher	Westbury-on-Trym	--	£10	died at sea
W	1754/26	Worrell, Thomas	City of Bristol	Hooper		
W	1704/37	Worrell, William (snr)	Stoke Gifford (Great Stoke)	Yeoman	£541	
W	1704/37	Worrole, William (snr)	(see Worrell)			
W	1705/38	Worwin, Thomas	<City of Bristol>	<Pin-maker>	£20	will states of Trowbridge, Wilts.
W	1753/30	Wotton, William	City of Bristol	Yeoman	£19	
W	1617/73	Woulven, Edward	(see Woolvin)			
W	1754/27	Wraight, Robert	City of Bristol	Mariner	£2	will states of Wellington, Som.
	1636/63	Wrayford, Richard	St. Stephen	--	£11	
	1678/63	Wrentmore, Hester	St. Augustine	Widow	£2	
W	1633/86	Wright, Anne	City of Bristol	Widow	£209	
	1634/79	Wright, Collinson	<Henbury> (Aust)	Inn-holder	£11	
W	1643/99	Wright, Erasmus	St. Werburgh	Merchant	£921	
	1662/51	Wright, Jane	All Saints	Widow	£5	

	Year ref.	Name	Parish or area	Occupation or status	Value	Notes
W	1742/63	Wright, John	City of Bristol	Mariner	£4	
	1694/CP	Wright, John	City of Bristol	Merchant	£9	inv. & account
W	1679/78	Wright, Mary	St. Werburgh	Widow	£121	
	1620/102	Wright, Nathaniel	St. John	Haulier	£123	
	1641/58	Wright, Ralph	City of Bristol	—	£392	
W	1640/87	Wright, Raphe	St. John	⟨Mercer⟩	£1,393	
	1617/75	Wright, Richard	St. Nicholas	—	£30	
	1741/51	Wright, Richard	City of Bristol	Mariner	£10	
	1684/69	Wright, Thomas	—	Inn-keeper	£493	
	1684/71	Wright, Thomas	—	Pin-maker	£3	
	1742/64	Wright, Thomas	City of Bristol	Mariner	£4	
W	1772/CP	Wright, Thomas	SS. Philip & Jacob	Victualer	£87	inv. & account 1760; will 1760
	1734/54	Wrinn, James	Stapleton	—	£21	
	1640/88	Wyatt, John	St. Mary, Redcliffe	—	—	
	1611/55	Wychill, Elizabeth	Mangotsfield	Widow	£4	
	1630/6	Wyckcom, Christian	St. Stephen	Wife or Widow	£17	
W	1613/68	Wyett, William	St. James	Whitawer	£21	
	1641/57	Wytheley, Thomas	(see Witherly)			
W	1643/13	Wytherly, Robert	(alias Brooks, which see)			
	1759/24	Wynn, John	City of Bristol	Physician	£15	
W	1730/63	Wynn, Ralph	(see Winn)			
W	1687/67	Yarington, John	Barton Regis	Nailer	£83	
W	1625/92	Yate, Elizabeth	Christchurch	Widow	£13	
	1675/75	Yate, Judith	St. Mary-le-Port	—	£59	
	1643/100	Yate, Thomas	St. Mary-le-Port	Baker	£372	
	1635/99	Yates, Margery	Henbury	Widow	£4	
	1720/35	Yealfe, John	City of Bristol	Saddler	£17	
W	1641/59	Yeamans, Catherine	SS. Philip & Jacob	Widow	£136	
W	1687/5	Yeamans, Mary	City of Bristol	Widow	£55	

	Reference	Name	Parish / Location	Occupation	Value
	1639/116	Yeamans, Richard	Henbury	—	£26
	1732/81	Yeamans, Richard	Westbury-on-Trym	—	£42
	1677/53	Yeamans, Robert	City of Bristol	Merchant	£25
	1693/35	Yeamans, Robert	City of Bristol	—	£8
	1680/63	Yeamans, William	City of Bristol	—	£23
	1734/55	Yeats, William	St. James	Mariner	£11
	:1694/66	Yemans, Richard	(see Yeamans)		
	1639/116	Yemans, William	SS. Philip & Jacob	House-carpenter	£31
W	1633/87	Yeo, Nicholas (jnr)	Temple	Clerk (Vicar)	£311
	1661/79	Yeo, Nicholas	Temple	Weaver	£42
	1661/80	Yeoman, William	(see Yemans)	Weaver	£6
W	1633/87	Yeomans, John	St. James	—	
	1637/73	Yeomans, Richard	Clifton	Chandler	£39+
	1662/56	Yeor, Abraham	(see Yower)	—	£185
	1634/80	Yerroth, Richard	Christchurch	Cooper	£21
W	1635/100	Yetman, Charles	City of Bristol	Mariner	£3
	1740/66	Yewer, Abraham	St. Peter	—	£30 3 documents (1634/80)
			(the account of Joan, relict: for inv. see Yower 1634/80)		
	1635/101	Yewins, John	St. Stephen	Mariner	£29
	1636/70	Yoiall, David	City of Bristol	Mariner	£6
W	1731/96	Yong, Thomas	(see Young)	Yeoman	£9
	1643/103	Yonge, John	Stoke Gifford		
W	1633/88	Yore, Abraham	(see Yower)	Soapmaker	£346
	1634/80	Yorke, Edward	Christchurch	—	£20
	1624/78	Yorke, Joan	St. Leonard		
	1642/50	Youill, David	(see Yoiall)	Mariner	£5
W	1731/96	Young, Alexander	City of Bristol	Mariner	£4
W	1727/41	Young, Alexander	City of Bristol	Spinster	£37
	1749/80	Young, Anne Phillis	City of Bristol	—	£28
	1731/97	Young, Arthur	Westbury-on-Trym (Redland)		
W	1624/79				

Year ref.	Name	Parish or area	Occupation or status	Value	Notes
W 1700/37	Young, Christopher	<Alveston> (Earthcott)	Yeoman	£294	
W 1625/93	Young, Edith	Abbots Leigh	Widow	£39	
1705/39	Young, Edward	—	—	£8	
1659/2	Young, Elizabeth	City of Bristol	Widow	£2,433	compare 1658/3
W 1742/65	Young, James	City of Bristol	Mariner	£9	
1754/28	Young, Joan	City of Bristol	Widow	£18	formerly Bright
1658/3	Young, John	City of Bristol	—	£2,961	compare 1659/2
W 1624/80	Young, Lewis	Temple	<Shearman>	£64	
W 1753/31	Young, Matthew	City of Bristol	Mariner	£9	
1692/1	Young, Moses	—	—	£6	
1711/51	Young, Nicholas	—	—	£773	
1623/79	Young, Peregrine	St. Thomas	Gent.	£21	
W 1702/26	Young, Roger	Almondsbury (Over)	Yeoman	£116	
1643/102	Young, Sarah	St. Mary-le-Port	—	—	
1643/103	Young, Thomas	Temple	Shearman	£238	
W 1751/22	Young, Thomas	City of Bristol	Mariner	£12	
1635/102	Younge, Edward	St. Thomas	Cloth-worker	£18	
W 1633/88	Younge, John	(see Yonge)			
W 1633/89	Younge, John	Temple	Shearman	£676	
W 1643/101	Younge, Nathaniel	St. Mary-le-Port	<Pewterer>	£24	
1634/80	Yower, Abraham	St. Peter	Pewterer	£30	
		(for account see Yewer, Abraham 1635/101)			
1648/20	Zouch, Welthian	(see Souch)			

APPENDIX I

Bristol Probate Inventories,
Distribution by Years

BRISTOL PROBATE INVENTORIES
DISTRIBUTION BY YEARS

The numbers given against each year are the number of inventories, accounts or other items in each year-bundle.

They include those inventories that remain attached to their wills and those with the Ecclesiastical Cause Papers.

Year	No.	Year	No.	Year	No.	Year	No.
1542	1	1650	14	1700	37	1740	66
1573	1	51	4	01	28	41	52
1588	1	52	3	02	26	42	68
1597	1	53	3	03	21	43	43
		54	–	04	37	44	16
1600	–	55	–	05	39	45	32
01	1	56	1	06	47	46	50
02	–	57	3	07	44	47	48
03	–	58	3	08	57	48	82
04	2	59	2	09	63	49	80
05	1	1660	29	1710	42	1750	50
06	–	61	80	11	51	51	23
07	1	62	57	12	56	52	35
08	2	63	73	13	49	53	31
09	84	64	59	14	43	54	37
1610	–	65	61	15	54	55	13
11	87	66	58	16	63	56	23
12	12	67	82	17	56	57	23
13	69	68	67	18	39	58	35
14	2	69	75	19	45	59	24
15	–	1670	46	1720	35	1760	37
16	–	71	56	21	37	61	38
17	75	72	57	22	28	62	12
18	82	73	47	23	32	63	12
19	–	74	49	24	22	64	7
1620	102	75	76	25	23	65	2
21	–	76	50	26	36	66	10
22	1	77	63	27	41	67	4
23	80	78	78	28	45	68	7
24	80	79	82	29	54	69	–
25	93	1680	69	1730	64	1770	–
26	2	81	63	31	97	71	2
27	28	82	56	32	81	72	4
28	84	83	62	33	85	73	7
29	74	84	77	34	55	74	1
1630	6	85	64	35	42	75	–
31	1	86	58	36	36	76	5
32	1	87	68	37	39	77	–
33	89	88	51	38	25	78	3
34	80	89	69	39	28	79	3
35	102	1690	49			1780	1
36	70	91	48			81	1
37	74	92	52			82	–
38	–	93	35			83	3
39	118	94	68				
1640	88	95	42			1792	1
41	59	96	33				
42	52	97	37			1804	1
43	103	98	36				
44	55	99	35				
45	–	1700	37				
46	51						
47	31						
48	20						
49	22						

Total of inventory documents 7133

APPENDIX II

Mariners' Inventories after 1704

MARINERS' INVENTORIES AFTER 1704

After 1704 more than half the Bristol probate inventories are those of mariners, surgeons, coopers, hoopers, carpenters, sailmakers and others who died while serving at sea. These form a distinct category of inventories. They do not list personal possessions or household goods but record only the wages due to the deceased for his last voyage, and usually the name and type of ship and the name of the master or captain. In the following table the number of such inventories is given for each year. The tabulation shows when the impact of the war at sea was at its greatest; the rate at which the usual local inventories continued to be produced and how they began to decline about 1760. There is a total of 1486 mariners 'Wages due . . .' inventories during this period.

Columns: (1) Total inventories
(2) City and rural inventories
(3) Mariners' 'Wages due' inventories
(4) Mariners' inventories as percentage of total

year	(1)	(2)	(3)	(4)	year	(1)	(2)	(3)	(4)
1703	21	28	–	–	1735	42	14	28	67%
04	37	36	1	3%	36	36	14	22	61
05	39	38	1	3	37	39	17	22	56
06	47	37	10	21	38	25	5	20	80
07	44	32	12	27	39	28	12	16	57
08	57	36	21	37	1740	66	10	56	85
09	63	36	27	43	41	52	13	39	75
1710	42	27	15	36	42	68	12	56	82
11	51	39	12	24	43	43	8	35	81
12	56	33	23	41	44	16	3	13	81
13	49	28	21	43	45	32	7	25	78
14	43	36	7	16	46	50	8	42	84
15	54	31	23	43	47	48	7	41	85
16	63	40	23	37	48	82	16	66	80
17	56	39	17	30	49	80	16	64	80
18	39	25	14	36	1750	50	23	27	54
19	45	28	17	38	51	23	9	14	61
1720	35	15	20	57	52	34	15	19	56
21	37	26	11	30	53	31	12	19	61
22	28	17	11	39	54	37	25	12	32
23	32	21	11	34	55	13	10	3	23
24	22	11	11	50	56	23	20	3	13
25	23	10	13	57	57	23	2	21	91
26	36	16	20	56	58	35	11	24	69
27	41	19	22	54	59	24	5	19	79
28	45	20	25	56	1760	37	4	33	89
29	54	26	28	52	61	38	6	32	84
1730	64	14	50	78	62	12	5	7	58
31	98	27	71	72	63	12	5	7	58
32	81	23	58	72	64	7	5	2	29
33	85	17	68	80	65	2	2	–	–
34	55	19	36	65	1766	10	10	–	–

INDEX OF
OCCUPATIONS AND STATUS

INDEX OF OCCUPATIONS AND STATUS

OCCUPATION INDEX

Indexed to page and parish

Each page entry is followed by a number in brackets indicating the parish or area if known. The numerical coding used is given below. Numbers in square brackets indicate the number of inventories relative to each occupation.

City Parishes or Wards		*Rural Parishes or areas*	
01	All Saints	51	Abbots Leigh
02	Castle Precinct	52	Almondsbury
03	Christchurch	53	Alveston
04	St. Augustine	54	Barton Regis
05	St. Ewen	55	Clifton
06	St. George (after 1756)	56	Compton Greenfield
07	St. James	57	Elberton
08	St. John	58	Filton
09	St. Leonard	59	Frenchay
10	St. Mark (le Gaunts)	60	Henbury
11	St. Mary-le-port	61	Horfield
12	St. Mary, Redcliffe	62	Littleton-on-Severn
13	St. Michael	63	Mangotsfield
14	St. Nicholas	64	Olveston
15	St. Peter	65	St. George, Easton-in-Gordano
16	SS. Philip & Jacob	66	Stapleton
17	St. Stephen	67	Stoke Gifford
18	St. Thomas	68	Westbury-on-Trym
19	St. Werburgh	69	Winterbourne
20	Temple	70	Bedminster
		99	Parishes outside the area

ale-draper/ale seller [2]
    222(04), 260(15)
anchor-smith [3]
    128(17), 131, 131(13)
apothecary [7]
    77, 116, 134, 169, 185(18), 203, 229
architector 159(20)
arms painter 20
artist (see PAINTER)

baker [47]
    3, 6, 6, 6(60), 11, 15(69), 20, 21(18), 34(17), 39, 45(04), 49, 58(19), 58(20),
    72(17), 77(07), 87(08), 88(17), 98, 100, 101(63), 105(04), 110, 110, 123,
    127(12), 140(03), 143(60), 153(14), 156, 164(18), 164(17), 166, 175(18),
    176, 180, 191, 195, 199, 199, 207, 212(18), 232, 232(16), 239(20), 247(12),
    262(11)
barber [5]
    38(19) 96(05), 141, 216(18), 217(05)
barber-surgeon [16]
    19(08), 25, 29(54), 37, 63, 83(03), 135(14), 166, 193(08), 203(17), 243(08),
    251, 252(15), 252(03), 252, 255
basket-maker [5]
    72(54), 87, 186, 204(03), 204(03)
bay-maker 47
bell founder 189
blacksmith [49]
    3(60), 8(64), 9, 13(04), 20(16), 27, 38, 44(54), 62(15), 63, 64(60), 69(12),
    71(64), 73, 81(16), 86, 86, 87(16), 99, 100(52), 105(64), 106(55),
    113(63), 115(60), 131(15), 134(16), 143(66), 143(11), 143(69), 146(58),
    151, 166(18), 173(08), 175(63), 180(13), 199(13), 207, 207(16), 208(54),
    209, 224(60), 225(16), 226(16), 231(13), 235(60), 240(15), 244(20),
    245(13)
blockmaker [9]
    11, 34(17), 38, 47(17), 47(17), 70(17), 105, 119, 211
boatman [2] (see also WATERMAN)
    17(60), 66(20)
boatswain 31[17]
bodice-maker [3]
    18(16), 44(18), 197(03)
bone-lace weaver (see also LACEMAKER)
    166(12)
book-binder 125
book seller 223
brass-founder [3]
    163, 189, 216
brazier [7]
    31, 48(16), 116, 179(12), 223, 223, 248
brass-worker [2] (see also LATTEN-PLATE WORKER)
    3(16), 168(99)
brewer/journey-man brewer [33]
    8(20), 19, 47(07), 60, 66(07), 76(16), 78(16), 89(18), 89(18), 98, 102(07),
    102(11), 111(18), 118(07), 119, 123, 123(18), 129(07), 140(07), 154(15),
    154(20), 177(07), 177(07), 187, 189, 210(12), 215, 227(18), 227(12),
    230(20), 235, 252(07), 257(20)

91(20), 95, 95(20), 130(20), 143(20), 166(20), 184(20), 204(20), 207(20), 209(19), 217(18), 219(20), 219(14), 231(20), 241(12), 258(20), 264(18)

coach-harness maker 62

coach-painter 56

coal-driver [7] (see also HORSE-DRIVER)
  46(54), 46(16), 53(16), 86(16), 132(16), 140(54), 144(16)

coal-miner [18]
54(66), 82(63), 89(63), 98(63), 111(54), 113(54), 140(63), 143(63), 145(63), 156(66), 156(66), 162(54), 162(54), 180(06), 230(66), 233(63), 252(63), 257(16)

coffee seller 133

collar-maker [2] (= HORSE-COLLAR MAKER)
  79(15), 248

collier [8]
  33(66), 79(66), 87(16), 100(66), 103(66), 112(66), 144(66), 235(66)

colour-merchant/colourman [2]
  24(16), 117

cook [9]
  28(19), 49(11), 104(18), 143(14), 146, 200(17), 209(13), 218(11), 231

cooper [141] (see also SET-COOPER and WINE-COOPER)
  3(09), 4(17), 5, 7, 8, 12, 13, 14, 14(17), 19(07), 20(08), 21(14), 21(14), 22(17), 23(14), 23(09), 24(14), 27, 33(09), 35, 35, 45, 45(17), 47, 48(99), 49(12), 50, 51, 51(17), 52, 55(14), 56, 56(17), 59(17), 59(17), 59, 60(08), 64(17), 64(14), 67, 71(17), 75(17), 77, 79, 80, 82, 83, 85, 87, 90(08), 90(17), 96(14), 97(12), 101(14), 101(14), 102, 105, 105, 106(08), 106(08), 108(63), 113, 118(17), 119(17), 121, 121, 123(12), 123(12), 124(14), 124, 126(17), 129, 131(01), 133(12), 134(12), 135, 140(14), 141, 142(14), 142(17), 144, 147(17), 150, 152, 152, 158(09), 158, 159, 161(17), 161, 163, 171, 179, 179, 180(08), 183(14), 183(15), 183, 183, 184(15), 185, 188(17), 189(14), 190, 193, 204, 205, 205, 207(07), 210(14), 212(14), 213, 220(17), 224, 224, 224(14), 225(12), 225(14), 225(17), 225(17), 227(18), 227(07), 230, 231, 233(14), 238, 243(15), 247, 247, 249, 250, 251(17), 253(17), 253(14), 256, 256(20), 256, 257(04), 258(14), 261(17), 263(03)

cordwainer [84]
  6, 6(60), 6(08), 7, 12(18), 13(68), 13(60), 13(60), 16(69), 17, 19(63), 20(63), 23(58), 26(52), 26(11), 29, 35(14), 35, 37(17), 39, 40, 41(16), 42(16), 43(13), 49, 52(11), 57, 59(63), 62, 67(54), 67(16), 69, 70(52), 71(69), 73(07), 78(03), 85(11), 86(56), 91, 91(02), 98(15), 104(16), 108, 111(54), 123(63), 124(13), 125(11), 125, 132, 133, 141, 143(02), 145, 148, 159, 161, 165, 167, 169, 174(07), 181(54), 189(66), 194, 197, 199, 201, 206(11), 207(18), 213, 221(16), 223(54), 226, 228, 229(01), 234(20), 239, 239, 241(18), 243(08), 243, 246(15), 246(68), 250(18), 250(64)

cork-cutter [3]
  63, 116, 149

corn-chandler [2]
  233(18), 253

corn-factor 160

cow keeper [2]
  209(52), 217(52)

curate 233(68)

currier [4]
  34(15), 136, 200, 217

cutler [9]
  20(16), 21(18), 40(16), 43, 97, 103(15), 219(18), 244(12), 259(03)

distiller [6]
  14(02), 14(16), 92(54), 125, 210, 218(08)
doctor (of Physic) [2] (see also PHYSICIAN)
  23, 42(13)
doctor (of Laws) 121(04)
draper [3]
  39(14), 163(17), 250(14)
dyer [9]
  17, 31, 31(02), 53(12), 111(20), 122(13), 201(12), 242(15), 243(18)

embroiderer 157(03)
exciseman 189

factor 42
fan-maker 81
farrier [13]
  33, 45(15), 56(16), 69(18), 83(15), 88(16), 94(18), 130, 130(18), 131, 208(16), 208(16), 258
felt-maker [20]
  7(54), 8, 16(07), 34(12), 62(16), 62(16), 82(63), 112(12), 113(12), 158(16), 181(18), 186(69), 187(12), 193(12), 197(12), 205(12), 216(12), 225(15), 247(07), 248(12)
fine-drawer (= INVISIBLE MENDER) 154(15)
fisherman 8(60)
fishman 177(60)
fishmonger [2]
  70(17), 141
fletcher 115(03)
freemason [3]
  7(18), 21, 77

gallipot maker [2]
  37(54), 240
gardener [21]
  18(16), 39(13), 42(07), 78, 154, 157(16), 157(16), 157(16), 157, 159(16), 160(16), 161(16), 169(16), 172(16), 174(07), 184(04), 209(54), 235(54), 248(20), 252, 260(16)
glass-bottle maker 169(16)
glass-maker/glassman [5]
  48(16), 62(12), 70(54), 138(16), 138(16)
glazier [16]
  4(07), 19, 67(02), 68(15), 92(12), 92(18), 92(18), 100, 130, 153(11), 180, 182, 204, 209(08), 230, 245(63)
glover [10]
  22(68), 42, 64(18), 65, 88, 117, 129(12), 132(16), 163(12), 252
goldsmith [9]
  47(03), 52(01), 65(17), 90(05), 90(05), 94(01), 103(03), 104(03), 111
grocer [17]
  9, 17(15), 17(15), 25, 28(16), 33, 39(18), 58, 64(18), 69(18), 85(16), 125(54), 132(01), 162(16), 164(08), 181(15), 251
gunner 204(14)
gunsmith [8]
  3(13), 104(13), 129, 129, 177(63), 201(16), 206, 257

haberdasher [16]
  30(18), 31, 46, 51, 60(17), 63(09), 75, 90(18), 92(07), 143, 149, 164(55),
  192(16), 207(18), 207, 236(07)
hair-weaver [2]
  50(12), 116(12)
hatter [7] (see also FELT-MAKER)
  30, 49, 115(16), 116(03), 181, 233(12), 235(12)
haulier [28]
  12, 27, 27, 27, 42(14), 59(14), 62, 62(08), 72(04), 79(08), 118, 118(20),
  118(18), 118(08), 140(08), 140(08), 149, 160(08), 167(08), 174(08),
  175(07), 193(08), 202(04), 224(66), 224, 225, 238(14), 262(08)
hooper [31]
  6, 10(18), 28(18), 35(17), 38, 51, 57, 61, 69, 80, 80, 83, 107, 125, 126, 129,
  131, 144, 149(16), 161(17), 164, 198, 198, 214, 214(17), 218, 224, 226, 247,
  256(16), 261
horner [3]
  50, 59, 258
horse-driver [6] (see also COAL-DRIVER)
  34(66), 143(63), 144(16), 180(54), 213(16), 230(66)
hosier [5]
  17(01), 31, 168(14), 229(01), 241
hot-presser 134
house-carpenter [24]
  3(07), 14, 30(17), 45, 45, 66(02), 69(02), 71(07), 95, 114, 115, 119, 122,
  143, 169, 170(16), 170, 178(07), 183(08), 196, 223, 225, 251(20), 263(07)
husbandman (214 entries)

inn-holder/inn-keeper [56]
  4(18), 5(16), 14, 16(15), 21, 21(03), 26(18), 30(16), 39(18), 41, 41(13),
  49(11), 50, 65(13), 70(15), 80(18), 84(54), 96, 102(18), 108(03), 108,
  109(16), 112, 114, 116, 124(18), 129(18), 136(18), 144(16), 145(16),
  145(54), 150(15), 155(68), 159, 161(54), 175(03), 176(03), 182, 183, 191,
  198(03), 199(68), 203(18), 203(64), 215(18), 215(15), 216(68), 220,
  220(18), 228(68), 238(69), 240(16), 243(52), 256(68), 261(60), 262
instrument maker 49(20)
ironmonger [2]
  102, 188

jeweller 80
joiner [39]
  2(17), 7(17), 9(14), 15, 21(14), 32(17), 32, 40, 44(17), 53(07), 67, 70(17),
  75(12), 78(17), 80, 83, 98(17), 103(08), 110(17), 115, 120, 124(17), 127(17),
  150(14), 157(13), 163(17), 163(09), 174(14), 190(17), 223(19), 235(04),
  238(09), 241(14), 244(19), 245(13), 250(19), 253, 256, 259(07)

keeper of the gaol of newgate 139

labourer [15]
  4(64), 23(20), 39(99), 77(68), 82(53), 92(16), 94(68), 99, 102(60), 125(52),
  166(60), 191, 198(64), 200(14), 247(60)
lacemaker (see also BONE-LACE WEAVER)
  261(04)
latten-plate worker 210
lay clerk 186(03)

lighterman [9]
   11, 12(55), 13(04), 41, 42(20), 86(14), 125(14), 126(14), 176(02)
lime-burner [6]
   29(16), 73(55), 154(20), 228, 230(20), 230
linen-draper [5]
   28(04), 28(02), 155(04), 192, 219(17)
locksmith [2]
   21, 167(13)

maltster/maltman [14]
   36(69), 49, 60, 109(69), 135(13), 154(03), 165(16), 180, 182(16), 183(63),
   237, 237(08), 253, 258
mariner (1675 entries) (see also SAILOR etc. and Appendix II)
mason [25] (see also STONEMASON and ROUGH MASON)
   4(69), 10(51), 11(64), 30(16), 30, 55(16), 61(16), 76, 77, 93(20), 104(64),
   106(07), 106(07), 115, 122(52), 130, 136(07), 148(60), 149(16), 149(16),
   153(18), 194, 203(07), 248, 255(52)
meal-man [2]
   144(14), 234
mercer [6]
   66, 134(14), 137(04), 181(69), 239(19), 262(08)
merchant [49]
   4(15), 9, 11(14), 11(19), 16, 25(12), 25(08), 26, 36(19), 41, 48, 50(08), 56,
   66(09), 79(18), 80, 80(08), 83(08), 84(12), 89, 89(08), 95(03), 105(04),
   105(07), 108(04), 126(17), 135(13), 136(08), 139(08), 145(18), 146, 153(05),
   155(01), 160(19), 165(68), 168(17), 182, 186, 216(13), 218(08), 223(12),
   231(20),   241(05),   245(14),   256(17),   256(17),   261(19),   262,
   263
merchant tailor [8]
   44(05), 51(03), 82, 90(08), 111(12), 199, 227, 251(12)
miller [13]
   15(66), 21, 36(69), 46(66), 50(68), 53(16), 97(69), 155(07), 160, 224(66),
   234(16), 251(66), 260(69)
milliner [6]
   106(07), 106(12), 107(03), 109(08), 151, 199
millwright [4]
37(15), 65, 232(16), 242(06)
minister/minister of the gospel [4]
   23, 28(18), 66(60), 75(04)
mould-maker 110(15). (= BUTTON-MOULD MAKER)
musician [4] (see also ORGANIST)
   31, 126(14), 137(03), 236

nailer [6]
   33(66), 112(18), 128(54), 214(16), 238(07), 262(54)
needle-maker 78(17)
notary public 169

oatmeal-maker [2]
   3(69), 151(16)
organist [2]
   3, 88
organ maker [2]
   163, 224(04)

122(04), 140(17), 141(52), 193(11), 212(04), 218, 224, 229(03), 249(64), 252(13), 255(64), 261(18)
shop-keeper 28
sieve-maker [2]
  34, 94(18)
silk-weaver [4]
  27(20), 64(20), 154(12), 241(02)
silversmith 202
skinner [7]
  20(15), 30(18), 219(19), 226, 235(16), 239(16), 259(07)
slaughterman 117(68)
smith [12]
  21(61), 50(18), 58, 82, 95, 130(13), 132(13), 181(69), 195(16), 198(15), 209(53), 234(18)
snuff-grinder 129
soap-boiler [13]
  21(17), 21, 42, 49(08), 85, 91, 95(05), 98(15), 141(07), 151, 164, 188(12), 218
soapmaker [23]
  7(16), 22(18), 47(11), 48, 64(18), 83(02), 85, 85, 102, 146(03), 146(03), 150(18), 169(15), 176, 180, 189(03), 193(17), 200(04), 219, 232(03), 241(12), 243(16), 263(03)
staymaker 48(16)
stocking-maker [2]
  26(16) 166(03)
stone-carver 198
stonemason 18(07)
strong-water distiller 5
stuff-maker 8
sugar-baker [2]
  150(12), 207
surgeon [56]
  4(13), 9(17), 9, 24, 27, 34, 34, 42, 51(13), 56, 57(13), 62, 70, 74, 84, 97, 105, 108, 111, 111, 119(65), 130, 131, 132, 132, 133, 134, 136(18), 144(07), 148, 149, 151, 152, 155, 157, 158(05), 165(02), 165, 169, 174(04), 176, 183, 185, 189, 199(05), 204(12), 207, 208(13), 217, 217, 223, 225, 231, 231, 245, 260(18)

tailor [86]
  2(18), 2, 5(66), 9, 10(60), 15(52), 18(16), 21(07), 22(20), 22, 26(02), 26, 27(54), 27(17), 28(14), 34(16), 37, 39(60), 41(04), 46(03), 53, 62(11), 62(07), 64(03), 68(60), 69(18), 81(08), 84(54), 84, 86(60), 94, 94(16), 106, 107(63), 108, 109(57), 112, 112(16), 115(19), 117, 117, 125(07), 126(68), 126, 126, 127(19), 128(55), 129(04), 130(07), 131(60), 134(17), 135, 138(52), 139(66), 142(60), 152(64), 152(60), 160(08), 171, 179(15), 185, 186(64), 187, 188(52), 188(16), 192, 207(17), 207(52), 214(60), 219(60), 221, 225, 229(19), 231, 232(16), 240(63), 241(17), 241(63), 250(12), 257(08), 257(08), 258(12), 259(60), 260(03), 260(03), 260
tanner [19]
  29(15), 36(12), 40(16), 46(07), 71(07), 118(12), 138(63), 138(63), 145, 182(15), 188(63), 188(16), 190, 202(15), 207(12), 219(63), 230(63), 246(16), 251
tallow-chandler 244(16)
tapster 63(60)

weaver [39] (see also BROADWEAVER)
5(18), 14, 16(20), 18(69), 22(12), 45(15), 46(20), 48(53), 53(20), 55(20), 55(20), 60(16), 71(64), 79, 82, 88(54), 91, 99(16), 106, 109(68), 122(20), 124(20), 144(20), 145, 149(20), 157(20), 167(69), 170(20), 175(52), 175, 215(16), 218(64), 240(52), 243, 244(68), 251(18), 260(20), 263(20), 263(20)
wheelwright [3]
31(12), 179(58), 182
whitawer [14]
10, 17(15), 58, 58(07), 123(07), 166, 167(15), 182(07), 208, 221(15), 221(15), 230, 238(07), 262(07)
white-smith (see also TIN-MAKER)
128(16)
whip-maker 8(16)
wine-cooper [7]
3(09), 11, 60, 110, 156, 217, 237
wine-merchant 70
wire-drawer [7]
8(12), 22, 39, 50(18), 75(18), 80, 203
wool-carder 84(12)
wool-comber [3]
102(16), 146, 170(12)
woollen-draper [6]
25, 75, 132(14), 144, 185(12), 260
writing master 19

yeoman [519 entries]

INDEX OF OCCUPATIONS AND STATUS

STATUS INDEX

Indexed to pages only. The number of entries on a
page is also included.

pauper [3]
    110, 125, 197
pensioner 6
prisoner 10

Sergeant at Mace [4]
    82, 131, 186, 251
spinster/single woman [135]
    3, 4, 8 x2, 12, 16, 18, 20, 22, 28, 29, 33, 36 x2, 39, 40 x2, 43, 45, 47, 51, 55,
    56, 57 x2, 59 x2, 60 x2, 61, 69, 70, 71 x2, 74, 77 x2, 82, 85, 86 x3, 87, 92 x3,
    93 x2, 96, 98, 102, 105, 106 x2, 107, 109 x2, 111, 113 x2, 114 x2, 117 x2,
    122 x3, 123, 125, 127, 134, 135, 136, 137, 139 x3, 145, 152, 153, 156, 158,
    159, 163, 165 x2, 168 x2, 169 x2, 171 x3, 174 x4, 178, 179 x2, 181, 186, 189,
    191, 193, 195, 196, 197, 199, 200 x2, 203, 204, 208 x2, 209 x2, 210, 211 x2,
    213, 216, 217, 221, 227, 228, 239, 240, 241 x2, 244, 245, 247, 253, 263

widow [total entries 910]
widow (valued over £100) [197]
    2 x2, 4, 6, 7 x3, 11, 12 x2, 14 x2, 15 x3, 16 x2, 19 x3, 21, 22 x2, 23 x2, 25,
    26 x2, 30, 34, 35, 36, 38, 39, 41 x2, 42 x2, 45, 48, 50, 53, 54 x3, 55, 57 x3, 59,
    62, 63, 64, 69 x2, 72, 73 x3, 75 x2, 78, 80, 83, 84 x2, 85, 86, 89, 95 x2, 96 x2,
    97, 99 x2, 100, 101, 104, 105 x3, 106, 107, 108, 113, 114, 115, 117, 118, 119,
    120, 122 x2, 124 x3, 125 x2, 127 x4, 129, 134 x2, 135 x2, 137, 138, 139, 144,
    145 x3, 146, 147, 151, 153, 154 x2, 155, 156 x2, 159, 161, 165, 167, 168 x2,
    170 x2, 172, 178 x2, 183, 184, 185, 188, 196 x2, 197, 199, 202, 204, 207 x3,
    208 x2, 210 x3, 211 x2, 213 x2, 214 x2, 216 x2, 218 x2, 219 x2, 220, 222, 223,
    224 x2, 226, 229, 230, 231, 232, 234, 237, 238, 239, 240, 241 x2, 242, 243,
    244 x3, 246 x2, 252, 253, 257, 259, 261, 262 x2, 264
wife/married [8]
    88, 92, 129, 143, 155, 209, 217, 262

INDEX TO INTRODUCTION

INDEX TO THE INTRODUCTION

INDEX TO THE INTRODUCTION